Home Plans

Publisher
Jim Schiekofer
The Family Handyman

Editor
Eric Englund
*Homestore™
Plans and Publications*

Marketing Director
William Cort
The Family Handyman

Production Manager
Judy Rodriguez
The Family Handyman

Production Associate
Lynn Colbjornsen
*Homestore™
Plans and Publications*

Graphic Designer
Jeff Harrison
*Homestore™
Plans and Publications*

The homes pictured here and on the cover may have been modified by the homeowners. Please refer to the floor plan and/or the drawn elevation for actual blueprint details.

Copyright 2002
by Home Service Publications, Inc., publishers of *The Family Handyman* Magazine,
2915 Commers Drive,
Suite 700,
Eagan, MN 55121.

The Family Handyman is a registered trademark of RD Publications, Inc.

RD Publications, Inc. is a subsidiary of The Reader's Digest Association, Inc.

Reader's Digest and the Pegasus logo are registered trademarks of The Reader's Digest Association, Inc.

All rights reserved. Unauthorized reproduction, in any manner, is prohibited.

A PUBLICATION OF

Reader's Digest
U.S. MAGAZINE PUBLISHING

Contents

Vol. 16, No. 4

Featured Homes

Plan E-1602 — page 260

Plan LS-97832-RE — page 316
Photo by Kieran J. Liebl

On the Cover

Plan AX-98368 — page 155

Sections

Home-Plan Chapters

Comfy Country Charmers	4
Nostalgic Farmhouses	129
Graceful Victorians	163
Stately Colonial-Style Homes	185
Southern Belles	215
Stylish Newcomers	273

Ordering Your Plans

What Our Plans Include	12
Important Ordering Information	13
Blueprint Order Form	15

Next-Day Delivery Available on All Plans
TO ORDER, CALL ANYTIME, TOLL-FREE:
1-800-820-1296

The Family Handyman magazine and Homestore™ Plans and Publications are pleased to join together to bring you this outstanding collection of home designs. Through our combined efforts, we have compiled the finest work from 55 of North America's leading home-design firms.

This edition features our top-rated designs, arranged to make it easier to find the home that meets your needs.

With an inventory of more than 11,000 plans, Homestore™ Plans and Publications has supplied blueprints for more than 250,000 new homes. We look forward to helping you find your dream home.

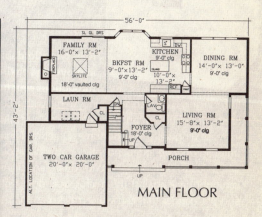
MAIN FLOOR

Unless otherwise noted, all photos on this page and on the cover by Mark Englund/Homestore™ Plans and Publications

Fight Allergens, Mold Spores and Dust, and Create a HEPA Healthy Home™

GuardianPlus™
AIR SYSTEMS

Now, one affordable unit improves the environment throughout your home.

Introducing GuardianPlus™ Air Systems with HEPA Filtration, Fresh Air Ventilation and Heat Recovery, a revolutionary way to increase air quality in your home. Quiet and lightweight, this unit can operate independently or attach to your HVAC system, where it stays out of sight. With GuardianPlus Air Systems, you can fight back against the microscopic dust, pollen, mold spores and pet dander that can worsen allergies and asthma. In short,

GuardianPlus Air Systems create dramatically cleaner air throughout your home, benefiting every member of your family. Better still, GuardianPlus Air Systems cost less than the multiple single-room units that you would need for filtration alone. To learn more about how you can keep your entire home cleaner and healthier, call 1-800-637-1453 (Broan) or 1-888-336-6151 (NuTone), or visit www.guardianplusairsystems.com.

Broan-NuTone,™ GuardianPlus™ and HEPA Healthy Home™ are trademarks of Broan-NuTone LLC. HEPA (High Efficiency Particulate Air) filters capture 99.97% of all particles that are 0.3 microns or larger.

BROAN·NUTONE™
A NORTEK COMPANY

Advertisement

Taking CONTROL of Indoor Air Quality

Scientific research has shown that indoor air can be up to 100 times more polluted than the air outside.

When your home has poor indoor air quality, airborne particles, gases and other pollutants are circulated throughout every room. This can lead to an unhealthy and uncomfortable environment and can put your family's health at risk. Resulting problems range from recurring colds and aggravated allergies to persistent coughs, headaches and poor concentration.

Now, there's a way to avoid these risks and provide a cleaner, healthier environment for you and your family through the innovative GuardianPlus™ Air Systems with Whole-House HEPA filtration, Fresh Air Ventilation and Heat Recovery.

HEPA filters capture 99.97% of all particles, even those as small as 0.3 microns (a human hair is 150 microns). Both HEPA filtration and fresh air ventilation are very important to improve indoor air quality, and the GuardianPlus™ Air Systems are the most effective and affordable ways to ensure fresh, clean indoor air throughout your home.

Options for *Every Home*

Unlike portable room air cleaners which can only cover isolated areas, GuardianPlus™ Air Systems address your entire indoor environment. The GuardianPlus™ family of products offers three types of customized systems to fit your needs:

- HEPA filtration throughout the house;
- HEPA filtration with Fresh Air Ventilation;
- HEPA filtration with Fresh Air Ventilation and Heat Recovery.

Breath Easier

GuardianPlus™ Air Systems are lightweight, and each unit will provide whole-house ventilation for up to 2,500 square feet. They can be installed in all types of homes, anywhere in the country, in approximately three hours. They are also efficient, using as much energy as two 100-watt lightbulbs. Best of all, they're affordable, with complete installation starting at under $600.

Your sales consultant will help you choose the system solution for your indoor air quality problem.
Call 1-800-637-1453 (Broan)
or 1-888-336-6151 (NuTone)
or visit

www.guardianplusairsystems.com
for more information.

COMFY COUNTRY CHARMERS

Cottage with Open Interior

- The exterior of this contemporary cottage features a delightful covered porch and a pair of matching dormers.
- The inviting entry is crowned by a dramatic ceiling and flows into the expansive vaulted Great Room. Tall windows brighten both corners, while a fireplace serves as a handsome centerpiece.
- Sliding glass doors between the Great Room and the breakfast nook open to an angled deck.
- The sunny nook provides a bright and cozy setting for family dining with a view of the backyard.
- Ample cabinets and counter space are offered in the efficient kitchen, which also features a handy snack counter that extends into the nook.
- The main-floor master bedroom boasts a walk-in closet and easy access to the full bath beyond.
- The upper floor offers another bedroom, plus a full bath with space for a laundry closet. The loft could serve as an extra sleeping space.

Plan JWB-9307	
Bedrooms: 2+	Baths: 2
Living Area:	
Upper floor	349 sq. ft.
Main floor	795 sq. ft.
Total Living Area:	**1,144 sq. ft.**
Standard basement	712 sq. ft.
Exterior Wall Framing:	2x4 or 2x6
Foundation Options:	
Standard basement	
(All plans can be built with your choice of foundation and framing. A generic conversion diagram is available. See order form.)	
BLUEPRINT PRICE CODE:	**A**

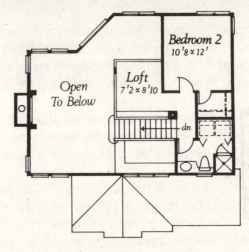

UPPER FLOOR

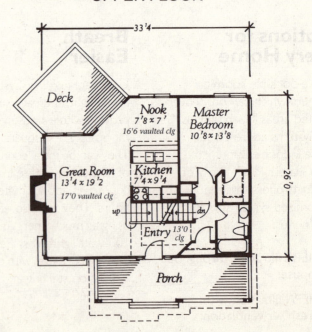

MAIN FLOOR

ORDER BLUEPRINTS ANYTIME!
CALL TOLL-FREE 1-800-820-1296

Plan JWB-9307
Plan copyright held by home designer/architect

PRICES AND DETAILS ON PAGES 12-15

Get More Out of Your basement

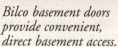

ScapeWEL® window wells create comfortable lower-level living areas.

Bilco basement doors provide convenient, direct basement access.

Better Living Basement® products will provide your home with comfort, convenience and enhanced value.

ScapeWEL® window wells create desirable new living space by adding unprecedented beauty and natural daylight to basement areas while providing safe emergency egress.

Create a lower-level family room, bedroom, home office or other living area to enhance the comfort and value of your home.

ScapeWEL window wells do not require pouring like concrete wells, are less expensive than site-built wells, and unlike metal wells, do not require unsightly ladders to meet emergency egress codes.

Available in a variety of sizes and with optional grates or clear domes, ScapeWEL window wells are landscape-ready and virtually maintenance-free.

Bilco basement doors, featuring counter-balanced lifting mechanisms, automatic safety latches, and weather-proof steel construction have been the first choice of homeowners, architects and contractors since 1926.

Bulky items are easily moved in and out without damage to first-floor walls or woodwork, trades people have easy access to basement-located mechanical systems, and security is enhanced by the positive action slide-lock or the optional keyed entry system.

Bilco doors are available in a variety of sizes, and can be supplied complete with precast concrete steps for new home construction.

ScapeWEL® Window wells and Bilco Basement doors are IRC 2000 compliant.

For more information call **(203)934-6363** or log on to www.bilco.com

Better Living Basements®

Since 1926

COMFY COUNTRY CHARMERS

Compact Three-Bedroom

- Both openness and privacy are possible in this economical three-bedroom home design.
- The inviting covered entry shelters visitors as they make their way into the sidelighted foyer.
- The bright living room boasts a vaulted ceiling, a warming fireplace and corner windows. A high clerestory window lets in additional natural light.
- The modern, U-shaped kitchen features a convenient pantry and a versatile snack bar.
- The adjacent open dining area provides access to a backyard deck through sliding glass doors.
- Lovely corner windows brighten the secluded master bedroom, which also includes a roomy walk-in closet and private access to a compartmentalized hall bath.
- On the upper floor, two good-sized secondary bedrooms share another handy split bath.

Plan B-101-8501

Bedrooms: 3	Baths: 2
Living Area:	
Upper floor	400 sq. ft.
Main floor	846 sq. ft.
Total Living Area:	**1,246 sq. ft.**
Garage	400 sq. ft.
Standard basement	846 sq. ft.
Exterior Wall Framing:	2x4

Foundation Options:
Standard basement
(All plans can be built with your choice of foundation and framing. A generic conversion diagram is available. See order form.)

BLUEPRINT PRICE CODE: A

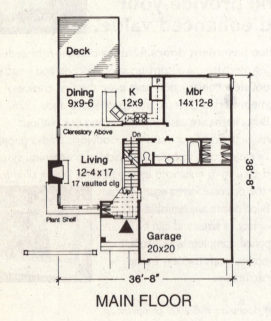

MAIN FLOOR

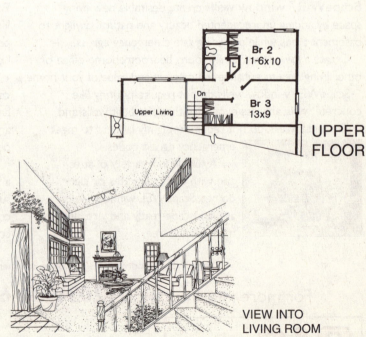

UPPER FLOOR

VIEW INTO LIVING ROOM

ORDER BLUEPRINTS ANYTIME!
CALL TOLL-FREE 1-800-820-1296

Plan B-101-8501
Plan copyright held by home designer/architect

PRICES AND DETAILS ON PAGES 12-15

COMFY COUNTRY CHARMERS

Formal Facade

- Formally balanced with twin dormers, gables and bay windows, a charming Southern-style exterior complements this home's informal interior. Its design boasts a compact, efficient plan with highly functional spaces.
- Featuring a fireplace, a built-in media center and a volume ceiling, the pavilion-style Great Room is flooded with light from the home's front and rear porches.
- Sliding glass doors to the back deck and a bay window highlight the dining room, which is easily served by the adjoining U-shaped kitchen.
- With a large walk-in closet, a private bath, a tray ceiling and a bay window, the secluded master bedroom offers wonderful respite from a busy day.
- Across the home, two secondary bedrooms share a full hall bath.
- An unfinished attic provides future expansion space, ideal for an additional bedroom or a home office.

Plan AX-97359

Bedrooms: 3+	Baths: 2

Living Area:
Main floor	1,380 sq. ft.
Total Living Area:	**1,380 sq. ft.**
Future upper floor	385 sq. ft.
Standard basement	1,380 sq. ft.
Garage	427 sq. ft.

Exterior Wall Framing: 2x4

Foundation Options:
Standard basement
Crawlspace
Slab
(All plans can be built with your choice of foundation and framing. A generic conversion diagram is available. See order form.)

BLUEPRINT PRICE CODE: A

VIEW INTO GREAT ROOM

UPPER FLOOR

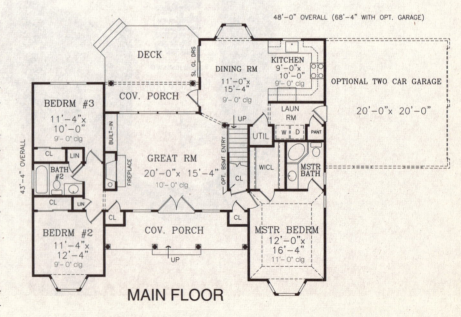

MAIN FLOOR

ORDER BLUEPRINTS ANYTIME!
CALL TOLL-FREE 1-800-820-1296

Plan AX-97359
Plan copyright held by home designer/architect

PRICES AND DETAILS
ON PAGES 12-15

300 Reasons to Own One

40 House Washes   200 Car Washes   60 Deck Cleanings

ZERO BREAKDOWNS*

The Most Important Reason of All

For the ultimate in durability, all Campbell Hausfeld pressure washers are Built to Last. And the fact that they provide the ultimate in versatility doesn't hurt either. Use them to clean decks, siding, cars, patios, and more. The pressure washer pictured above features a 5.5 HP Honda overhead cam engine and a durable axial pump with a long life brass manifold, all in a compact design. (Accessories sold separately.) Every one is Built to Last, so you can count on them 300 times. And beyond!

*Campbell Hausfeld stands by its reputation for quality and durability subject to conditions of our one, two, or three-year limited product warranties. Usage claims are estimates based upon product review and analysis.

© 2002 Campbell Hausfeld
CODE A45

Visit **www.chtools.com/washers** to get a free catalog and join the Powered Equipment Club for special offers.
Call toll-free: 1-866-CHTOOLS (1-866-248-6657)

COMFY COUNTRY CHARMERS

Charming Traditional

- The attractive facade of this traditional home features decorative fretwork and louvers in the gables, plus eye-catching window and door treatments.
- The entry area features a commanding view of the living room, which boasts a high ceiling and a corner fireplace. A rear porch and patio are visible through French doors.
- The bayed dining room shares an eating bar with the U-shaped kitchen. The nearby utility room includes a pantry and laundry facilities.
- The quiet master suite includes a big walk-in closet and a private bath with a dual-sink vanity.
- On the other side of the home, double doors close off the two secondary bedrooms from the living areas. A full bath services this wing.

Plan E-1428

Bedrooms: 3	Baths: 2
Living Area:	
Main floor	1,415 sq. ft.
Total Living Area:	**1,415 sq. ft.**
Garage	484 sq. ft.
Storage	60 sq. ft.
Exterior Wall Framing:	2x6
Foundation Options:	
Crawlspace	
Slab	

(All plans can be built with your choice of foundation and framing. A generic conversion diagram is available. See order form.)

BLUEPRINT PRICE CODE: A

VIEW INTO LIVING ROOM

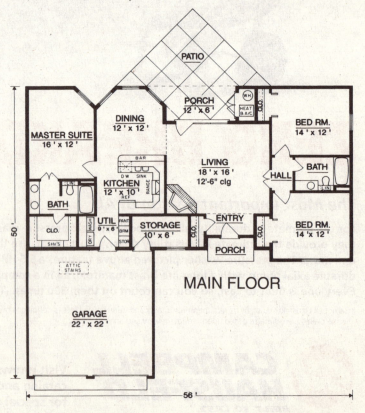

MAIN FLOOR

ORDER BLUEPRINTS ANYTIME!
CALL TOLL-FREE 1-800-820-1296

Plan E-1428
Plan copyright held by home designer/architect

PRICES AND DETAILS ON PAGES 12-15

The Package

Our construction blueprints are detailed, clear and concise. All blueprints are designed by licensed architects or members of the American Institute of Building Design (AIBD) or the Council of Publishing Home Designers (CPHD), and all plans are designed to meet one of the recognized North American building codes (the Uniform Building Code, the Standard Building Code, the Basic Building Code or the National Building Code of Canada) in effect at the time and place they are drawn.

The blueprints for most home designs include the elements listed below, but the presentation of these elements may vary depending on the size and complexity of the home and the style of the individual designer.

Exterior Elevations

Exterior elevations show the front, rear and sides of the house, including exterior materials, details and measurements.

Foundation Plans

Foundation plans include drawings for a full, daylight or partial basement, crawlspace, slab, or pole foundation. All necessary notations and dimensions are included. (Foundation options will vary for each plan. If the home you want does not have the type of foundation you desire, a foundation conversion diagram is available.)

Detailed Floor Plans

Detailed floor plans show the placement of interior walls and the dimensions for rooms, doors, windows, stairways, etc., of each level of the house.

Cross Sections

Cross sections show details of the house as though it were cut in slices from the roof to the foundation. The cross sections specify the home's construction, insulation, flooring and roofing details.

Interior Elevations

Interior elevations show the specific details of cabinets (kitchen, bathroom and utility room), fireplaces, built-in units, and other special interior features, depending on the nature and complexity of the item.

Note: To save money and to accommodate your own style and taste, we suggest contacting local cabinet and fireplace distributors for sizes and styles.

Roof Details

Roof details show slope, pitch and location of dormers, gables and other roof elements, including clerestory windows and skylights.

what our plans include

Other Helpful Building Aids

Every set of plans that you order will contain the details your builder needs. However, additional guides and information are also available:

Planning Sets

Planning sets are a great way to research the home that interests you. A planning set includes all four exterior elevations and the floor plans, shown to scale. Planning sets are stamped "Not for Construction," and may not be used to build a home. Receive full credit for the price of the planning set when you purchase a 4-, 8-, 12- or reproducible-set package of blueprints for that home within 60 days of your planning set purchase. See the chart on page 14 to see if a planning set is available for your design.

Reproducible Blueprint Set

Reproducible sets are useful if you will be making changes to the stock home plan you've chosen. This set consists of line drawings produced on erasable, reproducible paper for the purpose of modification. When alterations are complete, working copies can be made. *Bonus: Includes free working set

Mirror-Reversed Plans

Mirror-reversed plans are used when building the home in reverse of the illustrated floor plan. Reversed plans are available for an additional one-time surcharge. Since the lettering and dimensions read backward, we recommend ordering only one or two reversed sets in addition to the regular-reading sets.

Note: Full-reverse blueprints are available for a limited number of plans. Because lettering and dimensions read normally, all sets in your order will be reversed if your plan is available in full reverse. There is a $50 one-time surcharge for all reversed plans.

Itemized List of Materials

An itemized list of materials details the quantity, type and size of materials needed to build your home. This list is helpful in acquiring

These details may be shown on the elevation sheet or on a separate diagram.

Note: If trusses are used, we suggest using a local truss manufacturer to design your trusses to comply with local codes and regulations.

Electrical Layouts

Schematic electrical layouts show the suggested locations for switches, fixtures and outlets. These details may be shown on the floor plan or on a separate diagram.

General Specifications

General specifications provide general instructions and information regarding structure, excavating and grading, masonry and concrete work, carpentry and wood, thermal and moisture protection, and specifications about drywall, tile, flooring, glazing, caulking and sealants.

Note: Due to regional variations, local availability of materials, local codes, methods of installation, and individual preferences, it is impossible to include much detail on heating, plumbing and electrical work on your plans. The duct work, venting and other details will vary depending on the type of heating and cooling system (forced air, hot water, electric, solar) and the type of energy (gas, oil, electricity, solar) that you use. These details and specifications are easily obtained from your builder, contractor and/or local suppliers.

an accurate construction estimate. An expanded material workbook is available for some plans. Call for details.

Description of Materials

A description of materials may be required by your bank in order to secure a loan through the Federal Housing Administration or the Department of Veterans Affairs. The list specifies the minimum grade of building materials required to meet FHA or VA standards.

Generic "How-To" Diagrams

Plumbing, wiring, solar heating, and framing and foundation conversion diagrams are available. These diagrams detail the basic tools and techniques needed to plumb; wire; install a solar-heating system; convert plans with 2x4 exterior walls to 2x6 (or vice versa); or adapt a plan for a basement, crawlspace or slab foundation.

Note: These diagrams are general and not specific to any one plan.

Ordering Information

read before you buy

Blueprint Prices

Our pricing schedule is based on total heated living space. Garages, porches, decks and unfinished basements are not included in the total square footage.

Architectural and Engineering Seals

The increased concern over energy costs and safety has prompted many cities and states to require an architect or engineer to review and "seal" a blueprint prior to construction. There may be a fee for this service. Contact your local lumberyard, municipal building department, builders association, or local chapter of the AIBD or the American Institute of Architects (AIA).

Note: Plans for homes to be built in Nevada may have to be re-drawn and sealed by a Nevada-licensed design professional.

Foundation Options and Exterior Construction

Depending on your location and climate, your home will normally be built with a slab, crawlspace or basement foundation; the exterior walls will usually be of 2x4 or 2x6 framing. Most professional contractors and builders can easily adapt a home to meet the foundation and exterior wall requirements that you desire.

If the home you select does not offer your preferred type of foundation or exterior walls, you may wish to purchase a generic foundation and framing conversion diagram.

Note: These diagrams are not specific to any one plan.

Exchange Information

We want you to be happy with your home plans. If, for some reason, the blueprints that you ordered cannot be used, we will be pleased to exchange them within 30 days of the purchase date. A handling fee will be assessed for all exchanges. For more information, call toll-free.

Note: Reproducible sets may not be exchanged for any reason.

Estimating Building Costs

Building costs vary widely depending on the style and size of the home, the type of finishing materials you select, and the local rates for labor and building materials. A local average cost per square foot of construction can give you a rough estimate. You can learn this cost from a local contractor, your state or local builders association, the National Association of Home Builders (NAHB), or the AIBD. A more accurate estimate will require a professional review of the working blueprints and the materials you will be using.

13

How Many Blueprints Do You Need?

A single planning set is sufficient to study and review a home in greater detail (see page 12). However, if you are planning to get cost estimates or are planning to build, you will need at least four sets (see the checklist on page 15). If you will be modifying your home plan, we recommend ordering a reproducible set.

Revisions, Modifications and Customization

The tremendous variety of designs available from us allows you to choose the home that best suits your lifestyle, budget and building site. Through your choice of siding, roof, trim, decor, color, etc., your home can be customized easily.

Minor changes and material substitutions can be made by any professional builder without the need for expensive blueprint revisions. However, if you will be making major changes, we strongly recommend that you order a reproducible set and seek the services of an architect or professional designer.

Compliance with Codes

Every state, county and municipality has its own codes, zoning requirements, ordinances and building regulations. Modifications may be needed to comply with your specific requirements—snow loads, energy codes, seismic zones, etc. All of our plans are designed to meet the specifications of seismic zones I or II. We authorize the use of our blueprints expressly conditioned upon your obligation and agreement to strictly comply with all local building codes, ordinances, regulations and requirements, including permits and inspections at the time of construction.

License Agreement, Copy Restrictions and Copyright

When you purchase a blueprint or reproducible set, we, as Licensor, grant you, as Licensee, the right to use these documents to construct a single unit. All of the plans in this publication are protected under the Federal Copyright Act, Title XVII of the United States Code and Chapter 37 of the Code of Federal Regulations. Each designer retains title and ownership of the original documents. The blueprints licensed to you may not be resold or used by any other person, copied or reproduced by any means. When you purchase a reproducible set, you reserve the right to modify and reproduce the plan. Reproducible sets may not be resold or used by any other person. For more details, see our copyright notice on page 16.

Order Form

three ways to order

1.
Call toll-free anytime: 1-800-820-1296.

2.
Fax order form to (651) 602-5002.

3.
Mail your order to the address at the bottom of the form.

AVAILABILITY

plan prefix	planning set	reproducible set	itemized list of materials	description of materials	next-day delivery
A	●	●	C		●
ADI	●	●	C		●
AGH	●	●			●
AHP	●	●	●	●	●
APS	●	●	C		●
AX		●	C		●
B	●	●	C		●
BC	●	●			●
BOD		●	C		●
BRF	●	●			●
BSA	●	●			●
C	●	●	●		●
CC	●	●	C		●
CH	●	●			●
CL	●	●			●
COA	●	●			●
DBI		●	●		●
DD		●	C		●
DP		●			●
DW	●	●	●	●	●
E	C	●	C		●
EOF	●	●	C		●
FB		●	MW		●
FI	●	●			●
GA	●	●			●
GL	●	●			●
GS	●	●			●
H	●	●	●	●	●
HDC	●	●			●
HDS		●	C		●
HFL		●	●		●
HOM	●	●	●		●
HWG	●	●			●
I	●	●	C		●
J		●	C		●
JWB	●				●
K	●	●	●	●	●
KD	●	●			●
KLF	●	●			●
KP	●	●			●
KPS	●	●			●
L	●	●	C		●
LLM	●	●			●
LRK	●	●			●
LS	●	●			●
MIN	●	●			●
NW	●	●	C		●
OH	●	●			●
PI	●	●			●
PSC	●	●			●
RD	●	●			●
RLA	●	●			●
S	●	●	C		●
SDC	●	●			●
SUL	●	●	C		●
SUN	●	●	●		●
TS	●	●			●
UD	●	●	C		●
WAA	●	●			●
WH		●	C		●
Y	●	●		●	●

Legend

●   Available

C   Call for availability.

MW   An expanded material workbook is available for some plans. Call for details.

PRICING

Blueprints & Accessories

Price Code	Planning Set	4 Sets	8 Sets	12 Sets	Reproducible Set*
AAA	$99	$309	$349	$419	$484
AA	$99	$349	$389	$469	$524
A	$99	$419	$454	$529	$589
B	$99	$454	$494	$569	$629
C	$99	$494	$534	$609	$669
D	$99	$564	$609	$664	$704
E	$99	$619	$659	$739	$809
F	$99	$659	$699	$789	$854
G	$99	$704	$744	$829	$904
H	$99	$744	$789	$874	$949
I	$99	$789	$829	$914	$984

Prices subject to change

*A Reproducible Set is produced on erasable paper for the purpose of modification. See page 14 for availability.

Itemized List of Materials

Price Code	1 Set*	Price Code	1 Set*	Price Code	1 Set*
AAA	$60	C	$65	G	$75
AA	$60	D	$65	H	$75
A	$60	E	$70	I	$80
B	$60	F	$70		

See page 14 for availability.   *Additional sets are available for $15 each.

Generic How-To Diagrams

Quantity	Any 1	Any 2	Any 3	All 4
Price	$20	$30	$40	$45

Shipping & Handling

	1-3 sets	4-7 sets	8 sets or more	Reproducible Set
U.S. Regular (5-6 WORKING DAYS)	$15.00	$17.50	$20.00	$20.00
U.S. Express (2-3 WORKING DAYS)	$30.00	$32.50	$35.00	$35.00
U.S. Next Day* (1 WORKING DAY*)	$45.00	$47.50	$50.00	$50.00
Canada Regular (5-7 WORKING DAYS)	$35.00	$40.00	$45.00	$45.00
Canada Express (2-4 WORKING DAYS)	$50.00	$55.00	$60.00	$60.00
International (7-10 WORKING DAYS)	$60.00	$70.00	$80.00	$80.00

*Order before noon Central Time for next-day delivery to most locations.

BLUEPRINT CHECKLIST

_____ **OWNER'S SET(S)**

_____ **BUILDER** (usually requires at least three sets; one for legal document, one for inspections and a minimum of one set for subcontractors)

_____ **BUILDING PERMIT DEPT.** (at least one set; check with your local governing body for number of sets required)

_____ **LENDING INSTITUTION** (usually one set for conventional mortgage; three sets for FHA or VA loans)

_____ **TOTAL NUMBER OF SETS**

BLUEPRINT ORDER FORM

Your Order

Plan Number: FHTR164- _____   **Price Code:** _____

Foundation: _____
(Carefully review the foundation option(s) available for your plan—basement, crawlspace, pole, pier or slab. If several options are offered, choose only one.)

Blueprints

❑ **Planning Set** See page 14 for availability. $ _____ (see left)
  RECOMMENDED FOR REVIEW/STUDY STAMPED "NOT FOR CONSTRUCTION"

❑ **Four Sets**
  RECOMMENDED FOR BIDDING

❑ **Eight Sets**
  RECOMMENDED FOR CONSTRUCTION

❑ **Twelve Sets**
  RECOMMENDED FOR MULTIPLE CONTRACTOR BIDS

❑ **Reproducible Set** See page 14 for availability.
  RECOMMENDED FOR CONSTRUCTION/MODIFICATION INCLUDES ONE FREE BLUEPRINT

Additional Sets   QTY: _____ x $50 = $ _____ ($50 per set)
Additional sets of the plan ordered are $50 each. Available on all plans. With minimum 4-set order only.

Reversed Sets   QTY: _____ $ _____ ($50 surcharge)
If you wish your home to be the mirror image of the illustrated floor plan, please specify how many of your sets should be reversed. (Because the lettering on reversed plans reads backward, we recommend reversing only one or two of your sets.) There is a $50 one-time charge for any number of reversed sets.

Itemized List of Materials   QTY: _____ $ _____ (see left)
See pricing at left. See page 14 for availability.

Description of Materials $ _____ ($60 for set of two)
Sold only in sets of two for $60. See page 14 for availability.

Generic How-To Diagrams $ _____ (see left)
General guides on plumbing, wiring and solar heating, plus information on how to convert from one foundation or exterior framing to another. See pricing at left.
Note: These diagrams are not specific to any one plan.

❑ PLUMBING   ❑ WIRING   ❑ SOLAR HEATING   ❑ FRAMING & FOUNDATION CONVERSION

Order Total

Subtotal $ _____

Sales Tax $ _____
All U.S. residents add appropriate sales tax.
Attention Canadian customers: All sales are final, FOB St. Paul, Minnesota.

Shipping/Handling $ _____
See chart at left.

Total $ _____

Payment Information

❑ CHECK OR MONEY ORDER ENCLOSED (IN U.S. FUNDS)
❑ VISA   ❑ MASTERCARD   ❑ AMEX   ❑ DISCOVER

CARD NUMBER _____ EXP. DATE _____

NAME _____

ADDRESS _____

CITY _____ STATE _____ COUNTRY _____

ZIP CODE _____ DAYTIME PHONE (_____) _____

❑ CHECK HERE IF YOU ARE A BUILDER   HOME PHONE (_____) _____

MAIL TO **Homestore, Dept. FHTR164**
P.O. Box 75488
St. Paul, MN 55175-0488

OR FAX TO **(651) 602-5002**

SOURCE CODE: FHTR164

Copyright

Just like books, movies and songs, our plans are copyrighted. Federal copyright laws protect the intellectual property of architects and home designers. These laws allow for statutory penalties of up to $100,000 per incident, plus legal fees and actual damages, for copyright infringement involving any of the plans found in this publication or on our Web site. These laws stipulate the following:

Construction blueprints may not be duplicated.

If additional sets are required, they may be purchased at a nominal cost. With the purchase of a reproducible set, a license and copyright release are also provided, allowing you to make up to 12 copies of the design. But these copies may only be used for the construction of a single home.

Blueprints may be used for the construction of only one house.

For the construction of more than one unit, it is necessary to obtain an additional release or multiple licenses from the publisher, architect or designer.

You may not copy or adapt home designs found in any plan book, on a CD-ROM or on the Internet.

Creating your own plan by copying even part of a home design is called creating a derivative work and is illegal without permission from the original designer.

Ignorance of the law is not a valid defense! To avoid legal complications and damages, it is critical that you be certain of the original plan source and refuse to be a party to any copying or borrowing of designs.

Rustic Comfort

- Rustic charm highlights the exterior of this design, while the interior is filled with all the latest comforts.
- The sunken living room features a vaulted ceiling with exposed beams. Highlights include a fieldstone fireplace and access to a patio with planters.
- The U-shaped kitchen features a china niche with glass shelves. Other bonuses include the adjacent sewing/hobby room and the oversized utility room.
- The master suite hosts a sunken sleeping area with built-in bookshelves. One step up is a sitting area, where double doors open to the bath, which offers a niche with glass shelves.
- Across the home, two more bedrooms share a second full bath.

Plan E-1607	
Bedrooms: 3	**Baths:** 2
Living Area:	
Main floor	1,600 sq. ft.
Total Living Area:	**1,600 sq. ft.**
Standard basement	1,600 sq. ft.
Garage and workbench	484 sq. ft.
Storage	132 sq. ft.
Exterior Wall Framing:	2x6
Foundation Options:	
Standard basement	
Crawlspace	
Slab	
(All plans can be built with your choice of foundation and framing. A generic conversion diagram is available. See order form.)	
BLUEPRINT PRICE CODE:	**B**

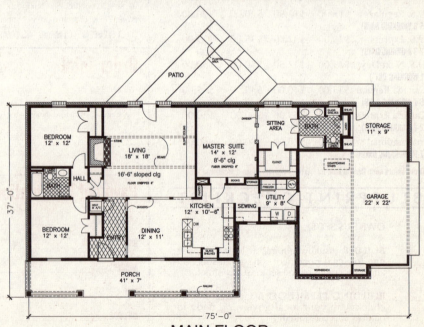

MAIN FLOOR

ORDER BLUEPRINTS ANYTIME!
CALL TOLL-FREE 1-800-820-1296

Plan E-1607
Plan copyright held by home designer/architect

PRICES AND DETAILS ON PAGES 12-15

COMFY COUNTRY CHARMERS

Classic Facade

- Shuttered windows, clapboard siding with corner board trim, a porch framed by slender posts and other Colonial-inspired touches imbue this one-story with the charm of Americana.
- The attractive, functional entry with a convenient coat closet leads into the spacious living room, which features a corner fireplace. The entrance to this room is thoughtfully secluded from the home's casual areas, making it a perfect spot for entertaining.
- Straight back from the entry, a pocket door hides the kitchen from immediate view. The kitchen's smart layout includes a snack bar that serves the adjoining room: a spacious family room in the basement version or a dining room in the crawlspace version.
- The home's sleeping quarters reside down a quiet hallway on the other side of the home. The master bedroom includes a private bath and a walk-in closet. Two secondary bedrooms share a full bath and ample linen storage. An optional playroom is ideal for storing toys or housing overnight visitors.

Plans H-3707-1 & -1A

Bedrooms: 3+	Baths: 2
Living Area:	
Main floor	1,486 sq. ft.
Total Living Area:	**1,486 sq. ft.**
Standard basement	1,486 sq. ft.
Garage	411 sq. ft.
Exterior Wall Framing:	2x4
Foundation Options:	**Plan #**
Standard basement	H-3707-1
Crawlspace	H-3707-1A
(All plans can be built with your choice of foundation and framing. A generic conversion diagram is available. See order form.)	
BLUEPRINT PRICE CODE:	**A**

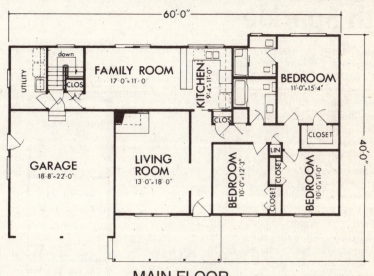

MAIN FLOOR
(Basement Version)

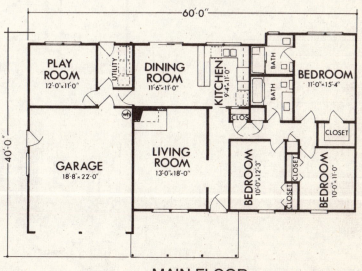

MAIN FLOOR
(Crawlspace Version)

ORDER BLUEPRINTS ANYTIME! CALL TOLL-FREE 1-800-820-1296

Plans H-3707-1 & -1A
Plan copyright held by home designer/architect

PRICES AND DETAILS ON PAGES 12-15

COMFY COUNTRY CHARMERS

Single-Story with Sparkle

- A lovely facade with bay windows and dormers give this home extra sparkle.
- The Great Room anchors the floor plan, adjoining both the dining room and a screened porch. It also has a fireplace, a tray ceiling and a built-in wet bar.
- The eat-in kitchen utilizes a half-wall to stay connected with the Great Room, while the dining room offers a bay window that overlooks the porch. A convenient two-car garage is nearby.
- The master suite is set apart from two secondary bedrooms for privacy, and it includes a bay window, a tray ceiling, and a luxurious private bath.
- The two smaller bedrooms are off the main foyer and separated by a full bath.
- A mudroom with washer and dryer is accessible from the two-car garage, which is disguised with a beautiful bay window.

Plan AX-91312

Bedrooms: 3	Baths: 2
Living Area:	
Main floor	1,595 sq. ft.
Total Living Area:	**1,595 sq. ft.**
Screened porch	178 sq. ft.
Basement	1,595 sq. ft.
Garage	469 sq. ft.
Storage	21 sq. ft.
Utility room	18 sq. ft.
Exterior Wall Framing:	2x4
Foundation Options:	
Daylight basement	
Standard basement	
Crawlspace	
Slab	
(All plans can be built with your choice of foundation and framing. A generic conversion diagram is available. See order form.)	
BLUEPRINT PRICE CODE:	**B**

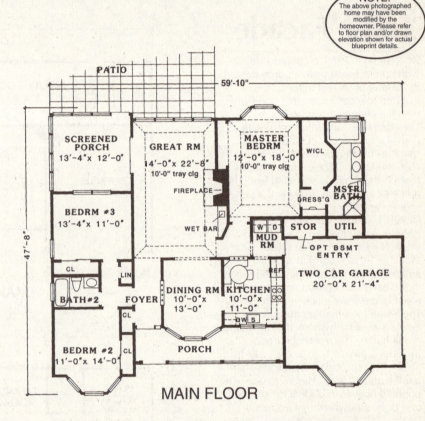

MAIN FLOOR

VIEW INTO GREAT ROOM

ORDER BLUEPRINTS ANYTIME!
CALL TOLL-FREE 1-800-820-1296

Plan AX-91312
Plan copyright held by home designer/architect

PRICES AND DETAILS ON PAGES 12-15

COMFY COUNTRY CHARMERS

Small Wonder

- This very affordable one-story home boasts an extremely efficient floor plan that maximizes the compact square footage. High ceilings in the shared living areas and in the master suite give the illusion of even more space.
- An elegant columned porch with gorgeous arched windows greets visitors and welcomes you home every day. Plenty of room is available here to sit and watch the day go by.
- The front entry opens directly into the good-sized living room, where you will enjoy years of memories in the making. A vaulted ceiling soars above, while a warm fireplace flanked by decorative plant shelves serves as the room's comforting focal point.
- The tiled dining room and U-shaped kitchen nearby share a vaulted ceiling. Easy access to the dining room will make family meals quick and easy. A patio provides a pleasing setting to enjoy a glass of fresh lemonade.
- The secluded master bedroom features a vaulted ceiling and a private bath.

Plan DD-1100-B

Bedrooms: 3	Baths: 2
Living Area:	
Main floor	1,100 sq. ft.
Total Living Area:	**1,100 sq. ft.**
Garage	416 sq. ft.
Exterior Wall Framing:	2x4

Foundation Options:
Crawlspace
Slab
(All plans can be built with your choice of foundation and framing. A generic conversion diagram is available. See order form.)

BLUEPRINT PRICE CODE: A

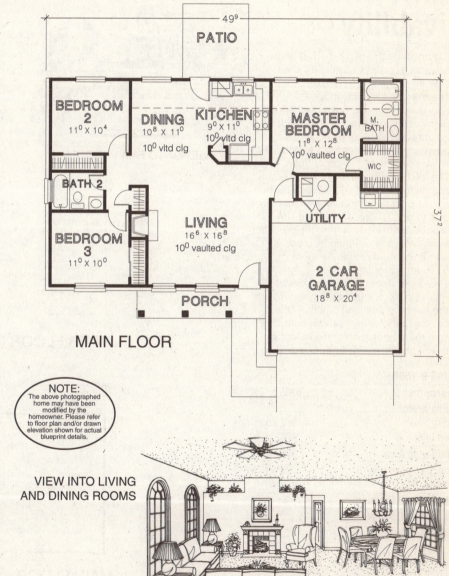

MAIN FLOOR

NOTE: The above photographed home may have been modified by the homeowner. Please refer to floor plan and/or drawn elevation shown for actual blueprint details.

VIEW INTO LIVING AND DINING ROOMS

ORDER BLUEPRINTS ANYTIME!
CALL TOLL-FREE 1-800-820-1296

Plan DD-1100-B
Plan copyright held by home designer/architect

PRICES AND DETAILS ON PAGES 12-15

19

COMFY COUNTRY CHARMERS

Luxury and Livability

- Big on style, this modest-sized home features a quaint Colonial-inspired exterior and an open interior.
- The front porch leads to a two-story foyer that opens to the formal living and dining rooms. A coat closet, an attractive display niche and a powder room are centrally located, as is the stairway to the upper floor.
- The kitchen, breakfast nook and family room are designed so that each room has its own definition yet also functions as part of a whole. The angled sink separates the kitchen from the breakfast nook, which is outlined by a bay window. The large family room includes a fireplace.
- The upper floor has an exceptional master suite, featuring a tray ceiling in the sleeping area and a high, vaulted ceiling in the deluxe private bath.
- Two more bedrooms and a balcony overlook add to this home's livability.

VIEW INTO FAMILY ROOM

NOTE: The above photographed home may have been modified by the homeowner. Please refer to floor plan and/or drawn elevation shown for actual blueprint details.

Plan FB-1600	
Bedrooms: 3	Baths: 2½
Living Area:	
Upper floor	772 sq. ft.
Main floor	828 sq. ft.
Total Living Area	**1,600 sq. ft.**
Daylight basement	828 sq. ft.
Garage	473 sq. ft.
Exterior Wall Framing	2x4
Foundation Options:	
Daylight basement	
Crawlspace	
Slab	
(All plans can be built with your choice of foundation and framing. A generic conversion diagram is available. See order form.)	
BLUEPRINT PRICE CODE:	**B**

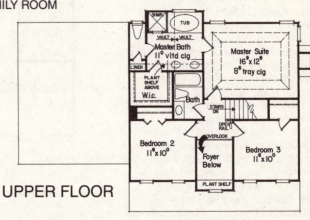

UPPER FLOOR

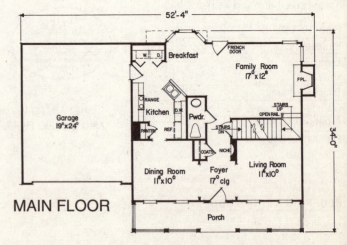

MAIN FLOOR

ORDER BLUEPRINTS ANYTIME!
CALL TOLL-FREE 1-800-820-1296

Plan FB-1600
Plan copyright held by home designer/architect

PRICES AND DETAILS ON PAGES 12-15

COMFY COUNTRY CHARMERS

Spacious Economy

- This economical country cottage features wide, angled spaces and 9-ft., 4-in. ceilings in both the Great Room and the master bedroom for roomy appeal and year-round comfort.
- The Great Room boasts a cozy fireplace with a raised hearth and a built-in niche for a TV, making this room perfect for winter gatherings. On warm nights, a homey covered porch at the rear can be accessed through sliding glass doors.
- Amenities in the luxurious master bedroom include a large walk-in closet, a private whirlpool bath and a dual-sink vanity.
- The nicely appointed kitchen offers nearby laundry facilities and porch access. A serving bar allows for casual dining and relaxed conversation.
- The optional daylight basement includes a tuck-under, two-car garage.

Plan AX-94322

Bedrooms: 3	Baths: 2½
Living Area:	
Upper floor	545 sq. ft.
Main floor	1,134 sq. ft.
Total Living Area:	**1,679 sq. ft.**
Daylight basement	618 sq. ft.
Standard basement	1,134 sq. ft.
Tuck-under garage	516 sq. ft.
Exterior Wall Framing:	2x4

Foundation Options:
Daylight basement
Standard basement
Crawlspace
Slab
(All plans can be built with your choice of foundation and framing. A generic conversion diagram is available. See order form.)

BLUEPRINT PRICE CODE: B

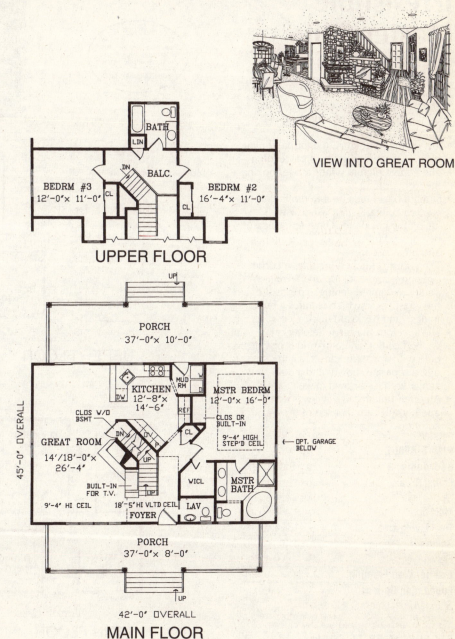

VIEW INTO GREAT ROOM

ORDER BLUEPRINTS ANYTIME!
CALL TOLL-FREE 1-800-820-1296

Plan AX-94322
Plan copyright held by home designer/architect

PRICES AND DETAILS
ON PAGES 12-15

COMFY COUNTRY CHARMERS

Irresistible Master Suite

- This home's main-floor master suite is hard to resist, with its inviting window seat and delightful bath.
- The home is introduced by a covered front entry, topped by a dormer with a half-round window.
- Just off the front entry, the formal dining room is distinguished by a tray ceiling and a large picture window overlooking the front porch.
- Straight back, the Great Room features a vaulted ceiling with a window wall facing the backyard. The fireplace can be enjoyed from the adjoining kitchen and breakfast area.
- The gourmet kitchen includes a corner sink, an island cooktop and a walk-in pantry. A vaulted ceiling expands the breakfast nook, which features a built-in desk and backyard deck access.
- The spacious master suite offers a vaulted ceiling and a luxurious private bath with a walk-in closet, a garden tub, a separate shower and a dual-sink vanity with a sit-down makeup area.
- An open-railed stairway leads up to another full bath that serves two additional bedrooms.

NOTE: The photographed home may have been modified by the homeowner. Please refer to floor plan and/or drawn elevation shown for actual blueprint details.

REAR VIEW

Plan B-89061	
Bedrooms: 3	**Baths:** 2½
Living Area:	
Upper floor	436 sq. ft.
Main floor	1,490 sq. ft.
Total Living Area:	**1,926 sq. ft.**
Standard basement	1,490 sq. ft.
Garage	400 sq. ft.
Exterior Wall Framing:	2x4
Foundation Options:	
Standard basement	
(All plans can be built with your choice of foundation and framing. A generic conversion diagram is available. See order form.)	
BLUEPRINT PRICE CODE:	**B**

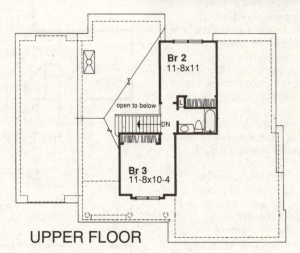
UPPER FLOOR

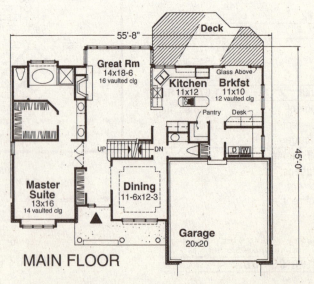
MAIN FLOOR

ORDER BLUEPRINTS ANYTIME!
CALL TOLL-FREE 1-800-820-1296

Plan B-89061
Plan copyright held by home designer/architect

PRICES AND DETAILS ON PAGES 12-15

COMFY COUNTRY CHARMERS

Classic Combo

- This snappy home combines classic touches with thoughtful design.
- Eye-catching arches frame the front porch. Inside, you'll be stunned by the expansive family room, where a cathedral ceiling and a majestic fireplace enhance the space.
- Double doors lead into the living room, where a vaulted ceiling and a Palladian window create an ideal spot for entertaining visitors.
- Through a graceful archway, the efficient kitchen includes a handy pantry and a serving bar overlooking the bayed breakfast nook.
- A screened porch with a vaulted ceiling opens to a deck for alfresco meals and relaxation.
- The dining room showcases a pair of tall windows and a tray ceiling.
- In the master suite, a cathedral ceiling, a separate sitting area, a lavish private bath and access to the deck create a wonderful retreat.
- Two more bedrooms share a bath on the other side of the home.
- The blueprints offer the choice of a two- or three-car garage.

Plan APS-1911

Bedrooms: 3	Baths: 2½

Living Area:
Main floor ..... 1,992 sq. ft.
Total Living Area: ..... **1,992 sq. ft.**
Screened porch ..... 192 sq. ft.
Standard basement ..... 1,992 sq. ft.
Garage ..... 649 sq. ft.

Exterior Wall Framing: 2x4

Foundation Options:
Standard basement
Crawlspace
Slab
(All plans can be built with your choice of foundation and framing. A generic conversion diagram is available. See order form.)

BLUEPRINT PRICE CODE: B

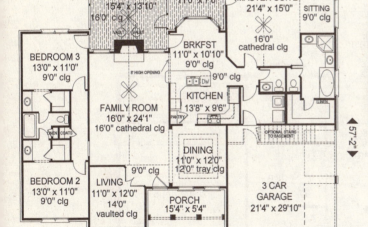

MAIN FLOOR

REAR VIEW

VIEW INTO FAMILY ROOM

ORDER BLUEPRINTS ANYTIME!
CALL TOLL-FREE 1-800-820-1296

Plan APS-1911
Plan copyright held by home designer/architect

PRICES AND DETAILS ON PAGES 12-15

COMFY COUNTRY CHARMERS

Memories in the Making

- You will enjoy years of memories in this peaceful country home.
- A tranquil covered porch opens into the foyer, where regal columns introduce the formal dining room. Raised ceilings enhance the foyer, dining room, kitchen and breakfast nook.
- Past two closets, a cathedral ceiling adds glamour to the living room. A grand fireplace flanked by French doors under beautiful quarter-round transoms will wow your guests! The French doors open to an inviting porch that is great for afternoon get-togethers.
- The sunny breakfast bay merges with the gourmet kitchen, which includes a large pantry and an island snack bar. Bifold doors above the sink create a handy pass-through to the living room.
- A neat computer room nearby allows the kids to do their homework under a parent's watchful eye.
- Across the home, a stylish tray ceiling crowns the master suite. The skylighted master bath features a refreshing whirlpool tub.
- A hall bath services two additional bedrooms. The larger bedroom is expanded by a vaulted ceiling.

Plan J-9294

Bedrooms: 3	Baths: 2

Living Area:
Main floor	2,018 sq. ft.
Total Living Area:	**2,018 sq. ft.**
Standard basement	2,018 sq. ft.
Garage and storage	556 sq. ft.

Exterior Wall Framing: 2x4

Foundation Options:
Standard basement
Crawlspace
Slab
(All plans can be built with your choice of foundation and framing. A generic conversion diagram is available. See order form.)

BLUEPRINT PRICE CODE: C

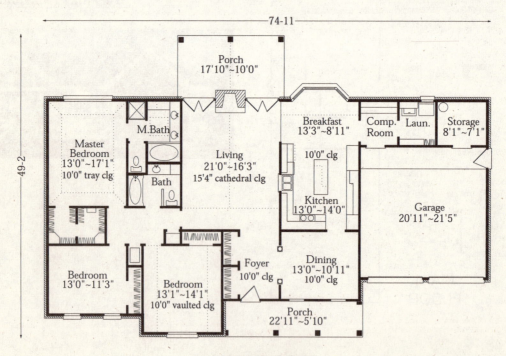

MAIN FLOOR

ORDER BLUEPRINTS ANYTIME! CALL TOLL-FREE 1-800-820-1296

Plan J-9294
Plan copyright held by home designer/architect

PRICES AND DETAILS ON PAGES 12-15

Open, Flowing Floor Plan

- Open, flowing rooms punctuated with wonderful windows enhance this spacious four-bedroom home.
- The two-story-high foyer is brightened by an arched window above. To the left lies the living room, which flows into the family room. An inviting fireplace and windows overlooking a rear terrace highlight the family room.
- The centrally located kitchen serves both the formal dining room and the bayed dinette, where sliding glass doors open to the terrace.
- Upstairs, the master suite features an arched window and a walk-in closet with a dressing area. The private master bath includes a dual-sink vanity, a skylighted whirlpool tub and a separate shower.
- The three remaining bedrooms share another skylighted bath.

Plan AHP-9020	
Bedrooms: 4	**Baths:** 2½
Living Area:	
Upper floor	1,021 sq. ft.
Main floor	1,125 sq. ft.
Total Living Area:	**2,146 sq. ft.**
Standard basement	1,032 sq. ft.
Garage and storage/workroom	543 sq. ft.
Exterior Wall Framing:	2x4 or 2x6
Foundation Options:	
Standard basement	
Crawlspace	
Slab	
(All plans can be built with your choice of foundation and framing. A generic conversion diagram is available. See order form.)	
BLUEPRINT PRICE CODE:	C

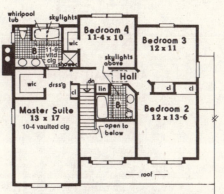

UPPER FLOOR

VIEW INTO MASTER BATH

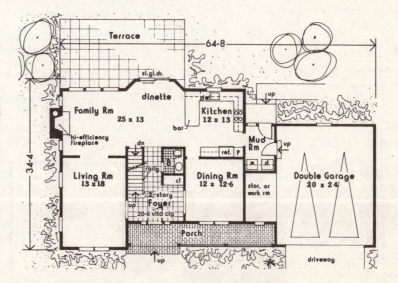

MAIN FLOOR

COMFY COUNTRY CHARMERS

ORDER BLUEPRINTS ANYTIME!
CALL TOLL-FREE 1-800-820-1296

Plan AHP-9020
Plan copyright held by home designer/architect

PRICES AND DETAILS ON PAGES 12-15

COMFY COUNTRY CHARMERS

Front Porch Invites Visitors

- This neat and well-proportioned design exudes warmth and charm, with an inviting front porch and a decorative sunburst in the gable.
- The broad foyer flows between the formal areas for special occasions. The living room and expansive family room join together, creating additional space for larger gatherings.
- The bright and airy kitchen, dinette and family room intermingle for great casual family living.
- Upstairs, the roomy master suite is complemented by a private bath available in two configurations. The alternate master bath adds 70 sq. ft. to the home.
- Two additional bedrooms share another full bath and a sunny library that overlooks the foyer.

Plan GL-2161

Bedrooms: 3	Baths: 2½
Living Area:	
Upper floor	991 sq. ft.
Main floor	1,170 sq. ft.
Total Living Area:	**2,161 sq. ft.**
Standard basement	1,170 sq. ft.
Garage	462 sq. ft.
Exterior Wall Framing:	2x6

Foundation Options:
Standard basement
(All plans can be built with your choice of foundation and framing. A generic conversion diagram is available. See order form.)

BLUEPRINT PRICE CODE: C

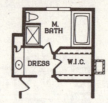

ALTERNATE BATH

VIEW INTO BREAKFAST NOOK AND KITCHEN

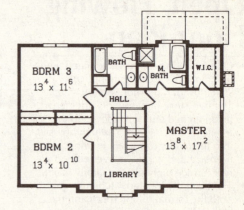

UPPER FLOOR

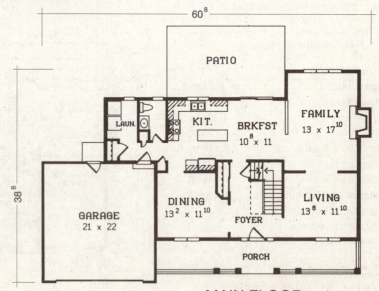

MAIN FLOOR

PRICES AND DETAILS ON PAGES 12-15

26 ORDER BLUEPRINTS ANYTIME! CALL TOLL-FREE 1-800-820-1296

Plan GL-2161
Plan copyright held by home designer/architect

A Move Up

- Narrow lap siding and repeated round-top windows with divided panes give this traditional home a different look.
- The roomy interior offers space for the upwardly mobile family, with four to five bedrooms and large activity areas.
- The two-story foyer welcomes guests into a spacious formal area that combines the living and dining rooms. The rooms share a dramatic cathedral ceiling, while a handsome fireplace adds a peaceful glow.
- A second fireplace and a media center make the family room a fun retreat. French doors open to a lovely terrace.
- Adjoining the family room is a well-designed kitchen with a bayed dinette.
- Double doors introduce the secluded master suite, which boasts a sloped ceiling and a quiet terrace. The private bath offers an invigorating whirlpool tub under a skylight.
- Behind double doors is a cozy study or fifth bedroom. Three more bedrooms and another bath occupy the upper floor.

Plan AHP-9396	
Bedrooms: 4+	**Baths:** 2½
Living Area:	
Upper floor	643 sq. ft.
Main floor	1,553 sq. ft.
Total Living Area:	**2,196 sq. ft.**
Standard basement	1,553 sq. ft.
Garage and storage	502 sq. ft.
Exterior Wall Framing:	2x4 or 2x6
Foundation Options:	
Standard basement	
Crawlspace	
Slab	
(All plans can be built with your choice of foundation and framing. A generic conversion diagram is available. See order form.)	
BLUEPRINT PRICE CODE:	**C**

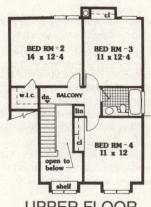

UPPER FLOOR

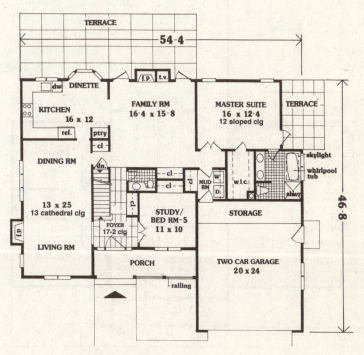

VIEW INTO LIVING AND DINING ROOMS

MAIN FLOOR

ORDER BLUEPRINTS ANYTIME!
CALL TOLL-FREE 1-800-820-1296

Plan AHP-9396
Plan copyright held by home designer/architect

PRICES AND DETAILS ON PAGES 12-15

COMFY COUNTRY CHARMERS

COMFY COUNTRY CHARMERS

Gracious Traditional

- This traditional home is perfect for a corner lot, with a quaint facade and an attached garage around back.
- Tall windows, elegant dormers and a covered front porch welcome guests to the front entry and into the foyer.
- Just off the foyer, the formal dining room boasts a built-in hutch and views to the front porch.
- The expansive, skylighted Great Room features a wet bar, a vaulted ceiling, a stunning fireplace and access to the screened back porch.
- The kitchen includes a large pantry and an eating bar to the bayed breakfast nook. A large utility room with garage access is nearby.
- The master bedroom offers a walk-in closet and a bath with a large corner tub and his-and-hers vanities.
- Two additional bedrooms have big walk-in closets, built-in desks and easy access to another full bath.
- Upstairs, a loft overlooks the Great Room and is perfect as an extra bedroom or a recreation area.

Plan C-8920	
Bedrooms: 3+	**Baths:** 3
Living Area:	
Upper floor	305 sq. ft.
Main floor	1,996 sq. ft.
Total Living Area:	**2,301 sq. ft.**
Screened porch	260 sq. ft.
Daylight basement	1,996 sq. ft.
Garage	469 sq. ft.
Storage	41 sq. ft.
Exterior Wall Framing:	2x4

Foundation Options:
Daylight basement
Crawlspace
(All plans can be built with your choice of foundation and framing. A generic conversion diagram is available. See order form.)

BLUEPRINT PRICE CODE: C

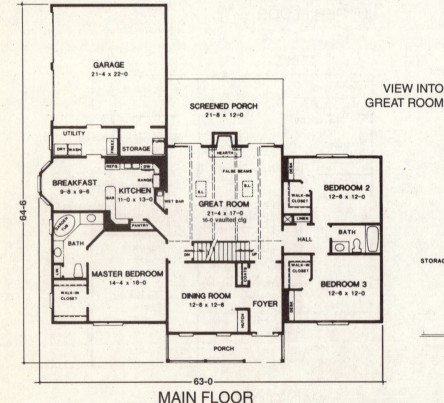

MAIN FLOOR

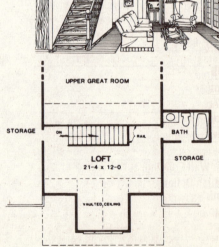

VIEW INTO GREAT ROOM

UPPER FLOOR

28   ORDER BLUEPRINTS ANYTIME! CALL TOLL-FREE 1-800-820-1296   **Plan C-8920**   PRICES AND DETAILS ON PAGES 12-15

Plan copyright held by home designer/architect

Enlightened Simplicity

- This stunning home draws its restful, nostalgic quality and elegant styling from its Craftsman heritage. But the comforts and amenities found inside reveal that the style is only a point of departure. You'll find luxuries you've only dreamed of!
- The front door opens into a gallery, perfect for displaying your artwork, textiles or pottery.
- Columns announce the Great Room beyond. A cheery fireplace anchors this expansive communal living space.
- The spacious island kitchen, served by a walk-in pantry and an angled counter bar, adjoins both the breakfast room and the formal dining room.
- An enormous walk-in closet, a garden tub, a separate shower and a dual-sink vanity update the master suite, which enjoys a sloped ceiling.
- The lavish guest quarters (the perfect in-law suite or media room) are nestled in a corner of the home for privacy.

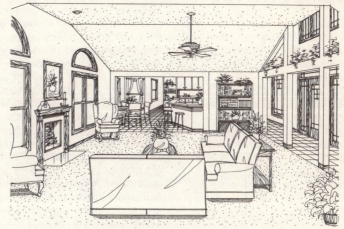

VIEW INTO GREAT ROOM, NOOK AND KITCHEN

Plan DD-2541-1B

Bedrooms: 4	Baths: 3
Living Area:	
Main floor	2,541 sq. ft.
Total Living Area:	**2,541 sq. ft.**
Standard basement	2,541 sq. ft.
Garage and workshop	498 sq. ft.
Exterior Wall Framing:	2x4

Foundation Options:
Standard basement
Crawlspace
Slab
(All plans can be built with your choice of foundation and framing. A generic conversion diagram is available. See order form.)

BLUEPRINT PRICE CODE: D

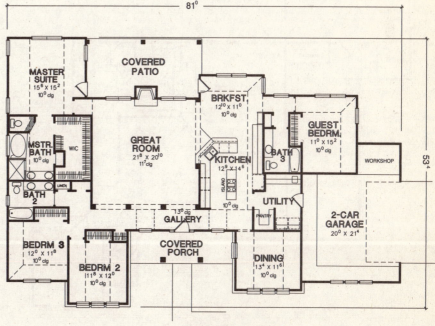

MAIN FLOOR

ORDER BLUEPRINTS ANYTIME!
CALL TOLL-FREE 1-800-820-1296

Plan DD-2541-1B
Plan copyright held by home designer/architect

PRICES AND DETAILS ON PAGES 12-15

COMFY COUNTRY CHARMERS

Award Winner!

- A successful combination of a traditional exterior and modern interior spaces makes this home a winner.
- A winning entry in a recent national design competition, this design has a facade that is filled with character and free of overbearing garage doors. The focus instead goes to the front entry, with decorative columns supporting a covered porch highlighted by a curved shed roof.

- A two-story foyer greets guests. Graceful arched openings and pillars separate the foyer from the formal dining room and the Great Room, which boasts a fireplace and views of a backyard patio.
- The gourmet kitchen features an island cooktop, a walk-in pantry and a snack bar to the sunny breakfast room.
- The main-floor master suite offers a private porch and a spacious personal bath with a garden tub, a separate shower and a large walk-in closet.
- Another bedroom and a full bath round out the main floor. Two more bedrooms are located upstairs, with a third full bath and a loft reading area under a dormer. A central game room features access to a sunny corner deck.

Plan BOD-26-8A

Bedrooms: 4	Baths: 3
Living Area:	
Upper floor	792 sq. ft.
Main floor	1,904 sq. ft.
Total Living Area:	**2,696 sq. ft.**
Standard basement	1,904 sq. ft.
Garage and storage	528 sq. ft.
Exterior Wall Framing:	2x4

Foundation Options:
Standard basement
Crawlspace
Slab
(All plans can be built with your choice of foundation and framing. A generic conversion diagram is available. See order form.)

BLUEPRINT PRICE CODE: D

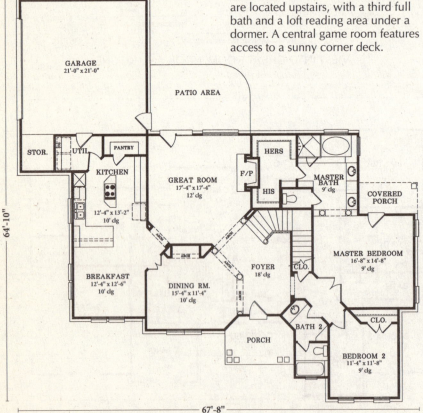

MAIN FLOOR

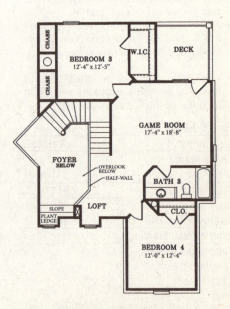

UPPER FLOOR

30   **ORDER BLUEPRINTS ANYTIME! CALL TOLL-FREE 1-800-820-1296**   **Plan BOD-26-8A** Plan copyright held by home designer/architect   **PRICES AND DETAILS ON PAGES 12-15**

Phillip Mueller

COMFY COUNTRY CHARMERS

Once Upon a Cottage

- Right out of a child's fairytale, this enchanting cottage is filled with treasures for the whole family.
- Stone walls, steep rooflines and tapered columns lend the Craftsman-style exterior a highly rustic and incredibly warm ambience. Wraparound decking adds considerable outdoor living space.
- Designed for family function and comfort, the interior is dramatically open and innovative. The kitchen's oversized island serves as the hub of the home and handles all of your meal preparation and entertaining needs.
- Built-in seating with tuck-under storage makes great use of space in the eating nook. A hutch, desk, pantry, buffet and media center offer other creative and attractive storage options.
- Upstairs, private baths and walk-in closets serve the three bedrooms.
- The blueprints include plans for optional rooms in the basement: a media room, a playroom and a guest room with a bath.

Plan FI-3120	
Bedrooms: 3+	**Baths:** 3½
Living Area:	
Upper floor	1,410 sq. ft.
Main floor	1,710 sq. ft.
Total Living Area:	**3,120 sq. ft.**
Screened porch	144 sq. ft.
Daylight basement	1,710 sq. ft.
Garage	559 sq. ft.
Exterior Wall Framing:	2x6

Foundation Options:
Daylight basement
(All plans can be built with your choice of foundation and framing. A generic conversion diagram is available. See order form.)

BLUEPRINT PRICE CODE: E

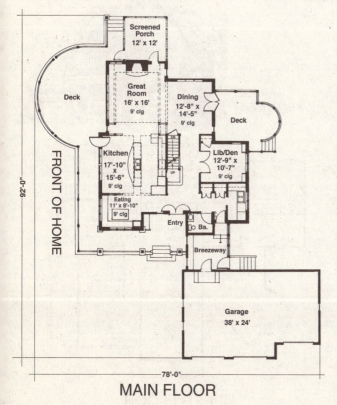

MAIN FLOOR

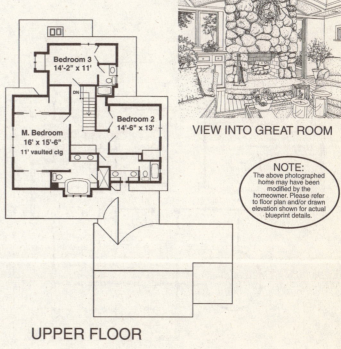

UPPER FLOOR

VIEW INTO GREAT ROOM

NOTE: The above photographed home may have been modified by the homeowner. Please refer to floor plan and/or drawn elevation shown for actual blueprint details.

ORDER BLUEPRINTS ANYTIME!
CALL TOLL-FREE 1-800-820-1296

Plan FI-3120
Plan copyright held by home designer/architect

PRICES AND DETAILS ON PAGES 12-15

31

COMFY COUNTRY CHARMERS

Extra Luxurious

- This luxurious home comes with every imaginable entertaining extra: a game room, a pub with a sit-down wet bar, two media centers and a media room!
- A nostalgic veranda highlights the shingled facade. Inside, the open foyer flows into the formal dining room.
- Double doors conceal a library, which unfolds to a bright circular study.
- The gourmet kitchen easily services the dining room and a sunny nook.
- A cozy fireplace makes the spacious living room warm and inviting.
- The game room offers another fireplace and French-door access to a second covered veranda. A cathedral ceiling tops the bayed pub and wet bar.
- Upstairs, the master suite boasts a sitting area with a high ceiling, plus an exciting corner Jacuzzi tub. Three more bedrooms—one with a high cathedral ceiling—share two baths. In the media room, shutters above the entertainment center offer dramatic views of the foyer.
- Plans for a detached three-car garage are included with the blueprints. A one-bedroom apartment (648 sq. ft.) is located above the garage.

Plan L-023-HD

Bedrooms: 4+	**Baths:** 3½
Living Area:	
Upper floor	1,938 sq. ft.
Main floor	2,083 sq. ft.
Total Living Area:	**4,021 sq. ft.**
Garage	843 sq. ft.
Exterior Wall Framing:	2x4
Foundation Options:	
Slab	

(All plans can be built with your choice of foundation and framing. A generic conversion diagram is available. See order form.)

BLUEPRINT PRICE CODE: G

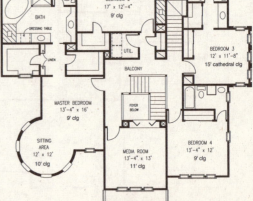

GARAGE/APARTMENT

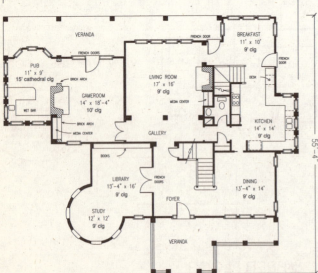

MAIN FLOOR

UPPER FLOOR

ORDER BLUEPRINTS ANYTIME!
CALL TOLL-FREE 1-800-820-1296

Plan L-023-HD
Plan copyright held by home designer/architect

PRICES AND DETAILS ON PAGES 12-15

COMFY COUNTRY CHARMERS

Easy Living for All

- This tidy home adopts the precepts of universal design to create an easy living environment for all ages and abilities.
- Wide halls and doorways facilitate passage between the common and private rooms. The bath is generously proportioned for easy mobility. Front and back entries are "no-step," meaning the thresholds are flush with both the inside and outside flooring surfaces.
- The living spaces themselves are warmly inviting. The front porch beckons you to enjoy a book and conversations with passersby.
- Inside, the living room flows smoothly into the dining room. The kitchenette at the rear of the home is just the ticket for meal preparation. Breakfast can be eaten quickly at the handy bar or enjoyed at your leisure on the back porch.
- The bedroom boasts open closet space and bright windows. Close by, the bathroom features a sit-down shower.

Plan PSC-786	
Bedrooms: 1	Baths: 1
Living Area:	
Main floor	786 sq. ft.
Total Living Area:	786 sq. ft.
Exterior Wall Framing:	2x4

Foundation Options:
Crawlspace
Slab
(All plans can be built with your choice of foundation and framing. A generic conversion diagram is available. See order form.)

BLUEPRINT PRICE CODE: AA

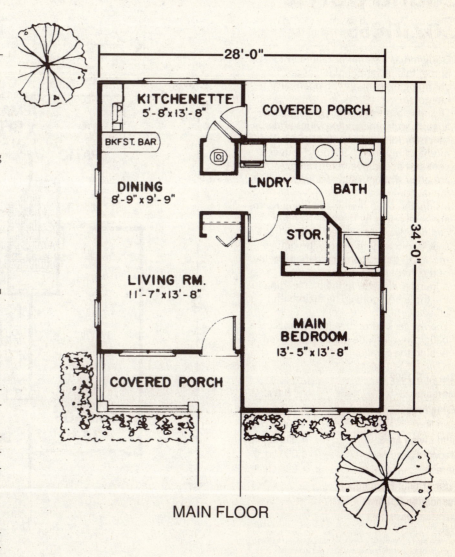

MAIN FLOOR

ORDER BLUEPRINTS ANYTIME!
CALL TOLL-FREE 1-800-820-1296

Plan PSC-786
Plan copyright held by home designer/architect

PRICES AND DETAILS ON PAGES 12-15

Country-Style Coziness

- Designed as a starter or retirement home, this delightful plan has a charming exterior and an open, airy interior.
- The spacious front porch gives guests a warm welcome and provides added space for relaxing or entertaining. The modified hip roof, half-round louver vent and decorative porch railings are other distinguishing features of the facade.
- Inside, the open dining and living rooms are heightened by dramatic vaulted ceilings. The streamlined kitchen has a snack counter joining it to the dining room. All three rooms reap the benefits of the fireplace.
- A laundry closet is in the hall leading to the three bedrooms. The main bath is close by.
- The master bedroom suite offers its own bath, plus a private patio sequestered behind the garage.

Plan APS-1002

Bedrooms: 3	Baths: 2
Living Area:	
Main floor	1,050 sq. ft.
Total Living Area:	**1,050 sq. ft.**
Standard basement	1,050 sq. ft.
Garage	288 sq. ft.
Exterior Wall Framing:	2x4

Foundation Options:
Standard basement
Slab
(All plans can be built with your choice of foundation and framing. A generic conversion diagram is available. See order form.)

BLUEPRINT PRICE CODE: A

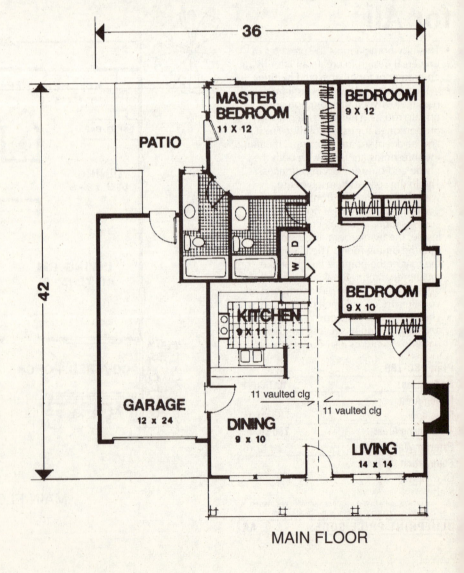

MAIN FLOOR

Plan APS-1002
Plan copyright held by home designer/architect

Affordable Comfort

- Compact and cozy, this attractive home gives you comfort and livability at an affordable price.
- The railed front porch is a nice touch; guests will certainly feel welcome when they come over to see you.
- Inside the front entry, the grand living room is immediately visible. A handsome fireplace sets a happy tone, while sliding glass doors give way to pleasant backyard landscaping.
- At the front of the home, a boxed-out corner window brightens the U-shaped kitchen. The open dining area is perfect for any meal, from a snack to a feast.
- Sleeping areas flank the living room, with each bedroom enjoying a measure of privacy. The quiet master suite boasts a walk-in closet and a personal bath. A corner window arrangement makes a nice spot to relax with a good book.
- Mirror-image secondary bedrooms share a nice-sized hall bath.
- Laundry facilities are located in the two-car garage, just off the foyer.

Plan L-1022

Bedrooms: 3	Baths: 2
Living Area:	
Main floor	1,078 sq. ft.
Total Living Area:	**1,078 sq. ft.**
Garage and utility	431 sq. ft.
Exterior Wall Framing:	2x4

Foundation Options:
Slab
(All plans can be built with your choice of foundation and framing. A generic conversion diagram is available. See order form.)

BLUEPRINT PRICE CODE: A

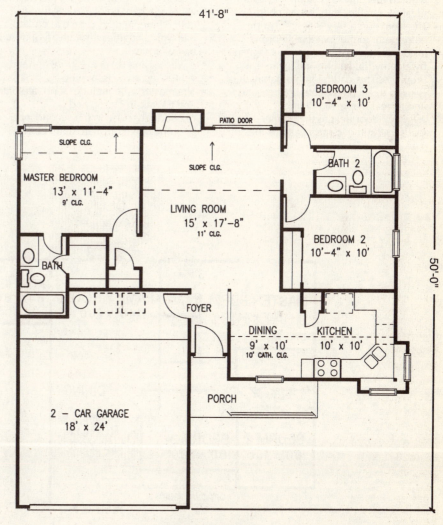

MAIN FLOOR

ORDER BLUEPRINTS ANYTIME!
CALL TOLL-FREE 1-800-820-1296

Plan L-1022
Plan copyright held by home designer/architect

PRICES AND DETAILS
ON PAGES 12-15

COMFY COUNTRY CHARMERS

35

COMFY COUNTRY CHARMERS

A Family Affair

- The thoughtful design of the sleeping wing in this one-story home makes it ideal for families with young children.
- The front porch serves as an inviting entry point to the spacious floor plan.
- Inside, the central living area is topped by a cathedral ceiling and features a fireplace. This natural hub of family life is sized to accommodate both casual and formal living and dining.
- A French door next to the fireplace leads to a sun deck that extends the living space into the backyard. The deck's proximity to the kitchen makes it a handy spot for outdoor grilling.
- A sunny breakfast nook lies just past the galley kitchen. Enjoy your Saturday coffee here, and keep an eye on backyard activities through an optional bay window.
- A washer and dryer are close at hand, yet tucked away from view.
- The master suite includes a private bath and a walk-in closet, and is reassuringly close to the secondary bedrooms, which share a full bath.

Plan APS-1004

Bedrooms: 3	Baths: 2

Living Area:
Main floor — 1,069 sq. ft.
Total Living Area: **1,069 sq. ft.**
Garage — 460 sq. ft.
Exterior Wall Framing: 2x4
Foundation Options:
Crawlspace
(All plans can be built with your choice of foundation and framing. A generic conversion diagram is available. See order form.)
BLUEPRINT PRICE CODE: **A**

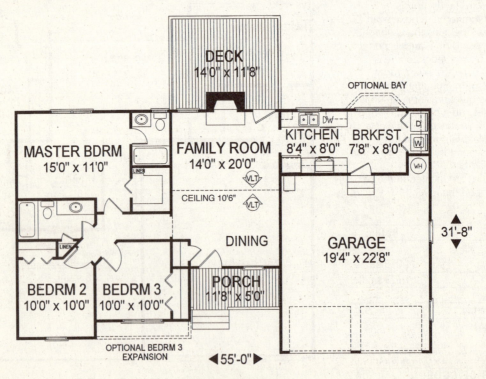

MAIN FLOOR

Plan APS-1004
Plan copyright held by home designer/architect

ORDER BLUEPRINTS ANYTIME! CALL TOLL-FREE 1-800-820-1296

PRICES AND DETAILS ON PAGES 12-15

Wonderfully Space-Efficient

- With multiple gables, big windows and a modern, free-flowing floor plan, this wonderfully space-efficient one-story home offers plenty of excitement.
- Past the inviting columned entrance, the expansive living room is highlighted by a dramatic vaulted ceiling and tall front windows.
- The adjoining dining room offers sliding glass doors to a backyard deck.
- The nearby U-shaped kitchen includes a sizable pantry and a convenient laundry closet. The garage is located just steps away, facilitating the unloading of groceries.
- The master bedroom boasts a vaulted ceiling, plenty of windows and a private bath.
- Rounding out the sleeping wing are two additional bedrooms with easy access to a linen closet and a full hall bath.

Plan B-89054

Bedrooms: 3	Baths: 2
Living Area:	
Main floor	1,135 sq. ft.
Total Living Area:	**1,135 sq. ft.**
Standard basement	1,135 sq. ft.
Garage	271 sq. ft.
Exterior Wall Framing:	2x4

Foundation Options:
Standard basement
(All plans can be built with your choice of foundation and framing. A generic conversion diagram is available. See order form.)

BLUEPRINT PRICE CODE: A

MAIN FLOOR

COMFY COUNTRY CHARMERS

ORDER BLUEPRINTS ANYTIME!
CALL TOLL-FREE 1-800-820-1296

Plan B-89054
Plan copyright held by home designer/architect

PRICES AND DETAILS
ON PAGES 12-15

COMFY COUNTRY CHARMERS

Warmth and Flexibility

- The hallmarks of this home are its open, flowing spaces, coupled with its cozy, intimate areas, giving it the warmth and flexibility you crave.
- A brief but stylish porch adjoins the tiled entry, which leads to the spacious Great Room. With a fireplace, bright windows and an airy ceiling, this room is a natural gathering spot.
- The adjacent dining nook is marked by large windows and direct access to a rear patio. This ensures an easy transition to backyard grilling or dining.
- A handy breakfast bar fronts the galley-style kitchen, lending an open feel.
- Down the hall are two secluded and sizable bedrooms that share a hall bath. The foremost bedroom, with its stunning window arrangement, might also be used as a home office.
- In a private corner of the home, the modest master suite enjoys the simple comforts of a private bath and a large walk-in closet. The nearby utility room has laundry facilities and leads to an attached two-car garage.

Plan KD-1145

Bedrooms: 3	Baths: 2
Living Area:	
Main floor	1,145 sq. ft.
Total Living Area:	**1,145 sq. ft.**
Garage	452 sq. ft.
Exterior Wall Framing:	2x4

Foundation Options:
Slab
(All plans can be built with your choice of foundation and framing. A generic conversion diagram is available. See order form.)

BLUEPRINT PRICE CODE: A

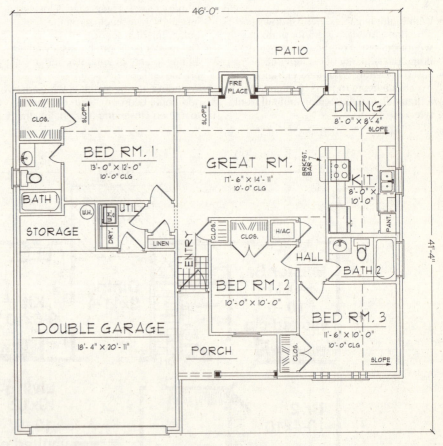

MAIN FLOOR

ORDER BLUEPRINTS ANYTIME!
CALL TOLL-FREE 1-800-820-1296

Plan KD-1145
Plan copyright held by home designer/architect

PRICES AND DETAILS
ON PAGES 12-15

Nostalgic Getaway

- Porches in the front and back of this country-style home make tempting mid-afternoon getaways in the summertime. Camp out with friends on the front porch and visit over a pitcher of lemonade and a plate of gingersnaps.
- As it cools off later in the evening, come in and sit by the living-room fireplace. Windows on either side of the hearth provide a view to the outdoors—though you'll hardly regret not being there.
- The setup of the dining room and kitchen allows for the easy flow of conversation.
- A nearby utility room and a snack bar servicing the living room highlight the kitchen. A door near the dining room invites you to enjoy your meals outside.
- Take advantage of the secluded master bedroom, which boasts a walk-in closet, a dressing area and private access to a full bath.

Plan DD-1141

Bedrooms: 3	Baths: 2
Living Area:	
Upper floor	338 sq. ft.
Main floor	819 sq. ft.
Total Living Area:	**1,157 sq. ft.**
Standard basement	819 sq. ft.
Exterior Wall Framing:	2x4

Foundation Options:
Standard basement
Crawlspace
Slab
(All plans can be built with your choice of foundation and framing. A generic conversion diagram is available. See order form.)

BLUEPRINT PRICE CODE: A

UPPER FLOOR

VIEW INTO LIVING ROOM, DINING ROOM AND KITCHEN

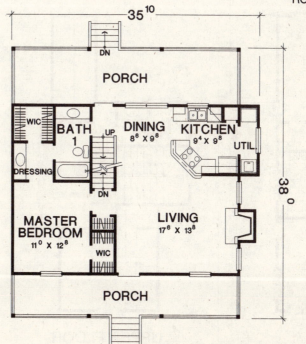

MAIN FLOOR

COMFY COUNTRY CHARMERS

ORDER BLUEPRINTS ANYTIME!
CALL TOLL-FREE 1-800-820-1296

Plan DD-1141
Plan copyright held by home designer/architect

PRICES AND DETAILS ON PAGES 12-15

COMFY COUNTRY CHARMERS

Delightful Bungalow

- Full of charm and dabbled with fine extras, this bungalow will delight smaller families, singles and empty nesters alike.
- A breezy side porch topped by a metal roof provides outdoor relaxation space and a serving bar under the kitchen window for easy grilling or beverage service. Inside, the spacious living and dining rooms offer your guests comfort.
- A second serving bar in the kitchen keeps dinner plates and glasses full, as it conveniently serves the dining room.
- A full bath and a bedroom on each floor promise privacy to their users.
- The bright, versatile loft on the upper floor works nicely as a hobby room, a play area or a library. It is crowned by a cathedral ceiling for added airiness.
- Plans for a detached, two-car garage are included in the blueprints.

Plan L-123-VACA	
Bedrooms: 2	**Baths:** 2
Living Area:	
Upper floor	342 sq. ft.
Main floor	693 sq. ft.
Total Living Area:	**1,035 sq. ft.**
Detached garage	440 sq. ft.
Exterior Wall Framing:	2x4
Foundation Options:	

Slab
(All plans can be built with your choice of foundation and framing. A generic conversion diagram is available. See order form.)

BLUEPRINT PRICE CODE: A

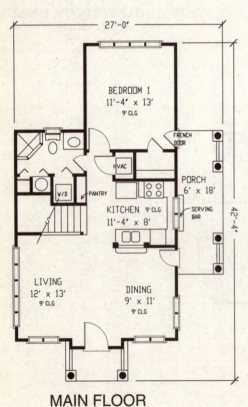

MAIN FLOOR

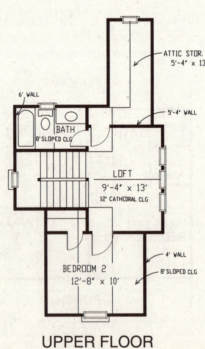

UPPER FLOOR

VIEW INTO LIVING AND DINING ROOMS

ORDER BLUEPRINTS ANYTIME!
CALL TOLL-FREE 1-800-820-1296

Plan L-123-VACA
Plan copyright held by home designer/architect

PRICES AND DETAILS ON PAGES 12-15

Cozy, Rustic Country Home

- This cozy, rustic home offers a modern, open interior that efficiently maximizes the modest square footage.
- A simple front porch stretches the width of the home and offers just enough room to set up a couple of rocking chairs and shoot the breeze.
- The large living room features a sloped ceiling accented by rustic beams. An eye-catching corner fireplace warms this inviting space.
- The living room flows into the adjoining dining room and the efficient U-shaped kitchen for a spacious, open feel.
- The master suite is separated from the two secondary bedrooms by the home's common living areas. The master suite includes a private bath and a separate dressing area with a dual-sink vanity. This arrangement will help make morning preparations less hectic.
- On the other side of the home, two good-sized secondary bedrooms share another full bath.

Plan E-1109

| Bedrooms: 3 | Baths: 2 |
|---|---|//
Living Area:	
Main floor	1,191 sq. ft.
Total Living Area:	**1,191 sq. ft.**
Garage, storage and utility	572 sq. ft.
Exterior Wall Framing:	2x6

Foundation Options:
Crawlspace
Slab
(All plans can be built with your choice of foundation and framing. A generic conversion diagram is available. See order form.)

BLUEPRINT PRICE CODE: A

VIEW INTO LIVING ROOM, DINING ROOM AND KITCHEN

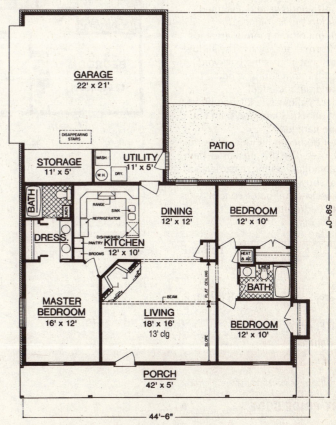

MAIN FLOOR

ORDER BLUEPRINTS ANYTIME!
CALL TOLL-FREE 1-800-820-1296

Plan E-1109
Plan copyright held by home designer/architect

PRICES AND DETAILS ON PAGES 12-15

COMFY COUNTRY CHARMERS

COMFY COUNTRY CHARMERS

Love at First Sight!

- Upon seeing its covered front porch and bright brick and siding exterior, it's easy to fall in love with this adorable home.
- Past the ornate and inviting entry, the spacious family room and its decorative plant shelf and dramatic fireplace offer an impressive introduction to the interior. Tall windows and a vaulted ceiling add to the ambience.
- The adjoining dining room is great for casual or formal occasions. The sliding glass doors that access the backyard may be built into a sunny window bay for a more dramatic effect.
- The efficient galley-style kitchen offers a pantry, an attached laundry room and a door to the garage.
- The master bedroom includes a roomy walk-in closet. The private master bath features a vaulted ceiling, a garden tub, a separate shower and a dual-sink vanity. A second full bath services two secondary bedrooms.

Plan APS-1103

Bedrooms: 3	Baths: 2
Living Area:	
Main floor	1,197 sq. ft.
Total Living Area:	**1,197 sq. ft.**
Garage	380 sq. ft.
Exterior Wall Framing:	2x4

Foundation Options:

Crawlspace
Slab
(All plans can be built with your choice of foundation and framing. A generic conversion diagram is available. See order form.)

BLUEPRINT PRICE CODE: A

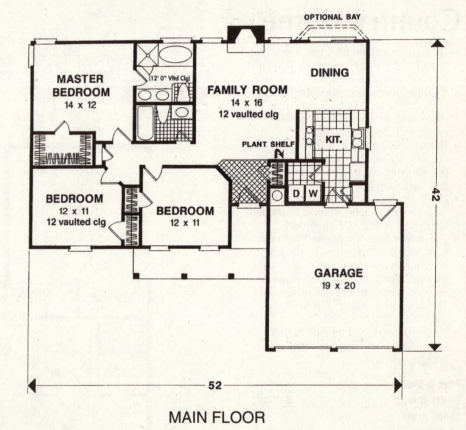

MAIN FLOOR

ORDER BLUEPRINTS ANYTIME!
CALL TOLL-FREE 1-800-820-1296

Plan APS-1103
Plan copyright held by home designer/architect

PRICES AND DETAILS ON PAGES 12-15

Good Gathering

- With its cheery fireplace and media center, and plenty of legroom, this country-style home's living room imbues family gatherings with special meaning.
- The adjoining dining room handles formal and casual meals easily; a French door leads to a backyard porch with enough room for a café table and, of course, the grill.
- A raised bar makes the walk-through kitchen extra serviceable. Nearby laundry facilities let you multi-task on the weekends.
- On the opposite side of the home, the master suite boasts ample wardrobe space, with a second closet augmenting a large walk-in closet. A private bath is the finishing touch for this sweet retreat.
- Two more bedrooms and a full hall bath complete the floor plan. The second bedroom has a sloped ceiling for an extra measure of spaciousness.

Plan RD-1223

Bedrooms: 3	Baths: 2
Living Area:	
Main floor	1,223 sq. ft.
Total Living Area:	**1,223 sq. ft.**
Garage and storage	487 sq. ft.
Exterior Wall Framing:	2x4

Foundation Options:
Crawlspace
Slab
(All plans can be built with your choice of foundation and framing. A generic conversion diagram is available. See order form.)

BLUEPRINT PRICE CODE: A

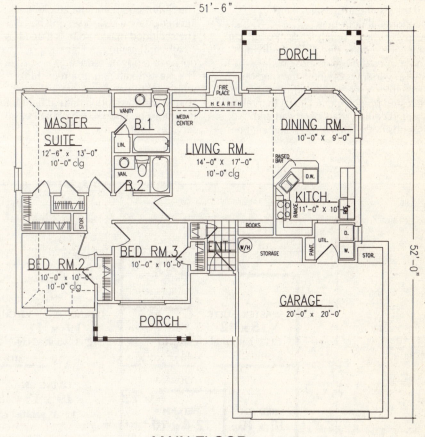

MAIN FLOOR

ORDER BLUEPRINTS ANYTIME!
CALL TOLL-FREE 1-800-820-1296

Plan RD-1223
Plan copyright held by home designer/architect

PRICES AND DETAILS
ON PAGES 12-15

COMFY COUNTRY CHARMERS

Classic Country

- This charming country-style home features a classic exterior and a luxurious interior design in an economical floor plan.
- A covered front porch leads through a sidelighted entry directly to the living room. A coat closet is close by.
- Stylish windows brighten the spacious living room, where a handsome recessed fireplace crackles. A marvelous vaulted ceiling soars overhead and extends to the dining room and kitchen.
- Stately columns set off the entry to the dining room, which offers French-door access to a backyard terrace that is perfect for summertime entertainment.
- The dining room and the efficient kitchen share a stylish serving bar.
- The secluded master suite is graced by a cathedral ceiling. A French door opens to a private terrace.
- The master bath flaunts a refreshing whirlpool tub and a separate shower.
- Lovely windows bring natural light into two more bedrooms. A hall bath easily services both rooms.

Plan AHP-9507

Bedrooms: 3	Baths: 2

Living Area:
Main floor	1,232 sq. ft.

Total Living Area:	**1,232 sq. ft.**
Standard basement	1,183 sq. ft.
Garage and storage	324 sq. ft.

Exterior Wall Framing: 2x4 or 2x6

Foundation Options:
Standard basement
Crawlspace
Slab
(All plans can be built with your choice of foundation and framing. A generic conversion diagram is available. See order form.)

BLUEPRINT PRICE CODE: A

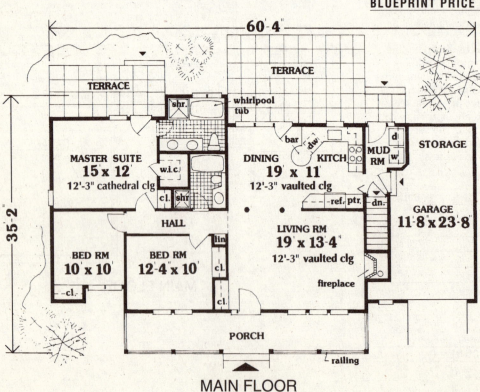

MAIN FLOOR

ORDER BLUEPRINTS ANYTIME!
CALL TOLL-FREE 1-800-820-1296

Plan AHP-9507
Plan copyright held by home designer/architect

PRICES AND DETAILS ON PAGES 12-15

COMFY COUNTRY CHARMERS

All in One!

- This plan puts today's most luxurious home-design features into one attractive, economical package.
- The covered front porch and the gabled roofline, accented by an arched window and a round louver vent, give the exterior a homey yet stylish appeal.
- Just inside the front door, the raised ceiling offers an impressive greeting. The spacious living room is flooded with light through a central skylight and a pair of French doors that frame the smart fireplace.
- The living room flows into the nice-sized dining room, also with a raised ceiling. The adjoining kitchen offers a handy laundry closet, lots of counter space and a sunny dinette that opens to an expansive backyard terrace.
- The bedroom wing includes a wonderful master suite with a sizable sleeping room and an adjacent dressing area with two closets. Glass blocks above the dual-sink vanity in the master bath let in light yet maintain privacy. A whirlpool tub completes the suite.
- The larger of the two remaining bedrooms boasts a high ceiling and an arched window.

Plan HFL-1680-FL

Bedrooms: 3	Baths: 2
Living Area:	
Main floor	1,367 sq. ft.
Total Living Area:	**1,367 sq. ft.**
Standard basement	1,367 sq. ft.
Garage	431 sq. ft.
Exterior Wall Framing:	2x6

Foundation Options:
Standard basement
Slab
(All plans can be built with your choice of foundation and framing. A generic conversion diagram is available. See order form.)

BLUEPRINT PRICE CODE: A

VIEW INTO LIVING ROOM

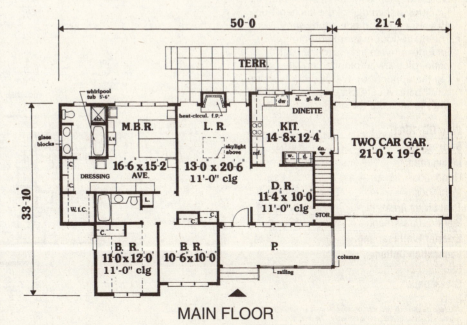

MAIN FLOOR

ORDER BLUEPRINTS ANYTIME!
CALL TOLL-FREE 1-800-820-1296

Plan HFL-1680-FL
Plan copyright held by home designer/architect

PRICES AND DETAILS ON PAGES 12-15

45

COMFY COUNTRY CHARMERS

Get Away— or Stay

- This rustic charmer is the right size for a vacation getaway or a starter home, and it's well equipped for day-to-day living.
- A deep porch at the front and and a covered patio out back are irresistible outdoor living spaces, not to mention delightful spots to watch a summer rain.
- The spacious living room with a focal-point fireplace can accommodate intimate gatherings or small parties with equal ease. The room flows freely into the dining area, which is served by the galley-style kitchen and topped by a rugged wood beam.
- Note the smart placement of the laundry facilities at the edge of the kitchen—do all your chores in one handy spot!
- The main-floor master bedroom includes private access to the back patio, plus a well-planned private bath.
- On the upper floor, two bedrooms share a full bath. A cute play area for the little ones rounds out the design.

Plan DD-1341	
Bedrooms: 3	**Baths:** 2½
Living Area:	
Upper floor	504 sq. ft.
Main floor	866 sq. ft.
Total Living Area:	**1,370 sq. ft.**
Standard basement	866 sq. ft.
Exterior Wall Framing:	2x4
Foundation Options:	
Standard basement	
Crawlspace	
Slab	
(All plans can be built with your choice of foundation and framing. A generic conversion diagram is available. See order form.)	
BLUEPRINT PRICE CODE:	**A**

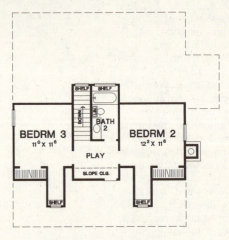

UPPER FLOOR

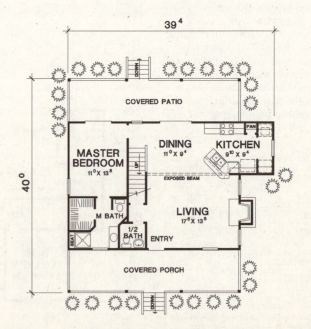

MAIN FLOOR

ORDER BLUEPRINTS ANYTIME! CALL TOLL-FREE 1-800-820-1296

Plan DD-1341
Plan copyright held by home designer/architect

PRICES AND DETAILS ON PAGES 12-15

COMFY COUNTRY CHARMERS

Instantly Welcome

- From the moment you set eyes on its rustic stone accents, charming railed porch and homey shingles, you're sure to fall in love with this delightful design.
- The front door opens directly into the family room, where a focal-point fireplace is topped by a smart TV niche. A door on one side of the fireplace leads out to a rear deck, which is perfect for sunning or barbecuing.
- Windows surround the bright dining area, creating an inviting spot for formal and casual meals. An angled serving counter in the kitchen enhances meal preparation and snack time. The kitchen also offers a sizable pantry and an out-of-the-way laundry room.
- On the opposite end of the home is the sleeping wing. Here, a large master bedroom is complemented by a private bath that includes a dual-sink vanity and both a tub and a shower. His-and-hers closets are an exciting feature.
- Two additional bedrooms share a full hall bath and linen storage.

Plan APS-1311

Bedrooms: 3	Baths: 2
Living Area:	
Main floor	1,381 sq. ft.
Total Living Area:	**1,381 sq. ft.**
Garage	429 sq. ft.
Exterior Wall Framing:	2x4

Foundation Options:
Slab
(All plans can be built with your choice of foundation and framing. A generic conversion diagram is available. See order form.)

BLUEPRINT PRICE CODE: A

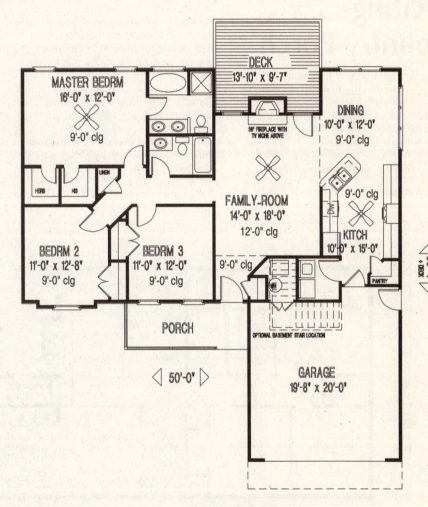

MAIN FLOOR

**ORDER BLUEPRINTS ANYTIME!
CALL TOLL-FREE 1-800-820-1296**

Plan APS-1311
Plan copyright held by home designer/architect

**PRICES AND DETAILS
ON PAGES 12-15**

47

COMFY COUNTRY CHARMERS

Inviting Country Porch

- A columned porch with double doors invites you into the rustic living areas of this ranch-style home.
- Inside, the entry allows views back to the expansive, central living room and the backyard beyond.
- The living room boasts an exposed-beam ceiling and a massive fireplace with a wide stone hearth, a wood box and built-in bookshelves. A sunny patio offers additional entertaining space.
- The dining room and the efficient kitchen combine for easy meal service, with a serving bar separating the two.
- The main hallway leads to the sleeping wing, which offers a large master bedroom with a walk-in closet and a private bath.
- Two additional bedrooms share another full bath, and a laundry closet is easily accessible to the entire bedroom wing.

Plan E-1304
Bedrooms: 3   **Baths:** 2
Living Area:
Main floor   1,395 sq. ft.
Total Living Area: **1,395 sq. ft.**
Garage   451 sq. ft.
Storage   30 sq. ft.
Exterior Wall Framing: 2x4
Foundation Options:
Crawlspace
Slab
(All plans can be built with your choice of foundation and framing. A generic conversion diagram is available. See order form.)
BLUEPRINT PRICE CODE: **A**

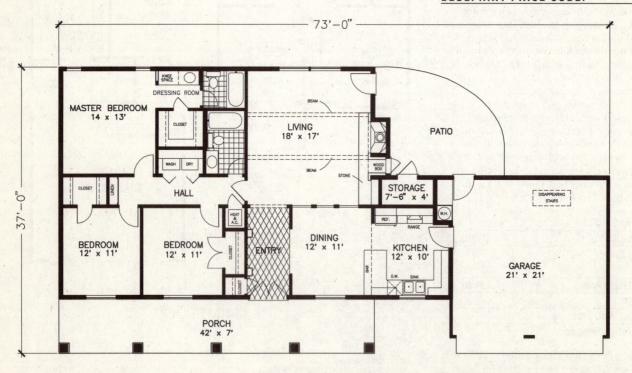

MAIN FLOOR

ORDER BLUEPRINTS ANYTIME!
CALL TOLL-FREE 1-800-820-1296

Plan E-1304
Plan copyright held by home designer/architect

PRICES AND DETAILS
ON PAGES 12-15

Timeless Charm

- With exterior charm comparable to that of an English country cottage, this delightful home combines timeless beauty and modern amenities.
- The covered entry opens to a spacious living room. Illuminated by a bright bay window and a comforting fireplace, this space also features a media center.
- In the dining room, French doors open to a rear porch. Enjoy this elegant backdrop for formal or casual meals.
- A pantry, a serving counter and views to the rear garden highlight the kitchen, which accesses the sunny utility room.
- A walk-in closet and a set of French doors to the porch embellish the master suite. The bath includes dual sinks, a garden tub and a separate shower.
- The blueprints for this plan give you the option of adding French doors between the living room and the front-facing bedroom, to turn this space into a den.
- With its generous area, the garage is big enough to accommodate a workshop.

Plan L-373-CSA

Bedrooms: 3	Baths: 2

Living Area:
Main floor .... 1,406 sq. ft.
Total Living Area: .... **1,406 sq. ft.**
Garage .... 533 sq. ft.
Exterior Wall Framing: 2x4
Foundation Options:
Slab
(All plans can be built with your choice of foundation and framing. A generic conversion diagram is available. See order form.)
BLUEPRINT PRICE CODE: A

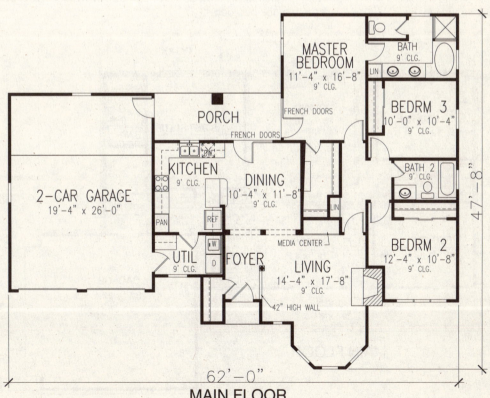

MAIN FLOOR

Plan L-373-CSA
Plan copyright held by home designer/architect

ORDER BLUEPRINTS ANYTIME!
CALL TOLL-FREE 1-800-820-1296

PRICES AND DETAILS ON PAGES 12-15

Rustic Ranch-Style Design

- This ranch-style home offers a rustic facade that is warm and inviting. The railed front porch and stone accents are an especially appealing complement to a wide-open lot.
- The interior is warm as well, with the the attractive living room at the heart. Features here include an eye-catching fireplace with a brick hearth, patio access, shelving that acts as a subtle divider between this room and the adjacent dining room, and a dramatic sloped ceiling with exposed beams.
- The open dining room lies off the foyer and adjoins the efficient U-shaped kitchen, which includes a pantry and a handy broom closet.
- Three windows in the large master suite provide a scenic view of the back patio. A deluxe walk-in closet and a roomy private bath round out this expansive retreat.
- Separated from the living areas by dual doors, two secondary bedrooms with abundant closet space share another full bath. A romantic window seat graces one of the bedrooms.

Plan E-1410

Bedrooms: 3	Baths: 2
Living Area:	
Main floor	1,418 sq. ft.
Total Living Area:	**1,418 sq. ft.**
Garage	484 sq. ft.
Storage	38 sq. ft.
Exterior Wall Framing:	2x4

Foundation Options:

Crawlspace
Slab
(All plans can be built with your choice of foundation and framing. A generic conversion diagram is available. See order form.)

BLUEPRINT PRICE CODE: A

COMFY COUNTRY CHARMERS

Tried and True

- Time-tested traditional touches abound in this appealing country-style home, which is fronted by a nostalgic railed porch and dormers.
- The spacious, central living room anchors the home. A tremendous fireplace flanked by built-in bookshelves serves as the focal-point of the room and adds warmth to family gatherings. Access to a cozy back porch is just steps away.
- An octagonal dining room borders the sunny kitchen, where you'll find a handy pantry and plenty of space to whip up any culinary masterpiece! The kitchen also adjoins a convenient utility room that leads to the attached garage.
- When you long for a good night's sleep, you'll appreciate the master suite, which offers a quiet sitting area that's perfect for spending leisure time. The private master bath is also quite well appointed, flaunting a stunning corner tub, a separate shower, his-and-hers walk-in closets and dual vanities.
- The kids get their space, too—a pair of good-sized bedrooms with ample closet space share a nearby hall bath.

Plan RD-1418

Bedrooms: 3	Baths: 2
Living Area:	
Main floor	1,418 sq. ft.
Total Living Area:	**1,418 sq. ft.**
Garage and storage	464 sq. ft.
Exterior Wall Framing:	2x4

Foundation Options:

Crawlspace
Slab

(All plans can be built with your choice of foundation and framing. A generic conversion diagram is available. See order form.)

BLUEPRINT PRICE CODE: A

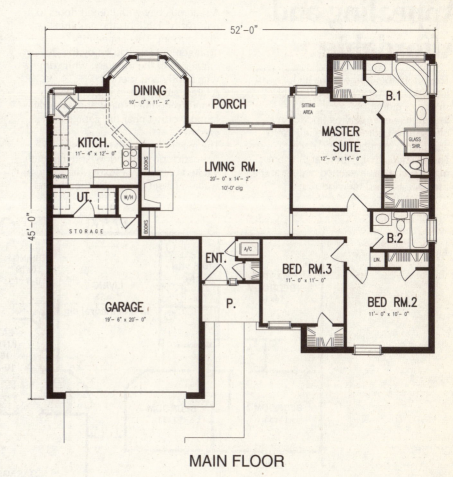

MAIN FLOOR

ORDER BLUEPRINTS ANYTIME!
CALL TOLL-FREE 1-800-820-1296

Plan RD-1418
Plan copyright held by home designer/architect

PRICES AND DETAILS
ON PAGES 12-15

COMFY COUNTRY CHARMERS

Appealing and Affordable

- This affordable home offers a choice of fetching exteriors—choose from brick, stucco or siding.
- Its simple, yet appealing floor plan offers three bedrooms, two full baths and plenty of open living space.
- The spacious living room at the center of the home has a vaulted ceiling and a fireplace flanked by windows.
- A spacious bay with French doors to a rear patio highlights the adjoining dining room. This appealing arrangement lets you enjoy the ambience of the fireplace while dining with family and friends.
- A large, sunny eat-in kitchen has generous counter space and a handy laundry closet near the garage entrance.
- The master bedroom features a dramatic corner window and a private, vaulted bath with a luxury tub; a large walk-in closet completes the picture.

Plan APS-1413

Bedrooms: 3	Baths: 2
Living Area:	
Main floor	1,428 sq. ft.
Total Living Area:	**1,428 sq. ft.**
Garage	419 sq. ft.
Exterior Wall Framing:	2x4

Foundation Options:
Slab
(All plans can be built with your choice of foundation and framing. A generic conversion diagram is available. See order form.)

BLUEPRINT PRICE CODE: A

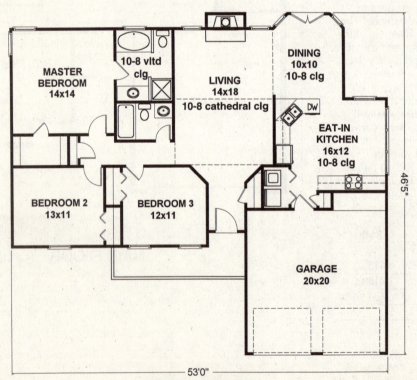

MAIN FLOOR

Plan APS-1413
Plan copyright held by home designer/architect

ORDER BLUEPRINTS ANYTIME! CALL TOLL-FREE 1-800-820-1296

PRICES AND DETAILS ON PAGES 12-15

View from the Veranda

- Welcome the new day from the kitchen's cheerful morning room and spend long summer evenings relaxing on the veranda.
- Past the foyer, a living room with a gas fireplace flows into the dining room, which offers sliding glass doors to a covered deck. These spaces will easily fulfill all your entertainment needs.
- The kitchen boasts an island workstation and a large walk-in pantry.
- A conveniently located laundry room is accessible from both the kitchen's morning room and the home's side-entry, two-car garage.
- The bedroom wing features a lavish master suite, where a French door leads out to a private covered deck. The master bath offers a luxurious jetted tub and a separate shower. A walk-in closet adds to the suite's amenities.
- Two additional bedrooms and a full bath complete this wing.

Plan WH-9518
Bedrooms: 3   **Baths:** 2
Living Area:
Main floor   1,463 sq. ft.
Total Living Area: **1,463 sq. ft.**
Standard basement   1,447 sq. ft.
Garage   407 sq. ft.
Exterior Wall Framing: 2x6
Foundation Options:
Standard basement
(All plans can be built with your choice of foundation and framing. A generic conversion diagram is available. See order form.)
BLUEPRINT PRICE CODE: **A**

MAIN FLOOR

ORDER BLUEPRINTS ANYTIME!
CALL TOLL-FREE 1-800-820-1296

Plan WH-9518
Plan copyright held by home designer/architect

PRICES AND DETAILS ON PAGES 12-15

COMFY COUNTRY CHARMERS

Pleasantly Peaceful

- The covered front porch of this lovely two-story traditional home offers a pleasant and peaceful welcome.
- Off the open foyer is an oversized family room, drenched with sunlight through a French door and surrounding windows. A handsome fireplace adds further warmth.
- The neatly arranged kitchen is conveniently nestled between the formal dining room and the sunny breakfast room. A pantry and a powder room are also within easy reach.
- A stairway off the family room accesses the upper floor, which houses three bedrooms. The isolated master bedroom features a tray ceiling, a huge walk-in closet and a private bath offering a vaulted ceiling, an oval garden tub and a separate shower.
- The two secondary bedrooms share another full bath.

Plan FB-1466	
Bedrooms: 3	Baths: 2½
Living Area:	
Upper floor	703 sq. ft.
Main floor	763 sq. ft.
Total Living Area:	**1,466 sq. ft.**
Daylight basement	763 sq. ft.
Garage	426 sq. ft.
Storage	72 sq. ft.
Exterior Wall Framing:	2x4 |//
Foundation Options:	
Daylight basement	
Crawlspace	
(All plans can be built with your choice of foundation and framing. A generic conversion diagram is available. See order form.)	
BLUEPRINT PRICE CODE:	**A**

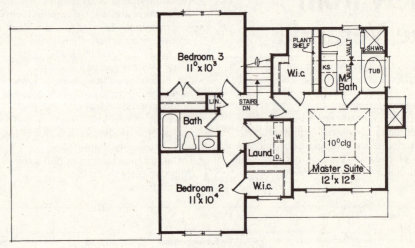

UPPER FLOOR

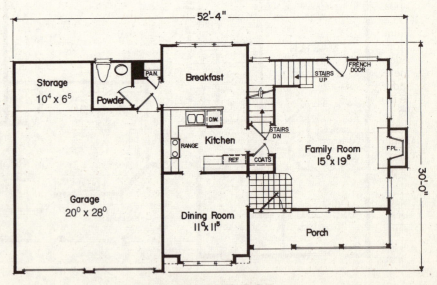

MAIN FLOOR

Plan FB-1466
Plan copyright held by home designer/architect

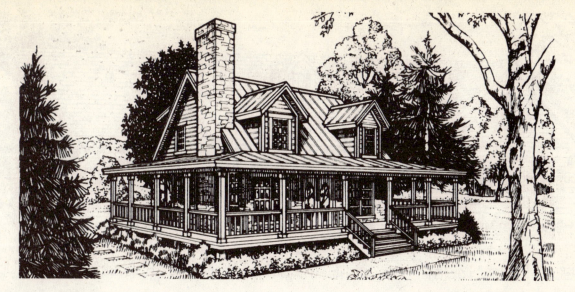

Smart and Smarter

- This country home's smart, appealing exterior covers a floor plan that is even smarter in its scope and execution.
- A deep porch borders three sides of the home, while a sturdy chimney and well-proportioned dormers exude a timeless charm. The metal roof will shrug off heavy snowfalls and make ice dams a forgotten headache.
- Inside, an impressive layout begins with the open living room, complete with a fireplace and three-step access to the kitchen. Here, you'll find an island cooktop, bright windows and an adjoining dining room.
- The master suite occupies the rear half of the main floor. Its impressive private bath boasts a tub and a separate shower, plus a dual-sink vanity. Even the laundry facilities are included! As a final touch, private porch access is provided from the suite.
- On the upper floor, two bedrooms and a second bath flank a beautiful overlook to the living room, below.

Plan RLA-309	
Bedrooms: 3	**Baths:** 2
Living Area:	
Upper floor	568 sq. ft.
Main floor	911 sq. ft.
Total Living Area:	**1,479 sq. ft.**
Standard basement	900 sq. ft.
Exterior Wall Framing:	2x4
Foundation Options:	
Standard basement	
(All plans can be built with your choice of foundation and framing. A generic conversion diagram is available. See order form.)	
BLUEPRINT PRICE CODE:	**A**

UPPER FLOOR

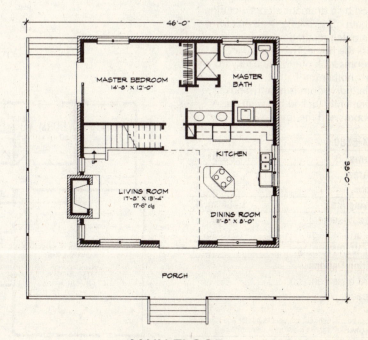

MAIN FLOOR

ORDER BLUEPRINTS ANYTIME!
CALL TOLL-FREE 1-800-820-1296

Plan RLA-309
Plan copyright held by home designer/architect

PRICES AND DETAILS
ON PAGES 12-15

COMFY COUNTRY CHARMERS

Pastoral Perfection

- An expansive front porch, quaint shutters and warm wood siding lend this home its look of pastoral perfection.
- With a striking stepped ceiling, a cozy fireplace and a built-in entertainment area, the Great Room is a natural gathering spot. Three sets of sliding French doors offer a view to the gentle beauty of the outdoors.
- The nearby dining room shares a snack counter with the kitchen. Here, a windowed sink brightens daily chores.
- Cleverly separated from the other bedrooms for privacy, the master suite is topped by a dramatic stepped ceiling. The bath offers a large walk-in closet and ample preparation space.
- Across the home, two secondary bedrooms look out to the backyard and share another full bath.
- The laundry room is quietly and conveniently tucked between these bedrooms and the foyer.

Plan AX-5380	
Bedrooms: 3	**Baths:** 2
Living Area:	
Main floor	1,480 sq. ft.
Total Living Area:	**1,480 sq. ft.**
Standard basement	1,493 sq. ft.
Garage and storage	610 sq. ft.
Exterior Wall Framing:	2x4
Foundation Options:	
Standard basement	
Crawlspace	
Slab	

(All plans can be built with your choice of foundation and framing. A generic conversion diagram is available. See order form.)

BLUEPRINT PRICE CODE: A

VIEW INTO GREAT ROOM

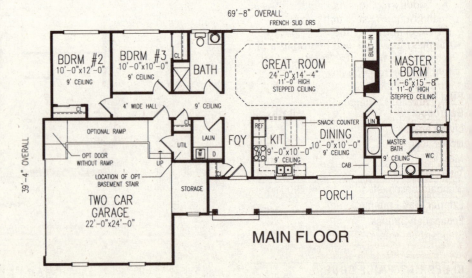

MAIN FLOOR

ORDER BLUEPRINTS ANYTIME!
CALL TOLL-FREE 1-800-820-1296

Plan AX-5380
Plan copyright held by home designer/architect

PRICES AND DETAILS ON PAGES 12-15

COMFY COUNTRY CHARMERS

Secluded Starter

- A secluded porch and cozy feel make this charming home perfect for any growing family.
- Inside, turn right and pass through the galley kitchen into the sun-drenched breakfast nook. A serving bar to the nook and the family room is the perfect place to set out snacks.
- The breakfast nook flows into the family room, where a fireplace and a vaulted ceiling create a comfortable space for guests and family alike.
- In the formal dining room, distinguished by decorative columns and a vaulted ceiling, serve a grand holiday dinner.
- A glorious master suite boasts a distinctive tray ceiling, an indulgent garden tub, a separate shower and a generous-sized walk-in closet.
- Two additional bedrooms and a full bath give your family plenty of room.
- A side-entry garage maintains the home's traditional facade.

Plan FB-5524-SCOF

Bedrooms: 3	Baths: 2
Living Area:	
Main floor	1,493 sq. ft.
Total Living Area:	**1,493 sq. ft.**
Daylight basement	1,493 sq. ft.
Garage	379 sq. ft.
Exterior Wall Framing:	2x4

Foundation Options:
Daylight basement
Crawlspace
(All plans can be built with your choice of foundation and framing. A generic conversion diagram is available. See order form.)

BLUEPRINT PRICE CODE: A

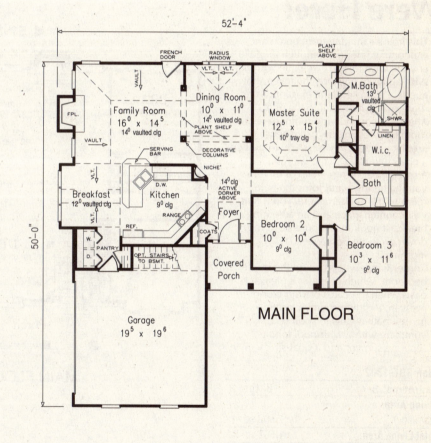

MAIN FLOOR

ORDER BLUEPRINTS ANYTIME!
CALL TOLL-FREE 1-800-820-1296

Plan FB-5524-SCOF
Plan copyright held by home designer/architect

PRICES AND DETAILS ON PAGES 12-15

COMFY COUNTRY CHARMERS

Wish You Were Here?

- This home's inviting front porch and welcoming interior is enough to make anyone wish for the sweet life within.
- With an air of mystery, the foyer allows guests a glimpse of the elegant dining room over a half-wall to the right.
- Ahead, the open living room leaves no room for guessing; its prominent fireplace practically begs you to pull up a chair and relax in the warmth.
- A serving bar brings a casual tone to your gatherings, and joins the living room to the kitchen. Here, you'll find vast counter space and an adjoining breakfast nook that should slow you down on those busy weekday mornings!
- Corner windows spruce up the master bedroom, which provides a pleasant oasis when the cares of your world press in. Past two roomy closets, a private bath awaits to spoil you, complete with a whirlpool tub, a separate shower and a dual-sink vanity.

Plan BRF-1502

Bedrooms: 3	Baths: 2
Living Area:	
Main floor	1,502 sq. ft.
Total Living Area:	**1,502 sq. ft.**
Daylight basement	1,502 sq. ft.
Garage	413 sq. ft.
Exterior Wall Framing:	2x4
Foundation Options:	
Daylight basement	

(All plans can be built with your choice of foundation and framing. A generic conversion diagram is available. See order form.)

BLUEPRINT PRICE CODE: B

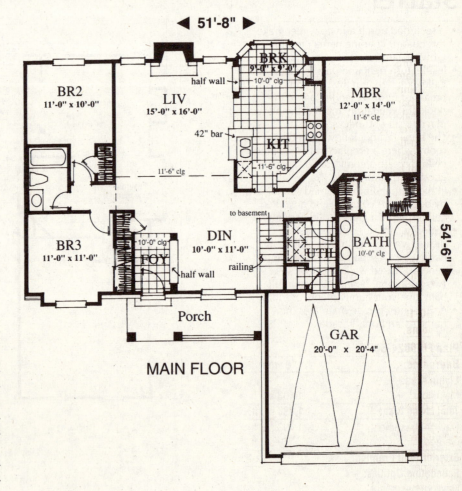

MAIN FLOOR

ORDER BLUEPRINTS ANYTIME! CALL TOLL-FREE 1-800-820-1296

Plan BRF-1502
Plan copyright held by home designer/architect

PRICES AND DETAILS ON PAGES 12-15

Outdoor Living

- This home's charming facade features a large wraparound front porch that sweeps into a wraparound side and rear deck, perfect for a neighborhood party.
- The living room boasts a bay window. A set of three large windows illuminates the greater area of this room.
- The stunning kitchen features an angled snack bar serving the dining room and the breakfast nook, which offers French-door access to the side deck.
- A main-floor bedroom provides access to a separate rear porch and is near a full hall bath.
- Upstairs, the master bedroom boasts French doors opening to a private deck, an exercise space and a private bath with a huge shower and dual sinks.
- Yet another set of French doors opens to the quiet study.
- Over the garage, a loft space provides room for a rec room for the kids, or for that workshop you've always wanted.

Plan BC-1500	
Bedrooms: 2+	**Baths:** 2
Living Area:	
Upper floor	576 sq. ft.
Main floor	665 sq. ft.
Loft	288 sq. ft.
Total Living Area:	**1,529 sq. ft.**
Garage	288 sq. ft.
Exterior Wall Framing:	2x6
Foundation Options:	
Crawlspace	

(All plans can be built with your choice of foundation and framing. A generic conversion diagram is available. See order form.)

BLUEPRINT PRICE CODE: B

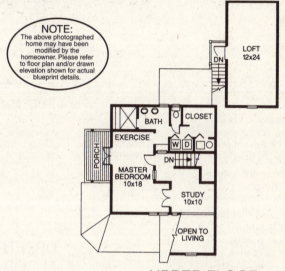

UPPER FLOOR

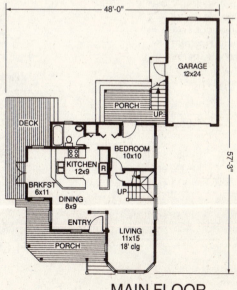

MAIN FLOOR

ORDER BLUEPRINTS ANYTIME!
CALL TOLL-FREE 1-800-820-1296

Plan BC-1500
Plan copyright held by home designer/architect

PRICES AND DETAILS ON PAGES 12-15

COMFY COUNTRY CHARMERS

A Country Classic

- The exterior of this cozy country-style home boasts a charming combination of woodwork and stone.
- A graceful, arched entryway leads into the spacious living room with a vaulted ceiling, tall windows and a fireplace.
- The dining area has a lovely view of a side patio and shares the living room's fireplace and vaulted ceiling.
- The impressive kitchen is brightened by a large window bank with skylights above, and it offers ample counter space, a full pantry and easy access to the dining room. For more casual meals, the kitchen offers ample space for a table and chairs near the windows.
- The main-floor master bedroom features a vaulted ceiling, plus a walk-in closet, a linen closet, a private, dual-sink master bath and sliding-door access to the patio. What a fabulous retreat!
- Two upper-floor bedrooms share another full bath and a view into the living and dining rooms below.

Plan B-87157

Bedrooms: 3	Baths: 2½
Living Area:	
Upper floor	452 sq. ft.
Main floor	1,099 sq. ft.
Total Living Area:	**1,551 sq. ft.**
Standard basement	1,099 sq. ft.
Garage	412 sq. ft.
Exterior Wall Framing:	2x4

Foundation Options:
Standard basement
(All plans can be built with your choice of foundation and framing. A generic conversion diagram is available. See order form.)

BLUEPRINT PRICE CODE: B

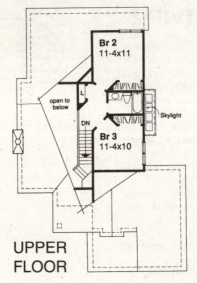

UPPER FLOOR

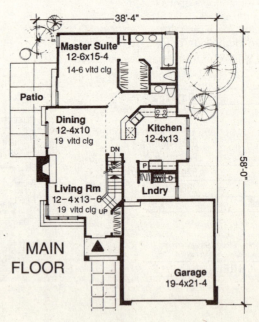

MAIN FLOOR

ORDER BLUEPRINTS ANYTIME! CALL TOLL-FREE 1-800-820-1296

Plan B-87157
Plan copyright held by home designer/architect

PRICES AND DETAILS ON PAGES 12-15

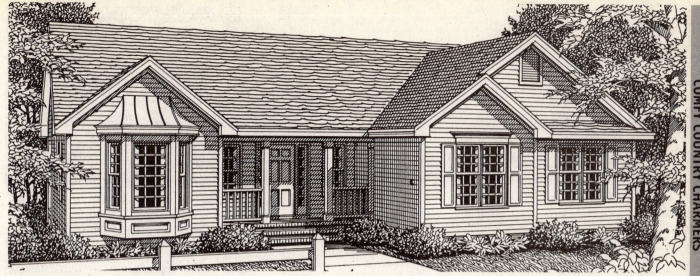

Simple Appeal

- This home's appeal comes from its simple exterior and practical floor plan.
- A charming copper-top bay window adorns the facade, which boasts classic gables and a darling front porch.
- The sidelighted entry leads to the bright foyer that acts as a gallery, connecting all parts of the home. Straight ahead, past decorative columns, is the spacious living room. It features a well-appointed fireplace, a soaring cathedral ceiling and French doors to a rear porch that's perfect for grilling or stargazing.
- The bay window brightens the dining room and the kitchen, which allows for casual dining at the snack bar. A door leads to the rear porch or, if you choose, to a detached garage out back.
- On the opposite side of the home, clever storage fills every corner of the hallway. Two sizable bedrooms share a hall bath that boasts a dual-sink vanity.
- The master suite is crowned by a visually stunning cathedral ceiling. A walk-in closet and a lush private bath with a garden tub are added amenities.
- Laundry facilities are tucked into a closet off the master suite.

Plan HWG-1559-N

Bedrooms: 3	Baths: 2

Living Area:
Main floor 1,559 sq. ft.
Total Living Area: 1,559 sq. ft.
Exterior Wall Framing: 2x4
Foundation Options:
Crawlspace
(All plans can be built with your choice of foundation and framing. A generic conversion diagram is available. See order form.)
BLUEPRINT PRICE CODE: B

COMFY COUNTRY CHARMERS

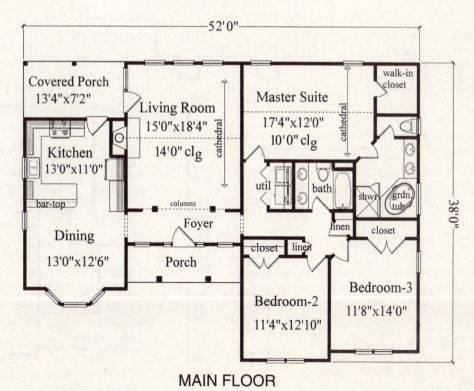

MAIN FLOOR

ORDER BLUEPRINTS ANYTIME!
CALL TOLL-FREE 1-800-820-1296

Plan HWG-1559-N
Plan copyright held by home designer/architect

PRICES AND DETAILS ON PAGES 12-15

COMFY COUNTRY CHARMERS

Here and Now

- This country home's mammoth upper-floor future area can flex to meet your coming needs, but the main-floor amenities are fit to suit your lifestyle right here, right now.
- A cozy porch fronts the home, promising hours of relaxation.
- The bright Great Room boasts a media unit, a fireplace, a wet bar and French doors to a lovely screened porch.
- Guests in the formal dining room will enjoy looking out on the front yard through a wide bay window.
- The master bedroom features a bay window in the sleeping chamber, plus a long walk-in closet and a private bath with an oversized tub, a separate shower and a dual-sink vanity.
- Another bay window enhances one of the two secondary bedrooms.

Plan AX-00306

Bedrooms: 3+	Baths: 2
Living Area:	
Main floor	1,595 sq. ft.
Total Living Area:	**1,595 sq. ft.**
Future upper floor	813 sq. ft.
Screened porch	178 sq. ft.
Basement	1,595 sq. ft.
Garage	466 sq. ft.
Storage	24 sq. ft.
Utility room	22 sq. ft.
Exterior Wall Framing:	2x4
Foundation Options:	
Daylight basement	
Standard basement	
Crawlspace	
Slab	

(All plans can be built with your choice of foundation and framing. A generic conversion diagram is available. See order form.)

BLUEPRINT PRICE CODE: B

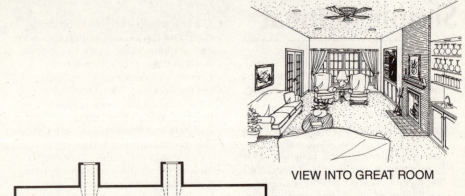

VIEW INTO GREAT ROOM

ORDER BLUEPRINTS ANYTIME!
CALL TOLL-FREE 1-800-820-1296

Plan AX-00306
Plan copyright held by home designer/architect

PRICES AND DETAILS ON PAGES 12-15

Simple Whimsy

- A gabled exterior and showy porches pair up in this whimsical design. Inside, the open floor plan showcases a winding staircase and an upper-floor balcony.
- The living room, dining room and island kitchen—all with hardwood floors—work together as a whole to unify family time. A fireplace graces the living room. The dining room features a built-in buffet and access to a back deck.
- In the front of the home, a multipurpose den features a built-in media center and bookshelves, as well as a charming window seat. When it's not being used as a media room, the den makes a nice guest room.
- The winding staircase leads to a balcony overlooking the living room. The master suite's amenities include a dressing area and private access to a balcony porch. The other two bedrooms boast ample closet space. A secret storage area is hidden behind one of the bedrooms.

Plan BC-1700

Bedrooms: 3+	Baths: 2½
Living Area:	
Upper floor	890 sq. ft.
Main floor	705 sq. ft.
Total Living Area:	**1,595 sq. ft.**
Garage	225 sq. ft.
Bike storage	36 sq. ft.
Exterior Wall Framing:	2x6

Foundation Options:
Crawlspace
(All plans can be built with your choice of foundation and framing. A generic conversion diagram is available. See order form.)

BLUEPRINT PRICE CODE: B

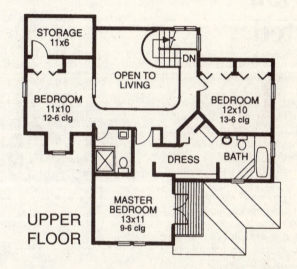

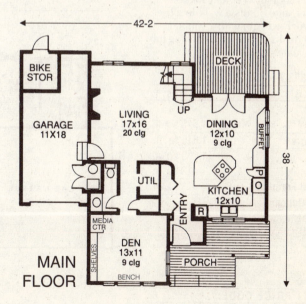

ORDER BLUEPRINTS ANYTIME!
CALL TOLL-FREE 1-800-820-1296

Plan BC-1700
Plan copyright held by home designer/architect

PRICES AND DETAILS ON PAGES 12-15

COMFY COUNTRY CHARMERS

Tradition Updated

- The nostalgic exterior of this home gives way to dramatic cathedral ceilings and illuminating skylights inside.
- The front porch welcomes guests into the stone-tiled foyer. Beyond, the living and dining rooms merge together, forming an open entertaining area under a cathedral ceiling.
- The family room shares a cathedral ceiling and a cozy three-sided fireplace with the living room. A sunny skylight and sliding glass doors to a patio brighten the room.
- The skylighted island kitchen offers yet another cathedral ceiling and adjoins a cheery breakfast nook, which serves as the perfect spot for everyday meals.
- The master suite boasts a walk-in closet and a skylighted bath with a vaulted ceiling, a dual-sink vanity, a soaking tub and a separate shower.

Plan AX-90303-A

Bedrooms: 3	Baths: 2

Living Area:
Main floor	1,615 sq. ft.
Total Living Area:	**1,615 sq. ft.**
Basement	1,615 sq. ft.
Garage	412 sq. ft.

Exterior Wall Framing: 2x4

Foundation Options:
Daylight basement
Standard basement
Crawlspace
Slab
(All plans can be built with your choice of foundation and framing. A generic conversion diagram is available. See order form.)

BLUEPRINT PRICE CODE: B

VIEW INTO FAMILY ROOM

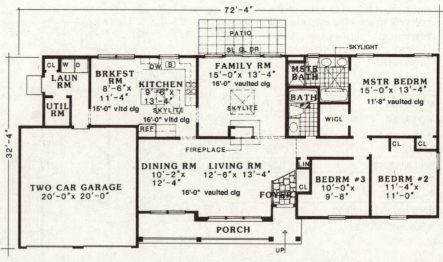

MAIN FLOOR

ORDER BLUEPRINTS ANYTIME!
CALL TOLL-FREE 1-800-820-1296

Plan AX-90303-A
Plan copyright held by home designer/architect

PRICES AND DETAILS ON PAGES 12-15

COMFY COUNTRY CHARMERS

Welcome Home

- An inviting covered porch welcomes you home to this country-kissed ranch.
- Inside, a cathedral ceiling soars over the expansive living room, which boasts a fireplace flanked by windows.
- Bathed in sunlight from more windows, the dining room flaunts an elegant French door that opens to a delightful backyard porch.
- The gourmet kitchen features a planning desk, a pantry and a unique, angled bar—a great place to settle for an afternoon snack. Garage access is conveniently nearby.

- Smartly secluded in one corner of the home is the lovely and spacious master bedroom, crowned by a tray ceiling. Other amenities include huge his-and-hers walk-in closets and a private bath with a garden tub and a dual-sink vanity.
- Just outside the door to the master bedroom, a neat laundry closet is handy for last-minute loads.
- Two secondary bedrooms round out this wonderful design. The front-facing bedroom is complemented by a vaulted ceiling, while the rear bedroom offers a sunny window seat. A full bath accented by a stylish round window is shared by both rooms.

Plan J-91085

Bedrooms: 3	Baths: 2

Living Area:

Main floor	1,643 sq. ft.
Total Living Area:	**1,643 sq. ft.**
Standard basement	1,643 sq. ft.
Garage	443 sq. ft.
Storage	37 sq. ft.
Exterior Wall Framing:	2x4

Foundation Options:

Standard basement
Crawlspace
Slab

(All plans can be built with your choice of foundation and framing. A generic conversion diagram is available. See order form.)

BLUEPRINT PRICE CODE:	B

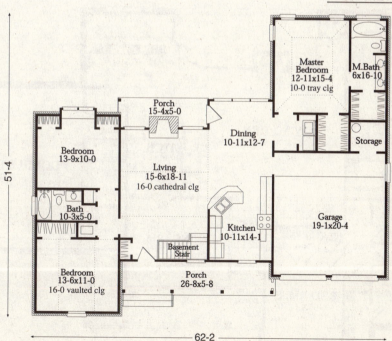

MAIN FLOOR

ORDER BLUEPRINTS ANYTIME!
CALL TOLL-FREE 1-800-820-1296

Plan J-91085

Plan copyright held by home designer/architect

PRICES AND DETAILS ON PAGES 12-15

COMFY COUNTRY CHARMERS

Just Perfect

- This well-planned design is the perfect solution for a family in search of an affordable yet comfortable home.
- A quiet porch out front gives you a peaceful spot to retreat to with a book or just your thoughts. A charming rail lends warmth to the home.
- Inside, the formal dining room sits to the right of the entry. This is the ideal spot to entertain friends or celebrate a promotion with a good meal.
- At the core of the home, the living room awaits years of visiting, good conversation, homework, TV watching and other regular activities. A handy bar between the living room and the kitchen holds chips, sodas and other refreshments during get-togethers.
- You will enjoy everyday dinners and leisurely breakfasts with coffee and the Sunday paper in the casual breakfast nook. A nearby door offers escape to a nice-sized covered patio.
- The cozy master suite makes getting out of bed even harder. In the skylighted bath, a dual-sink vanity and an oversized tub give the heads of the household extra-special treatment.

Plan KD-1648

Bedrooms: 3	Baths: 2

Living Area:
Main floor ..... 1,648 sq. ft.
Total Living Area: ..... **1,648 sq. ft.**
Garage ..... 446 sq. ft.
Storage ..... 61 sq. ft.
Exterior Wall Framing: 2x4
Foundation Options:
Slab
(All plans can be built with your choice of foundation and framing. A generic conversion diagram is available. See order form.)

BLUEPRINT PRICE CODE: **B**

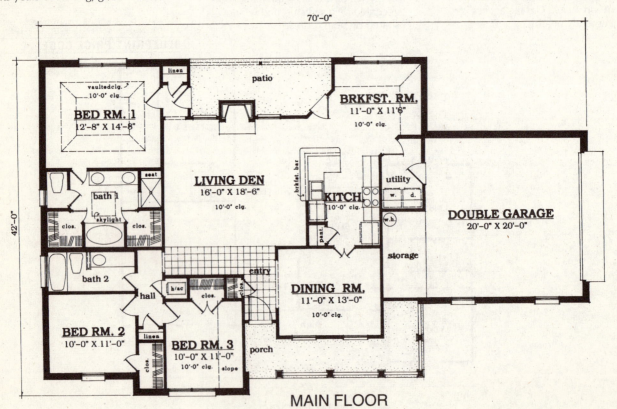

MAIN FLOOR

**ORDER BLUEPRINTS ANYTIME!
CALL TOLL-FREE 1-800-820-1296**

Plan KD-1648
Plan copyright held by home designer/architect

PRICES AND DETAILS ON PAGES 12-15

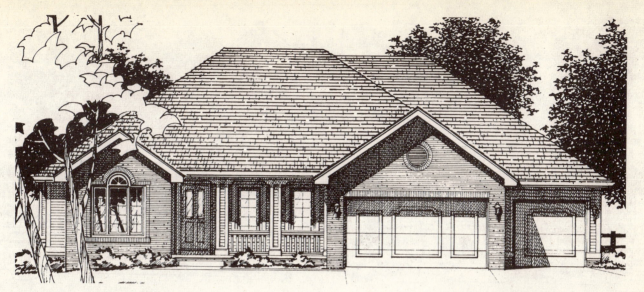

REAR VIEW

Suite Sensation

- Go ahead, you deserve it! Pamper yourself every day in this sensational master suite.
- A stepped ceiling adds space to the bedroom. The oversized bath is a treat, with its corner whirlpool tub, separate shower and dual-sink vanity. The adjacent den, complete with a built-in wet bar, is quite versatile: Convert it to a guest room, or expand the master suite to include this area as an anteroom.
- A vaulted ceiling expands the front-facing secondary bedroom. The highlight of this room is a beautiful Palladian window.
- The rest of the design is equally luxurious—perfect for entertaining. The Great Room and the breakfast nook feature high ceilings and tall, transom-topped windows. The kitchen lies between the two eating areas, and a butler's pantry separates the kitchen and the dining room for serving ease.
- The home's two porches accommodate outdoor entertaining, while the three-car garage meets your storage needs.

Plan DBI-2818

Bedrooms: 2+	Baths: 2
Living Area:	
Main floor	1,651 sq. ft.
Total Living Area:	**1,651 sq. ft.**
Standard basement	1,651 sq. ft.
Garage	677 sq. ft.
Exterior Wall Framing:	2x4
Foundation Options:	

Standard basement
(All plans can be built with your choice of foundation and framing. A generic conversion diagram is available. See order form.)

BLUEPRINT PRICE CODE: B

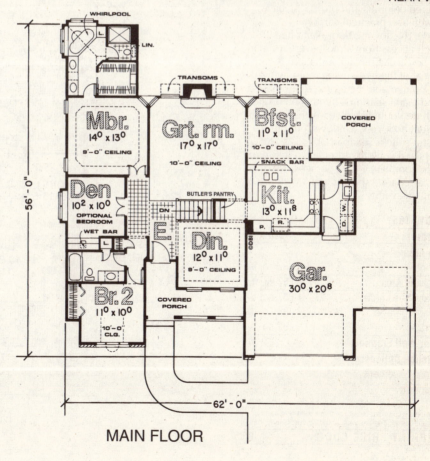

MAIN FLOOR

ORDER BLUEPRINTS ANYTIME!
CALL TOLL-FREE 1-800-820-1296

Plan DBI-2818
Plan copyright held by home designer/architect

PRICES AND DETAILS
ON PAGES 12-15

COMFY COUNTRY CHARMERS

Something for Everyone

- The charming porches and Craftsman-inspired details of this home will capture your heart; the sensible layout will appeal to the utilitarian in you.
- The design's exterior is marked by tapered columns and projecting eaves, as well as a practical carport.
- Inside, the flowing floor plan offers porch access from almost every room in the house. A fireplace enhances the appeal of the large living room, while the kitchen and the dining room make a good team, sharing a handy peninsula.
- Each bedroom is blessed with a walk-in closet and lovely windows, but the master suite is set apart. It boasts an oversized walk-in closet and a luxurious bath, complete with a corner garden tub, a separate shower and a wide, dual-sink vanity.

Plan DW-1657

Bedrooms: 3	Baths: 2
Living Area:	
Main floor	1,657 sq. ft.
Total Living Area:	**1,657 sq. ft.**
Standard basement	1,657 sq. ft.
Detached garage	484 sq. ft.
Carport	282 sq. ft.
Exterior Wall Framing:	2x4

Foundation Options:
Standard basement
Crawlspace
Slab
(All plans can be built with your choice of foundation and framing. A generic conversion diagram is available. See order form.)
BLUEPRINT PRICE CODE: B

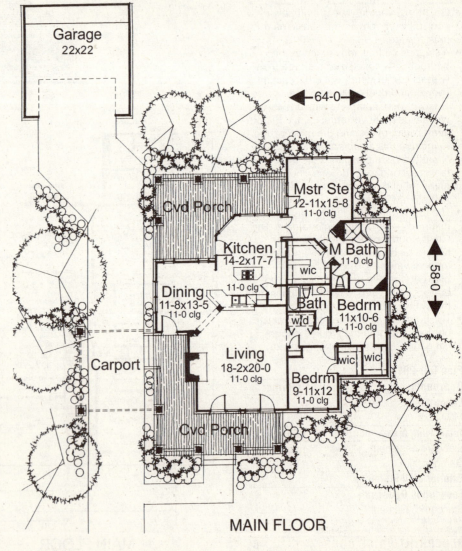

MAIN FLOOR

Plan DW-1657
Plan copyright held by home designer/architect

Rustic Welcome

- This rustic design boasts an appealing exterior with a covered front porch that offers guests a friendly welcome.
- Inside, the centrally located Great Room features a cathedral ceiling with exposed wood beams. A massive fireplace separates the living area from the large dining room, which offers access to a nice backyard patio.
- The galley-style kitchen flows between the formal dining room and the bayed breakfast room, which offers a handy pantry and access to laundry facilities.
- The master suite features a walk-in closet and a compartmentalized bath.
- Across the Great Room, two additional bedrooms have extra closet space and share a second full bath.
- The side-entry garage gives the front of the home an extra-appealing and uncluttered look.
- The optional daylight basement offers expanded living space. The stairway (not shown) would be located along the wall between the dining room and the back bedroom.

Plan C-8460

Bedrooms: 3	**Baths:** 2

Living Area:	
Main floor	1,670 sq. ft.
Total Living Area:	**1,670 sq. ft.**
Daylight basement	1,600 sq. ft.
Garage	427 sq. ft.
Storage	63 sq. ft.

Exterior Wall Framing: 2x4

Foundation Options:
Daylight basement
Crawlspace
Slab
(All plans can be built with your choice of foundation and framing. A generic conversion diagram is available. See order form.)

BLUEPRINT PRICE CODE: B

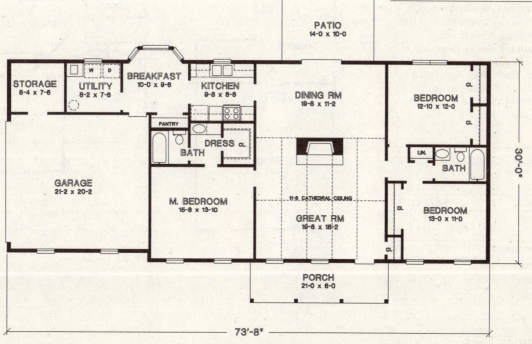

MAIN FLOOR

ORDER BLUEPRINTS ANYTIME!
CALL TOLL-FREE 1-800-820-1296

Plan C-8460
Plan copyright held by home designer/architect

PRICES AND DETAILS ON PAGES 12-15

COMFY COUNTRY CHARMERS

Smashing Master Suite!

- Corniced gables accented with arched louvers and a covered front porch with striking columns take this one-story design beyond the ordinary.
- The vaulted ceiling in the foyer rises to join the vaulted ceiling in the family room. A central fireplace heats the casual areas and is framed by a window and a French door.
- An angled serving bar/snack counter connects the family room to the sunny dining room and kitchen. The adjoining breakfast room has easy access to the garage, the optional basement and the laundry room with a plant shelf.
- The master suite is simply smashing, with a tray ceiling and private access to the backyard. The master bath has a vaulted ceiling and all the amenities, while the vaulted sitting area offers an optional fireplace.

Plan FB-1671	
Bedrooms: 3	**Baths:** 2
Living Area:	
Main floor	1,671 sq. ft.
Total Living Area:	**1,671 sq. ft.**
Daylight basement	1,671 sq. ft.
Garage	400 sq. ft.
Exterior Wall Framing:	2x4

Foundation Options:
Daylight basement
Crawlspace
Slab
(All plans can be built with your choice of foundation and framing. A generic conversion diagram is available. See order form.)

BLUEPRINT PRICE CODE: B

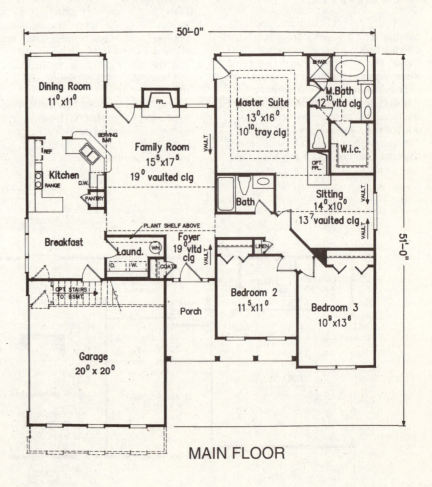

MAIN FLOOR

ORDER BLUEPRINTS ANYTIME!
CALL TOLL-FREE 1-800-820-1296

Plan FB-1671
Plan copyright held by home designer/architect

PRICES AND DETAILS
ON PAGES 12-15

COMFY COUNTRY CHARMERS

Perfect Repose

- This perfectly planned home is well suited to serve as the haven your family retreats to for repose and relaxation.
- The front porch includes just the right amount of space for your favorite two rocking chairs and a side table.
- Inside, the foyer flows into the generous Great Room, which will serve as home base for family gatherings. A fireplace flanked by a media center turns this room into a home theater.
- Nearby, sunlight pours into the versatile dining room. Along one wall, a beautiful built-in cabinet holds linens, china and other fine collectibles.
- For easy serving, the kitchen's snack bar extends to a peninsula counter. Serve casual meals on the back porch.
- A tray ceiling and a bay window in the master suite help to create a stylish oasis. A dressing area with a vanity table for morning preening leads to the master bath, where a skylight and a lofty vaulted ceiling brighten the room.

Plan AX-95347

Bedrooms: 3	Baths: 2½
Living Area:	
Main floor	1,709 sq. ft.
Total Living Area:	**1,709 sq. ft.**
Standard basement	1,709 sq. ft.
Garage and storage	448 sq. ft.
Enclosed storage	12 sq. ft.
Utility room	13 sq. ft.
Exterior Wall Framing:	2x4

Foundation Options:
Standard basement
Crawlspace
Slab
(All plans can be built with your choice of foundation and framing. A generic conversion diagram is available. See order form.)

BLUEPRINT PRICE CODE: B

REAR VIEW

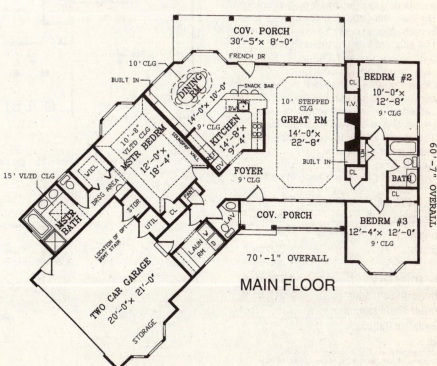

MAIN FLOOR

ORDER BLUEPRINTS ANYTIME!
CALL TOLL-FREE 1-800-820-1296

Plan AX-95347
Plan copyright held by home designer/architect

PRICES AND DETAILS ON PAGES 12-15

71

COMFY COUNTRY CHARMERS

Charming Guest Cottage

- A charming guest cottage makes this home a unique find.
- Incorporated with the detached garage, the cottage's cozy covered porch opens to a comfortable living area, which shares an efficient serving counter with the galley-style kitchen.
- A full bath and a bedroom with a large walk-in closet complete the cottage.
- The foyer of the main home unfolds to the spacious living room, which boasts a cathedral ceiling and a cozy fireplace.
- The sun-drenched dining room features French-door access to a covered porch.
- The efficient kitchen includes a neat serving counter and a handy laundry area behind pocket doors.
- Elegant double doors open to the master bedroom, which features another cathedral ceiling and attractive plant ledges above the two walk-in closets. The master bath flaunts a garden tub and a separate shower.
- French doors open to a cozy study, which could serve as a second bedroom.

Plan L-270-SA

Bedrooms: 2+	Baths: 3
Living Area:	
Main floor	1,268 sq. ft.
Guest cottage	468 sq. ft.
Total Living Area:	**1,736 sq. ft.**
Garage and storage	573 sq. ft.
Exterior Wall Framing:	2x4
Foundation Options:	
Slab	
(All plans can be built with your choice of foundation and framing. A generic conversion diagram is available. See order form.)	
BLUEPRINT PRICE CODE:	**B**

REAR VIEW

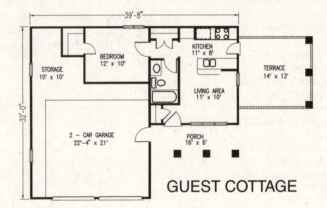

GUEST COTTAGE

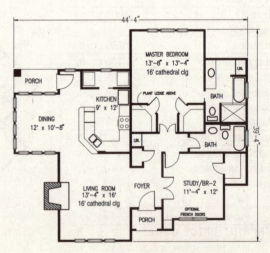

MAIN FLOOR

Plan L-270-SA
Plan copyright held by home designer/architect

COMFY COUNTRY CHARMERS

Designed for Livability

- With the removal of the master suite from the rest of the home, this design is ideal for the maturing family.
- Off the columned porch, the sidelighted front entry offers views through the bright living room to the backyard.
- An elegant column visually sets off the formal dining room from the adjacent living room.
- The kitchen offers a sunny morning room, a pantry and handy access to the laundry facilities and the garage.
- The sunny bay created by the morning room and the sitting area of the master suite adds interior and exterior excitement to this plan.
- The master bath boasts an exciting oval garden tub and a separate shower, as well as a spacious walk-in closet and a dressing area with a dual-sink vanity.
- All of the rooms mentioned above feature soaring ceilings.
- Across the home, three additional bedrooms share another full bath.

REAR VIEW

VIEW INTO LIVING ROOM, KITCHEN AND DINING ROOM

Plan DD-1696	
Bedrooms: 4	**Baths:** 2
Living Area:	
Main floor	1,748 sq. ft.
Total Living Area:	**1,748 sq. ft.**
Standard basement	1,748 sq. ft.
Garage	393 sq. ft.
Exterior Wall Framing:	2x4
Foundation Options:	
Standard basement	
Crawlspace	
Slab	
(All plans can be built with your choice of foundation and framing. A generic conversion diagram is available. See order form.)	
BLUEPRINT PRICE CODE:	**B**

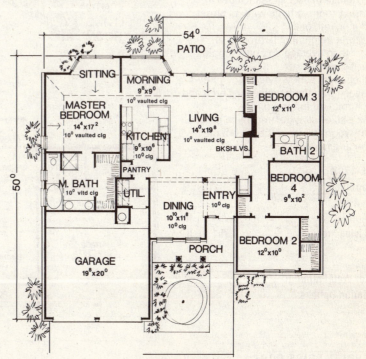

MAIN FLOOR

ORDER BLUEPRINTS ANYTIME!
CALL TOLL-FREE 1-800-820-1296

Plan DD-1696
Plan copyright held by home designer/architect

PRICES AND DETAILS ON PAGES 12-15

Simply Beautiful

- This four-bedroom design offers simplistic beauty, economical construction and ample space for both family life and formal entertaining—all on one floor.
- The charming cottage-style exterior gives way to a spacious interior. A vaulted, beamed ceiling soars above the huge living room, which features a massive fireplace, built-in bookshelves and access to a backyard patio.
- The deluxe master suite includes a dressing room, a large walk-in closet and a private bath.
- The three remaining bedrooms are larger than average and offer ample closet space.
- The efficient galley-style kitchen flows between a sunny bayed eating area and the formal dining room.
- A nice-sized storage area and a deluxe utility room are accessible from the two-car garage.

Plan E-1702

Bedrooms: 4	Baths: 2
Living Area:	
Main floor	1,751 sq. ft.
Total Living Area:	**1,751 sq. ft.**
Garage	484 sq. ft.
Storage	105 sq. ft.
Exterior Wall Framing:	2x4

Foundation Options:
Crawlspace
Slab
(All plans can be built with your choice of foundation and framing. A generic conversion diagram is available. See order form.)

BLUEPRINT PRICE CODE: B

VIEW INTO LIVING ROOM

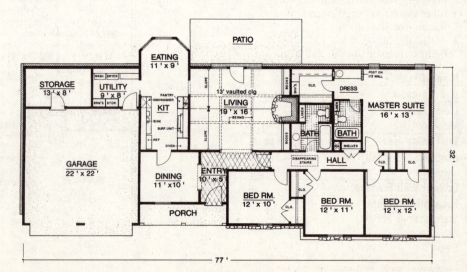

MAIN FLOOR

Plan E-1702
Plan copyright held by home designer/architect

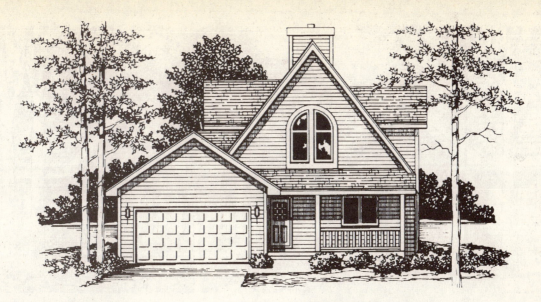

Very Versatile!

- You won't find a more versatile design than this one! The attractive traditional facade gives way to a dramatic rear deck, making the home suitable for a lakeside lot. With its modest width and daylight basement, the home also adapts to a narrow or sloping site.
- A railed porch welcomes guests into the main entry and into the Great Room straight ahead. The Great Room flaunts a vaulted ceiling, a metal fireplace and sliding glass doors to the deck.
- The efficient U-shaped kitchen offers a pantry and presents a serving bar to the dining room.
- A convenient hall bath serves the quiet main-floor bedroom, which overlooks the scenic rear wood porch.
- Upstairs, a spacious loft allows dramatic views of the Great Room over a wood rail. A commodious storage closet is accessed from the loft.
- Double doors introduce the posh master suite, which boasts a walk-in closet, a whirlpool bath and attic access.
- The loft and the master bedroom are visually expanded by high ceilings.

Plan PI-92-373

Bedrooms: 2	Baths: 2
Living Area:	
Upper floor	546 sq. ft.
Main floor	1,212 sq. ft.
Total Living Area:	**1,758 sq. ft.**
Daylight basement	1,212 sq. ft.
Garage	475 sq. ft.
Exterior Wall Framing:	2x6
Foundation Options:	
Daylight basement	

(All plans can be built with your choice of foundation and framing. A generic conversion diagram is available. See order form.)

BLUEPRINT PRICE CODE: B

REAR VIEW

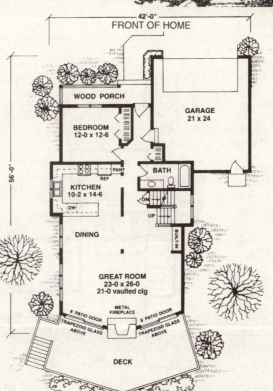

MAIN FLOOR

UPPER FLOOR

ORDER BLUEPRINTS ANYTIME!
CALL TOLL-FREE 1-800-820-1296

Plan PI-92-373
Plan copyright held by home designer/architect

PRICES AND DETAILS ON PAGES 12-15

75

COMFY COUNTRY CHARMERS

Enticing Interior

- Filled with elegant features, this modern country home's exciting floor plan is as impressive as it is innovative.
- Past the inviting columned porch, the entrance gallery flows into the spacious living room/dining room area.
- Boasting a high sloped ceiling, the living room is enhanced by a semi-circular window bay and includes a handsome fireplace. A low wall further distinguishes this space from the gallery. The adjoining dining room offers sliding glass doors to a spacious backyard terrace.
- The skylighted kitchen features an eating bar that serves the sunny bayed dinette. A convenient half-bath and a laundry/mudroom are nearby.
- Brightened by a bay window, the luxurious master bedroom shows off his-and-hers walk-in closets. The master bath showcases a whirlpool garden tub under a glass sunroof.
- Two additional bedrooms—the smaller of which might make a nice home office or study—have plenty of closet space and share a skylighted hall bath.

Plan K-685-DA	
Bedrooms: 3	**Baths:** 2½
Living Area:	
Main floor	1,760 sq. ft.
Total Living Area:	1,760 sq. ft.
Standard basement	1,700 sq. ft.
Garage	482 sq. ft.
Exterior Wall Framing:	2x4 or 2x6
Foundation Options:	
Standard basement	
Slab	
(All plans can be built with your choice of foundation and framing. A generic conversion diagram is available. See order form.)	
BLUEPRINT PRICE CODE:	B

VIEW INTO LIVING AND DINING ROOMS

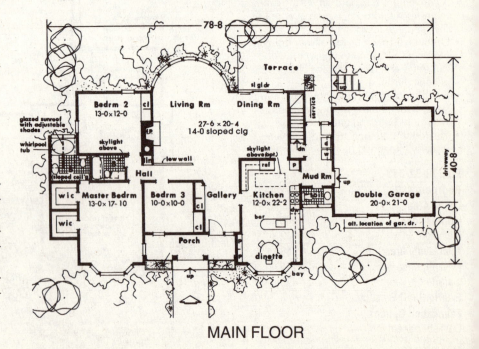

MAIN FLOOR

Plan K-685-DA
Plan copyright held by home designer/architect

COMFY COUNTRY CHARMERS

Fresh Country Air

- A skylighted screen porch, a fun backyard deck and an abundance of windows infuse this country-style home with air and light.
- An inviting front porch ushers neighbors into the spacious, centrally-located family room, where a fireplace warms chilly nights. On sunny days, enjoy the screened-in back porch, or head out onto the rear deck.
- The roomy kitchen boasts a built-in desk, a closet pantry and serving bars overlooking both the breakfast nook and the family room.
- A tray ceiling, his-and-hers walk-in closets and a light-filled sitting area highlight the master bedroom. The private master bath flaunts a dual-sink vanity and a garden tub.
- A versatile bonus room above the garage offers expansion opportunities.

Plan APS-1717

Bedrooms: 3+	Baths: 2
Living Area:	
Main floor	1,787 sq. ft.
Total Living Area:	**1,787 sq. ft.**
Future area	263 sq. ft.
Screen porch	153 sq. ft.
Standard basement	1,787 sq. ft.
Garage	466 sq. ft.
Exterior Wall Framing:	2x4

Foundation Options:
Standard basement
Crawlspace
(All plans can be built with your choice of foundation and framing. A generic conversion diagram is available. See order form.)

BLUEPRINT PRICE CODE: B

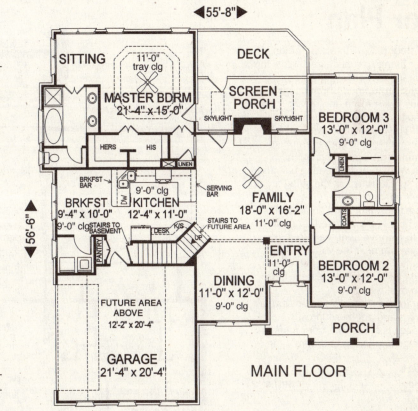

MAIN FLOOR

VIEW INTO KITCHEN AND BREAKFAST NOOK

ORDER BLUEPRINTS ANYTIME!
CALL TOLL-FREE 1-800-820-1296

Plan APS-1717
Plan copyright held by home designer/architect

PRICES AND DETAILS ON PAGES 12-15

77

COMFY COUNTRY CHARMERS

Free-Flowing Floor Plan

VIEW INTO LIVING ROOM

REAR VIEW

- A fluid floor plan with open indoor/outdoor living spaces characterizes this exciting luxury home.
- The stylish columned porch opens to a spacious living room and dining room expanse that overlooks the outdoor spaces. The breathtaking view also includes a dramatic corner fireplace.
- The dining area opens to a bright kitchen with an angled eating bar. The overall spaciousness of the living areas is increased with raised ceilings.
- A sunny, informal eating area adjoins the kitchen, and an angled set of doors opens to a convenient main-floor laundry room near the garage entrance.
- The vaulted master bedroom has a walk-in closet and a sumptuous bath with an oval tub.
- A separate wing houses two additional bedrooms and another full bath.
- Attic space is accessible from stairs in the garage and in the bedroom wing.

Plan E-1710

Bedrooms: 3	Baths: 2
Living Area:	
Main floor	1,792 sq. ft.
Total Living Area:	**1,792 sq. ft.**
Standard basement	1,792 sq. ft.
Garage	484 sq. ft.
Storage	96 sq. ft.
Exterior Wall Framing:	2x6

Foundation Options:
Standard basement
Crawlspace
Slab
(All plans can be built with your choice of foundation and framing. A generic conversion diagram is available. See order form.)

BLUEPRINT PRICE CODE: B

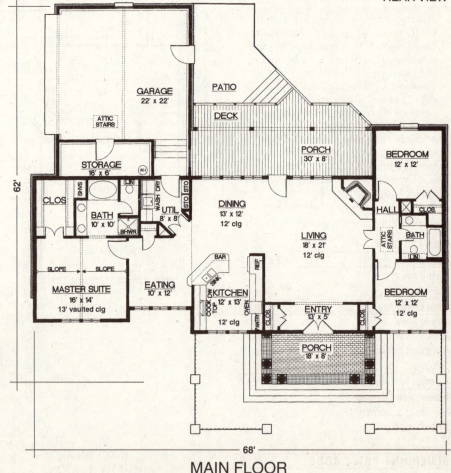
MAIN FLOOR

ORDER BLUEPRINTS ANYTIME!
CALL TOLL-FREE 1-800-820-1296

Plan E-1710
Plan copyright held by home designer/architect

PRICES AND DETAILS ON PAGES 12-15

A Perfect Fit

- Whether built in the city, a suburb or a rural area, this design, with its charming facade and access to the outdoors, is a perfect fit.
- The front porch and the two-story entry lead to the home's main living spaces. The formal living room lies through an archway and flaunts a two-way fireplace and built-in bookshelves.
- Everyday living takes place in the family room, the eating nook and the kitchen. Large windows brighten the space. These rooms are clearly defined, yet they work together as a whole.
- The family room shares the fireplace with the living room and displays built-in shelves, a TV cabinet and a unique art niche. The island kitchen features a substantial pantry and a handy snack bar. The nook provides a bright eating spot, as well as outdoor access.
- A nearby powder room contains a convenient laundry closet.
- Upstairs, the master bedroom boasts a large walk-in closet and a private bath. The home's two additional bedrooms share a full bath.

Plan KPS-60202

Bedrooms: 3	Baths: 2½
Living Area:	
Upper floor	890 sq. ft.
Main floor	902 sq. ft.
Total Living Area:	**1,792 sq. ft.**
Garage	392 sq. ft.
Exterior Wall Framing:	2x4

Foundation Options:
Crawlspace
(All plans can be built with your choice of foundation and framing. A generic conversion diagram is available. See order form.)
BLUEPRINT PRICE CODE: B

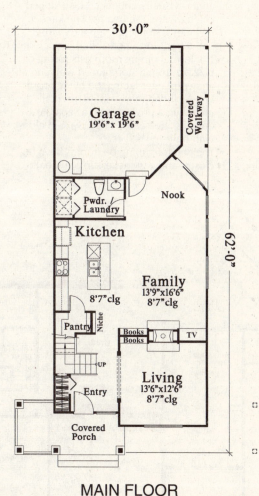

MAIN FLOOR

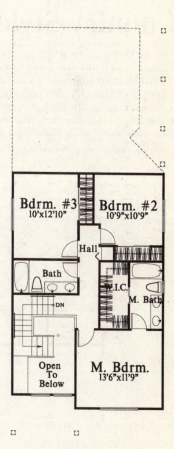

UPPER FLOOR

ORDER BLUEPRINTS ANYTIME!
CALL TOLL-FREE 1-800-820-1296

Plan KPS-60202
Plan copyright held by home designer/architect

PRICES AND DETAILS ON PAGES 12-15

79

Classic Country-Style

- At the center of this rustic country-style home is an enormous living room with a flat beamed ceiling and a massive stone fireplace. A sunny patio and a covered rear porch are just steps away.
- The adjoining eating area and kitchen provide plenty of room for casual dining and meal preparation. The eating area is visually enhanced by a sloped ceiling with false beams. The kitchen includes a snack bar, a pantry closet and a built-in spice cabinet.
- The formal dining room gets plenty of pizzazz from a stone-faced wall and an arched planter facing the living room.
- The secluded master suite has it all, including a private bath, a separate dressing area and a large walk-in closet with built-in shelves.
- The two remaining bedrooms have big closets and easy access to a full bath.

Plan E-1808

Bedrooms: 3	**Baths:** 2

Living Area:
Main floor — 1,800 sq. ft.
Total Living Area: — **1,800 sq. ft.**
Garage — 506 sq. ft.
Storage — 99 sq. ft.
Exterior Wall Framing: 2x4
Foundation Options:
Crawlspace
Slab
(All plans can be built with your choice of foundation and framing. A generic conversion diagram is available. See order form.)

BLUEPRINT PRICE CODE: B

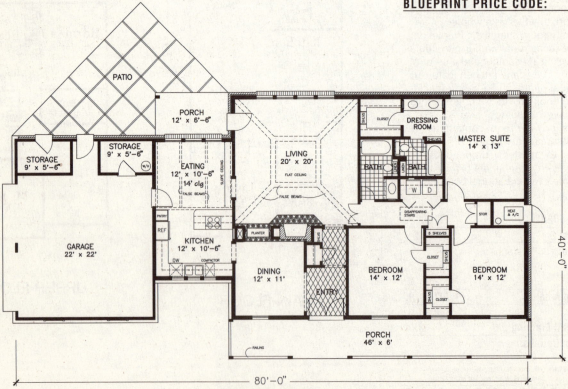

MAIN FLOOR

Plan E-1808
Plan copyright held by home designer/architect

COMFY COUNTRY CHARMERS

Exciting Perks

- Traditional doesn't have to be dull—this neat two-story is full of exciting perks.
- The idyllic front porch is one nice detail. To the rear, a just-right deck invites outdoor dining.
- The living and dining rooms team up to provide ample space for your family to gather or for guests to mingle. An eating bar fronting the kitchen is perfect for serving snacks or buffet spreads.
- An efficient layout allows the open kitchen to function well for all types of meals. A handy pantry closet provides extra storage space.
- Pocket doors open to the main-floor master suite's walk-in closet, creating a simple barrier between the sleeping area and storage. A private bath is a thoughtful addition to this smart, relaxing retreat.
- Upstairs, two generous bedrooms, each with a built-in desk and a pretty dormer, share a full bath.
- Off the kitchen, a half-bath and laundry facilities offer practical necessities and lead to the two-car garage.

Plan Y-1801

Bedrooms: 3	Baths: 2½
Living Area:	
Upper floor	670 sq. ft.
Main floor	1,131 sq. ft.
Total Living Area:	**1,801 sq. ft.**
Standard basement	1,131 sq. ft.
Garage	517 sq. ft.
Exterior Wall Framing:	2x6

Foundation Options:
Standard basement
Crawlspace
(All plans can be built with your choice of foundation and framing. A generic conversion diagram is available. See order form.)

BLUEPRINT PRICE CODE: B

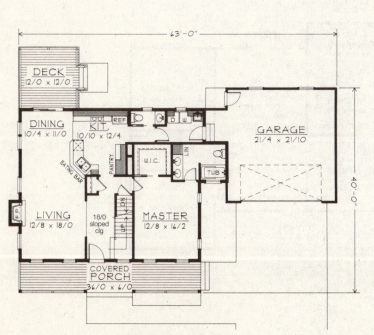

MAIN FLOOR

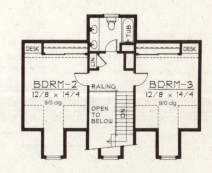

REAR VIEW

UPPER FLOOR

ORDER BLUEPRINTS ANYTIME!
CALL TOLL-FREE 1-800-820-1296

Plan Y-1801
Plan copyright held by home designer/architect

PRICES AND DETAILS ON PAGES 12-15

81

COMFY COUNTRY CHARMERS

Treasure Trove

- This home is quite a find! It's loaded with thoughtful amenities that will enrich your daily life for years to come.
- A covered front porch provides outdoor space for visiting with neighbors.
- The foyer precedes a Great Room topped by an airy cathedral ceiling. A fireplace at one end of the room invites you to gather around its comforting hearth. A door beside the fireplace leads out to a backyard deck that's perfect for summer fun.
- The U-shaped kitchen boasts a walk-in pantry and plenty of counter space for preparing holiday meals. It is situated between a sunny breakfast nook and a formal dining room crowned by a tray ceiling.
- The master bedroom is secluded in a rear corner of the home for privacy. It features a tray ceiling and a lush bath with a handy dual-sink vanity, a whirlpool tub and a separate shower, plus two walk-in closets.
- Across the home, two more bedrooms share a convenient hall bath.

Plan C-9715

Bedrooms: 3	Baths: 2

Living Area:
Main floor 1,804 sq. ft.
Total Living Area: **1,804 sq. ft.**
Daylight basement 1,804 sq. ft.
Garage 506 sq. ft.
Exterior Wall Framing: 2x4
Foundation Options:
Daylight basement
Crawlspace
Slab
(All plans can be built with your choice of foundation and framing. A generic conversion diagram is available. See order form.)
BLUEPRINT PRICE CODE: B

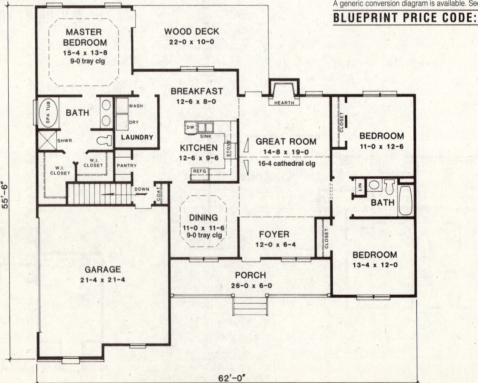

MAIN FLOOR

Plan C-9715
Plan copyright held by home designer/architect

ORDER BLUEPRINTS ANYTIME! CALL TOLL-FREE 1-800-820-1296

PRICES AND DETAILS ON PAGES 12-15

COMFY COUNTRY CHARMERS

Something Familiar

- This is what you've always wanted—a familiar home that reminds you of treasured past family times and inspires you to create good times of your own.
- The inherent friendliness of this home's design is evident at first glance: The welcoming windows, the charming front porch and the traditional lines all lend to its open, familiar and approachable feel.

- The formal dining room and inviting family room create a perfectly elegant setting for your first Thanksgiving dinner in your new home.
- Preparation of any meal is a breeze in the large, work-friendly kitchen. Casual meals and gatherings can be held in the spacious Keeping Room, which opens to the backyard.
- Luxury awaits you in the master suite, where a tray ceiling presides over the sleeping chamber. A pair of walk-in closets flanks the passage to the private bath, which offers twin sinks, a garden tub and a separate shower.

Plan LRK-96037-C

Bedrooms: 3	Baths: 2½

Living Area:
| Upper floor | 880 sq. ft. |
| Main floor | 935 sq. ft. |

Total Living Area:	**1,815 sq. ft.**
Porte cochere	481 sq. ft.
Optional storage	42 sq. ft.

Exterior Wall Framing: 2x4

Foundation Options:
Slab
(All plans can be built with your choice of foundation and framing. A generic conversion diagram is available. See order form.)

BLUEPRINT PRICE CODE: B

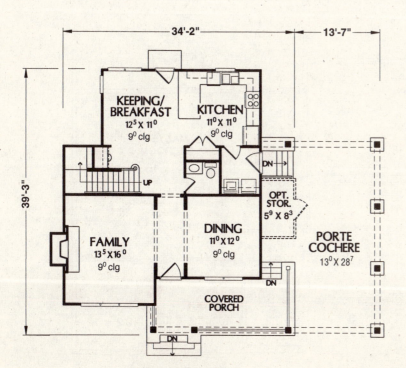

MAIN FLOOR

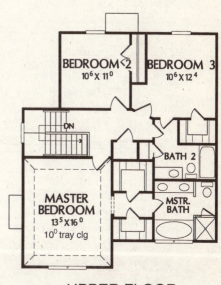

UPPER FLOOR

ORDER BLUEPRINTS ANYTIME!
CALL TOLL-FREE 1-800-820-1296

Plan LRK-96037-C
Plan copyright held by home designer/architect

PRICES AND DETAILS
ON PAGES 12-15

COMFY COUNTRY CHARMERS

Kitchen Takes All

- With an island workstation, a large pantry closet and a built-in menu desk, this home's kitchen truly has it all.
- The adjoining dining area is flooded with natural light and boasts a French door that leads to a spacious backyard patio and the flora beyond.
- From the dining area, a few quick steps take you to the family room, where built-in shelves and a handsome fireplace promise warm (and educating) weekend nights.
- For more formal gatherings, the living room lies off the foyer.
- The master bedroom offers a big walk-in closet and a private bath. An extra plus is its direct access to the patio.
- Two more bedrooms and a second full bath complete this home's floor plan.

Plan WH-9402

Bedrooms: 3	Baths: 2

Living Area:
Main floor 1,818 sq. ft.
Total Living Area: 1,818 sq. ft.
Standard basement 1,818 sq. ft.
Garage 485 sq. ft.
Exterior Wall Framing: 2x6
Foundation Options:
Standard basement
(All plans can be built with your choice of foundation and framing. A generic conversion diagram is available. See order form.)
BLUEPRINT PRICE CODE: B

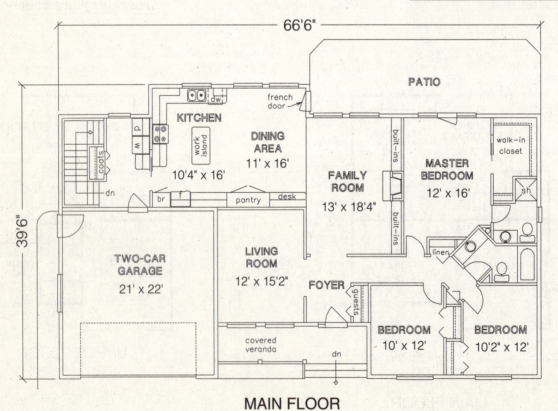

MAIN FLOOR

84   ORDER BLUEPRINTS ANYTIME! CALL TOLL-FREE 1-800-820-1296

Plan WH-9402
Plan copyright held by home designer/architect

PRICES AND DETAILS ON PAGES 12-15

COMFY COUNTRY CHARMERS

Take a Look!

- Once you take a look at this delightful home, you're sure to be enchanted by its many amenities. Out front, a perfectly sized porch offers a warm welcome to visitors.
- Inside, the entry leads back to the Great Room, where a cathedral ceiling with exposed wood beams draws admiring glances from guests. The handsome fireplace maximizes the room's comforting nature.
- To the left, the bayed dining room and kitchen merge together, creating an efficient space for family meals. A breakfast bar between the two rooms holds bulky serving dishes during dinner, while a pantry stores sundries.
- Across the home, a coffered ceiling, a private bath and two huge walk-in closets distinguish the master suite from the other bedrooms.
- A vaulted ceiling also tops the front-facing secondary bedroom.
- Above the garage, a bonus room provides space to grow. Depending on your needs, this spot would be great as a home office, a workshop or an extra bedroom. You decide!

Plan KD-1577

Bedrooms: 3+	Baths: 2
Living Area:	
Main floor	1,577 sq. ft.
Bonus room	274 sq. ft.
Total Living Area:	**1,851 sq. ft.**
Garage	438 sq. ft.
Exterior Wall Framing:	2x4

Foundation Options:

Crawlspace
Slab

(All plans can be built with your choice of foundation and framing. A generic conversion diagram is available. See order form.)

BLUEPRINT PRICE CODE: B

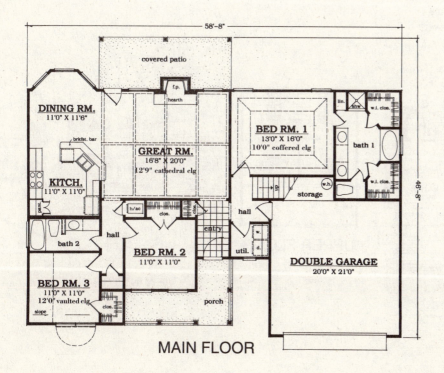

MAIN FLOOR

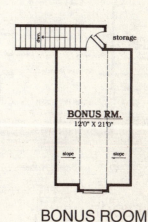

BONUS ROOM

ORDER BLUEPRINTS ANYTIME!
CALL TOLL-FREE 1-800-820-1296

Plan KD-1577
Plan copyright held by home designer/architect

PRICES AND DETAILS ON PAGES 12-15

COMFY COUNTRY CHARMERS

Unique Inside and Out

- This delightful design is as striking on the inside as it is on the outside.
- The focal point of the home is the huge Grand Room, which features a soaring, vaulted ceiling, high plant shelves and lots of glass, including a clerestory window. French doors flanking the fireplace lead to a spacious porch and two adjoining sun decks.
- The open, centrally located kitchen enjoys easy access from any room; a full bath and a laundry area are located nearby.
- The two main-floor master suites are another unique design element of the home. Each suite showcases an airy, vaulted ceiling, a sunny window seat, a private bath, a walk-in closet and French doors that open to a sun deck.
- Upstairs, two guest suites under a vaulted peak overlook the gorgeous Grand Room below.
- The multiple suites make this design a perfect shared vacation home.
- The one-car garage at the rear of the home offers convenient access and additional storage space.

Plan EOF-13

Bedrooms: 4	Baths: 3
Living Area:	
Upper floor	443 sq. ft.
Main floor	1,411 sq. ft.
Total Living Area:	**1,854 sq. ft.**
Garage	264 sq. ft.
Storage	50 sq. ft.
Exterior Wall Framing:	2x6

Foundation Options:
Crawlspace
(All plans can be built with your choice of foundation and framing. A generic conversion diagram is available. See order form.)

BLUEPRINT PRICE CODE: B

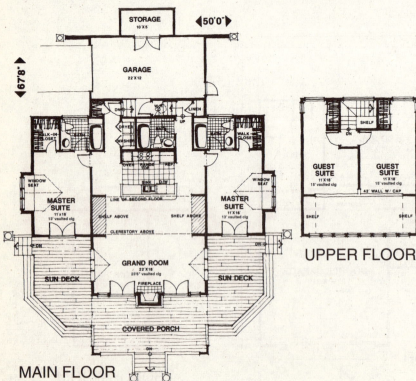

VIEW INTO GRAND ROOM

ORDER BLUEPRINTS ANYTIME!
CALL TOLL-FREE 1-800-820-1296

Plan EOF-13
Plan copyright held by home designer/architect

PRICES AND DETAILS ON PAGES 12-15

Classic Blend

- With decorative brick quoins, a columned porch and stylish dormers, the exterior of this classic one-story provides an interesting blend of Early American and European design.
- Just off the foyer, the bay-windowed formal dining room is enhanced by an stepped ceiling.
- The spacious Great Room, separated from the dining room by a columned arch, features a stepped ceiling, a built-in media center and a striking fireplace. Lovely French doors lead to a big backyard patio.
- The breakfast room, which shares an eating bar with the kitchen, boasts a sloped ceiling. French doors access a covered rear porch.
- The master bedroom has a tray ceiling, a sunny bay window and a roomy walk-in closet. The master bath features a whirlpool tub in a bayed nook and a separate shower.
- The front-facing bedroom is enhanced by a vaulted area over an arched transom window.

Plan AX-93304

Bedrooms: 3	Baths: 2
Living Area:	
Main floor	1,860 sq. ft.
Total Living Area:	**1,860 sq. ft.**
Standard basement	1,860 sq. ft.
Garage	434 sq. ft.
Exterior Wall Framing:	2x4

Foundation Options:
Standard basement
Crawlspace
Slab
(All plans can be built with your choice of foundation and framing. A generic conversion diagram is available. See order form.)

BLUEPRINT PRICE CODE:	**B**

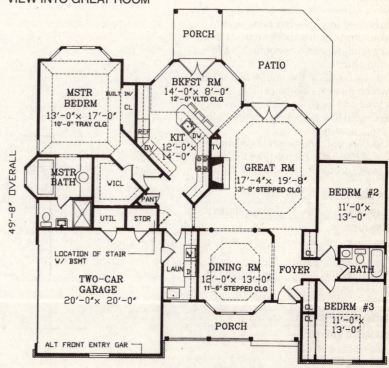

VIEW INTO GREAT ROOM

MAIN FLOOR

COMFY COUNTRY CHARMERS

ORDER BLUEPRINTS ANYTIME!
CALL TOLL-FREE 1-800-820-1296

Plan AX-93304
Plan copyright held by home designer/architect

PRICES AND DETAILS ON PAGES 12-15

COMFY COUNTRY CHARMERS

Overflowing With Luxury

- This compact home overflows with luxurious details, offering built-ins and boxed-out windows throughout.
- From the front porch, the open foyer leads into the expansive Great Room, which features a see-through fireplace and stunning transom windows overlooking the backyard.
- Lighted by a garden window, the roomy kitchen serves the bayed breakfast nook via a convenient snack bar. A menu desk is housed in a compact nook nearby.
- The formal dining room enjoys a boxed-out window and a beautiful built-in china hutch.
- Luxury awaits in the master bedroom, which includes a high ceiling, a walk-in closet and a private bath with an enclosed toilet, a lavish whirlpool tub and a dual-sink vanity.
- Upstairs, two additional bedrooms share a full hall bath. Each enjoys lots of closet space.

Plan DBI-1330

Bedrooms: 3	Baths: 2½
Living Area:	
Upper floor	448 sq. ft.
Main floor	1,421 sq. ft.
Total Living Area:	**1,869 sq. ft.**
Standard basement	1,384 sq. ft.
Garage	480 sq. ft.
Exterior Wall Framing:	2x4

Foundation Options:
Standard basement
(All plans can be built with your choice of foundation and framing. A generic conversion diagram is available. See order form.)

BLUEPRINT PRICE CODE: B

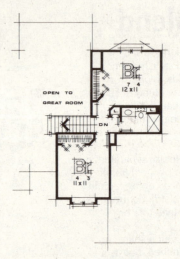

UPPER FLOOR

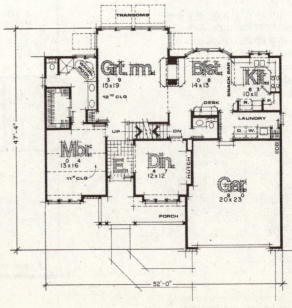

MAIN FLOOR

ORDER BLUEPRINTS ANYTIME!
CALL TOLL-FREE 1-800-820-1296

Plan DBI-1330
Plan copyright held by home designer/architect

PRICES AND DETAILS ON PAGES 12-15

Dramatic Heights

- Brick lends a rich look to this two-story traditional home.
- Interior highlights begin with a dramatic two-story foyer with a decorative corner niche. The formal spaces are located on either side of the foyer, with the living room showing off a lovely bay window.
- The informal spaces are incorporated into a large activity area at the back of the home. A handsome corner fireplace and a window wall are featured in the spectacular two-story family room.
- The roomy kitchen offers an angled snack bar and a pantry closet. The sunny adjoining breakfast room opens to the outdoors.
- The upper floor houses three bedrooms and is accessed from stairs in the family room. The large master bedroom features a tray ceiling and the option of an added sitting room. A huge walk-in closet and a luxurious vaulted bath with an oval tub and his-and-hers dressing areas are also included.

Plan FB-5014-SOME

Bedrooms: 3	Baths: 2½
Living Area:	
Upper floor	963 sq. ft.
Main floor	915 sq. ft.
Total Living Area:	**1,878 sq. ft.**
Daylight basement	915 sq. ft.
Garage and storage	444 sq. ft.
Exterior Wall Framing:	2x4

Foundation Options:
Daylight basement
(All plans can be built with your choice of foundation and framing. A generic conversion diagram is available. See order form.)

BLUEPRINT PRICE CODE: B

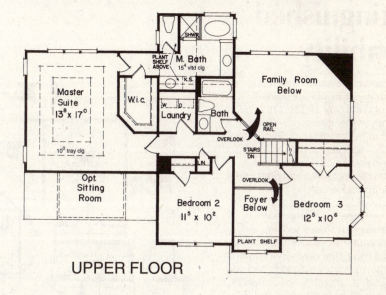

UPPER FLOOR

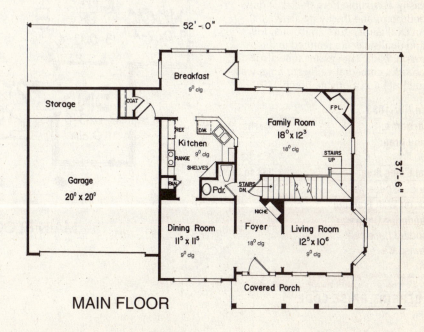

MAIN FLOOR

Plan FB-5014-SOME
Plan copyright held by home designer/architect

COMFY COUNTRY CHARMERS

Distinguished Durability

- Sturdy tapered columns with brick pedestals give this unique home a feeling of durability and security.
- Off the foyer, the spacious living room is brightened by the incoming light of the double dormers above. The high ceiling and the glass-framed fireplace add further ambience. An atrium door opens to the wraparound porch.
- Decorative wood columns and a high ceiling enhance the dining room.
- The neat kitchen shares serving counters with the breakfast nook and the living room, for easy service to both locations. A central cooktop island and a built-in desk are other conveniences.
- The main bath has twin sinks and is easily accessible from the secondary bedrooms and the living areas.
- An oval garden tub, an isolated toilet and dual sinks are featured in the master bath. The master suite also boasts a cathedral ceiling, a huge walk-in closet and a private porch.

Plan DW-1883

Bedrooms: 3	Baths: 2

Living Area:
Main floor	1,883 sq. ft.
Total Living Area:	**1,883 sq. ft.**
Standard basement	1,883 sq. ft.
Exterior Wall Framing:	**2x4**

Foundation Options:
Standard basement
Crawlspace
Slab
(All plans can be built with your choice of foundation and framing. A generic conversion diagram is available. See order form.)

BLUEPRINT PRICE CODE: B

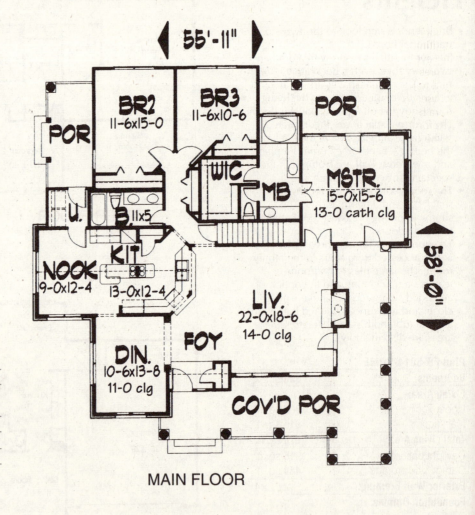

MAIN FLOOR

Plan DW-1883
Plan copyright held by home designer/architect

COMFY COUNTRY CHARMERS

Fantastic Family Living Space

- Luxury begins at the front door with this exciting one-story traditional home.
- The eye-catching front entry opens to an impressive vaulted foyer. Double doors lead to an unusual living room that can be used as a den, a home office or an extra bedroom.
- The formal dining room has easy access to the combination kitchen, breakfast room and family room. This fantastic family living space is punctuated by floor-to-ceiling windows, a tray ceiling, a fireplace and views of the rear deck.
- Double doors open to the vaulted master suite, which features French doors leading to the deck, just right for romantic moonlight strolls. There's also a luxurious bath with a corner spa tub, as well as a large walk-in closet.
- Two more bedrooms and another full bath are set apart across the home.
- A utility room near the two-car garage rounds out the floor plan.

Plan APS-1812

Bedrooms: 3+	Baths: 2
Living Area:	
Main floor	1,886 sq. ft.
Total Living Area:	**1,886 sq. ft.**
Standard basement	1,886 sq. ft.
Garage	400 sq. ft.
Exterior Wall Framing:	2x4

Foundation Options:
Standard basement
Crawlspace
Slab
(All plans can be built with your choice of foundation and framing. A generic conversion diagram is available. See order form.)

BLUEPRINT PRICE CODE: B

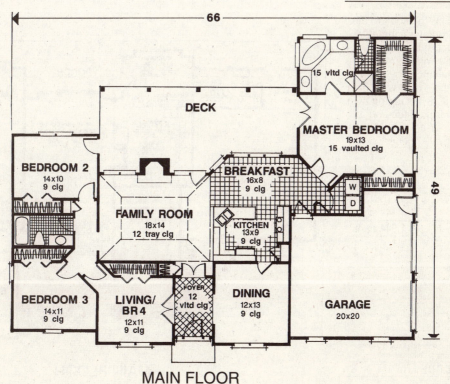

MAIN FLOOR

ORDER BLUEPRINTS ANYTIME!
CALL TOLL-FREE 1-800-820-1296

Plan APS-1812
Plan copyright held by home designer/architect

PRICES AND DETAILS ON PAGES 12-15

COMFY COUNTRY CHARMERS

Morning Glory

- This melodious country-style home opens itself to the sights and sounds of nature with front and rear porches, and dazzling window treatments.
- From the sidelighted entry, a long hall leads to the right, introducing three secondary bedrooms. Along the way, you'll find plenty of storage closets.
- There's plenty of space to gather in the family room, where a fireplace warms the spirit. Bird-watchers will enjoy a boxed-out window to the rear.
- The cheery breakfast nook flaunts its own boxed-out window and a door to the backyard porch.
- A raised snack bar joins the nook to the kitchen, which incorporates cabinets into its center island. Just a few steps bring you to the formal dining room.
- The master suite is enhanced by a charming window seat. The private bath is packed with essentials, including twin walk-in closets, a whirlpool tub and a dual-sink vanity. The sit-down shower is sure to be a morning eye-opener!

Plan RD-1944	
Bedrooms: 4	Baths: 2
Living Area:	
Main floor	1,944 sq. ft.
Total Living Area:	**1,944 sq. ft.**
Standard basement	1,750 sq. ft.
Garage and storage	538 sq. ft.
Exterior Wall Framing:	2x4

Foundation Options:
Standard basement
Crawlspace
Slab
(All plans can be built with your choice of foundation and framing. A generic conversion diagram is available. See order form.)

BLUEPRINT PRICE CODE:	B

VIEW INTO FAMILY ROOM

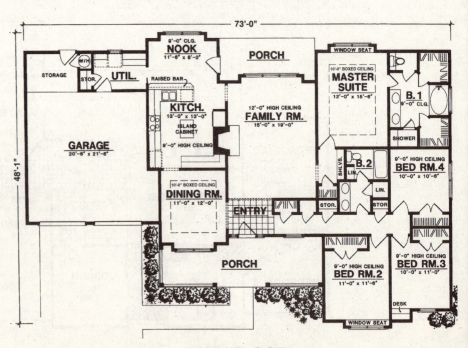

MAIN FLOOR

ORDER BLUEPRINTS ANYTIME!
CALL TOLL-FREE 1-800-820-1296

Plan RD-1944
Plan copyright held by home designer/architect

PRICES AND DETAILS
ON PAGES 12-15

COMFY COUNTRY CHARMERS

Wonderfully Warm

- Wonderfully warm and beautifully livable, this two-story design turns a welcoming face to friends and neighbors.
- The exterior is highlighted by round-top windows, keystones and an interesting covered stoop that's the perfect spot to sit and soak up the sunshine.
- Inside, events will naturally gravitate to the sizable Great Room, where folks can gather around the handsome fireplace and bask in its warm glow.
- Nearby, the island kitchen is designed for all your culinary moods. Casual meals have a home in the skylighted breakfast nook, while your formal affairs are meant for the elegant, bayed dining room. A huge pantry lets you store everything you need.
- Incredibly equipped, the master suite adds a welcome dose of luxury. It features a walk-in closet, a bay window and a cozy, secluded bath.
- Upstairs in the loft, three bedrooms share a full bath.

Plan CC-2006-M	
Bedrooms: 4	**Baths:** 2½
Living Area:	
Upper floor	583 sq. ft.
Main floor	1,423 sq. ft.
Total Living Area:	**2,006 sq. ft.**
Standard basement	1,423 sq. ft.
Garage	398 sq. ft.
Exterior Wall Framing:	2x4
Foundation Options:	
Standard basement	

(All plans can be built with your choice of foundation and framing. A generic conversion diagram is available. See order form.)

BLUEPRINT PRICE CODE: C

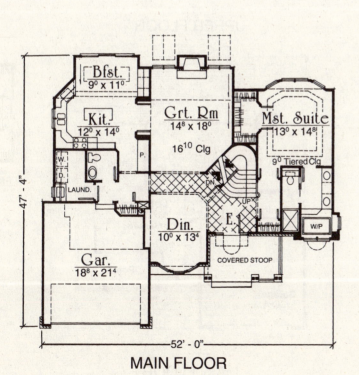

MAIN FLOOR

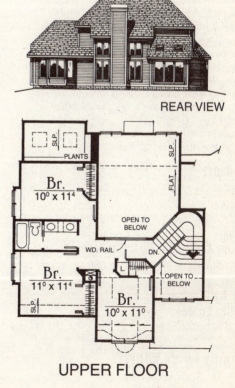

REAR VIEW

UPPER FLOOR

ORDER BLUEPRINTS ANYTIME!
CALL TOLL-FREE 1-800-820-1296

Plan CC-2006-M
Plan copyright held by home designer/architect

PRICES AND DETAILS ON PAGES 12-15

COMFY COUNTRY CHARMERS

Quaint Country

- A quaint porch with a striking wall of windows introduces this country home.
- The foyer opens to the living room, which features a vaulted ceiling and porch access. Elegant columns introduce the formal dining room.
- A convenient island cooktop in the nearby kitchen allows for maximum use of space. The kitchen extends to a sunny bayed breakfast nook.
- A handy serving counter between the kitchen and the family room makes entertaining a breeze.
- The family room features a warm fireplace with a raised hearth and sliding glass doors to a rear deck.
- Centrally located stairs lead up to a balcony with a great view of the living room below. An adjacent loft could serve as a bedroom or a game room.
- The master suite features a soaring vaulted ceiling and a walk-in closet. The master bath boasts a whirlpool tub, and a dual-sink vanity.
- Two additional bedrooms share a compartmentalized hall bath.

Plan B-88077

Bedrooms: 3+	Baths: 2½
Living Area:	
Upper floor	991 sq. ft.
Main floor	1,056 sq. ft.
Total Living Area:	**2,047 sq. ft.**
Standard basement	1,056 sq. ft.
Garage	442 sq. ft.
Exterior Wall Framing:	2x4

Foundation Options:
Standard basement
(All plans can be built with your choice of foundation and framing. A generic conversion diagram is available. See order form.)

BLUEPRINT PRICE CODE: C

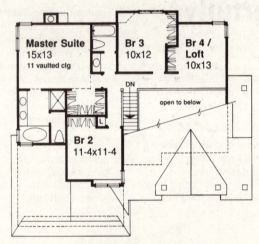

UPPER FLOOR

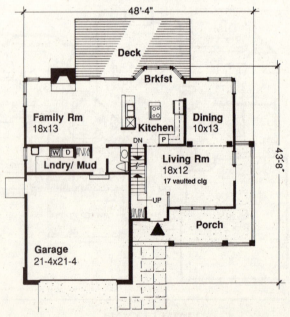

MAIN FLOOR

Plan B-88077
Plan copyright held by home designer/architect

Create a New Tradition

- Keystones, arched windows and a hip roof give this home its traditional character, while its functional floor plan fits your life today.
- The living areas occupy the front of the home. A fireplace and access to a screen porch and the deck beyond enhance the appeal of the living room.
- The kitchen's peninsula maximizes counter space, and the adjacent eating area is perfect for everyday meals. Garage access nearby makes unloading groceries convenient.
- The bedrooms lie along the design's perimeter for privacy. Two of the bedrooms, each with a private vanity and a walk-in closet, share a bath.
- The master suite boasts a space-adding tray ceiling and features a private bath and a large walk-in closet. A clever door arrangement in the closet's linen storage allows access to the utility room for easy loading on laundry day.
- Above the garage, a bonus room makes an ideal studio, office or playroom.

Plan E-1719

Bedrooms: 3+	Baths: 2½

Living Area:
Main floor	1,704 sq. ft.
Bonus room	364 sq. ft.

Total Living Area:	2,068 sq. ft.
Screen porch	128 sq. ft.
Garage	484 sq. ft.
Storage	216 sq. ft.

Exterior Wall Framing: 2x4

Foundation Options:
Crawlspace
Slab
(All plans can be built with your choice of foundation and framing. A generic conversion diagram is available. See order form.)

BLUEPRINT PRICE CODE: C

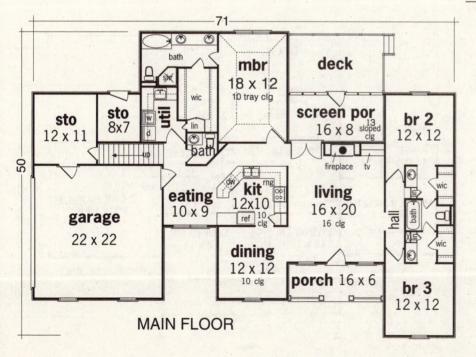

MAIN FLOOR

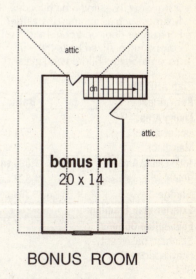

BONUS ROOM

Plan E-1719
Plan copyright held by home designer/architect

COMFY COUNTRY CHARMERS

Country Charm

- With its inviting porch, quaint shutters and trio of dormers, the exterior of this home exudes old-fashioned charm.
- Inside, plenty of space allows you to entertain in style. The two-story foyer draws guests into the living and dining rooms, which overlook the front porch through tall windows.
- On autumn nights, enjoy a crackling blaze in the spacious family room, which features a fireplace, a built-in media center and deck access.
- A circular dinette offers stunning views of the backyard and a sunny space for casual meals.
- The kitchen easily serves the formal and informal eating areas and includes an ample pantry and a built-in desk.
- Across the home, the secluded master suite boasts a cathedral ceiling, a walk-in closet and a bath loaded with luxuries such as an amazing garden tub.
- Four upper-floor bedrooms and a full, compartmentalized bath gracefully accommodate children and guests.

Plan AHP-9612	
Bedrooms: 5	**Baths:** 2½
Living Area:	
Upper floor	771 sq. ft.
Main floor	1,328 sq. ft.
Total Living Area:	**2,099 sq. ft.**
Standard basement	1,328 sq. ft.
Garage	399 sq. ft.
Exterior Wall Framing:	2x4 or 2x6
Foundation Options:	
Standard basement	
Crawlspace	
Slab	
(All plans can be built with your choice of foundation and framing. A generic conversion diagram is available. See order form.)	
BLUEPRINT PRICE CODE:	**C**

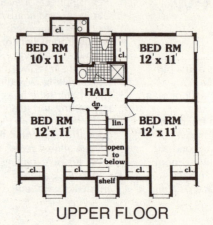

UPPER FLOOR

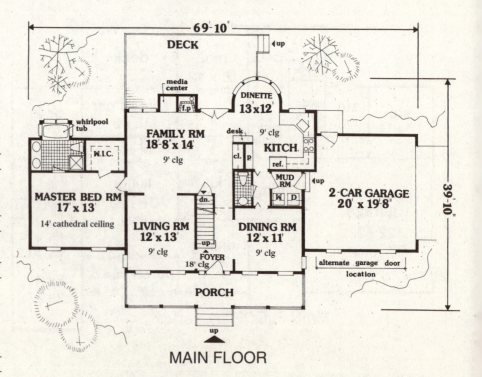

MAIN FLOOR

ORDER BLUEPRINTS ANYTIME! CALL TOLL-FREE 1-800-820-1296

Plan AHP-9612
Plan copyright held by home designer/architect

PRICES AND DETAILS ON PAGES 12-15

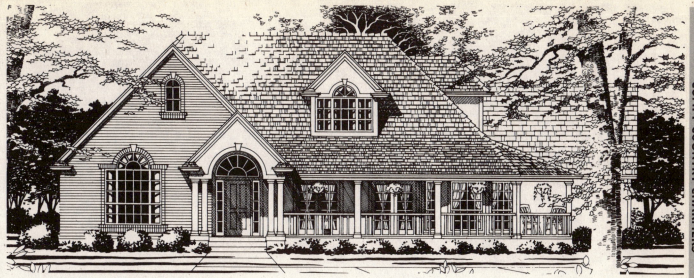

COMFY COUNTRY CHARMERS

Stunning Porch

- This home's stunning wraparound porch and covered rear patio provide fantastic spaces for outdoor entertaining.
- Through the entry, the living room boasts a cathedral ceiling, a built-in entertainment center, a handsome fireplace and access to the covered patio at the back of the design.
- The gourmet kitchen's angled snack bar serves the octagonal morning room. The formal dining room gives your family a place to share a special holiday meal together.
- The opulent master bedroom boasts a cathedral ceiling and a private bath that features a dual-sink vanity, two walk-in closets, a garden tub and an oversized shower.
- Two additional bedrooms are blessed with generous closet space. The bedrooms share a full hall bath that includes its own dual-sink vanity—a must-have amenity for a busy family.

Plan DD-2117

Bedrooms: 3	Baths: 2½
Living Area:	
Main floor	2,104 sq. ft.
Total Living Area:	**2,104 sq. ft.**
Standard basement	2,112 sq. ft.
Garage	544 sq. ft.
Exterior Wall Framing:	2x4
Foundation Options:	
Standard basement	
Crawlspace	
Slab	
(All plans can be built with your choice of foundation and framing. A generic conversion diagram is available. See order form.)	
BLUEPRINT PRICE CODE:	**C**

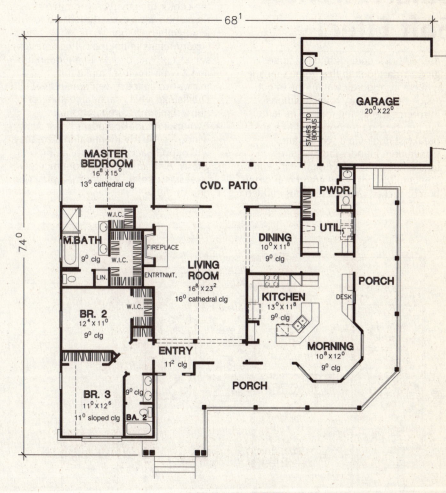

MAIN FLOOR

ORDER BLUEPRINTS ANYTIME!
CALL TOLL-FREE 1-800-820-1296

Plan DD-2117
Plan copyright held by home designer/architect

PRICES AND DETAILS
ON PAGES 12-15

COMFY COUNTRY CHARMERS

Smart Arches, Soft Effect

- Arched brick courses and keystones give a smart look to this home's facade, while a front porch softens the effect.
- Inside the two-story foyer, columns introduce the dining room. The large kitchen beyond is connected to a sunny breakfast nook via a serving bar. Convenient laundry facilities are located near this functional work zone.
- The family room is the grand hub of the home. Tucked under a glorious vaulted ceiling, this sunny space is sure to be the center of activity. A prominent fireplace adds a cozy dimension to this ideal gathering spot.
- Luxury reigns in the main-floor master suite. A private bath with a garden tub and a walk-in closet make this marvelous space a welcome retreat. Dual sinks are a practical feature for hurried morning preparations.
- Two upper-floor bedrooms boast sunny windows. Nearly identical in size, they will happily accommodate family or guests. A sizable bonus room nicely serves as an extra bedroom, a playroom or a studio.

Plan FB-5723-WILL

Bedrooms: 3+	Baths: 2½

Living Area:
Upper floor	436 sq. ft.
Main floor	1,382 sq. ft.
Bonus room	298 sq. ft.
Total Living Area:	**2,116 sq. ft.**
Daylight basement	1,382 sq. ft.
Garage	436 sq. ft.

Exterior Wall Framing: 2x4

Foundation Options:
Daylight basement
Crawlspace
(All plans can be built with your choice of foundation and framing. A generic conversion diagram is available. See order form.)

BLUEPRINT PRICE CODE: C

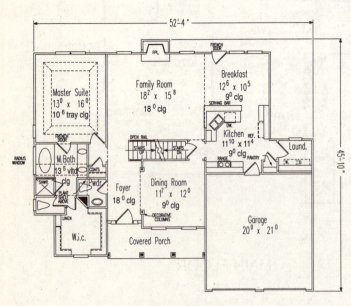

MAIN FLOOR

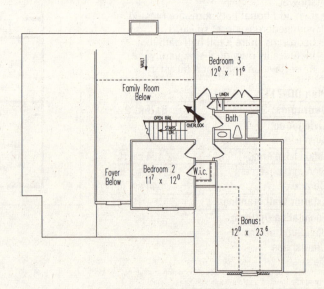

UPPER FLOOR

ORDER BLUEPRINTS ANYTIME!
CALL TOLL-FREE 1-800-820-1296

Plan FB-5723-WILL
Plan copyright held by home designer/architect

PRICES AND DETAILS ON PAGES 12-15

High Ceilings Throughout

- High ceilings throughout this home will give you a sense of spaciousness and airy comfort.
- Just in from the front porch and sidelighted entry, the sunny, high foyer stands between the formal living and dining rooms.
- Straight ahead, the family room is the perfect place for gathering, with its fireplace flanked by built-in media shelves. In addition, sliding glass doors open to a covered rear patio.
- Nearby, a sunny, bayed breakfast nook flows into the kitchen, which features a corner pantry closet and an angled eating bar. A pocket door reveals the adjoining dining room.
- Double doors give way to a roomy master suite, which features a private bath with a walk-in closet, plant shelves, a garden tub and a dual-sink vanity with knee space.
- To the other side of the home, three large bedrooms share two full baths. Each features a lovely plant shelf.

Plan HDS-99-303	
Bedrooms: 4	**Baths:** 3
Living Area:	
Main floor	2,116 sq. ft.
Total Living Area:	**2,116 sq. ft.**
Garage	441 sq. ft.
Exterior Wall Framing:	2x4

Foundation Options:
Slab
(All plans can be built with your choice of foundation and framing. A generic conversion diagram is available. See order form.)

BLUEPRINT PRICE CODE: C

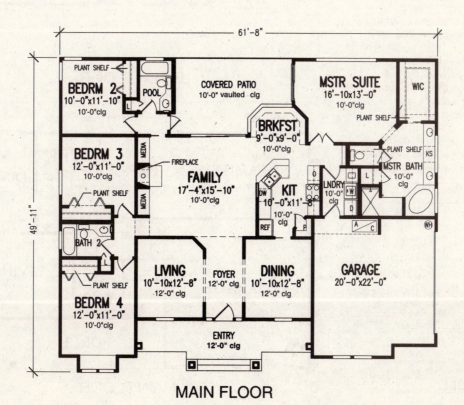

MAIN FLOOR

ORDER BLUEPRINTS ANYTIME!
CALL TOLL-FREE 1-800-820-1296

Plan HDS-99-303
Plan copyright held by home designer/architect

PRICES AND DETAILS ON PAGES 12-15

COMFY COUNTRY CHARMERS

Comfortable Country Home

- A central gable and a wide, welcoming front porch with columns give this home comfortable country charm.
- The large living room is open to the dining room, which features a tray ceiling and views to the backyard.
- The kitchen offers an oversized island counter with a snack bar. The adjoining breakfast area has a sliding glass door to the backyard and a half-wall that separates it from the family room. The inviting family room includes a central fireplace and a bay window with a cozy window seat.
- Upstairs, the master suite boasts three windows—including a lovely arched window—that overlook the front yard. The adjoining private bath offers a whirlpool tub and a separate shower.
- Three more bedrooms, a second full bath and a multipurpose den make this a great family-sized home that's flexible enough to meet your changing needs.

Plan OH-165

Bedrooms: 4+	Baths: 2½
Living Area:	
Upper floor	1,121 sq. ft.
Main floor	1,000 sq. ft.
Total Living Area:	**2,121 sq. ft.**
Standard basement	1,000 sq. ft.
Garage	400 sq. ft.
Exterior Wall Framing:	2x4

Foundation Options:
Standard basement
(All plans can be built with your choice of foundation and framing. A generic conversion diagram is available. See order form.)

BLUEPRINT PRICE CODE: C

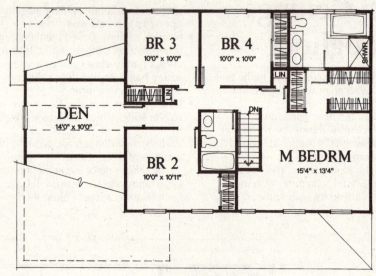

UPPER FLOOR

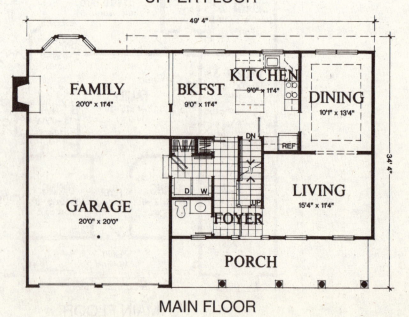

MAIN FLOOR

100   ORDER BLUEPRINTS ANYTIME! CALL TOLL-FREE 1-800-820-1296   Plan OH-165   PRICES AND DETAILS ON PAGES 12-15

Plan copyright held by home designer/architect

COMFY COUNTRY CHARMERS

Irresistible Design

- High ceilings, plenty of floor space and lots of thoughtful design touches make this country-style home irresistible.
- A shady front porch, and plant shelves in the foyer, create an inviting entryway.
- Decorative columns set off the formal living room and dining room, which flank the foyer. Use these rooms separately, or take advantage of their openness on grand occasions.
- The family room lies directly ahead. Large windows bathe the room in light by day; a fireplace glows at night.
- You'll find all sorts of handy features in the kitchen: an island countertop, double ovens, a pantry and a serving bar overlooking the breakfast nook.
- A built-in desk in the nook is perfect for paying bills or finishing homework.
- A tray ceiling heightens the master bedroom, which features French doors opening to the porch, as well as to the luxurious vaulted bath.
- Across the home, two secondary bedrooms share another full bath.

Plan FB-5665-SABR

Bedrooms: 3	Baths: 2½
Living Area:	
Main floor	2,170 sq. ft.
Total Living Area:	**2,170 sq. ft.**
Daylight basement	2,170 sq. ft.
Garage	484 sq. ft.
Exterior Wall Framing:	2x4

Foundation Options:
Daylight basement
Crawlspace
(All plans can be built with your choice of foundation and framing. A generic conversion diagram is available. See order form.)

BLUEPRINT PRICE CODE: C

MAIN FLOOR

ORDER BLUEPRINTS ANYTIME!
CALL TOLL-FREE 1-800-820-1296

Plan FB-5665-SABR
Plan copyright held by home designer/architect

PRICES AND DETAILS ON PAGES 12-15

101

COMFY COUNTRY CHARMERS

Country Kitchen

- A lovely front porch, dormers and shutters give this home a country-style exterior and complement its comfortable and informal interior.
- The roomy country kitchen connects with the sunny breakfast nook and the formal dining room. Bay windows brighten both eating areas.
- The central portion of the home consists of a large family room with a handsome fireplace and easy access to a backyard deck. A powder room services this area.
- The main-floor master suite, particularly impressive for a home of this size, features a majestic master bath with a corner garden tub, two walk-in closets and a dual-sink vanity with knee space.
- Upstairs, you will find two more good-sized bedrooms, a double bath and a large storage area.
- Another storage room is accessed through the two-car garage.

Plan C-8645

Bedrooms: 3	Baths: 2½
Living Area:	
Upper floor	704 sq. ft.
Main floor	1,477 sq. ft.
Total Living Area:	**2,181 sq. ft.**
Daylight basement	1,400 sq. ft.
Garage	476 sq. ft.
Storage	52 sq. ft.
Exterior Wall Framing:	2x4
Foundation Options:	
Daylight basement	
Crawlspace	
Slab	
(All plans can be built with your choice of foundation and framing. A generic conversion diagram is available. See order form.)	
BLUEPRINT PRICE CODE:	**C**

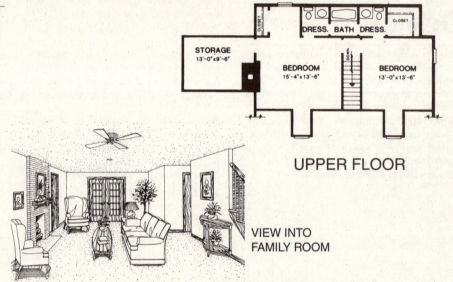

VIEW INTO FAMILY ROOM

UPPER FLOOR

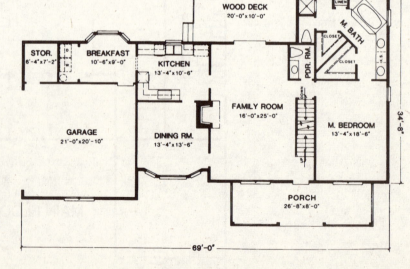

MAIN FLOOR

ORDER BLUEPRINTS ANYTIME!
CALL TOLL-FREE 1-800-820-1296

Plan C-8645
Plan copyright held by home designer/architect

PRICES AND DETAILS ON PAGES 12-15

Traditional Family

- A cute columned porch adds character to this traditional family home.
- A walk-in closet and a half-bath in the two-story foyer accommodate guests.
- To the right, the formal living and dining rooms make entertaining a snap because of their openness to each other.
- The roomy kitchen includes a space-saving island and a windowed sink. Sliding glass doors in the bright dinette extend dining to an enormous patio that's perfect for a barbecue.
- A striking cathedral ceiling soars over the family room, which is warmed by a cozy fireplace. You'll spend countless evenings together in this attractive, comfortable space.
- An open staircase leads up to the magnificent master bedroom, which is embellished with a tray ceiling and a private bath, where a whirlpool tub pampers you after a long day.
- Three secondary bedrooms share a conveniently located full bath.

Plan GL-2223

Bedrooms: 4	Baths: 2½

Living Area:	
Upper floor	1,007 sq. ft.
Main floor	1,216 sq. ft.
Total Living Area:	**2,223 sq. ft.**
Standard basement	1,207 sq. ft.
Garage	484 sq. ft.
Exterior Wall Framing:	2x6

Foundation Options:
Standard basement
(All plans can be built with your choice of foundation and framing. A generic conversion diagram is available. See order form.)

BLUEPRINT PRICE CODE: C

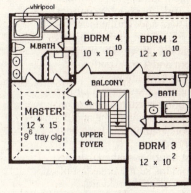

UPPER FLOOR

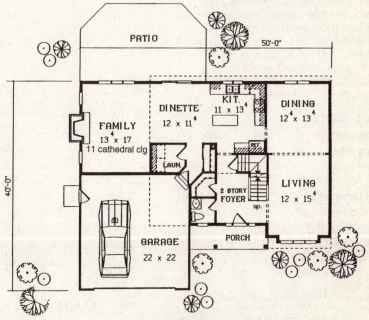

MAIN FLOOR

ORDER BLUEPRINTS ANYTIME!
CALL TOLL-FREE 1-800-820-1296

Plan GL-2223
Plan copyright held by home designer/architect

PRICES AND DETAILS
ON PAGES 12-15

COMFY COUNTRY CHARMERS

Sunny Charmer

- A huge wraparound porch highlights this bright and airy country charmer.
- Inside, the two-story vaulted foyer is bathed in sunlight from the expansive arched window above. The formal dining room and a cozy parlor complete the front area.
- Straight ahead is the spectacular family room, featuring a vaulted ceiling, a unique three-sided fireplace and double French doors leading to a large back porch and deck.
- A breakfast bar divides the U-shaped kitchen from the sunny breakfast nook, which overlooks the backyard.
- The expansive master bedroom features a large walk-in closet and private access to the front porch. The master bath includes dual vanities, a garden tub, a private toilet and a tray ceiling.
- Upstairs, the two remaining bedrooms share a second full bath.
- A two-car detached garage with an optional studio and bath above is included in the blueprints.

Plan APS-2218

Bedrooms: 3	Baths: 2½
Living Area:	
Upper floor	607 sq. ft.
Main floor	1,632 sq. ft.
Total Living Area:	**2,239 sq. ft.**
Standard basement	1,600 sq. ft.
Detached garage	624 sq. ft.
Exterior Wall	2x4
Foundation Options:	
Standard basement	
Crawlspace	
(All plans can be built with your choice of foundation and framing. A generic conversion diagram is available. See order form.)	
BLUEPRINT PRICE CODE:	**C**

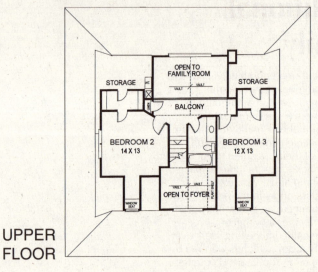

UPPER FLOOR

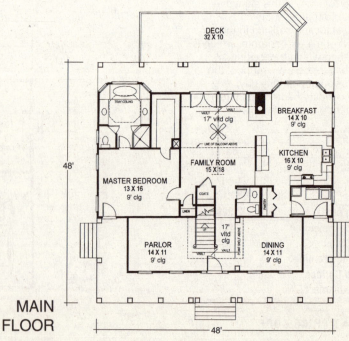

MAIN FLOOR

104   **ORDER BLUEPRINTS ANYTIME! CALL TOLL-FREE 1-800-820-1296**   **Plan APS-2218**   Plan copyright held by home designer/architect   **PRICES AND DETAILS ON PAGES 12-15**

COMFY COUNTRY CHARMERS

Great Family Living Areas

- The covered front porch and multi-windowed facade give this home its countrypolitan appeal and comfort.
- Inside, a wonderful kitchen, breakfast nook and family room combination makes a statement. The step-saving kitchen includes a large pantry closet, an oversized worktop island/snack bar and a built-in desk. The bay-windowed breakfast nook steps down to the vaulted family room.
- Options include a living room fireplace, and a bay window in the dining room.
- A half-bath is just off the foyer, as is a charming study.
- The upper floor features a spectacular master suite, offering a vaulted ceiling in the sleeping area, a dressing area with a walk-in closet, and a skylighted bath with a corner platform tub.
- Blueprints include details for finishing the exterior with brick or wood siding.

Plan CH-240-A

Bedrooms: 4+	Baths: 2½

Living Area:
Upper floor	1,019 sq. ft.
Main floor	1,300 sq. ft.
Total Living Area:	**2,319 sq. ft.**
Basement	1,300 sq. ft.
Garage	384 sq. ft.

Exterior Wall Framing: 2x4

Foundation Options:
Daylight basement
Standard basement
Crawlspace
(All plans can be built with your choice of foundation and framing. A generic conversion diagram is available. See order form.)

BLUEPRINT PRICE CODE: C

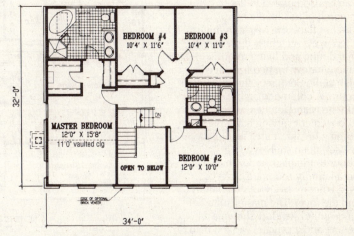

UPPER FLOOR

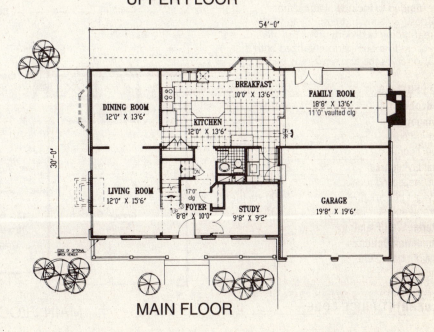

MAIN FLOOR

ORDER BLUEPRINTS ANYTIME!
CALL TOLL-FREE 1-800-820-1296

Plan CH-240-A
Plan copyright held by home designer/architect

PRICES AND DETAILS ON PAGES 12-15

COMFY COUNTRY CHARMERS

Arched Accents

- Elegant arches add drama to the covered porch of this lovely home.
- Interior arches flank the two-story-high foyer, offering eye-catching entrances to the formal dining and living rooms.
- A dramatic window-framed fireplace and a high ceiling enhance the spacious family room. A columned archway leads into the island kitchen, which offers a convenient serving bar.
- The adjoining breakfast area features a pantry closet, open shelves and a French door to the backyard. A half-bath and a laundry room are close by.
- Upstairs, a balcony overlooks the family room and the foyer. The master suite flaunts a beautiful window showpiece, a tray ceiling and a private, vaulted bath with a garden tub. The bedroom may be extended to include a sitting area.
- Boasting its own dressing vanity, the rear-facing bedroom offers private access to a compartmentalized bath that also serves the two remaining bedrooms.

Plan FB-2368

Bedrooms: 4	Baths: 2½
Living Area:	
Upper floor	1,179 sq. ft.
Main floor	1,200 sq. ft.
Total Living Area:	**2,379 sq. ft.**
Optional sitting room	90 sq. ft.
Daylight basement	1,200 sq. ft.
Garage and storage	537 sq. ft.
Exterior Wall Framing:	2x4

Foundation Options:
Daylight basement
Slab
(All plans can be built with your choice of foundation and framing. A generic conversion diagram is available. See order form.)

BLUEPRINT PRICE CODE: C

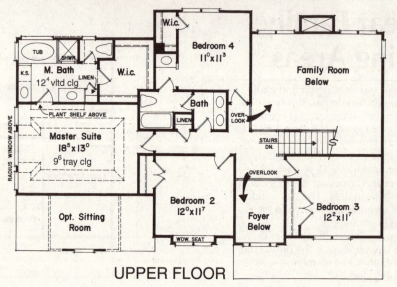

UPPER FLOOR

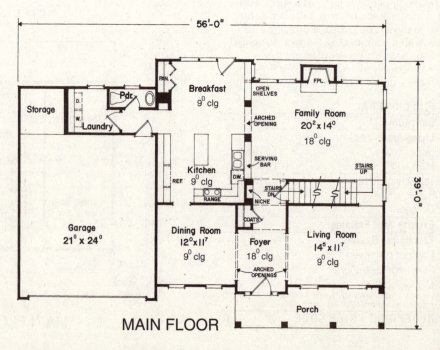

MAIN FLOOR

106 ORDER BLUEPRINTS ANYTIME!
CALL TOLL-FREE 1-800-820-1296

Plan FB-2368
Plan copyright held by home designer/architect

PRICES AND DETAILS
ON PAGES 12-15

Then and Now

- This home's brick-and-stone facade, wooden shutters and gently arched windows evoke images of a rustic past, yet its floor plan is surprisingly modern.
- A pretty porch leads to the foyer, which offers a useful built-in bench. Beyond, the open living areas meet the need for space most families experience today.
- The huge living room is amazing in its versatility: use it as one space or divide it into cozy sitting and entertaining areas. A built-in media center resides alongside the fireplace.
- The kitchen's island provides extra work space and lets the cook spend extra time with company. The adjoining dining room accesses the back porch.
- A quiet resource center with subtle pocket doors makes a nice library or a study area for the kids.
- Three bedrooms—each with double closets—share one side of the home. The deluxe master bedroom offers a pleasant sitting area and a private bath.
- Guest quarters adjoining the garage are ideal for extended visits. The future area upstairs poses even more options.

Plan L-0001-UDA

Bedrooms: 3+	Baths: 3
Living Area:	
Main floor	2,070 sq. ft.
Guest quarters	311 sq. ft.
Total Living Area:	**2,381 sq. ft.**
Future area	328 sq. ft.
Garage and storage	593 sq. ft.
Exterior Wall Framing:	2x4
Foundation Options:	
Slab	
(All plans can be built with your choice of foundation and framing. A generic conversion diagram is available. See order form.)	
BLUEPRINT PRICE CODE:	**C**

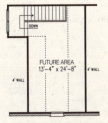

FUTURE AREA

MAIN FLOOR

ORDER BLUEPRINTS ANYTIME!
CALL TOLL-FREE 1-800-820-1296

Plan L-0001-UDA
Plan copyright held by home designer/architect

PRICES AND DETAILS
ON PAGES 12-15

COMFY COUNTRY CHARMERS

At the Heart

- A natural place to gather, the versatile Great Room lies at the heart of this home and offers access to a spacious back deck. An elegant hip roof and arched windows distinguish the facade, where a porch is a classic touch.
- The kitchen boasts not one but two islands, the larger of the two offering a serving bar. A huge corner pantry lets you tuck away scads of goodies. Several windows in the breakfast room allow light to flood the area from two directions.
- Elegant columns define the formal dining room, while a high, coffered ceiling tops the area. An airy study offers a quiet retreat across the hall.
- The secluded master suite occupies one wing of the home. A coffered ceiling and a bay window accent the sleeping area, while the spacious bath pampers you from head to toe.
- Three additional bedrooms, each with ample closet space, share a hall bath.

Plan DD-2500	
Bedrooms: 4+	Baths: 2½
Living Area:	
Main floor	2,494 sq. ft.
Total Living Area:	**2,494 sq. ft.**
Standard basement	2,494 sq. ft.
Garage	411 sq. ft.
Exterior Wall Framing:	2x4

Foundation Options:
Standard basement
Crawlspace
Slab
(All plans can be built with your choice of foundation and framing. A generic conversion diagram is available. See order form.)
BLUEPRINT PRICE CODE: C

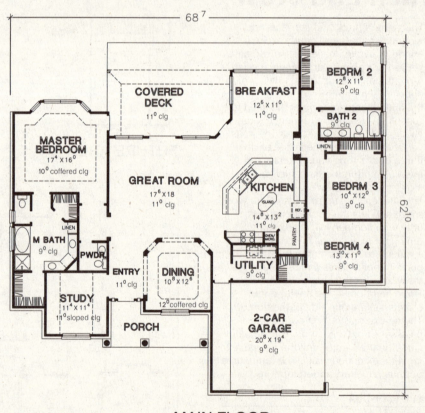

MAIN FLOOR

ORDER BLUEPRINTS ANYTIME!
CALL TOLL-FREE 1-800-820-1296

Plan DD-2500
Plan copyright held by home designer/architect

PRICES AND DETAILS
ON PAGES 12-15

Formal Meets Informal

- The charming, columned front porch of this appealing home leads visitors into a two-story-high foyer with a beautiful turned staircase.
- The gracious formal living room shares a cathedral ceiling and a dramatic see-through fireplace with the adjoining family room.
- A railing separates the family room from the spacious breakfast area and the island kitchen. A menu desk and plenty of pantry storage are helpful additions. A unique butler's pantry joins the kitchen to the dining room, which is enhanced by a tray ceiling.
- A convenient laundry room is located between the kitchen and the entrance to the garage.
- All four bedrooms are located on the upper level. The master suite boasts an cathedral ceiling, a walk-in closet and a large, luxurious bath.

Plan OH-132

Bedrooms: 4	Baths: 2½

Living Area:	
Upper floor	1,118 sq. ft.
Main floor	1,396 sq. ft.
Total Living Area:	**2,514 sq. ft.**
Standard basement	1,396 sq. ft.
Garage	413 sq. ft.
Storage/workshop	107 sq. ft.
Exterior Wall Framing:	2x4

Foundation Options:
Standard basement
(All plans can be built with your choice of foundation and framing. A generic conversion diagram is available. See order form.)

BLUEPRINT PRICE CODE: D

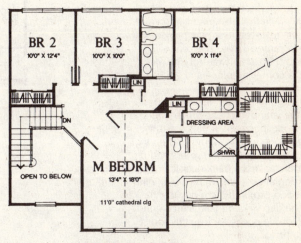

UPPER FLOOR

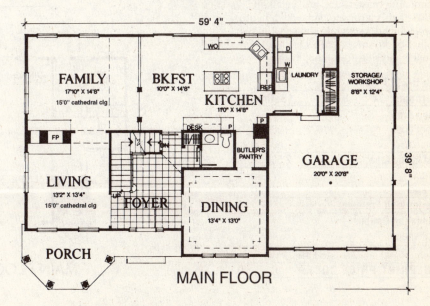

MAIN FLOOR

ORDER BLUEPRINTS ANYTIME!
CALL TOLL-FREE 1-800-820-1296

Plan OH-132
Plan copyright held by home designer/architect

PRICES AND DETAILS
ON PAGES 12-15

COMFY COUNTRY CHARMERS

Wowsers!

- A striking exterior wows you with an array of window treatments: Dormers, an arch-topped window and a bay window grace this design's facade.
- Inside, the tri-level floor plan provides unique common areas. The central living room boasts a two-story vaulted ceiling, a corner fireplace and a breathtaking bay window.
- The bright dining room lies two steps below the island kitchen, which offers ample work space and a handy pantry.
- Double doors open from the kitchen to the spacious family room, where sliding glass doors access a back deck.
- A cozy den also opens to the deck. With a closet and proximity to a powder room, the den would make a nice guest room. Double doors enclose this room for extra privacy.
- Three bedrooms reside on the upper floor. The master suite has a walk-in closet, plus a private bath with a hydro-spa tub and a separate shower. The two other bedrooms have lots of closet space and share a full hall bath.

Plan H-2123-1A

Bedrooms: 3+	Baths: 2½
Living Area:	
Upper floor	989 sq. ft.
Main floor	1,597 sq. ft.
Total Living Area:	**2,586 sq. ft.**
Garage	473 sq. ft.
Storage	48 sq. ft.
Exterior Wall Framing:	2x6
Foundation Options:	
Crawlspace	
(All plans can be built with your choice of foundation and framing. A generic conversion diagram is available. See order form.)	
BLUEPRINT PRICE CODE:	**D**

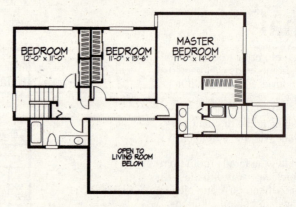

UPPER FLOOR

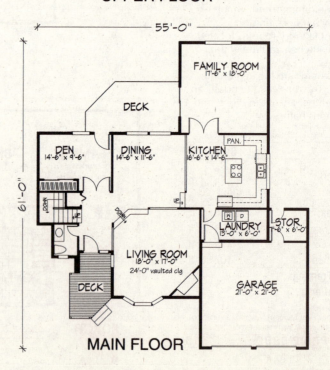

MAIN FLOOR

ORDER BLUEPRINTS ANYTIME! CALL TOLL-FREE 1-800-820-1296

Plan H-2123-1A
Plan copyright held by home designer/architect

PRICES AND DETAILS ON PAGES 12-15

Elegant Arches

- Elegant arched windows and decorative dormers grace this home's entry.
- A cozy study with a sloped ceiling lies just to the left of the entry, while columns set off the formal dining room on the right.
- Straight ahead, the spacious Great Room, the kitchen and the breakfast nook all flow into each other. An angled snack bar serves both the Great Room and the breakfast nook, while the island in the center of the kitchen facilitates easy meal preparation.
- Secluded in its own wing, the master bedroom features a bayed sitting area, a tray ceiling and a private bath with two walk-in closets, dual sinks, a spa tub and a separate shower.
- On the other side of the home, three secondary bedrooms share two full baths—one with outdoor access.

Plan DD-2579

Bedrooms: 4+	Baths: 3½
Living Area:	
Main floor	2,587 sq. ft.
Total Living Area:	**2,587 sq. ft.**
Standard basement	2,587 sq. ft.
Garage	411 sq. ft.
Exterior Wall Framing:	2x4

Foundation Options:
Standard basement
Crawlspace
Slab
(All plans can be built with your choice of foundation and framing. A generic conversion diagram is available. See order form.)

BLUEPRINT PRICE CODE: D

REAR VIEW

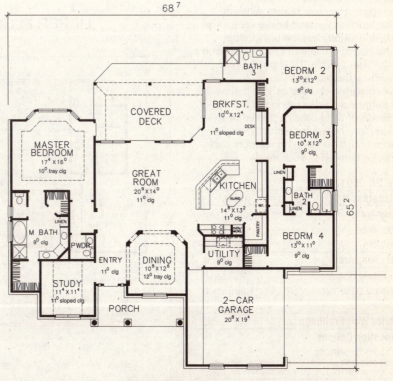

MAIN FLOOR

Plan DD-2579
Plan copyright held by home designer/architect

COMFY COUNTRY CHARMERS

True Grit

- Traditional Arts and Crafts styling gives this bungalow grit and durability. Its bold, low-maintenance exterior combines natural stone and cedar.
- Inside, skylights and transom windows produce plenty of natural light for the thoroughly modern floor plan.
- A high ceiling soars above the foyer and the Great Room, which are separated by a stone fireplace and a balcony.
- A decorative arch and wood-framed glass doors surround the Great Room's large-screen media center, while skylights overhead radiate sunshine.
- The functional island kitchen enjoys an ideal location near the busy living spaces and the laundry room. You won't miss your favorite TV show as you're washing the dinner dishes!
- A compartmentalized private bath with a delightful garden tub keeps the owners of this home pampered in style.
- Two more bedrooms share the upper floor with a versatile bonus room that can be tailored to your needs.

Plan GA-9601

Bedrooms: 3+	Baths: 2½
Living Area:	
Upper floor	594 sq. ft.
Main floor	1,996 sq. ft.
Total Living Area:	**2,590 sq. ft.**
Unfinished bonus room	233 sq. ft.
Standard basement	1,996 sq. ft.
Garage	576 sq. ft.
Exterior Wall Framing:	2x6
Foundation Options:	
Standard basement	
(All plans can be built with your choice of foundation and framing. A generic conversion diagram is available. See order form.)	
BLUEPRINT PRICE CODE:	D

UPPER FLOOR

VIEW INTO GREAT ROOM

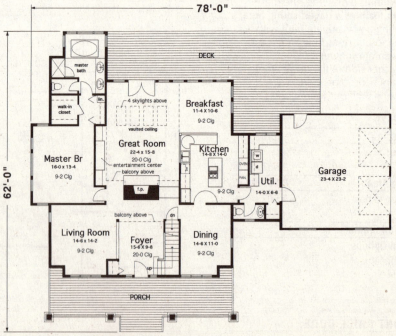

MAIN FLOOR

112   ORDER BLUEPRINTS ANYTIME! CALL TOLL-FREE 1-800-820-1296

Plan GA-9601
Plan copyright held by home designer/architect

PRICES AND DETAILS ON PAGES 12-15

COMFY COUNTRY CHARMERS

This Is Your New Home

- Unique angles update this otherwise traditional design. Arched windows, a stone chimney and a railed porch give the facade a homey, welcoming quality.
- A graceful staircase punctuates the foyer, which leads to the sunken Great Room. A fireplace makes this huge space feel cozy and intimate. A vaulted ceiling crowns the room, while sliding glass doors lead to a fantastic wraparound deck.
- The breakfast room, which opens to the deck and the Great Room, adjoins the spacious, enviable island kitchen.
- The master suite features a fireplace for the romantic in you; the main-floor location and a huge walk-in closet cater to your practical side.
- At the top of the stairs, a balcony overlooking the Great Room leads to a bedroom with a private bath, plus a versatile loft and two bedrooms that share a full hall bath.

Plan AX-00305

Bedrooms: 4+	Baths: 3½
Living Area:	
Upper floor	1,070 sq. ft.
Main floor	1,530 sq. ft.
Total Living Area:	**2,600 sq. ft.**
Daylight basement	1,530 sq. ft.
Garage	539 sq. ft.
Utility room	21 sq. ft.
Exterior Wall Framing:	2x4

Foundation Options:
Daylight basement
(All plans can be built with your choice of foundation and framing. A generic conversion diagram is available. See order form.)

BLUEPRINT PRICE CODE: D

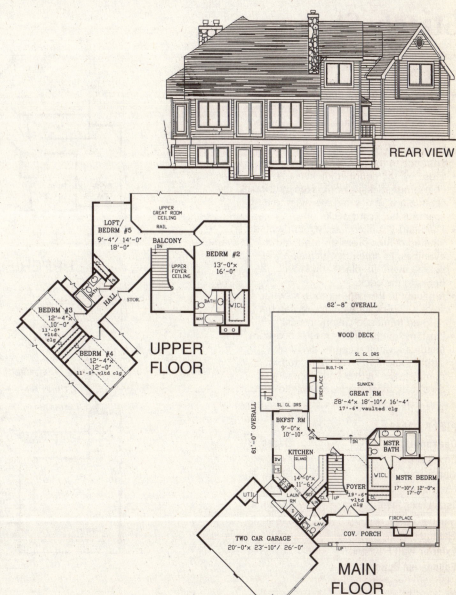

ORDER BLUEPRINTS ANYTIME!
CALL TOLL-FREE 1-800-820-1296

Plan AX-00305
Plan copyright held by home designer/architect

PRICES AND DETAILS ON PAGES 12-15

COMFY COUNTRY CHARMERS

Stately Style

- Classic columns and half-round windows enhance the facade of this beautiful two-story home.
- The bright, sidelighted foyer offers views across a columned half-wall into the living room, which boasts a vaulted ceiling and a cozy fireplace.
- Decorative columns also flank the entrance to the formal dining room.
- Close by, the gourmet kitchen adjoins a charming breakfast nook. French doors set into a wall of windows open to a spacious backyard deck.
- The nearby sunken family room with a vaulted ceiling promises fun-filled evenings. Its amenities include a wet bar, a cheery fireplace and French doors to the deck.
- Adjacent to the family room, a swing suite with private bath access can be tailored to meet changing needs.
- Upstairs, the luxurious master bedroom features a vaulted ceiling and a quiet sitting room for private reflection in comfort. The master bath is enhanced by a walk-through closet, a platform tub and a dual-sink vanity.

Plan B-93019

Bedrooms: 4+	Baths: 3
Living Area:	
Upper floor	1,190 sq. ft.
Main floor	1,433 sq. ft.
Total Living Area:	**2,623 sq. ft.**
Standard basement	1,433 sq. ft.
Garage	450 sq. ft.
Exterior Wall Framing:	2x4
Foundation Options:	
Standard basement	
(All plans can be built with your choice of foundation and framing. A generic conversion diagram is available. See order form.)	
BLUEPRINT PRICE CODE:	**D**

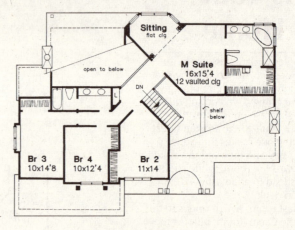

UPPER FLOOR

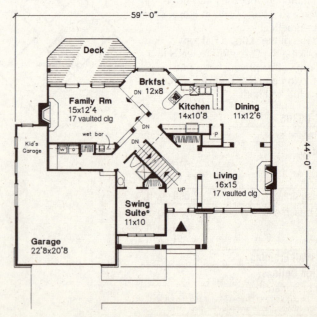

MAIN FLOOR

ORDER BLUEPRINTS ANYTIME!
CALL TOLL-FREE 1-800-820-1296

Plan B-93019
Plan copyright held by home designer/architect

PRICES AND DETAILS ON PAGES 12-15

Double Take

- Family entertainment is a priority in one corner of this stunning home, where you'll find a joined family room and media room that will double your fun!
- For lively conversation, settle down in front of the family room's fireplace. When the evening calls for a movie, treat yourselves to a big-screen flick in the media room. Even your in-laws' home movies will look great!
- The nearby island kitchen lends itself easily to formal entertaining and daily chores. Note the big walk-in pantry and the wraparound serving bar.
- A morning room offers access to a partially covered backyard deck. Here you can barbecue, rain or shine; and there is plenty of room for a hot tub, if you like.
- Escape to the master suite for a little pampering. You can slip out to the deck on cool spring mornings or curl up with a crossword puzzle by the bay window. The master bath offers two walk-in closets and a dual-sink vanity.

Plan DD-2665

Bedrooms: 3+	Baths: 2½
Living Area:	
Main floor	2,666 sq. ft.
Total Living Area:	**2,666 sq. ft.**
Standard basement	2,666 sq. ft.
Garage	411 sq. ft.
Exterior Wall Framing:	2x4

Foundation Options:
Standard basement
Crawlspace
Slab
(All plans can be built with your choice of foundation and framing. A generic conversion diagram is available. See order form.)

BLUEPRINT PRICE CODE: D

REAR VIEW

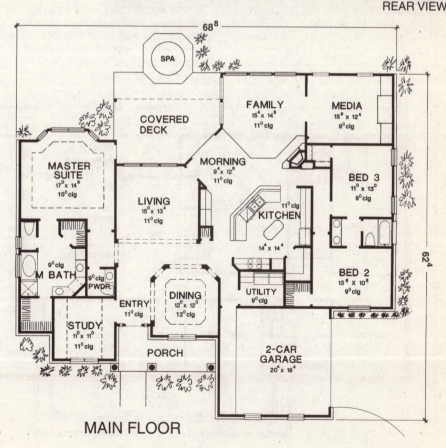

MAIN FLOOR

ORDER BLUEPRINTS ANYTIME!
CALL TOLL-FREE 1-800-820-1296

Plan DD-2665
Plan copyright held by home designer/architect

PRICES AND DETAILS ON PAGES 12-15

115

Easy-Living Atmosphere

- Clean lines and a functional, well-designed floor plan create a relaxed, easy-living atmosphere for this sprawling ranch-style home.
- An inviting front porch with attractive columns and planter boxes opens to an airy entry, which flows into the living room and the family room.
- The huge central family room features a vaulted, exposed-beam ceiling and a handsome fireplace with a built-in wood box. A nice desk and plenty of bookshelves give the room a distinguished feel. A French door opens to a versatile covered rear porch.
- The large gourmet kitchen is highlighted by an arched brick pass-through to the family room. Double doors open to the intimate formal dining room, which hosts a built-in china hutch. The sunny informal eating area features lovely porch views on either side.
- The isolated sleeping wing includes four bedrooms. The enormous master bedroom has a giant walk-in closet and a private bath. A compartmentalized bath with two vanities serves the remaining bedrooms.

Plan E-2700	
Bedrooms: 4	**Baths:** 2½
Living Area:	
Main floor	2,719 sq. ft.
Total Living Area:	**2,719 sq. ft.**
Garage	533 sq. ft.
Storage	50 sq. ft.
Exterior Wall Framing:	2x6

Foundation Options:
Crawlspace
Slab
(All plans can be built with your choice of foundation and framing. A generic conversion diagram is available. See order form.)

BLUEPRINT PRICE CODE: D

MAIN FLOOR

Plan E-2700

Plan copyright held by home designer/architect

COMFY COUNTRY CHARMERS

Gracious Days

- As it brings a touch of Victorian flair to this country-style home, a charming gazebo provides a gracious spot for afternoon visits and lemonade.
- Inside, the living and dining rooms flank the foyer, creating an elegant setting for parties. With a closet and private access to a bath, the living room could also be used as a bedroom or a home office.
- Straight ahead, columns frame the Great Room, where sunshine pools under two skylights. Sliding glass doors let in the fresh scent of spring blooms. A corner fireplace warms chilled fingers after an afternoon of raking leaves.
- In the kitchen, a sizable island doubles as a workstation and a snack bar. The sunny bay in the breakfast nook will rouse the sleepiest child.
- Across the home, the owners receive some extra special treatment in the master suite. Features here include a pair of walk-in closets, a linen closet and a bath with a dual-sink vanity.

VIEW INTO GREAT ROOM

Plan AX-95349

Bedrooms: 3+	Baths: 3
Living Area:	
Upper floor	728 sq. ft.
Main floor	2,146 sq. ft.
Total Living Area:	**2,874 sq. ft.**
Unfinished loft	300 sq. ft.
Standard basement	2,146 sq. ft.
Garage	624 sq. ft.
Exterior Wall Framing:	2x6

Foundation Options:
Standard basement
Crawlspace
Slab
(All plans can be built with your choice of foundation and framing. A generic conversion diagram is available. See order form.)

BLUEPRINT PRICE CODE: D

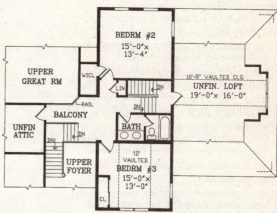

UPPER FLOOR

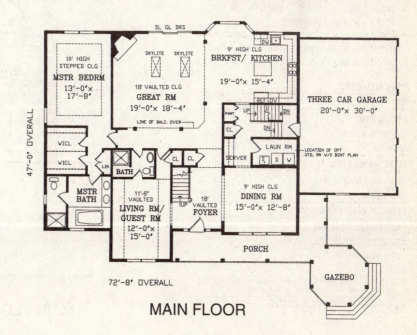

MAIN FLOOR

ORDER BLUEPRINTS ANYTIME!
CALL TOLL-FREE 1-800-820-1296

Plan AX-95349
Plan copyright held by home designer/architect

PRICES AND DETAILS ON PAGES 12-15

COMFY COUNTRY CHARMERS

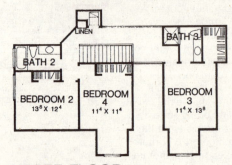

REAR VIEW

Dramatic Rear Views

- Columned front and rear porches offer country styling to this elegant two-story.
- The formal dining room and living room flank the two-story-high foyer.
- A dramatic array of windows stretches along the informal, rear-oriented living areas, where the central family room features a high vaulted ceiling and a striking fireplace.
- The modern kitchen features an angled snack counter, a walk-in pantry and a work island, in addition to the bayed morning room.
- The exciting and secluded master suite has a sunny bayed sitting area with its own fireplace. Large walk-in closets lead to a luxurious private bath with angled dual vanities, a garden spa tub and a separate shower.
- The centrally located stairway leads to three extra bedrooms and two full baths on the upper floor.

Plan DD-2912

Bedrooms: 4	Baths: 3½
Living Area:	
Upper floor	916 sq. ft.
Main floor	2,046 sq. ft.
Total Living Area:	**2,962 sq. ft.**
Standard basement	1,811 sq. ft.
Garage	513 sq. ft.
Exterior Wall Framing:	2x4

Foundation Options:
Standard basement
Crawlspace
Slab
(All plans can be built with your choice of foundation and framing. A generic conversion diagram is available. See order form.)

BLUEPRINT PRICE CODE: D

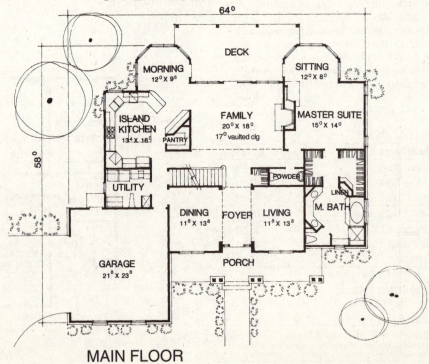

UPPER FLOOR

MAIN FLOOR

ORDER BLUEPRINTS ANYTIME!
CALL TOLL-FREE 1-800-820-1296

Plan DD-2912
Plan copyright held by home designer/architect

PRICES AND DETAILS ON PAGES 12-15

COMFY COUNTRY CHARMERS

Luxury Lodge

- Bringing to mind the hunting lodges of English royalty, this plan is at home in the country or on a city cul-de-sac. Brick arches highlight multi-paned windows against a subtle stone facade.
- Stepping into the Great Room from the broad entry, you can see a back deck through a wall of windows. Built-ins flank a grand fireplace to one side, while a single step leads up to a nook.
- One corner of the bayed eating nook hosts a huge walk-in pantry, while another accesses a three-season porch. The kitchen is vast enough to satisfy even the most exacting chef.
- Across the main floor, the master suite boasts bright windows and access to the deck. In the suite's private bath, a garden tub tempts you to forget work and soak stress away.
- Two more bedrooms share a generous split bath on the upper floor. One bedroom features a cathedral ceiling, while the other has dual closets.
- Double doors open into a sunny game room that's perfect for family time. Two closets also make it a good possibility for an extra-large bedroom.

Plan ADI-74197

Bedrooms: 3+	**Baths:** 2½
Living Area:	
Upper floor	970 sq. ft.
Main floor	1,826 sq. ft.
Three-season porch	213 sq. ft.
Total Living Area:	**3,009 sq. ft.**
Standard basement	2,039 sq. ft.
Garage	781 sq. ft.
Exterior Wall Framing:	2x6

Foundation Options:
Standard basement
(All plans can be built with your choice of foundation and framing. A generic conversion diagram is available. See order form.)

BLUEPRINT PRICE CODE: E

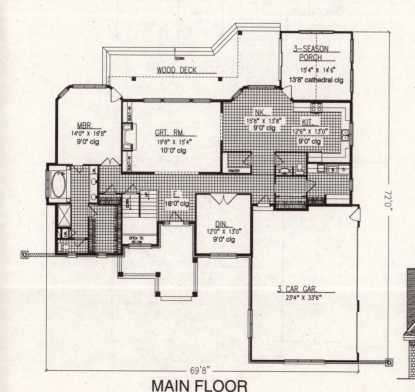

MAIN FLOOR

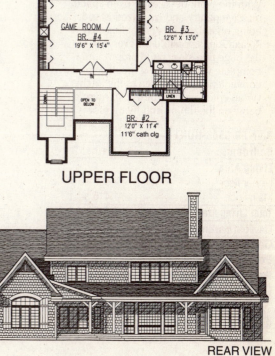

UPPER FLOOR

REAR VIEW

ORDER BLUEPRINTS ANYTIME!
CALL TOLL-FREE 1-800-820-1296

Plan ADI-74197
Plan copyright held by home designer/architect

PRICES AND DETAILS ON PAGES 12-15

COMFY COUNTRY CHARMERS

High Comfort

- Metal roof overhangs, paneled shutters and an ornate arched entry are appropriate adornments for this exquisite luxury home.
- From the three-car garage to the sprawling master suite, this home is designed for maximum comfort.
- All four of the bedrooms have generous closet space and private access to a bath. The master bedroom suite includes a private garden bath and also enjoys a plush octagonal sitting room.
- Another bonus? Dirty clothes can be piled up in the central laundry room without climbing any stairs!
- The kitchen below has so much cabinet space, you may be pressed to fill it. With the work desk, extra oven space, massive pantry and oversized island, being organized was never this easy!
- Relaxation is possible for everyone in the huge two-story family room, complete with a blazing fireplace and a convenient pass-through to the kitchen.
- When entertaining, guests can mingle between the dining and living rooms.

Plan FB-5545-HUNT	
Bedrooms: 4	Baths: 3½
Living Area:	
Upper floor	1,632 sq. ft.
Main floor	1,415 sq. ft.
Total Living Area:	**3,047 sq. ft.**
Daylight basement	1,415 sq. ft.
Garage	766 sq. ft.
Exterior Wall Framing:	2x4
Foundation Options:	
Daylight basement	
(All plans can be built with your choice of foundation and framing. A generic conversion diagram is available. See order form.)	
BLUEPRINT PRICE CODE:	E

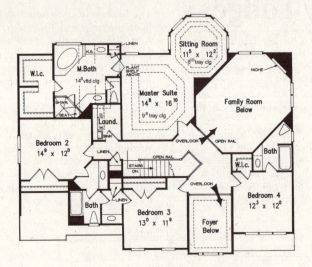

UPPER FLOOR

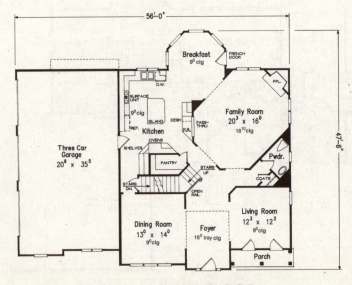

MAIN FLOOR

ORDER BLUEPRINTS ANYTIME! **CALL TOLL-FREE 1-800-820-1296**

Plan FB-5545-HUNT
Plan copyright held by home designer/architect

PRICES AND DETAILS ON PAGES 12-15

Tall Two-Story

- This gorgeous two-story is introduced by a barrel-vaulted entry and supporting columns. Inside, a spectacular curved staircase leads to a balcony overlook.
- Off the two-story-high foyer, a library with a lofty vaulted ceiling is the perfect spot for reading or study.
- A formal dining room opposite the library opens to the fabulous island kitchen. The kitchen offers an angled serving bar to the bayed breakfast area and the adjoining living room.
- The spacious living room opens to a backyard patio. A fireplace flanked by built-in bookshelves warms the area.
- The master bedroom boasts a gambrel ceiling, a sunny bay window and direct patio access. The private master bath offers two walk-in closets, a dual-sink vanity, a splashy garden tub and a separate shower.
- Upstairs, a railed balcony connects three secondary bedrooms, two more full baths and a versatile storage room.

Plan DD-3125

Bedrooms: 4+	Baths: 3½

Living Area:	
Upper floor	933 sq. ft.
Main floor	2,184 sq. ft.
Total Living Area:	**3,117 sq. ft.**
Bonus room	210 sq. ft.
Standard basement	2,184 sq. ft.
Garage	734 sq. ft.
Exterior Wall Framing:	2x4

Foundation Options:
Standard basement
Crawlspace
Slab
(All plans can be built with your choice of foundation and framing. A generic conversion diagram is available. See order form.)

BLUEPRINT PRICE CODE: E

REAR VIEW

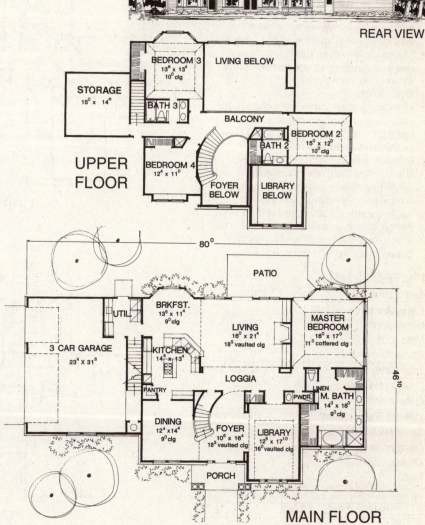

UPPER FLOOR

MAIN FLOOR

ORDER BLUEPRINTS ANYTIME!
CALL TOLL-FREE 1-800-820-1296

Plan DD-3125
Plan copyright held by home designer/architect

PRICES AND DETAILS ON PAGES 12-15

COMFY COUNTRY CHARMERS

High on Luxury

- With an exterior of stucco and stone and an interior enhanced by arched openings and climbing ceilings, this two-story home is high on luxury.
- Beyond the towering entry, the foyer reveals a high tray ceiling and an elegant stairway to an overlook above.
- Alongside the foyer, the living room boasts a tray ceiling; the formal dining room offers French doors to a covered front porch.
- The casual areas converge at the family room, where bold columns, a warm fireplace and a lofty ceiling equal pure excitement. A cozy breakfast bay extends from the adjoining kitchen.
- You'll enjoy the extra space in the sprawling master suite, which includes a romantic sitting area and a lavish, vaulted garden bath. A tray ceiling hovers above your bed.
- Three more bedrooms and a versatile bonus room occupy the upper floor.

Plan FB-5551-SHEL	
Bedrooms: 4+	**Baths:** 3½
Living Area:	
Upper floor	896 sq. ft.
Main floor	2,044 sq. ft.
Bonus room	197 sq. ft.
Total Living Area:	**3,137 sq. ft.**
Daylight basement	2,044 sq. ft.
Garage and storage	682 sq. ft.
Exterior Wall Framing:	2x4
Foundation Options:	
Daylight basement	
Crawlspace	
Slab	
(All plans can be built with your choice of foundation and framing. A generic conversion diagram is available. See order form.)	
BLUEPRINT PRICE CODE:	E

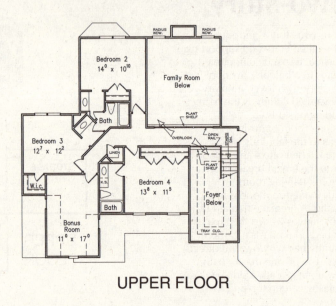

UPPER FLOOR

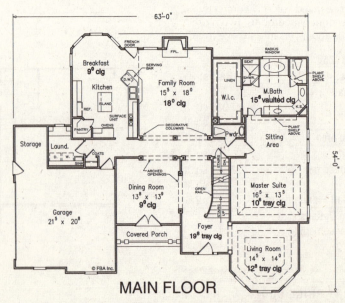

MAIN FLOOR

ORDER BLUEPRINTS ANYTIME! CALL TOLL-FREE 1-800-820-1296

Plan FB-5551-SHEL
Plan copyright held by home designer/architect

PRICES AND DETAILS ON PAGES 12-15

Subtle Appeal

- Lovely stone accents, charming shutters and a darling front porch contribute to the cottage-style look of this sizable family home. A hidden garage with an attached guest suite adds further appeal.
- Off the foyer, the spacious study offers niches for books and for displaying prized treasures. This room makes a nice den, home office or guest room.
- Columns mark the living room nearby. A fireplace centers the room, while a built-in media center adds to its versatility as a family room. A high, sloped ceiling adds drama and light to this enticing gathering spot.
- The kitchen's layout is sure to please the family chef! A pass-through and dual islands aid meal or snack service, while abundant counter space makes it easy to create delectable gourmet dishes.
- A resource center nearby allows you to pay bills in peace, while smart storage cabinets near the back door prevent the kids from leaving an after-school trail!
- The main-floor master suite includes a well-planned private bath and a large walk-in closet. Two more bedrooms upstairs share a loft and a full bath.

Plan L-0004-UDA

Bedrooms: 4+	Baths: 3½
Living Area:	
Upper floor	545 sq. ft.
Main floor	2,358 sq. ft.
Guest quarters	245 sq. ft.
Total Living Area:	**3,148 sq. ft.**
Garage	514 sq. ft.
Exterior Wall Framing:	2x4

Foundation Options:
Slab
(All plans can be built with your choice of foundation and framing. A generic conversion diagram is available. See order form.)

BLUEPRINT PRICE CODE: E

ORDER BLUEPRINTS ANYTIME!
CALL TOLL-FREE 1-800-820-1296

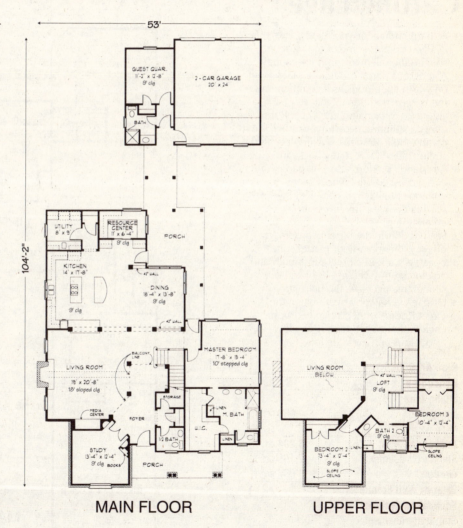

MAIN FLOOR   UPPER FLOOR

Plan L-0004-UDA
Plan copyright held by home designer/architect

PRICES AND DETAILS ON PAGES 12-15

COMFY COUNTRY CHARMERS

Cutting Edge

- A sharp choice for your next home, this design contains some of the most sought-after elements in homes today.
- A generous porch provides a place to sit on warm afternoons as it complements the home's traditional facade.
- Living up to its name, the Great Room offers a stunning two-story, vaulted ceiling, built-in shelves, a fireplace and sliding glass doors to the backyard.
- An island cooktop, a step-in pantry and easy access to the laundry room enhance the kitchen's efficient layout. A serving counter simplifies casual entertaining.
- Secluded from the other bedrooms for privacy, the main-floor master suite boasts a walk-in closet, a lush bath and an elegant tray ceiling. Its boxed-out sitting area accesses the backyard.
- Upstairs, a balcony overlooking the Great Room connects two bedrooms—each with a sweet dormer window—to a spacious and versatile loft.

Plan AX-00309	
Bedrooms: 3+	Baths: 4
Living Area:	
Upper floor	1,008 sq. ft.
Main floor	2,196 sq. ft.
Total Living Area:	**3,204 sq. ft.**
Standard basement	2,196 sq. ft.
Garage	667 sq. ft.
Exterior Wall Framing:	2x4
Foundation Options:	
Standard basement	
Crawlspace	
(All plans can be built with your choice of foundation and framing. A generic conversion diagram is available. See order form.)	
BLUEPRINT PRICE CODE:	E

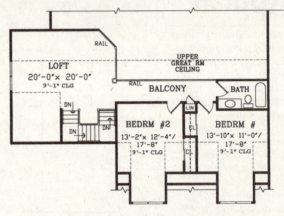

UPPER FLOOR

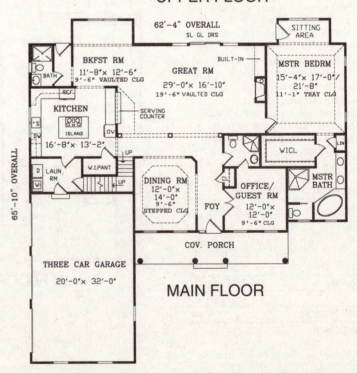

MAIN FLOOR

ORDER BLUEPRINTS ANYTIME!
CALL TOLL-FREE 1-800-820-1296

Plan AX-00309
Plan copyright held by home designer/architect

PRICES AND DETAILS
ON PAGES 12-15

Striking Details

- Thoughtful details perfectly complement this home's striking outer design.
- Inside, the spacious living room boasts a traditional stone fireplace and a modern, built-in media center.
- Usher your family in for meals in the dining room, or through French doors for dinner alfresco. The island kitchen, complete with a corner pantry and stacked ovens, makes entertaining easy.
- Mom's office, an activity center and a utility room ease day-to-day tasks.
- The master suite is amazing! Its large private bath has a Jacuzzi, his-and-hers walk-in closets and a makeup desk. An exercise room is a useful addition.
- Two upper-floor bedrooms—each with a built-in desk—share a Jacuzzi bath. Future areas allow for a third bedroom or extra storage. A quiet office over the garage is a nice place to receive clients.
- Plentiful storage off the garage safely houses utility vehicles and a workshop.

Plan HDC-3220

Bedrooms: 4+	Baths: 3½–4½

Living Area:

Upper floor	735 sq. ft.
Main floor	2,278 sq. ft.
Office	207 sq. ft.
Total Living Area:	**3,220 sq. ft.**
Future area	738 sq. ft.
Garage and storage	621 sq. ft.
Shop and tractor storage	383 sq. ft.
Motor home cover	410 sq. ft.
Exterior Wall Framing:	2x4

Foundation Options:
Slab
(All plans can be built with your choice of foundation and framing. A generic conversion diagram is available. See order form.)

BLUEPRINT PRICE CODE: E

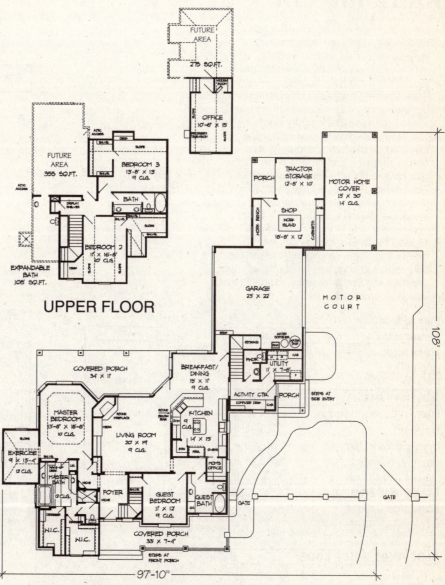

UPPER FLOOR

MAIN FLOOR

ORDER BLUEPRINTS ANYTIME!
CALL TOLL-FREE 1-800-820-1296

Plan HDC-3220
Plan copyright held by home designer/architect

PRICES AND DETAILS ON PAGES 12-15

COMFY COUNTRY CHARMERS

COMFY COUNTRY CHARMERS

Ramblin' On

- Pretty porches in front and back add a nice touch to this rambling country-style home. Other exterior details include shutters and fishscale shingles.
- Inside, the main floor boasts open, airy living spaces. The high-ceilinged foyer benefits from a large plant shelf and an angled staircase to the upper floor.
- The dining and living rooms flank the foyer, while the family room—with a corner fireplace and double doors to the rear covered porch—lies straight ahead.
- The kitchen features a large pantry, an island cooktop with a built-in table, a snack bar shared with the family room and nearby access to a screened porch.
- Topped by an elegant tray ceiling, the master suite offers a symmetrical private bath with a corner whirlpool tub, a separate shower, dual sinks and two vast walk-in closets.

Plan APS-3405

Bedrooms: 4+	Baths: 3½

Living Area:

Upper floor	1,013 sq. ft.
Main floor	2,480 sq. ft.
Total Living Area:	**3,493 sq. ft.**
Future area above garage	394 sq. ft.
Screened porch	168 sq. ft.
Unfinished storage	513 sq. ft.
Daylight basement	2,480 sq. ft.
Garage and storage	802 sq. ft.
Exterior Wall Framing	2x4

Foundation Options:
Daylight basement
(All plans can be built with your choice of foundation and framing. A generic conversion diagram is available. See order form.)

BLUEPRINT PRICE CODE: E

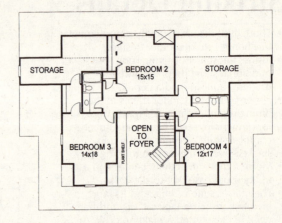

UPPER FLOOR

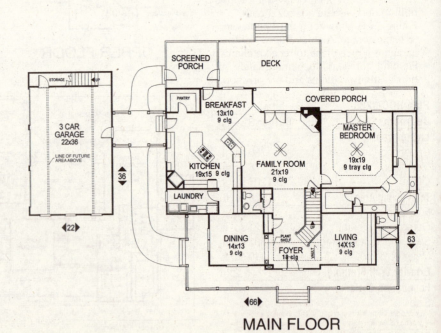

MAIN FLOOR

ORDER BLUEPRINTS ANYTIME!
CALL TOLL-FREE 1-800-820-1296

Plan APS-3405
Plan copyright held by home designer/architect

PRICES AND DETAILS ON PAGES 12-15

COMFY COUNTRY CHARMERS

Very Impressive

- With its regal columns and keystone-topped arches, this home's stunning entry will easily impress the neighbors.
- The grand image continues inside, where the beautiful foyer will wow the guests at your annual holiday ball.
- On the right, four columns define the formal yet versatile dining room.
- When spring arrives, swing open the French doors in the living room and savor the gentle breezes. The porch outside provides a pretty setting for tea.
- Most of your family's daily living will take place in the casual area. Here, the kitchen, nook and family room open to one another, letting family members concentrate on different tasks while still being able to visit.
- If you're craving some time alone, retreat to the master suite. In the private bath, a sunny whirlpool tub is just the prescription for weary spirits.
- Upstairs, a fun game room gives the kids a place to carry on without bothering the adults of the household.

Plan BOD-34-6A

Bedrooms: 3+	Baths: 3½
Living Area:	
Upper floor	1,025 sq. ft.
Main floor	2,469 sq. ft.
Total Living Area:	**3,494 sq. ft.**
Standard basement	2,469 sq. ft.
Garage and storage	793 sq. ft.
Exterior Wall Framing:	2x4

Foundation Options:
Standard basement
Crawlspace
Slab
(All plans can be built with your choice of foundation and framing. A generic conversion diagram is available. See order form.)

BLUEPRINT PRICE CODE: E

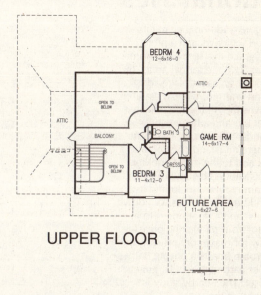

UPPER FLOOR

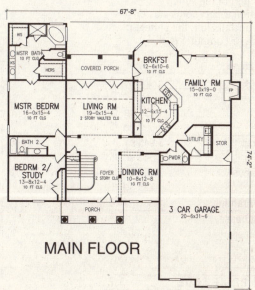

MAIN FLOOR

ORDER BLUEPRINTS ANYTIME!
CALL TOLL-FREE 1-800-820-1296

Plan BOD-34-6A
Plan copyright held by home designer/architect

PRICES AND DETAILS ON PAGES 12-15

COMFY COUNTRY CHARMERS

Traditional Ties

- Clean lines and traditional elements, like shuttered windows and a pretty front porch, grace this sprawling home.
- Bay windows light the formal areas. In the living room, a gas fireplace adds character and warmth, while a coffered ceiling crowns the dining room in style.
- A handy wet bar and a huge pantry—a walk-in wonder—flank passage to the kitchen, where an island cooktop and a sunny nook add to the joy of cooking.
- The kitchen's vaulted ceiling also soars above the family room, including its fireplace and built-in shelves. Windows line the walls, and a door opens to a back deck for your picnicking pleasure.
- Tucked away for maximum privacy, the master bedroom boasts a private bath with a corner garden tub and a huge walk-in closet. The nearby study is practically part of the suite.
- Three additional bedrooms cluster around an upstairs loft, the perfect place for an office or computer desk.

Plan SUN-3425

Bedrooms: 4+	Baths: 3
Living Area:	
Upper floor	1,254 sq. ft.
Main floor	2,692 sq. ft.
Total Living Area:	**3,946 sq. ft.**
Future area	563 sq. ft.
Daylight basement	2,106 sq. ft.
Garage	835 sq. ft.
Exterior Wall Framing:	2x6
Foundation Options:	
Daylight basement	
Slab	
(All plans can be built with your choice of foundation and framing. A generic conversion diagram is available. See order form.)	
BLUEPRINT PRICE CODE:	**F**

UPPER FLOOR

MAIN FLOOR

Plan SUN-3425
Plan copyright held by home designer/architect

Porch Watch

- Set up for lazy afternoons on the idyllic wraparound porch, the highlight of this country-style home's exterior.
- Move your guests inside to the picture perfect bayed dining room when dinner is ready. This room enjoys pocket-door access to the efficiently planned kitchen—a life-saver for the host!
- A snack bar augments the sunny breakfast nook. Utilitarian built-ins include a handy computer desk and a niche for photos or works of art.
- Built-in cabinets, a media center and a lovely fireplace grace the sprawling Great Room. A wall of windows allows light in; a French door allows you out.
- The vaulted master bedroom's corner of windows serves as the room's focal point. The private, compartmentalized bath features a spa tub and a dual-sink vanity. A walk-in closet is nearby.
- Down the hall, two more bedrooms share a full bath.
- The utility room doubles as a mudroom and accesses the garage.

Plan S-110496-B

Bedrooms: 3	Baths: 2
Living Area:	
Main floor	1,613 sq. ft.
Total Living Area:	**1,613 sq. ft.**
Standard basement	1,613 sq. ft.
Garage	400 sq. ft.
Exterior Wall Framing:	2x6
Foundation Options:	
Standard basement	
Crawlspace	
Slab	

(All plans can be built with your choice of foundation and framing. A generic conversion diagram is available. See order form.)

BLUEPRINT PRICE CODE: B

REAR VIEW

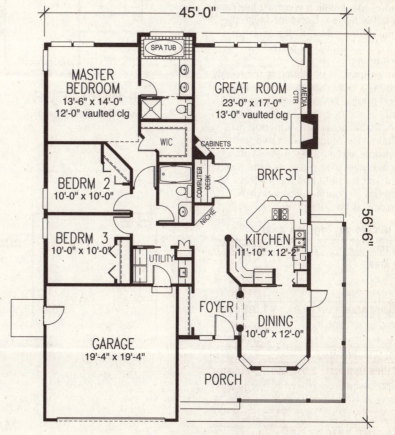

MAIN FLOOR

ORDER BLUEPRINTS ANYTIME!
CALL TOLL-FREE 1-800-820-1296

Plan S-110496-B
Plan copyright held by home designer/architect

PRICES AND DETAILS ON PAGES 12-15

NOSTALGIC FARMHOUSES

Friendly and Flexible

- Inside this home's engaging facade, flexibility is the key. Alternate plans for the upper floor allow for a growing family or an extra-posh master retreat.
- Cross the deep front porch and step into the entry. To one side, the living room is a sunny space with a warming fireplace and tall windows. Combined with the formal dining room, which accesses a back deck, this area is perfect for entertaining.
- Counter space is unrivaled in the roomy kitchen, which also features a bright bayed nook. This enormous casual family space opens to a huge utility room that accesses the front porch.
- Upstairs, one plan calls for two sunny bedrooms and a roomy master suite. The alternate plan provides extra room in the master suite and the second bedroom. An open-railed staircase enhances both floor plans.

Plans H-1439-2A, -2C, -3A & -3C

Bedrooms: 2+	Baths: 2½
Living Area:	
Upper floor	678 sq. ft.
Main floor	940 sq. ft.
Total Living Area:	**1,618 sq. ft.**
Standard basement	940 sq. ft.
Garage	544 sq. ft.
Exterior Wall Framing:	2x6

Foundation Options:	2-bedroom	3-bedroom
Standard basement	H-1439-2C	H-1439-3C
Crawlspace	H-1439-2A	H-1439-3A

(All plans can be built with your choice of foundation and framing. A generic conversion diagram is available. See order form.)

BLUEPRINT PRICE CODE:	B

UPPER FLOOR
(with Two Bedrooms)

UPPER FLOOR
(with Three Bedrooms)

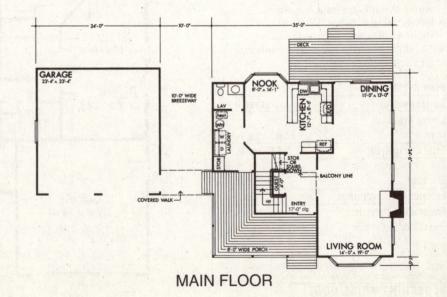

MAIN FLOOR

Plans H-1439-2A/2C/3A/3C

Made for the Shade!

- Finely tuned interior features and vintage Victorian-style looks satisfy your appetite for relaxed, easy living. Time will seem to stand still when you enjoy it on the shady wraparound veranda.
- Inside, 9-ft. ceilings on both floors lend volume to every room.
- The family room flows from the foyer and serves as your indoor rendezvous for warmth and entertainment. A central serving counter extending from the kitchen is ideal for pouring drinks and displaying munchies.
- For sit-down meals, the dining room is quite fitting. A French door entices you to savor dessert on the cool veranda.
- Secluded to the rear, the master suite includes a large private bath with a spa tub, a separate shower, dual vanities and an isolated toilet.
- A charming sun room, a walk-in storage closet and a big bookshelf cater to the two bedrooms on the upper floor.
- Plans for a detached two-car garage are included in the blueprints.

Plan L-680-VSA

Bedrooms: 3	Baths: 2½
Living Area:	
Upper floor	631 sq. ft.
Main floor	1,051 sq. ft.
Total Living Area:	**1,682 sq. ft.**
Detached garage	480 sq. ft.
Exterior Wall Framing:	2x4

Foundation Options:
Slab
(All plans can be built with your choice of foundation and framing. A generic conversion diagram is available. See order form.)

BLUEPRINT PRICE CODE: B

VIEW INTO FAMILY ROOM

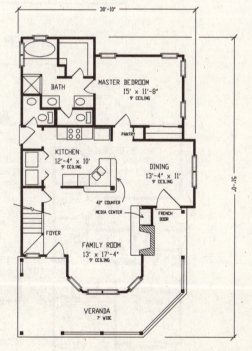

MAIN FLOOR

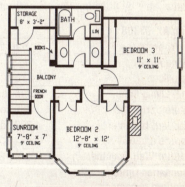

UPPER FLOOR

NOSTALGIC FARMHOUSES

ORDER BLUEPRINTS ANYTIME!
CALL TOLL-FREE 1-800-820-1296

Plan L-680-VSA
Plan copyright held by home designer/architect

PRICES AND DETAILS ON PAGES 12-15

Fresh Air

- With its nostalgic look and country style, this lovely home brings a breath of fresh air into any neighborhood.
- Past the inviting wraparound porch, the foyer is brightened by an elliptical transom window above the front door.
- The adjoining formal dining room is defined by decorative columns and a stylish stepped ceiling.
- The bright and airy kitchen includes a pantry, a windowed sink and a sunny breakfast area with porch access.
- A stepped ceiling enhances the spacious Great Room, where a fireplace warms the area. Two sets of sliding glass doors open to a back porch.
- The lush master bedroom and a bayed sitting area boast high ceilings. The master bath showcases a circular spa tub embraced by a glass-block wall.
- Two more bedrooms share a second bath. The protruding bedroom includes a dramatic vaulted ceiling.
- Additional living space can be made available by finishing the upper floor.

VIEW INTO GREAT ROOM

Plan AX-93308

Bedrooms: 3+	Baths: 2

Living Area:
Main floor	1,793 sq. ft.
Total Living Area:	**1,793 sq. ft.**
Future upper floor	779 sq. ft.
Standard basement	1,793 sq. ft.
Garage and utility	471 sq. ft.
Exterior Wall Framing:	2x4

Foundation Options:
Standard basement
Crawlspace
Slab

(All plans can be built with your choice of foundation and framing. A generic conversion diagram is available. See order form.)

BLUEPRINT PRICE CODE: B

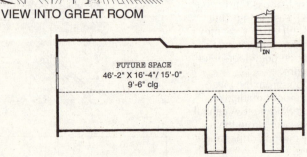

UPPER FLOOR

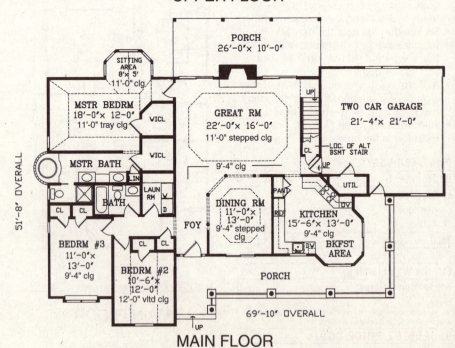

MAIN FLOOR

ORDER BLUEPRINTS ANYTIME!
CALL TOLL-FREE 1-800-820-1296

Plan AX-93308
Plan copyright held by home designer/architect

PRICES AND DETAILS ON PAGES 12-15

Rugged Look, Regal Feel

- This home's wraparound porch, stone exterior and metal roof give it the look of a rustic country lodge. Inside, you'll find amenities that treat you like royalty.
- Sunlight streams through a dormer window into the living room, where a vaulted ceiling adds to the space's generous proportions. A fireplace casts a golden glow on winter evenings.
- The adjoining kitchen is fronted by a long serving bar that makes entertaining as easy as pointing guests to the head of the buffet line. A center island provides needed extra work space.
- Brightened by a bay window, the master suite boasts a private bath with an oval soaking tub and a large walk-in closet.
- At the top of an open-railed staircase, a balcony loft overlooks the living room and the dining area. The loft connects two secondary bedrooms and an expansive full bath.

Plan DD-1850

Bedrooms: 3	Baths: 2½
Living Area:	
Upper floor	690 sq. ft.
Main floor	1,156 sq. ft.
Total Living Area:	**1,846 sq. ft.**
Standard basement	1,156 sq. ft.
Exterior Wall Framing:	2x4

Foundation Options:
Standard basement
Crawlspace
Slab
(All plans can be built with your choice of foundation and framing. A generic conversion diagram is available. See order form.)

BLUEPRINT PRICE CODE: B

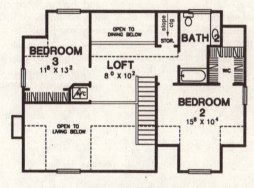

UPPER FLOOR

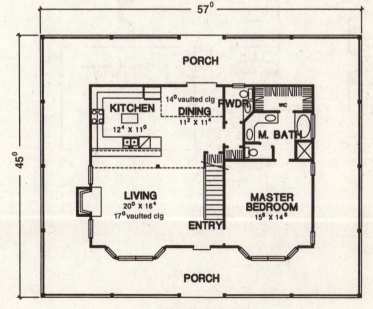

MAIN FLOOR

NOSTALGIC FARMHOUSES

ORDER BLUEPRINTS ANYTIME!
CALL TOLL-FREE 1-800-820-1296

Plan DD-1850
Plan copyright held by home designer/architect

PRICES AND DETAILS ON PAGES 12-15

Octagonal Dining Bay

- Classic traditional styling is recreated with a covered front porch and triple dormers with half-round windows.
- Off the entry porch, double doors reveal the reception area, with a walk-in closet and a half-bath.
- The living room features a striking fireplace and leads to the dining room, with its octagonal bay.
- The island kitchen overlooks the dinette and the family room, which features a second fireplace and sliding glass doors to a rear deck.
- Upstairs, the master suite boasts a walk-in closet and a whirlpool bath. A skylighted hallway connects three more bedrooms and another full bath.

Plan K-680-R	
Bedrooms: 4	Baths: 2½
Living Area:	
Upper floor	853 sq. ft.
Main floor	1,047 sq. ft.
Total Living Area:	**1,900 sq. ft.**
Standard basement	1,015 sq. ft.
Garage and storage	472 sq. ft.
Exterior Wall Framing:	2x4 or 2x6
Foundation Options:	
Standard basement	
Slab	

(All plans can be built with your choice of foundation and framing. A generic conversion diagram is available. See order form.)

BLUEPRINT PRICE CODE: B

NOSTALGIC FARMHOUSES

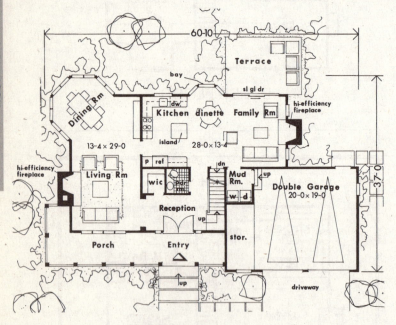

MAIN FLOOR

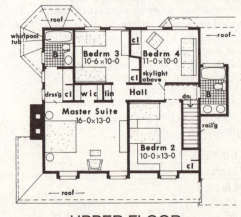

UPPER FLOOR

VIEW INTO LIVING AND DINING ROOMS

ORDER BLUEPRINTS ANYTIME!
CALL TOLL-FREE 1-800-820-1296

Plan K-680-R
Plan copyright held by home designer/architect

PRICES AND DETAILS ON PAGES 12-15

Relax on the Front Porch

- With its wraparound covered porch, this quaint two-story home makes summer evenings a breeze.
- Inside, a beautiful open stairway welcomes guests into the vaulted foyer, which connects the formal areas. The front-facing living and dining rooms have views of the covered front porch.
- French doors open from the living room to the family room, where a fireplace and corner windows warm and brighten this spacious activity area.
- The breakfast nook, set off by a half-wall, hosts a handy work desk and opens to the back porch.
- The country kitchen offers an oversized island, a pantry closet and illuminating windows flanking the corner sink.
- The upper-floor master suite boasts two walk-in closets and a private bath with a tub and a separate shower. Two more bedrooms, another full bath and a laundry room are also included.

Plan AGH-1997	
Bedrooms: 3	Baths: 2½
Living Area:	
Upper floor	933 sq. ft.
Main floor	1,064 sq. ft.
Total Living Area:	**1,997 sq. ft.**
Standard basement	1,064 sq. ft.
Garage	662 sq. ft.
Exterior Wall Framing:	2x6
Foundation Options:	
Standard basement	
(All plans can be built with your choice of foundation and framing. A generic conversion diagram is available. See order form.)	
BLUEPRINT PRICE CODE:	**B**

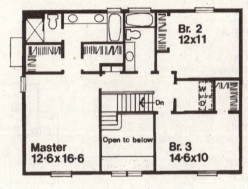

UPPER FLOOR

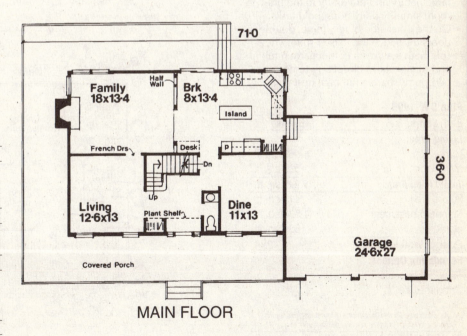

MAIN FLOOR

ORDER BLUEPRINTS ANYTIME!
CALL TOLL-FREE 1-800-820-1296

Plan AGH-1997
Plan copyright held by home designer/architect

PRICES AND DETAILS
ON PAGES 12-15

Well-Crafted

- Craftsman-style details pair up with an ingenious use of both indoor and outdoor space in this charming home. A versatile future area makes the design a perfect choice for growing families.
- A deep porch introduces the foyer, which opens into a formal dining room. To the left of the foyer, double doors enclose a unique bayed study.
- In the living room beyond, a high ceiling rises above the warming fireplace, and sliding French doors along one wall access a back deck.
- The living room lies adjacent to a bayed nook, which leads out to a sizable sun deck. The kitchen's island cooktop, large pantry and proximity to the utility room simplify daily household tasks.
- On the other side of the home, double doors introduce the master suite. The split bath features a corner garden tub and dual walk-in closets. Two more bedrooms share a full bath upstairs.

NOSTALGIC FARMHOUSES

Plan DW-1999

Bedrooms: 3+	**Baths:** 2½
Living Area:	
Upper floor	469 sq. ft.
Main floor	1,530 sq. ft.
Total Living Area:	**1,999 sq. ft.**
Future area	413 sq. ft.
Standard basement	1,530 sq. ft.
Garage	639 sq. ft.
Exterior Wall Framing:	2x4
Foundation Options:	
Standard basement	
Crawlspace	
Slab	

(All plans can be built with your choice of foundation and framing. A generic conversion diagram is available. See order form.)

BLUEPRINT PRICE CODE: B

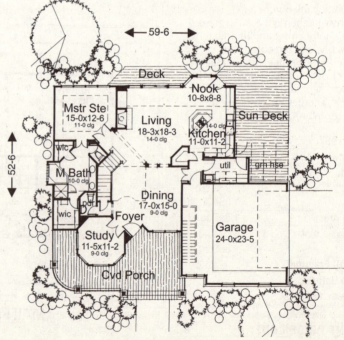

UPPER FLOOR

MAIN FLOOR

136 ORDER BLUEPRINTS ANYTIME! CALL TOLL-FREE 1-800-820-1296

Plan DW-1999
Plan copyright held by home designer/architect

PRICES AND DETAILS ON PAGES 12-15

Today's Tradition

- This two-story country home combines traditional standards with the exciting new designs of today.
- Visitors are welcomed by the nostalgic wraparound porch and the symmetrical bay windows of the formal living and dining rooms.
- The front half of the main floor lends itself to entertaining, as the angled entry creates a flow between the formal areas.
- French doors lead from the living room into the spacious family room, which boasts a beamed ceiling, a warming fireplace and rear access to the porch.
- The super kitchen features an island cooktop with a snack bar. The overall layout of the kitchen is conducive to all culinary endeavors! A nice-sized laundry room is conveniently nearby.
- The spacious upper floor hosts a master suite with two walk-in closets and a large bath with a dual-sink vanity, a tub and a separate shower. Three more bedrooms share another full bath.

Plan AGH-2143

Bedrooms: 4	Baths: 2½
Living Area:	
Upper floor	1,047 sq. ft.
Main floor	1,096 sq. ft.
Total Living Area:	**2,143 sq. ft.**
Daylight basement	1,096 sq. ft.
Garage and storage	852 sq. ft.
Exterior Wall Framing:	2x6
Foundation Options:	
Daylight basement	
(All plans can be built with your choice of foundation and framing. A generic conversion diagram is available. See order form.)	
BLUEPRINT PRICE CODE:	**C**

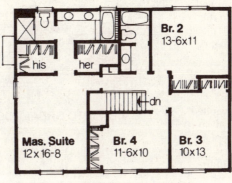

UPPER FLOOR

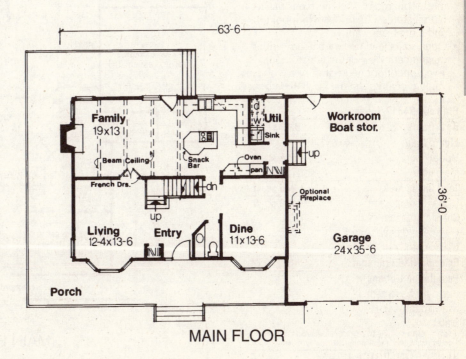

MAIN FLOOR

ORDER BLUEPRINTS ANYTIME!
CALL TOLL-FREE 1-800-820-1296

Plan AGH-2143
Plan copyright held by home designer/architect

PRICES AND DETAILS
ON PAGES 12-15

Sunny Comfort

- A wraparound porch and lovely arched windows give this home a comfortable country style. Oval glass, a fantail transom window, and sidelights bathe the foyer in light for a memorable introduction.
- An elegant columned archway introduces the formal dining room.
- The huge Great Room features a vaulted ceiling, a wall of windows and built-in wall units on either side of the fireplace.
- Ample counter space and a convenient work island allow maximum use of the roomy kitchen. The sunny breakfast nook opens to a rear porch through sliding glass doors.
- On the other side of the home, a dramatic bay window highlights the master bedroom. The enormous master bath features a luxurious whirlpool tub and a dual-sink vanity.
- Open stairs lead up to a balcony with a magnificent view of the Great Room. Two upper-floor bedrooms, one with a vaulted ceiling, share a full hall bath.

Plan AX-94317

Bedrooms: 3	Baths: 2½

Living Area:	
Upper floor	525 sq. ft.
Main floor	1,720 sq. ft.
Total Living Area:	**2,245 sq. ft.**
Upper-floor storage	149 sq. ft.
Standard basement	1,720 sq. ft.
Garage and storage	525 sq. ft.
Utility room	29 sq. ft.
Exterior Wall Framing:	2x4

Foundation Options:
Standard basement
Crawlspace
Slab
(All plans can be built with your choice of foundation and framing. A generic conversion diagram is available. See order form.)

BLUEPRINT PRICE CODE: C

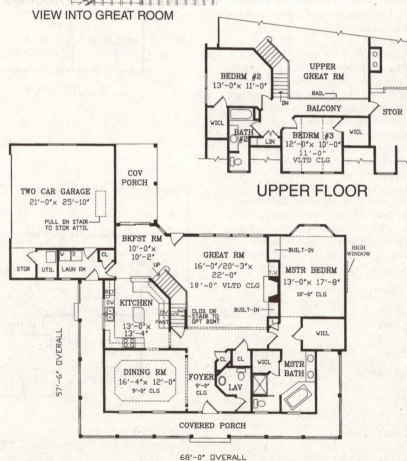

VIEW INTO GREAT ROOM

UPPER FLOOR

MAIN FLOOR

NOSTALGIC FARMHOUSES

138 ORDER BLUEPRINTS ANYTIME!
CALL TOLL-FREE 1-800-820-1296

Plan AX-94317
Plan copyright held by home designer/architect

PRICES AND DETAILS ON PAGES 12-15

All-American Country Home

- The covered wraparound porch of this popular all-American home creates an old-fashioned country appeal.
- Off the entryway is the generous-sized living room, which offers a fireplace and French doors that open to the porch.
- The large adjoining dining room further expands the entertaining area.
- The country kitchen has a handy island and flows into the cozy family room, which is enhanced by exposed beams. A handsome fireplace warms the entire informal area, while windows overlook the porch.
- The quiet upper floor hosts four good-sized bedrooms and two baths. The master suite includes a walk-in closet, a dressing area and a private bath with a sit-down shower.
- This home is available with or without a basement and with or without a garage.

Plans H-3711-1, -1A, -2 & -2A

Bedrooms: 4	Baths: 2½
Living Area:	
Upper floor	1,176 sq. ft.
Main floor	1,288 sq. ft.
Total Living Area:	**2,464 sq. ft.**
Standard basement	1,176 sq. ft.
Garage	505 sq. ft.
Exterior Wall Framing:	2x6
Foundation Options:	Plan #
Basement with garage	H-3711-1
Basement without garage	H-3711-2
Crawlspace with garage	H-3711-1A
Crawlspace without garage	H-3711-2A

(All plans can be built with your choice of foundation and framing. A generic conversion diagram is available. See order form.)

BLUEPRINT PRICE CODE: C

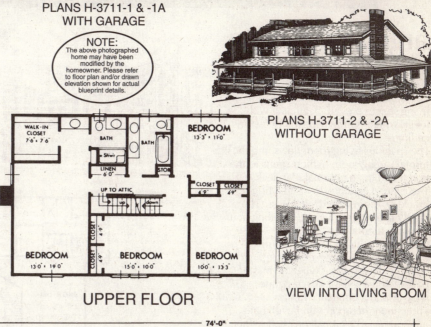

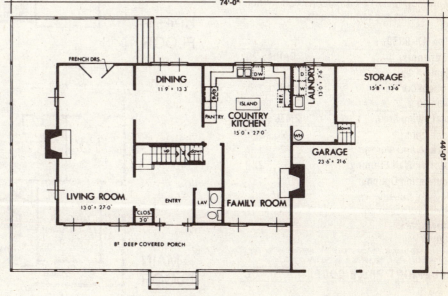

NOSTALGIC FARMHOUSES

ORDER BLUEPRINTS ANYTIME!
CALL TOLL-FREE 1-800-820-1296

Plans H-3711-1/1A/2/2A
Plan copyright held by home designer/architect

PRICES AND DETAILS ON PAGES 12-15

Large-Scale Living

- Eye-catching windows and a wrap-around porch highlight this home.
- Inside, high ceilings and large-scale living spaces prevail, beginning with the foyer, which is crowned by a two-story ceiling.
- The spacious living room flows into the formal dining room, which opens to the porch and to an optional rear deck.
- The island kitchen extends to a bright breakfast room with deck access. The family room offers a vaulted ceiling and a corner fireplace.
- Upstairs, the lush master bedroom boasts its own vaulted ceiling and two walk-in closets. The skylighted master bath features a spa tub, a separate shower and a dual-sink vanity.
- Three more bedrooms and a full bath are connected by a balcony hall, which overlooks the family room.

Plan AX-93309

Bedrooms: 4	Baths: 2½
Living Area:	
Upper floor	1,180 sq. ft.
Main floor	1,290 sq. ft.
Total Living Area:	**2,470 sq. ft.**
Basement	1,290 sq. ft.
Garage and storage	421 sq. ft.
Exterior Wall Framing:	2x4

Foundation Options:
Daylight basement
Standard basement
Crawlspace
Slab
(All plans can be built with your choice of foundation and framing. A generic conversion diagram is available. See order form.)

BLUEPRINT PRICE CODE: C

NOSTALGIC FARMHOUSES

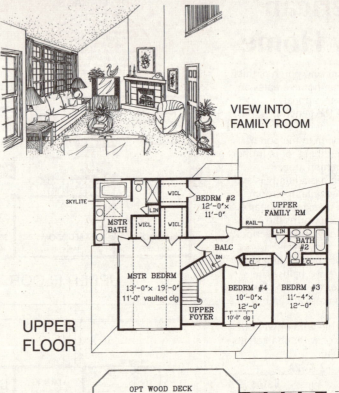

VIEW INTO FAMILY ROOM

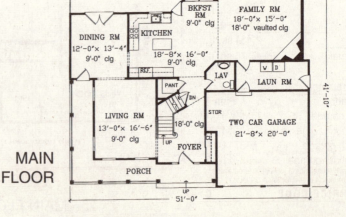

UPPER FLOOR

MAIN FLOOR

ORDER BLUEPRINTS ANYTIME!
CALL TOLL-FREE 1-800-820-1296

Plan AX-93309
Plan copyright held by home designer/architect

PRICES AND DETAILS ON PAGES 12-15

Home at Last!

- Whether you're returning from a business trip or a personal vacation, you'll never get tired of coming home to this spectacular stucco delight.
- Breezy outdoor spaces parade around the home, starting with a nostalgic front porch and ending at a relaxing spa tub on a sprawling backyard deck.
- The spacious interior is bright and open. Past the entry, a gallery with French doors leads to the superb kitchen and the sunny bayed morning room.
- For activities of a larger scale, the living room offers an engaging fireplace, exciting views and enough space to house your entertainment equipment.
- A two-sided fireplace adds a romantic glow to the master bedroom and private sitting area. The elegant, skylighted master bath promises luxury for two!
- The upper-floor bedrooms are furnished with a shared bath and their own walk-in closets and sunny sitting spaces.

Plan DD-2617

Bedrooms: 4	Baths: 3
Living Area:	
Upper floor	609 sq. ft.
Main floor	2,034 sq. ft.
Total Living Area:	**2,643 sq. ft.**
Standard basement	2,034 sq. ft.
Garage	466 sq. ft.
Storage	78 sq. ft.
Exterior Wall Framing:	2x4

Foundation Options:
Standard basement
Crawlspace
Slab
(All plans can be built with your choice of foundation and framing. A generic conversion diagram is available. See order form.)

BLUEPRINT PRICE CODE: D

REAR VIEW

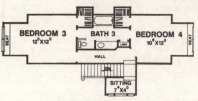

UPPER FLOOR

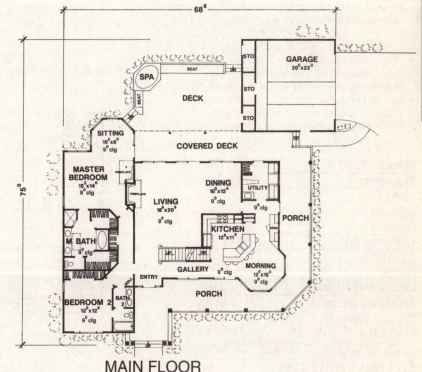

MAIN FLOOR

NOSTALGIC FARMHOUSES

ORDER BLUEPRINTS ANYTIME!
CALL TOLL-FREE 1-800-820-1296

Plan DD-2617
Plan copyright held by home designer/architect

PRICES AND DETAILS ON PAGES 12-15

Great Room Grandeur

- Hidden at the rear of this unique design, the vast, sunken Great Room features a wood-burning stove and access to a rear deck, and anchors the home's casual living areas.
- From the Great Room, step up into the bayed eating nook, which, like the formal dining room, is easily served by the huge island kitchen. A bright corner sink and a fireplace make cooking and household chores more pleasant.
- Move to the front-facing dining room to appreciate a bay window and an elegant built-in china closet. Across the two-story entry, a large library features a handsome built-in desk and bookcases.
- Climb the steps and peer down into the Great Room from a cozy reading area—bedtime stories will never be the same!
- Step to the end of the hall and enter the spacious master suite. A walk-in closet and a private bath surround a raised, hydro-spa tub.

Plans H-2125-1 & -1A

Bedrooms: 3	Baths: 2½
Living Area:	
Upper floor	1,105 sq. ft.
Main floor	1,554 sq. ft.
Total Living Area:	**2,659 sq. ft.**
Standard basement	1,554 sq. ft.
Garage	475 sq. ft.
Exterior Wall Framing:	2x6
Foundation Options:	Plan #
Standard basement	H-2125-1
Crawlspace	H-2125-1A
(All plans can be built with your choice of foundation and framing. A generic conversion diagram is available. See order form.)	
BLUEPRINT PRICE CODE:	**D**

NOSTALGIC FARMHOUSES

UPPER FLOOR

BASEMENT STAIRWAY LOCATION

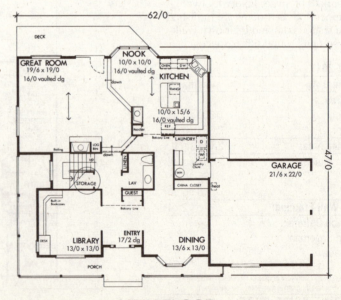

MAIN FLOOR

Plans H-2125-1 & -1A
Plan copyright held by home designer/architect

Warm Country

- Three beautiful fireplaces exude wonderful warmth and ambience throughout this stately country home.
- A wide wraparound porch encloses the facade and frames the sidelighted entry. The fantastic foyer shows off a sweeping stairway as it flows into the formal dining room.
- On the opposite side of the foyer, a roomy study is accessed by French doors and features a handsome fireplace accented by built-in bookshelves.
- A gallery unfolds to the family room, where a French door opens to a porch.
- This porch can also be accessed from the master bedroom. The master bath boasts a large walk-in closet, a Jacuzzi tub and a separate shower.
- The kitchen has a long snack/serving bar that is also great for meal preparation. The adjacent nook sports a built-in breakfast booth and a French door to another porch.
- Along the balcony hall are three more bedrooms. One bedroom flaunts a convenient private bath; another has a handy built-in desk.

REAR VIEW

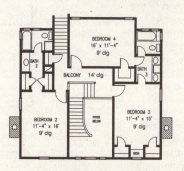

UPPER FLOOR

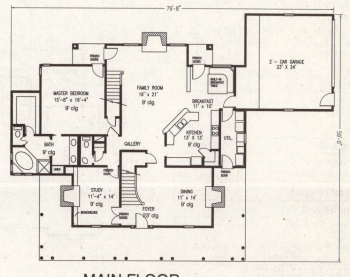

MAIN FLOOR

Plan L-934-VSB	
Bedrooms: 4+	**Baths:** 3½
Living Area:	
Upper floor	933 sq. ft.
Main floor	1,999 sq. ft.
Total Living Area:	**2,932 sq. ft.**
Garage	530 sq. ft.
Exterior Wall Framing:	2x4
Foundation Options:	
Slab	
(All plans can be built with your choice of foundation and framing. A generic conversion diagram is available. See order form.)	
BLUEPRINT PRICE CODE:	**D**

**ORDER BLUEPRINTS ANYTIME!
CALL TOLL-FREE 1-800-820-1296**

Plan L-934-VSB
Plan copyright held by home designer/architect

**PRICES AND DETAILS
ON PAGES 12-15**

NOSTALGIC FARMHOUSES

Southern Blend

- This striking home—a stylish blend of European and country elements—has a look that bespeaks its Southern roots.
- A columned wraparound porch gives way to a two-story entry flanked by the formal dining and living rooms.
- The generous Great Room is open to the second floor. Its fireplace is sided by built-in cabinets.
- The U-shaped kitchen puts everything within easy reach of the family chef. A center island provides needed work space, a pantry closet gives you extra storage, and a pass-through serves the adjoining Great Room.
- French doors open from the breakfast nook onto a covered rear porch.
- Upstairs, double doors access the master suite, where a quiet sitting area offers French doors to a private deck. The master bath features his-and-hers vanities, a spa tub, a separate oversized shower and a walk-in closet.
- One of three other bedrooms boasts its own bath, making it a nice guest suite.

NOSTALGIC FARMHOUSES

Plan C-9630	
Bedrooms: 4+	**Baths:** 4
Living Area:	
Upper floor	1,445 sq. ft.
Main floor	1,609 sq. ft.
Total Living Area:	**3,054 sq. ft.**
Daylight basement	1,609 sq. ft.
Garage	527 sq. ft.
Exterior Wall Framing:	2x4
Foundation Options:	
Daylight basement	
Crawlspace	
(All plans can be built with your choice of foundation and framing. A generic conversion diagram is available. See order form.)	
BLUEPRINT PRICE CODE:	D

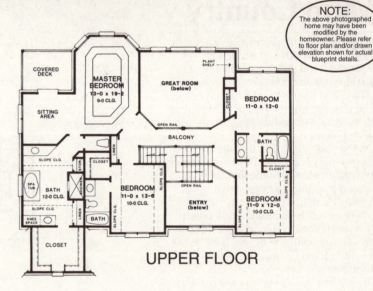

UPPER FLOOR

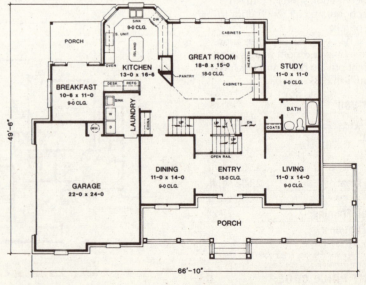

MAIN FLOOR

ORDER BLUEPRINTS ANYTIME!
CALL TOLL-FREE 1-800-820-1296

Plan C-9630
Plan copyright held by home designer/architect

PRICES AND DETAILS ON PAGES 12-15

Catch of the Day

- Inspired by the late 19th century summer cottages along the East Coast, this versatile shingle-style design is suitable as a primary residence or as a cozy weekend retreat.
- The floor plan is practically sized and is expanded by a deep veranda and a screened porch, which serve as additional entertaining areas. Hardwood floors and raised ceilings lend beauty and volume to the living spaces.
- At the entry, a leaded glass door opens to a dramatic two-story foyer and turned staircase. A view into the living area reveals a warm woodstove and plenty of space for unwinding after work or a long day of fishing.
- A dining area is nestled between two sets of sliding French doors—one to the veranda and one to the porch.
- Its central location and convenient serving bar to the living area make the kitchen simple yet functional.
- Enticing double doors gain access to the master bedroom on the main floor. Enjoy stepping out to the porch or into your private bath with a handy pocket door to the laundry room.
- Two more bedrooms, each with a high ceiling and lots of space, share another bath on the upper floor.
- The blueprints include plans for a detached two-car garage.

Plan L-444-VACA	
Bedrooms: 3	**Baths:** 2
Living Area:	
Upper floor	464 sq. ft.
Main floor	978 sq. ft.
Total Living Area:	**1,442 sq. ft.**
Screened porch	100 sq. ft.
Detached garage	528 sq. ft.
Exterior Wall Framing:	2x4
Foundation Options:	
Slab	

(All plans can be built with your choice of foundation and framing. A generic conversion diagram is available. See order form.)

BLUEPRINT PRICE CODE: A

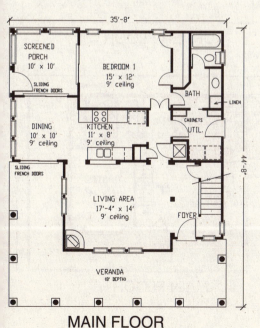

MAIN FLOOR

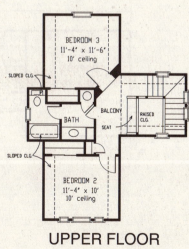

UPPER FLOOR

REAR VIEW

Plan L-444-VACA
Plan copyright held by home designer/architect

Cape Cod Variation

- A handsome wraparound porch and stylish dormers with transom glass dress up this Cape Cod variation.
- Inside, a dramatic balcony creates immediate interest as it overlooks the living room and entry from high above. Complementing the lofty vaulted ceiling is a lovely boxed-out window.
- The kitchen and the dining area unite at the back of the home and include a neat pantry, a versatile island and access to the backyard. With everything at your fingertips, why dine out?
- When the dishes are done, slip into the private master suite on the main floor. Your daily worries will be long gone as you relax in the bubbly whirlpool tub.
- A skylighted bath shares the upper floor with two secondary bedrooms and a large attic storage area.
- A laundry room and a half-bath connect the home to the two-car garage.

NOSTALGIC FARMHOUSES

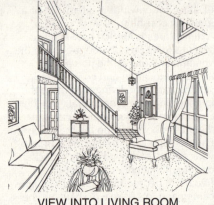

VIEW INTO LIVING ROOM

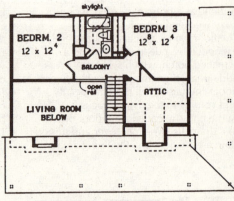

UPPER FLOOR

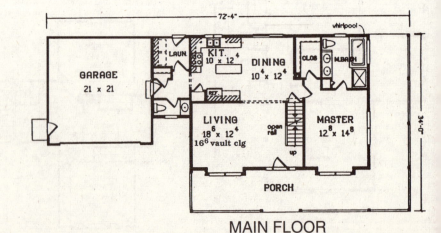

MAIN FLOOR

Plan GL-1581

Bedrooms: 3	Baths: 2½
Living Area:	
Upper floor	506 sq. ft.
Main floor	1,075 sq. ft.
Total Living Area:	**1,581 sq. ft.**
Attic storage space	137 sq. ft.
Standard basement	1,059 sq. ft.
Garage	441 sq. ft.
Exterior Wall Framing:	2x6

Foundation Options:
Standard basement
(All plans can be built with your choice of foundation and framing. A generic conversion diagram is available. See order form.)

BLUEPRINT PRICE CODE: B

146   **ORDER BLUEPRINTS ANYTIME! CALL TOLL-FREE 1-800-820-1296**   Plan GL-1581   **PRICES AND DETAILS ON PAGES 12-15**

Plan copyright held by home designer/architect

Either Choice Is a Winner

- Win either way in this charming home, offering a choice of two or three bedrooms on the upper floor.
- The L-shaped front porch greets visitors and leads to both the main entry and the service entry.
- The main entry is flanked by the living room and the stairway to the upper floor. The living room features a warm fireplace and a large bay window.
- The rear-oriented kitchen offers a sunny sink area, a pantry closet and a bayed breakfast nook that connects the kitchen to the family room.
- Sliding glass doors open from the family room to a backyard deck. An oversized laundry room and a half-bath are convenient to the family living area as well as to the service entry.
- Both upper floor plans include a master suite with a private bath, a second full bath and a railing overlooking the front entry below.

Plans H-1439-2D, -2E, -3D & -3E

Bedrooms: 2+	Baths: 2½
Living Area:	
Upper floor	678 sq. ft.
Main floor	940 sq. ft.
Total Living Area:	**1,618 sq. ft.**
Standard basement	940 sq. ft.
Garage	544 sq. ft.
Exterior Wall Framing:	2x6
Foundation Options:	2-bedroom 3-bedroom
Standard basement	H-1439-2E H-1439-3E
Crawlspace	H-1439-2D H-1439-3D

(All plans can be built with your choice of foundation and framing. A generic conversion diagram is available. See order form.)

BLUEPRINT PRICE CODE: B

UPPER FLOOR (with two bedrooms)

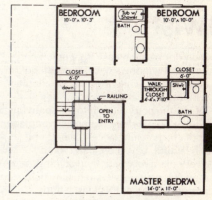

UPPER FLOOR (with three bedrooms)

NOSTALGIC FARMHOUSES

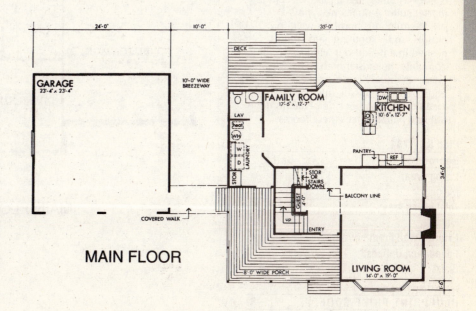

MAIN FLOOR

ORDER BLUEPRINTS ANYTIME! CALL TOLL-FREE 1-800-820-1296

Plans H-1439-2D/2E/3D/3E
Plan copyright held by home designer/architect

PRICES AND DETAILS ON PAGES 12-15

Countrytime Twist

- Twin dormers, an easy front porch and beautiful windows with shutters lend a country feel, while a stunning Palladian window adds a new twist.
- Inside, the entry leads into the sprawling Great Room, where a dramatic fireplace and a high ceiling accentuate its appeal.
- A beautiful, bayed breakfast room overlooks a rear patio and adjoins the efficient, galley-style kitchen, which presents a corner breakfast bar for serving snacks at parties.
- Dine in style in the formal dining room, crowned by a sloped ceiling and the front Palladian window that lets the sun splash inside.
- A sloped ceiling highlights the secluded master suite. A dual-sink vanity, a private toilet, his-and-hers walk-in closets, and a soothing garden tub nestled in a boxed-out window complete the master bath.
- Three secondary bedrooms, each equipped with a walk-in closet, are located on the other side of the home. A full hall bath services these rooms.

Plan KD-1784

Bedrooms: 4	Baths: 2
Living Area:	
Main floor	1,783 sq. ft.
Total Living Area:	**1,783 sq. ft.**
Garage	442 sq. ft.
Exterior Wall Framing:	2x4
Foundation Options:	
Slab	
(All plans can be built with your choice of foundation and framing. A generic conversion diagram is available. See order form.)	
BLUEPRINT PRICE CODE:	**B**

NOSTALGIC FARMHOUSES

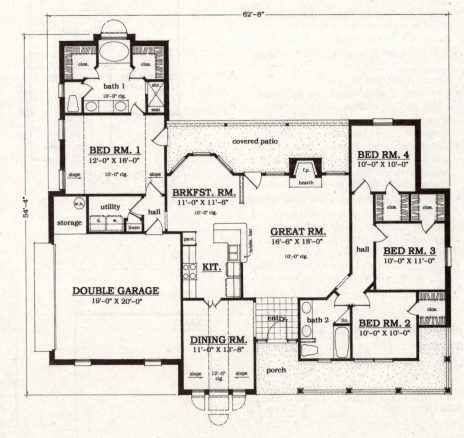

MAIN FLOOR

ORDER BLUEPRINTS ANYTIME!
CALL TOLL-FREE 1-800-820-1296

Plan KD-1784
Plan copyright held by home designer/architect

PRICES AND DETAILS ON PAGES 12-15

Room to Spare

- You'll be amazed at the roominess of this livable, space-efficient home.
- The fanciful facade showcases dormers up top, keystones, a bay window and a beautiful wraparound porch.
- Inside, the spacious living room offers a cozy fireplace, as well as a window overlook and access to a rear porch.
- Both dining spaces feature bay windows and are bridged by the kitchen, with its corner sink and useful snack bar. A nearby utility room offers a sizable pantry and storage space.
- The posh master suite sits on the opposite end of the home, where it enjoys privacy among other exciting amenities. A boxed-out window and a stepped ceiling mark the bedroom, while a corner tub, a separate shower and dual walk-in closets grace the private bath, accessed by double doors.
- Two additional bedrooms in the home's sleeping wing bask in spaciousness while sharing a full hall bath and ample storage.
- An attached, two-car garage and storage is located off the utility room and provides passage to the rear porch.

Plan RD-1948	
Bedrooms: 3	**Baths:** 2
Living Area:	
Main floor	1,948 sq. ft.
Total Living Area:	**1,948 sq. ft.**
Garage and storage	581 sq. ft.
Exterior Wall Framing:	2x4
Foundation Options:	
Crawlspace	
Slab	

(All plans can be built with your choice of foundation and framing. A generic conversion diagram is available. See order form.)

BLUEPRINT PRICE CODE: B

NOSTALGIC FARMHOUSES

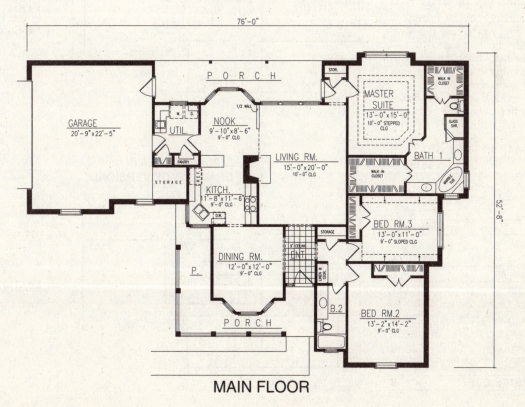

MAIN FLOOR

ORDER BLUEPRINTS ANYTIME!
CALL TOLL-FREE 1-800-820-1296

Plan RD-1948
Plan copyright held by home designer/architect

PRICES AND DETAILS ON PAGES 12-15

Low Profile

- This home's dramatic low roofline hides a spacious, versatile floor plan within a smart package. Choose one of two kitchen layouts: a country kitchen or a dining-room-and-nook combination.
- A deep porch shades a series of wide front windows. Inside, the living room stretches to meet a warming fireplace surrounded by more windows.
- In both designs, the kitchen features plenty of dining space and access to a rear deck or patio for meals al fresco. Long stretches of counter space and windows over the sink are pluses.
- The nearby laundry room also opens to the deck, inviting you to hang the wash out to dry in the summer sun.
- Located on the main floor, the master suite features twin closets and a private bath. A quiet study across the hall would make an ideal spare bedroom.
- On the upper floor, two more bedrooms share a sunny full bath.

NOSTALGIC FARMHOUSES

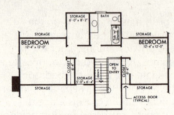

UPPER FLOOR

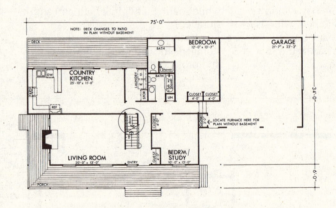

MAIN FLOOR
(with Country Kitchen)

STAIRWAY AREA IN
CRAWLSPACE VERSIONS

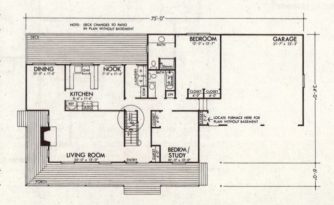

MAIN FLOOR
(with Dining Room)

Plans H-3732, -1A, -1B, -1C & -1D	
Bedrooms: 3+	Baths: 3
Living Area:	
Upper floor	626 sq. ft.
Main floor	1,359 sq. ft.
Total Living Area:	**1,985 sq. ft.**
Daylight basement	1,359 sq. ft.
Garage	528 sq. ft.
Exterior Wall Framing:	2x6
Foundation Options:	Plan #
Daylight basement, Country kitchen	H-3732-1B
Daylight basement, Dining room	H-3732-1D
Crawlspace, Country kitchen	H-3732-1A
Crawlspace, Dining room	H-3732-1C
(All plans can be built with your choice of foundation and framing. A generic conversion diagram is available. See order form.)	
BLUEPRINT PRICE CODE:	**B**

ORDER BLUEPRINTS ANYTIME!
CALL TOLL-FREE 1-800-820-1296

Plans H-3732-1A/1B/1C/1D
Plan copyright held by home designer/architect

PRICES AND DETAILS
ON PAGES 12-15

Masterfully Planned

- A wraparound porch highlights the exterior of this charming two-story.
- Inside, a vaulted entry impressively divides the formal living room from the dining room. The living room includes a built-in entertainment center, while the dining room hosts a china shelf.
- The well-planned island kitchen, family room and bayed nook open up at the rear of the home. The family room has patio doors to the backyard and another built-in entertainment center.
- A secluded stairway leads to the bedrooms on the upper floor. The master suite is truly masterful, with its vaulted sleeping area and views of the backyard. The opulent bath is also vaulted and features a long, dual-sink vanity, a makeup table and a garden spa tub. A walk-in closet and a shower round out the suite.
- The two remaining bedrooms are also vaulted and share a skylighted bath. The balcony hall overlooks the foyer and is accented by a planter.

Plan I-2075-A

Bedrooms: 3+	Baths: 2½
Living Area:	
Upper floor	980 sq. ft.
Main floor	1,096 sq. ft.
Total Living Area:	**2,076 sq. ft.**
Garage and shop	526 sq. ft.
Exterior Wall Framing:	2x6

Foundation Options:
Crawlspace
(All plans can be built with your choice of foundation and framing. A generic conversion diagram is available. See order form.)

BLUEPRINT PRICE CODE: C

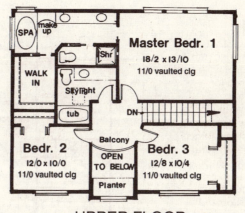

UPPER FLOOR

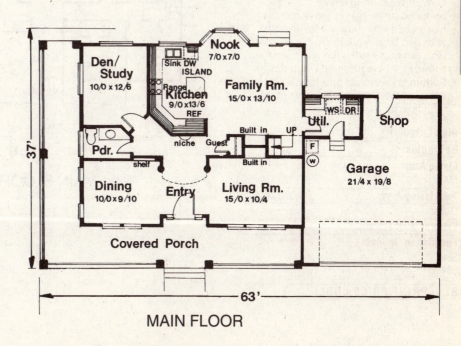

MAIN FLOOR

ORDER BLUEPRINTS ANYTIME!
CALL TOLL-FREE 1-800-820-1296

Plan I-2075-A
Plan copyright held by home designer/architect

PRICES AND DETAILS ON PAGES 12-15

Decorative Distinction

- A wraparound porch gives a decorative country look to this traditional farmhouse, which is designed for distinctive yet practical living.
- Amble through the foyer into the living room, where you'll find the welcoming warmth of a fireplace. Built-in cabinets incorporate a media center. Graceful French doors lead out to a bright, beautiful sun room.
- Enjoy a hearty meal prepared at the kitchen's handy island cooktop and served in either the breakfast area or the adjacent dining room. The kitchen also features a pantry for extra storage and a convenient built-in desk.
- Secluded at the rear of the home, the master bedroom boasts a lavish bath with two large walk-in closets, a dual-sink vanity, a garden tub and a separate shower for ease in starting your day.
- Built-in bookshelves and large closets enhance the two secondary bedrooms, which share a full bath.

Plan L-320-FHB

Bedrooms: 3	Baths: 2
Living Area:	
Main floor	2,320 sq. ft.
Total Living Area:	**2,320 sq. ft.**
Garage	528 sq. ft.
Exterior Wall Framing:	2x4

Foundation Options:
Slab
(All plans can be built with your choice of foundation and framing. A generic conversion diagram is available. See order form.)

BLUEPRINT PRICE CODE: C

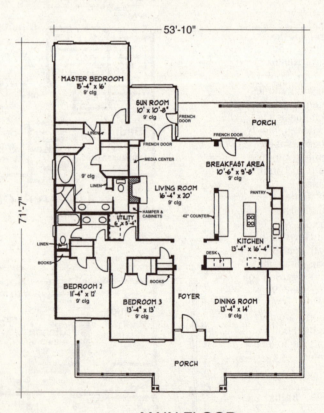

MAIN FLOOR

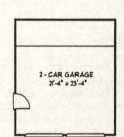

NOSTALGIC FARMHOUSES

152 ORDER BLUEPRINTS ANYTIME! CALL TOLL-FREE 1-800-820-1296

Plan L-320-FHB
Plan copyright held by home designer/architect

PRICES AND DETAILS ON PAGES 12-15

Traditional Two-Story

- This traditional two-story home's facade shows off classic shuttered windows, a roomy wraparound porch and a sidelighted entry.
- At the center of the home, the versatile Great Room lets you entertain many options. Enjoy the fireplace or step past French doors to a back porch. Slip into the breakfast nook for a bite from the snack bar, or step through double doors to an office or home school area.
- To the right of the foyer, the formal dining room nicely hosts elegant events. French doors separate the area from the efficient, U-shaped kitchen.
- The main-floor master suite features a tray ceiling and a private bath with a Jacuzzi tub, dual sinks and a walk-in closet, plus access to the front porch.
- Two bedrooms and a split bath share the upper floor with a spacious rec room and a sitting area.

Plan UD-161-D	
Bedrooms: 3+	Baths: 2½
Living Area:	
Upper floor	843 sq. ft.
Main floor	1,484 sq. ft.
Total Living Area:	**2,327 sq. ft.**
Standard basement	1,484 sq. ft.
Garage and shop/storage	652 sq. ft.
Exterior Wall Framing:	2x4
Foundation Options:	
Standard basement	
Crawlspace	
Slab	
(All plans can be built with your choice of foundation and framing. A generic conversion diagram is available. See order form.)	
BLUEPRINT PRICE CODE:	**C**

UPPER FLOOR

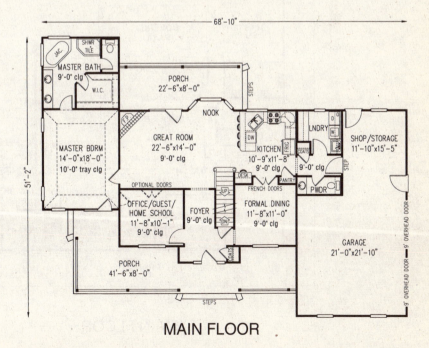

MAIN FLOOR

ORDER BLUEPRINTS ANYTIME!
CALL TOLL-FREE 1-800-820-1296

Plan UD-161-D
Plan copyright held by home designer/architect

PRICES AND DETAILS ON PAGES 12-15

Perfect—Inside and Out

- Charming as can be on the outside, it's the thoughtful interior of this country-style gem that sets it apart from the rest.
- Distinguished by handsome columns, the Great Room truly is the heart of the design. A corner fireplace casts a cozy glow on winter nights. A matching set of French doors leads out to a covered patio for warm-weather fun.
- The kitchen is fronted by a long serving bar for ease in entertaining, and it boasts a walk-in pantry as well. The nearby bayed breakfast nook provides a sunny spot for casual meals.
- A mudroom is handily located near the utility room. An adjacent powder room may serve as a pool bath.
- The formal dining room just off the foyer may be converted into a home office, a bedroom or a hobby room.
- At day's end, relax in the quiet master suite. Two walk-in closets flank the hall to the private bath, which has a garden tub, a separate shower and a dual-sink vanity. French doors open to the patio.
- Two more bedrooms share a split bath featuring a dual-sink vanity.

Plan DD-2436

Bedrooms: 3+	Baths: 2½

Living Area:
Main floor — 2,436 sq. ft.
Total Living Area: **2,436 sq. ft.**
Standard basement — 2,436 sq. ft.
Garage — 478 sq. ft.

Exterior Wall Framing: 2x4

Foundation Options:
Standard basement
Crawlspace
Slab
(All plans can be built with your choice of foundation and framing. A generic conversion diagram is available. See order form.)

BLUEPRINT PRICE CODE: C

MAIN FLOOR

Plan DD-2436
Plan copyright held by home designer/architect

Just Right!

- This home boasts a magnificent vaulted family room. All you need is there: a skylight to make the room sunny and bright, a fireplace for warmth and elegance, and sliding glass doors leading to the backyard.
- With plenty of counter space, a pantry and a convenient central location, the open island kitchen is ideal for even the most discriminating chef.
- A surprisingly spacious laundry room is located just off the garage.
- Upstairs, the deluxe master suite is set off by an angled balcony overlooking the foyer. Double doors lead into the master bedroom, which enjoys a vaulted ceiling and a well-appointed private bath with a garden tub and a dual-sink vanity.
- A large unfinished storage area rounds out the upper-floor design. An alternate upper-floor layout offers a loft or fourth bedroom, as well as an optional alcove above the garage.

Plan AX-98368

Bedrooms: 3+	Baths: 2½
Living Area:	
Upper floor	863/1,198 sq. ft.
Main floor	1,240 sq. ft.
Total Living Area:	**2,103/2,438 sq. ft.**
Standard basement	1,240 sq. ft.
Garage	425 sq. ft.
Exterior Wall Framing:	2x6
Foundation Options:	
Standard basement	
Crawlspace	

(All plans can be built with your choice of foundation and framing. A generic conversion diagram is available. See order form.)

BLUEPRINT PRICE CODE: C

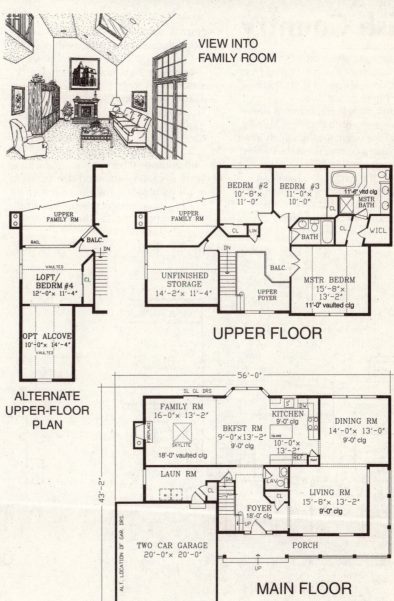

ORDER BLUEPRINTS ANYTIME!
CALL TOLL-FREE 1-800-820-1296

Plan AX-98368
Plan copyright held by home designer/architect

PRICES AND DETAILS ON PAGES 12-15

Stylish Country

- A stylish wraparound porch fronts this symmetrical, country-style home. Three winsome dormers promise great views from the future upper floor.
- In the sidelighted foyer, columns frame the entrances to both the formal dining room and the Great Room, which offers built-ins and a central fireplace flanked by windows.
- Just around the corner, the breakfast nook also enjoys a backyard view. Fronted by a handy bar serving the nook, the kitchen is a true chef's haven.
- A small corridor leads to the generous utility room and a convenient powder room. Garage access makes unloading groceries a snap, and extra storage space hides tools away from view.
- The master suite is so luxurious, it needs its own wing! An extravagant garden tub, an oversized shower and vast walk-in closets in the private bath are truly winning features.
- Two additional bedrooms—one with a walk-in closet—share private access to a full bath with a dual-sink vanity. The entire sleeping wing is separated from the common areas by double doors.

Plan BOD-24-25A

Bedrooms: 3+	Baths: 2½–3½
Living Area:	
Main floor	2,465 sq. ft.
Total Living Area:	**2,465 sq. ft.**
Future upper floor	788 sq. ft.
Garage	512 sq. ft.
Storage	132 sq. ft.
Exterior Wall Framing:	2x4

Foundation Options:
Crawlspace
Slab
(All plans can be built with your choice of foundation and framing. A generic conversion diagram is available. See order form.)

BLUEPRINT PRICE CODE: C

NOSTALGIC FARMHOUSES

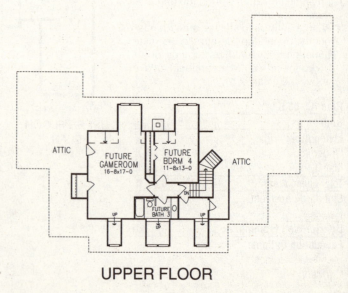

MAIN FLOOR

UPPER FLOOR

Plan BOD-24-25A
Plan copyright held by home designer/architect

Fabulous Family Room

- This traditional home's wide front porch introduces a lovely sidelighted entry.
- Topped by a high ceiling, the airy foyer features inviting French doors that open to a flexible study or parlor.
- The fabulous family room warms all your guests, with sun-splashed windows to the rear and a handsome corner fireplace at the front.
- The well-designed kitchen boasts an island eating bar that services a sunny, bayed breakfast nook.
- For formal affairs, the front-facing dining room sports a built-in china hutch to protect your delicate collectibles.
- Upstairs, the unsurpassed master suite pampers you with a superb private bath. Note the convenient dual-sink vanity, the luxurious corner tub and the roomy walk-in closet.
- Utilize the bonus room as a game room, an office or an extra bedroom.

Plan Y-2197

Bedrooms: 3+	Baths: 2½

Living Area:
Upper floor	1,029 sq. ft.
Main floor	1,168 sq. ft.
Bonus room	358 sq. ft.
Total Living Area:	**2,555 sq. ft.**
Standard basement	1,152 sq. ft.
Garage	572 sq. ft.

Exterior Wall Framing: 2x6

Foundation Options:
Standard basement
Crawlspace
(All plans can be built with your choice of foundation and framing. A generic conversion diagram is available. See order form.)

BLUEPRINT PRICE CODE: D

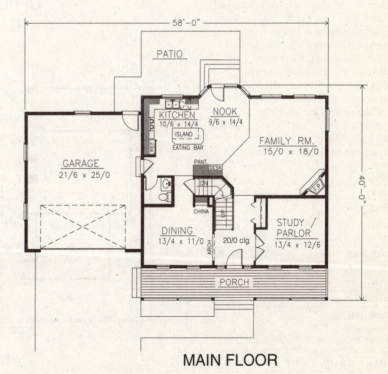

UPPER FLOOR

MAIN FLOOR

ORDER BLUEPRINTS ANYTIME!
CALL TOLL-FREE 1-800-820-1296

Plan Y-2197
Plan copyright held by home designer/architect

PRICES AND DETAILS ON PAGES 12-15

NOSTALGIC FARMHOUSES

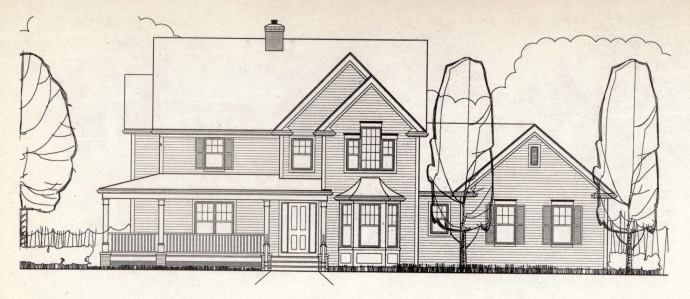

Clever Touches

- Clever touches and a timeless facade add to this home's livability and beauty.
- A wraparound porch adds charming farmhouse appeal, while a bay window and other lovely arrangements add a bit of flair to the home's clean lines.
- Twin closets in the foyer handily store your family's or guests' outerwear. Dual doors lead to a versatile den, which may be used in place of a formal living room. It could also serve as a room for guests when the need arises.
- The formal dining room opens from the foyer and lies near the pantry and a built-in desk. The rest of the kitchen is well planned to serve a bayed breakfast nook and the Great Room, which share a two-sided fireplace. Utility areas, including a laundry room and a half-bath, flank the garage entry.
- Upstairs, all four bedrooms enjoy privacy. The secondary bedrooms boast ample storage and utilize a full hall bath. The master suite includes a cavernous walk-in closet and a spacious private bath. There is even room for a sitting area in this luxurious retreat.

Plan MIN-9751

Bedrooms: 4+	Baths: 2½
Living Area:	
Upper floor	1,262 sq. ft.
Main floor	1,385 sq. ft.
Total Living Area:	**2,647 sq. ft.**
Partial basement	849 sq. ft.
Garage	580 sq. ft.
Exterior Wall Framing:	2x4

Foundation Options:
Partial basement
(All plans can be built with your choice of foundation and framing. A generic conversion diagram is available. See order form.)

BLUEPRINT PRICE CODE: D

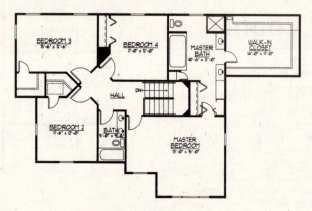

UPPER FLOOR

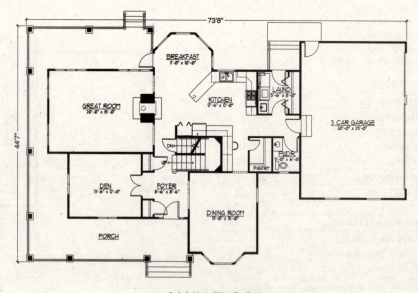

MAIN FLOOR

Plan MIN-9751

A Sure Bet!

- With its wraparound covered porch and repeating gables, this beautiful country home is sure to be noticed.
- The high foyer is flanked by the formal dining room and the gracious living room, where French doors offer expansion to the porch.
- The adjacent family room is enhanced by a soaring ceiling and features a handsome window-flanked fireplace and its own porch access.
- An open rail defines the breakfast nook, which includes a walk-in pantry and a French door to the backyard.
- An angled serving bar highlights the walk-through kitchen. A butler's pantry simplifies serving in the dining room.
- Upstairs, an open-railed balcony bridge overlooks the family room and the foyer. The master bedroom is crowned by a tray ceiling and adjoins an optional sitting room. The private master bath flaunts a vaulted ceiling, a corner garden tub, a separate shower and dual vanities.
- Three additional upper-floor bedrooms share a clever compartmentalized bath.

Plan FB-5102-CARR

Bedrooms: 4	Baths: 2½
Living Area:	
Upper floor	1,257 sq. ft.
Main floor	1,351 sq. ft.
Optional sitting room	115 sq. ft.
Total Living Area:	**2,723 sq. ft.**
Daylight basement	1,351 sq. ft.
Garage and storage	467 sq. ft.
Exterior Wall Framing:	2x4

Foundation Options:
Daylight basement
(All plans can be built with your choice of foundation and framing. A generic conversion diagram is available. See order form.)

BLUEPRINT PRICE CODE: **D**

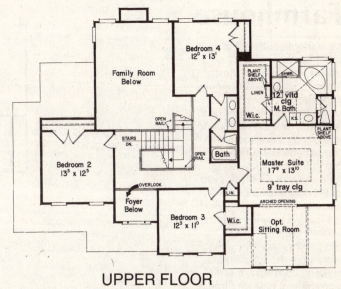

UPPER FLOOR

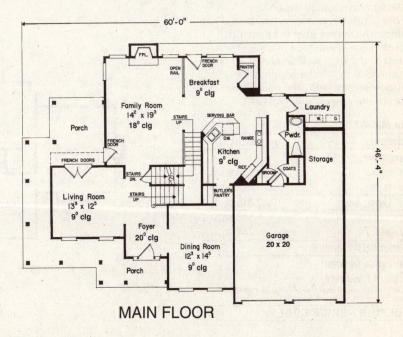

MAIN FLOOR

ORDER BLUEPRINTS ANYTIME!
CALL TOLL-FREE 1-800-820-1296

Plan FB-5102-CARR
Plan copyright held by home designer/architect

PRICES AND DETAILS ON PAGES 12-15

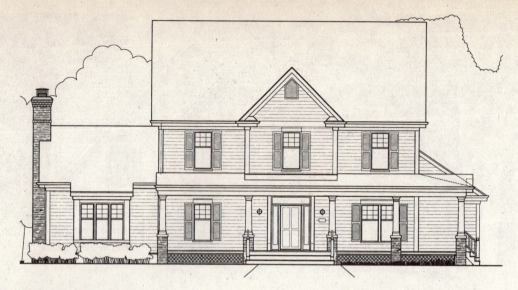

Fine Farmhouse

- Drawing on the simple charm of a traditional farmhouse, this design features plenty of fine touches. Most obvious is a porch, which wraps around two sides of the home.
- From the side porch, double doors open into a formal dining room. A colonnade leads to the adjoining living room—an ideal place for after-dinner coffee.
- Across the broad foyer, a study works well as a home office or a well-stocked library. A pocket door separates the study from the large family room, which is sure to host many a relaxing night of movies and board games.
- A huge step-in pantry graces the dinette, just a step away from the spacious kitchen. The island cooktop is a sure bonus, as is convenient passage through the laundry room to the porch.
- Four bedrooms reside on the upper floor. The master suite is a particularly posh place, featuring a boxed-out sitting area and a large walk-in closet. An oval tub and twin vanities highlight the roomy private bath. The other three bedrooms share a split hall bath.

NOSTALGIC FARMHOUSES

Plan MIN-9739

Bedrooms: 4+	Baths: 2½
Living Area:	
Upper floor	1,236 sq. ft.
Main floor	1,579 sq. ft.
Total Living Area:	**2,815 sq. ft.**
Standard basement	1,518 sq. ft.
Garage	741 sq. ft.
Exterior Wall Framing:	2x4
Foundation Options:	
Standard basement	
(All plans can be built with your choice of foundation and framing. A generic conversion diagram is available. See order form.)	
BLUEPRINT PRICE CODE:	**D**

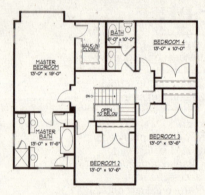

UPPER FLOOR

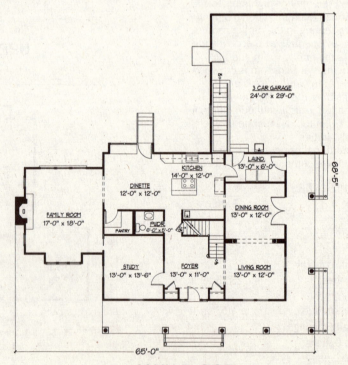

MAIN FLOOR

ORDER BLUEPRINTS ANYTIME!
CALL TOLL-FREE 1-800-820-1296

Plan MIN-9739
Plan copyright held by home designer/architect

PRICES AND DETAILS ON PAGES 12-15

Quite a Pair

- A breezeway connects this home's two structures, which combine to form a unique design and flexible living space.
- A wraparound porch fronts the home. The foyer leads to the formal dining room on the left, which features a tray ceiling and a stunning, arch-topped window. To the right, a quiet library offers built-in bookshelves.
- A fireplace warms the Great Room, which opens to the kitchen. An island provides extra work space and a handy snack bar. Nearby, a built-in desk is the perfect place for the family computer.
- The main-floor master suite boasts a fireplace and a private bath with a whirlpool tub. Upstairs, three bedrooms and a study are serviced by a full bath.
- Above the three-car garage, a versatile studio might be used as a home office, a playroom or a secluded guest quarters.

Plan AHP-9915	
Bedrooms: 4+	**Baths:** 3½
Living Area:	
Upper floor	1,062 sq. ft.
Main floor	1,729 sq. ft.
Studio	315 sq. ft.
Total Living Area:	**3,106 sq. ft.**
Basement	1,729 sq. ft.
Garage	750 sq. ft.
Exterior Wall Framing:	2x4 or 2x6
Foundation Options:	
Daylight basement	
Standard basement	
Crawlspace	
Slab	
(All plans can be built with your choice of foundation and framing. A generic conversion diagram is available. See order form.)	
BLUEPRINT PRICE CODE:	E

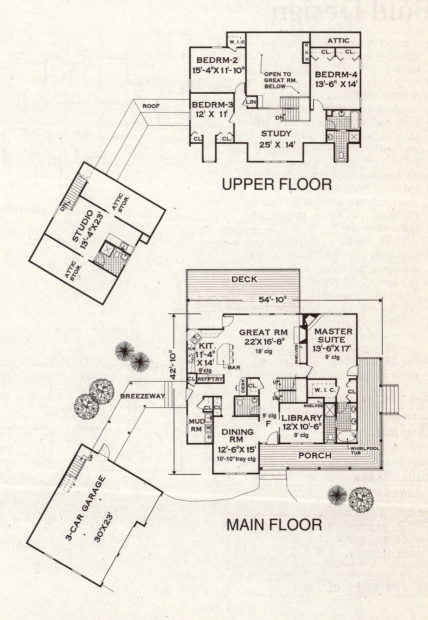

ORDER BLUEPRINTS ANYTIME!
CALL TOLL-FREE 1-800-820-1296

Plan AHP-9915
Plan copyright held by home designer/architect

PRICES AND DETAILS ON PAGES 12-15

Bold Design

- A broad front porch, a wealth of windows and an expansive floor plan speak boldly of this home's design.
- A vaulted entry introduces the formal areas of the home: a living room with a fireplace and a coffered dining room.
- Sunshine filters through skylights into the spacious family room, where built-ins flank the fireplace and sliding glass doors lead onto the rear porch.
- A bayed breakfast nook adjoins the kitchen, which features an island cooktop and a large walk-in pantry.
- The main-floor master suite boasts a coffered ceiling, a bay window, private access to the back porch, a luxurious bath with a garden tub and a separate shower, and a roomy walk-in closet.
- The secluded den is the perfect place to establish a home office.
- Two upper-floor bedrooms with walk-in closets and skylighted vanities share a bath, while a fourth bedroom offers private access to an additional full bath.
- The unfinished bonus room would make a nice guest suite or exercise area.

Plan SUN-3390

Bedrooms: 4+	Baths: 3½

Living Area:
Upper floor	1,197 sq. ft.
Main floor	2,833 sq. ft.
Total Living Area:	**4,030 sq. ft.**
Future area	671 sq. ft.
Garage	1,012 sq. ft.
Exterior Wall Framing:	2x6

Foundation Options:
Crawlspace
(All plans can be built with your choice of foundation and framing. A generic conversion diagram is available. See order form.)

BLUEPRINT PRICE CODE: G

NOSTALGIC FARMHOUSES

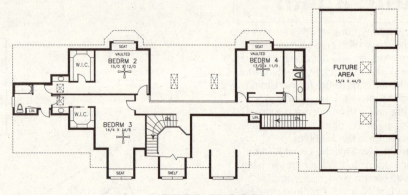

UPPER FLOOR

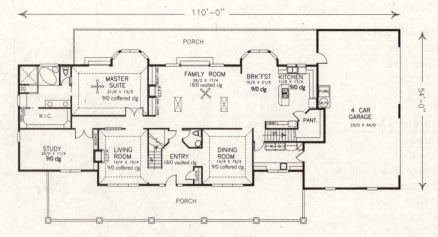

MAIN FLOOR

ORDER BLUEPRINTS ANYTIME!
CALL TOLL-FREE 1-800-820-1296

Plan SUN-3390
Plan copyright held by home designer/architect

PRICES AND DETAILS ON PAGES 12-15

Appealing One-Story

- This appealing one-story design boasts a shady and inviting front porch accented by decorative railings. It's the perfect spot to chat with the neighbors or enjoy an inspiring sunset.
- Inside, a coat closet stands at the ready, while a cathedral ceiling expands the living and dining rooms. This large area is brightened by multiple bay windows and is warmed by a unique two-way fireplace. Sliding glass doors lead to a sunny backyard patio.
- The efficient, U-shaped kitchen includes a pantry closet and plenty of cabinet space. The kitchen is fronted by a serving bar that makes itself available to the adjacent dining room and serves as a great place for light meals, snacks or buffet-style meals.
- The master bedroom boasts abundant closet space, a dressing area lined with mirrors, and a private bath with an oversized shower.
- Two additional bedrooms share another full bath. The front-facing bedroom includes a cozy window seat.

Plan NW-521

Bedrooms: 3	Baths: 2
Living Area:	
Main floor	1,187 sq. ft.
Total Living Area:	**1,187 sq. ft.**
Garage	448 sq. ft.
Exterior Wall Framing:	2x6

Foundation Options:
Crawlspace
(All plans can be built with your choice of foundation and framing. A generic conversion diagram is available. See order form.)

BLUEPRINT PRICE CODE: A

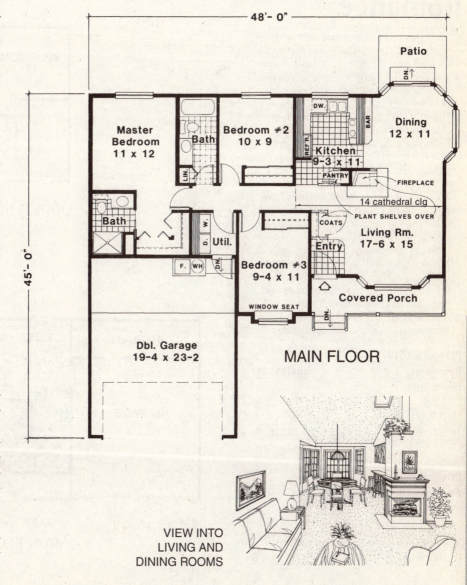

MAIN FLOOR

VIEW INTO LIVING AND DINING ROOMS

ORDER BLUEPRINTS ANYTIME!
CALL TOLL-FREE 1-800-820-1296

Plan NW-521
Plan copyright held by home designer/architect

PRICES AND DETAILS ON PAGES 12-15

GRACEFUL VICTORIANS

A Hint of Romance

- An ornate front porch and a decorative gable with fishscale shingles give this lovely home a romantic Victorian look.
- The central foyer flows to all areas of the home, including the convenient powder room to the left.
- Directly ahead, the airy kitchen features a functional eating bar and a sunny breakfast area with sliding glass doors to a backyard deck. Access to both the garage and a fully appointed laundry room is also a cinch.
- The formal dining room expands into the spacious bayed family room, where a handsome fireplace adds warmth and character to the room.
- Upstairs, the master bedroom boasts a bay window and an optional vaulted ceiling. Two closets and a private bath with a spa tub, a separate shower and twin vanities are also included.
- A second full bath and two more bedrooms complete the upper floor.

Plan APS-1514	
Bedrooms: 3	Baths: 2½
Living Area:	
Upper floor	786 sq. ft.
Main floor	812 sq. ft.
Total Living Area:	**1,598 sq. ft.**
Garage	420 sq. ft.
Storage	140 sq. ft.
Exterior Wall Framing:	2x4
Foundation Options:	
Crawlspace	
Slab	
(All plans can be built with your choice of foundation and framing. A generic conversion diagram is available. See order form.)	
BLUEPRINT PRICE CODE:	**B**

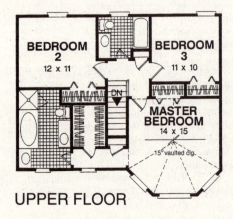

UPPER FLOOR

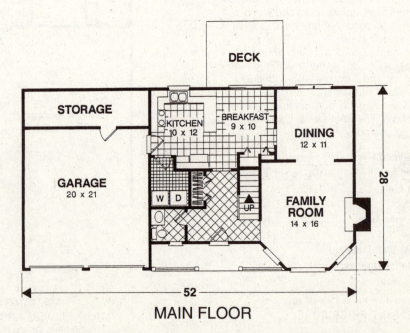

MAIN FLOOR

ORDER BLUEPRINTS ANYTIME!
CALL TOLL-FREE 1-800-820-1296

Plan APS-1514
Plan copyright held by home designer/architect

PRICES AND DETAILS ON PAGES 12-15

Rural Roots

- This nostalgic farmhouse reminds you of country life, bringing back memories or maybe just fond daydreams.
- Authentic Victorian details contribute to the comforting facade. Lovely fishscale shingles above the bay window and oval glass in the front door will command attention from visitors.
- Receive the long-awaited kinfolk on the delightful wraparound porch; you may want to sit a spell and catch up on family news!
- Then usher everyone into the family room, for memorable moments in front of the corner fireplace.
- When the feast is ready, eyes will sparkle as the turkey is presented in the bay-windowed dining room. A French door leads to the back porch for after-dinner chatting in the cool evening.
- The efficient kitchen handles meal preparation with ease. The "east" wall features a pantry and double ovens.
- The secluded master suite lets you unwind before a good night's rest. A fabulous bath and direct porch access make this suite really sweet!
- Two secondary bedrooms share a split bath. The bayed front bedroom boasts a raised ceiling and a walk-in closet.
- The blueprints include plans for a detached, two-car garage (not shown).

Plan L-1772	
Bedrooms: 3	Baths: 2
Living Area	
Main floor	1,772 sq. ft.
Total Living Area:	**1,772 sq. ft.**
Detached garage	576 sq. ft.
Exterior Wall Framing:	2x4
Foundation Options:	
Slab	

(All plans can be built with your choice of foundation and framing. A generic conversion diagram is available. See order form.)

BLUEPRINT PRICE CODE: B

VIEW INTO FAMILY ROOM

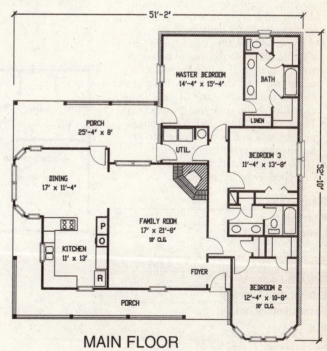

MAIN FLOOR

ORDER BLUEPRINTS ANYTIME!
CALL TOLL-FREE 1-800-820-1296

Plan L-1772
Plan copyright held by home designer/architect

PRICES AND DETAILS ON PAGES 12-15

GRACEFUL VICTORIANS

Details, Details!

- The wonderful Victorian details in this lovely one-story home create a stylish, yet practical, charm.
- Fishscale shingles, a railed wraparound porch and dual bay windows highlight the inviting exterior. You'll be tempted to stretch a hammock and spend the weekend relaxing on the cozy porch.
- Inside, the immense living room features a huge brick hearth and built-in book shelves. Three large windows in front help to bring in the warmth of the sun.
- The galley-style kitchen comes equipped with a large walk-in pantry and enough conveniences to make gourmet meals a breeze. The bayed dining room provides a sparkling setting for those culinary delights.
- A lavish bath awaits as just one of the alluring details in the master bedroom suite. A cathedral ceiling adds drama, while two walk-in closets, twin vanities, built-in bookshelves and its own linen closet make the suite smartly functional.
- Two more bedrooms, each with ample closet space and one with a gorgeous bay window, complete the design.
- The blueprints include plans for a detached, two-car garage.

Plan L-1659	
Bedrooms: 3	**Baths:** 2
Living Area:	
Main floor	1,659 sq. ft.
Total Living Area:	**1,659 sq. ft.**
Detached garage	576 sq. ft.
Exterior Wall Framing:	2x4
Foundation Options:	
Slab	
(All plans can be built with your choice of foundation and framing. A generic conversion diagram is available. See order form.)	
BLUEPRINT PRICE CODE:	B

GRACEFUL VICTORIANS

VIEW INTO LIVING ROOM

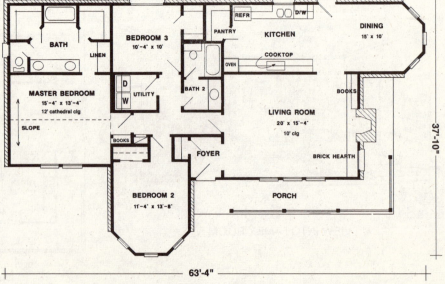

MAIN FLOOR

Plan L-1659
Plan copyright held by home designer/architect

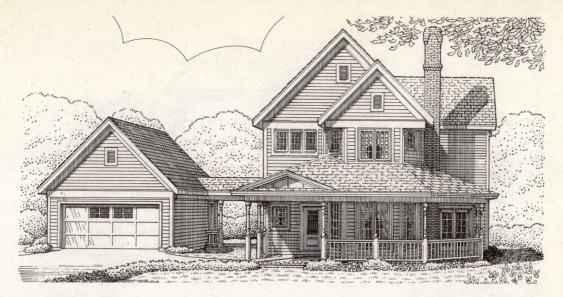

The Good Life

- The good life beckons from the rustic wraparound veranda of this charming farmhouse design.
- Inside, the living room features a cozy fireplace, a media center and a huge bay looking out to the veranda.
- Just past the living room, the dining room offers access to the veranda through a lovely set of French doors.
- A corner snack bar serving both the living and dining rooms highlights the galley kitchen.
- The main-floor master suite boasts a luxurious private bath with a corner garden tub and a separate shower, dual sinks, a private toilet and a spacious walk-in closet.
- Upstairs, two secondary bedrooms share a full hall bath. One flaunts a gorgeous bay while the other enjoys a walk-in closet.
- The upper floor also includes a storage closet, built-in bookshelves and French doors to a wonderful sun room reminiscent of a turn-of-the-century sleeping porch. Soak up the rays in this resplendent retreat.

Plan L-830-VACA

Bedrooms: 3+	Baths: 2½

Living Area:

Upper floor	578 sq. ft.
Main floor	1,141 sq. ft.
Sun room	78 sq. ft.
Storage	35 sq. ft.
Total Living Area:	**1,832 sq. ft.**
Garage	480 sq. ft.
Exterior Wall Framing:	2x4

Foundation Options:
Slab
(All plans can be built with your choice of foundation and framing. A generic conversion diagram is available. See order form.)

BLUEPRINT PRICE CODE: B

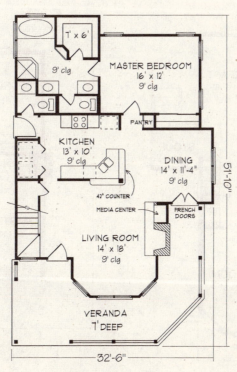

MAIN FLOOR

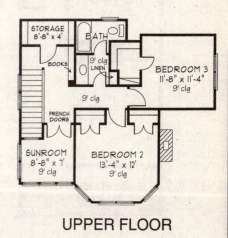

UPPER FLOOR

ORDER BLUEPRINTS ANYTIME! CALL TOLL-FREE 1-800-820-1296

Plan L-830-VACA
Plan copyright held by home designer/architect

PRICES AND DETAILS ON PAGES 12-15

GRACEFUL VICTORIANS

Affordable Victorian

- This compact Victorian design incorporates four bedrooms and three full baths into an attractive, affordable home that's only 30 ft. wide.
- Just in from the covered front porch, family members and guests will gather in the spacious parlor to relax in front of the soothing fireplace. A beautiful bay window adds cheer and elegance to the formal dining room nearby.
- The galley-style kitchen offers efficient service to the breakfast nook. A laundry closet and a pantry are nearby.
- The main-floor bedroom makes a great office or guest bedroom, with a convenient full bath nearby.
- Upstairs, the master suite features an adjoining sitting room with a cathedral ceiling. The luxurious master bath includes a dual-sink vanity and a whirlpool tub with a shower. Two more bedrooms share another bath.
- An attached two-car garage off the kitchen is available upon request.

Plan C-8347-A

Bedrooms: 3+	Baths: 3
Living Area:	
Upper floor	783 sq. ft.
Main floor	954 sq. ft.
Total Living Area:	**1,737 sq. ft.**
Exterior Wall Framing:	2x4

Foundation Options:
Crawlspace
Slab
(All plans can be built with your choice of foundation and framing. A generic conversion diagram is available. See order form.)

BLUEPRINT PRICE CODE: B

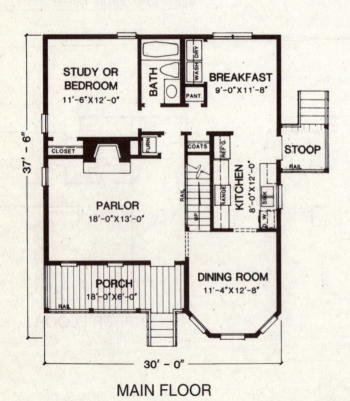

MAIN FLOOR

UPPER FLOOR

Plan C-8347-A
Plan copyright held by home designer/architect

ORDER BLUEPRINTS ANYTIME! CALL TOLL-FREE 1-800-820-1296

PRICES AND DETAILS ON PAGES 12-15

Quite a Cottage

- This cottage's inviting wraparound veranda is topped by an eye-catching metal roof that will draw admiring gazes from neighbors out for a stroll.
- Inside, the raised foyer ushers guests into your home in style. Straight ahead, built-in bookshelves line one wall in the living room, creating a look reminiscent of an old-fashioned library. A neat pass-through to the wet bar in the kitchen saves trips back and forth when you entertain friends.
- The family chef will love the gourmet kitchen, where an island cooktop frees counter space for other projects. For morning coffee and casual meals, the breakfast nook sets a cheery, relaxed tone. When appearances count, move out to the formal dining room.
- Across the home, the master suite serves as an oasis of peace and quiet. First thing in the morning, step out to the veranda to watch the rising sun soak up the mist. When you want a little extra special treatment, sink into the oversized garden tub for a long bath.
- The foremost bedroom boasts a large walk-in closet and built-in bookshelves for the student of the house.

Plan L-893-VSA

Bedrooms: 3	Baths: 2
Living Area:	
Main floor	1,891 sq. ft.
Total Living Area:	**1,891 sq. ft.**
Exterior Wall Framing:	2x4

Foundation Options:
Slab
(All plans can be built with your choice of foundation and framing. A generic conversion diagram is available. See order form.)

BLUEPRINT PRICE CODE: B

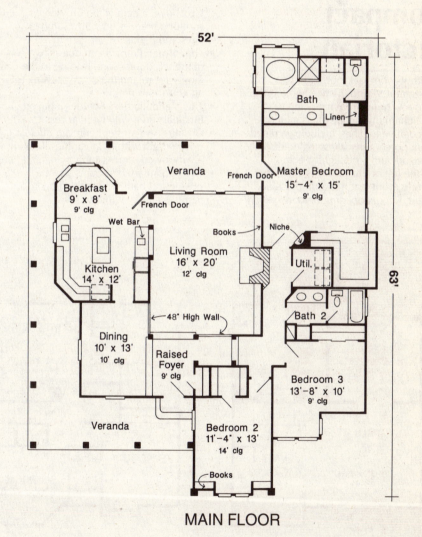

MAIN FLOOR

ORDER BLUEPRINTS ANYTIME!
CALL TOLL-FREE 1-800-820-1296

Plan L-893-VSA
Plan copyright held by home designer/architect

PRICES AND DETAILS ON PAGES 12-15

Compact Victorian

- With its compact footprint, this delightful Victorian-style home is the perfect choice for narrow lots.
- The charming facade offers multiple decorative touches, including a railed front porch, fishscale shingles, delicate fretwork and a sidelighted entry.
- To the left of the spacious entry, the family room features a fireplace and French doors opening onto the porch. Up above, a ceiling fan provides soothing breezes on warm summer days and nights.
- The formal dining room boasts two sets of French doors—one leading to the family room and the other opening to an enormous rear deck.
- The island kitchen includes a bayed breakfast area with deck access.
- Upstairs, the master bedroom offers a private bath with twin vanities flanking a windowed, corner tub.
- Two secondary bedrooms share a private full bath. The second bedroom features a cozy window seat.

Plan APS-1912

Bedrooms: 3	Baths: 2½
Living Area:	
Upper floor	976 sq. ft.
Main floor	1,009 sq. ft.
Total Living Area:	**1,985 sq. ft.**
Partial daylight basement	474 sq. ft.
Exterior Wall Framing:	2x4

Foundation Options:
Partial daylight basement
(All plans can be built with your choice of foundation and framing. A generic conversion diagram is available. See order form.)

BLUEPRINT PRICE CODE: B

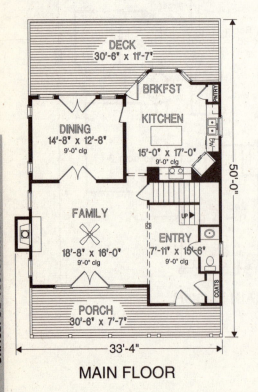

MAIN FLOOR

UPPER FLOOR

VIEW INTO KITCHEN

Plan APS-1912
Plan copyright held by home designer/architect

Some Romantic Feeling

- Seemingly saved from some romantic era, this picturesque Victorian-style home will capture your heart.
- You can spend almost the entire day outside if you want; a great wraparound veranda in front and a covered porch in back are nice spots to while away a sunny day.
- Indoors, the family room offers an incredible amount of space, highlighted by a huge bay window and a heartwarming fireplace.
- Gourmets will appreciate the ambience of the formal dining room, while casual meals in the breakfast room are sparked by the bright bay window.
- Upstairs, the deluxe master suite handles you with care. A bayed sitting area, a skylighted private bath and an L-shaped walk-in closet ensure the peacefulness of this gorgeous retreat.
- Included in the blueprints is an optional attached garage off the utility room.

Plan L-2066

Bedrooms: 3	Baths: 2½
Living Area:	
Upper floor	1,069 sq. ft.
Main floor	997 sq. ft.
Total Living Area:	**2,066 sq. ft.**
Optional attached garage	506 sq. ft.
Exterior Wall Framing:	2x4

Foundation Options:
Slab
(All plans can be built with your choice of foundation and framing. A generic conversion diagram is available. See order form.)

BLUEPRINT PRICE CODE: C

UPPER FLOOR

MAIN FLOOR

ORDER BLUEPRINTS ANYTIME!
CALL TOLL-FREE 1-800-820-1296

Plan L-2066
Plan copyright held by home designer/architect

PRICES AND DETAILS ON PAGES 12-15

GRACEFUL VICTORIANS

Regal Namesake

- Fanciful spindlework at the wraparound veranda, an elaborate Palladian window and octagon-shaped turrets with leaded-glass transom windows capture the essence of the Queen Anne style.
- A gorgeous bay window brightens the living room. Nearby, a handsome fireplace casts a warm glow that invites you to settle in on long winter nights.
- Two handy serving bars flank the entrance to the efficient kitchen.
- The screened porch is the perfect spot for relaxing on a lovely spring day.
- The master bedroom boasts French doors that open to a rear veranda. A spectacular private bath is highlighted by a raised Jacuzzi tub set into an octagonal alcove.
- Upstairs, French doors open to a game room. Two secondary bedrooms, each with its own walk-in closet, share a split bath that includes twin vanities.
- Plans for a two-car detached garage are included in the blueprints.

Plan L-73-VB

Bedrooms: 3+	Baths: 2½
Living Area:	
Upper floor	835 sq. ft.
Main floor	1,236 sq. ft.
Total Living Area:	**2,071 sq. ft.**
Screened porch	171 sq. ft.
Detached garage	576 sq. ft.
Exterior Wall Framing:	2x4
Foundation Options:	
Slab	

(All plans can be built with your choice of foundation and framing. A generic conversion diagram is available. See order form.)

BLUEPRINT PRICE CODE: C

REAR VIEW

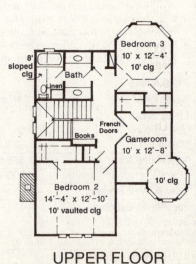

MAIN FLOOR

UPPER FLOOR

GRACEFUL VICTORIANS

ORDER BLUEPRINTS ANYTIME! CALL TOLL-FREE 1-800-820-1296

Plan L-73-VB
Plan copyright held by home designer/architect

PRICES AND DETAILS ON PAGES 12-15

Panoramic Porch

- A gracious, ornately rounded front porch and a two-story turreted bay lend Victorian charm to this home.
- A two-story foyer with round-top transom windows and a plant ledge above greets guests at the entry.
- The living room enjoys a high ceiling and a panoramic view.
- The formal dining room and den each feature a bay window for added style.
- The sunny kitchen incorporates an angled island cooktop with an eating bar to the bayed breakfast room.
- A step down, the family room offers a corner fireplace that may be enjoyed throughout the casual living spaces.
- The upper floor is highlighted by a stunning master suite, which flaunts an octagonal sitting area with a high, tray ceiling and turreted bay. The master bath offers a corner spa tub.

Plan AX-90307

Bedrooms: 3+	Baths: 3
Living Area:	
Upper floor	956 sq. ft.
Main floor	1,499 sq. ft.
Total Living Area:	**2,455 sq. ft.**
Standard basement	1,499 sq. ft.
Garage and storage	469 sq. ft.
Utility room	38 sq. ft.
Exterior Wall Framing:	2x4

Foundation Options:
Standard basement
Crawlspace
Slab
(All plans can be built with your choice of foundation and framing. A generic conversion diagram is available. See order form.)

BLUEPRINT PRICE CODE: C

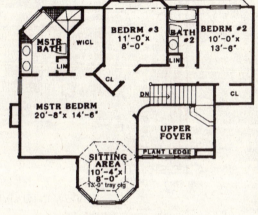

UPPER FLOOR

VIEW INTO LIVING ROOM

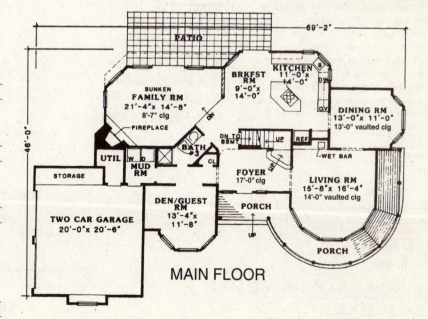

MAIN FLOOR

ORDER BLUEPRINTS ANYTIME!
CALL TOLL-FREE 1-800-820-1296

Plan AX-90307
Plan copyright held by home designer/architect

PRICES AND DETAILS ON PAGES 12-15

Peaceful Days

- This beautiful home's wraparound veranda and adjacent piazza recall the peaceful days of the past when friends spent restful afternoons mingling at pretty garden parties.
- Inside, a series of handsome columns creates a dignified gallery that ushers guests into the living and dining rooms. When appearances count, serve dinner in the dining room. Afterwards, step out to the piazza for a breath of night air.
- Day to day, the kitchen and breakfast nook will bustle with activity. Perfect for family meals, the nook is also a great spot for a student to do homework under the watchful eye of a parent in the kitchen. Nearby access to the garage saves steps when unloading groceries.
- In the master suite, a number of perks provide special treatment for the home owners. Access to the veranda offers a romantic escape, while a Jacuzzi tub in the bath pampers a weary spirit.
- Upstairs, all three bedrooms include sizable walk-in closets. The front-facing bedroom also boasts a soaring vaulted ceiling and a separate vanity. A laundry chute helps keep kids' bedrooms neat.

VIEW INTO LIVING ROOM

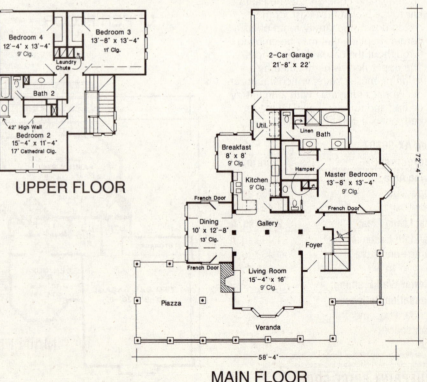

UPPER FLOOR

MAIN FLOOR

Plan L-215-VSB	
Bedrooms: 4	**Baths:** 2½
Living Area:	
Upper floor	862 sq. ft.
Main floor	1,351 sq. ft.
Total Living Area:	**2,213 sq. ft.**
Garage	477 sq. ft.
Exterior Wall Framing:	2x4
Foundation Options:	
Slab	
(All plans can be built with your choice of foundation and framing. A generic conversion diagram is available. See order form.)	
BLUEPRINT PRICE CODE:	**C**

Plan L-215-VSB
Plan copyright held by home designer/architect

Poised and Pure

- This pure country-style home stands poised with plenty of eye-catching features to grab your attention.
- Relaxation is the rule on the railed veranda in front; on starry summer nights it's the perfect place to cuddle up with your loved ones.
- From the raised foyer you can step down to the living room or dining room. The living room features a cozy boxed-out window and a pleasant fireplace to cheer up the large space.
- The dining room also contains a boxed-out window, and is just a step from the island kitchen, which helps to make serving and cleaning up meals fast and easy.
- Sunshine pours into the corner breakfast nook via two walls of windows. Sit down and enjoy the great views or step outside via a handy French door.
- French doors are also a key feature in the beautiful master suite—they invite you to a private patio. Other highlights include a huge bath and an equally spacious walk-in closet.
- Two more bedrooms complete the main floor. A large game room upstairs converts easily to a fourth bedroom.

Plan L-284-VB	
Bedrooms: 3+	**Baths:** 3
Living Area:	
Upper floor	445 sq. ft.
Main floor	1,837 sq. ft.
Total Living Area:	**2,282 sq. ft.**
Exterior Wall Framing:	2x4

Foundation Options:
Slab
(All plans can be built with your choice of foundation and framing. A generic conversion diagram is available. See order form.)

BLUEPRINT PRICE CODE: C

UPPER FLOOR

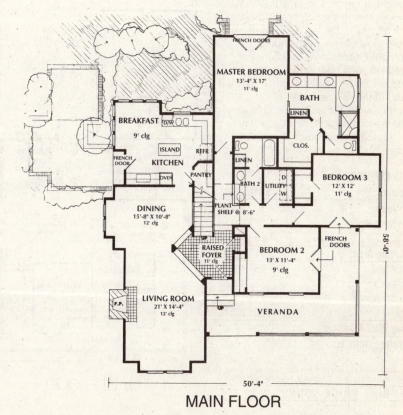

MAIN FLOOR

ORDER BLUEPRINTS ANYTIME!
CALL TOLL-FREE 1-800-820-1296

Plan L-284-VB
Plan copyright held by home designer/architect

PRICES AND DETAILS ON PAGES 12-15

Victorian Flair

- A wraparound veranda and an octagonal turret lend a Victorian air to this splendid home.
- Pocket doors lead from the foyer to the study, which is lined with bookshelves and brightened by a bay window.
- Imagine a crackling fire in the living room. During warmer months, step out to the veranda or the rear screened porch through beautiful French doors.
- The kitchen and adjoining breakfast nook are warmed by a cozy fireplace.
- Thoughtful touches abound upstairs: a window seat in the balcony, a private deck off one of the bedrooms and ample closet space throughout.
- A romantic sitting area in the master suite features a high ceiling and windows on four sides. Further luxury is found in the private bath.
- The blueprints include plans for a third-floor exercise loft off the master bath and a handy home office above the garage.

Plan L-438-VSB

Bedrooms: 3+	Baths: 2½
Living Area:	
Upper floor	1,079 sq. ft.
Main floor	1,233 sq. ft.
Total Living Area:	**2,312 sq. ft.**
Exercise loft	167 sq. ft.
Office/storage	228 sq. ft.
Screened porch	124 sq. ft.
Garage	503 sq. ft.
Exterior Wall Framing:	2x4
Foundation Options:	
Slab	

(All plans can be built with your choice of foundation and framing. A generic conversion diagram is available. See order form.)

BLUEPRINT PRICE CODE: C

GRACEFUL VICTORIANS

REAR VIEW

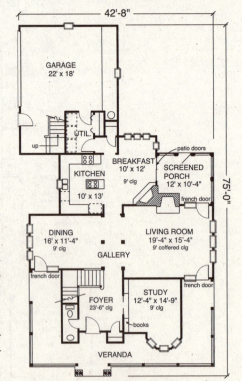

MAIN FLOOR

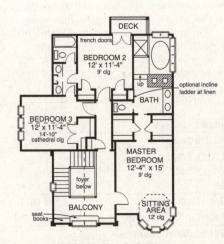

UPPER FLOOR

ORDER BLUEPRINTS ANYTIME!
CALL TOLL-FREE 1-800-820-1296

Plan L-438-VSB
Plan copyright held by home designer/architect

PRICES AND DETAILS ON PAGES 12-15

Alluring Look

- A nostalgic wraparound porch and a plethora of windows are a preview of this home's alluring features.
- A cathedral ceiling lends a dramatic touch to the foyer, which opens to the impressive living room. A bay window looking out to the front porch fills this room with natural light. Flowing easily into the formal dining room, this area is ideal for entertaining. A lovely French door leads to the front porch.
- With views of the backyard and high ceilings throughout, the spacious family room, the sunny breakfast room and the convenient island kitchen blend together to create an incomparably relaxed space for you and your family.
- The upper-floor master bedroom enjoys a bay window, two walk-in closets and a private bath with a dual-sink vanity and a corner garden tub. What a perfect retreat at day's end!
- Two more bedrooms share a full hall bath, while a loft at the end of the hallway could easily be used as a fourth bedroom. You may also decide to create a game room or a playroom from this ample space.

Plan AX-00307	
Bedrooms: 3+	**Baths:** 2½
Living Area:	
Upper floor	1,258 sq. ft.
Main floor	1,551 sq. ft.
Total Living Area:	**2,809 sq. ft.**
Standard basement	1,551 sq. ft.
Garage	494 sq. ft.
Exterior Wall Framing:	2x4
Foundation Options:	
Standard basement	
Crawlspace	

(All plans can be built with your choice of foundation and framing. A generic conversion diagram is available. See order form.)

BLUEPRINT PRICE CODE: D

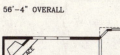

REAR VIEW

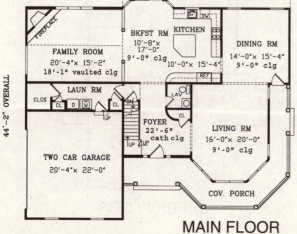

MAIN FLOOR

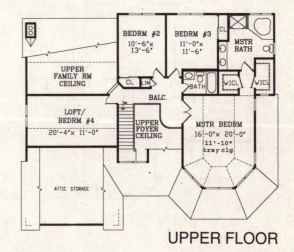

UPPER FLOOR

ORDER BLUEPRINTS ANYTIME!
CALL TOLL-FREE 1-800-820-1296

Plan AX-00307
Plan copyright held by home designer/architect

PRICES AND DETAILS
ON PAGES 12-15

Victorian Romance

- If the romance of Victorian-style living is in your blood, consider life in this charming two-story.
- Delightful exterior features, including diamond-cut cedar shingles, metal roof accents, decorative fretwork and a nifty arbor, lend character to any boulevard.
- Inside, large and comfortable living spaces radiate from a central stairway. Rich hardwood floors sweep across the foyer, living room, dining room and study, which is accessible through two sets of French doors.
- A room you'll always cherish, the study features 30-in.-high bookcases that create functional wraparound seating.
- The big kitchen offers a convenient serving counter to the family room.
- Upstairs, four generous-sized bedrooms are arranged for ultimate privacy; each includes a walk-in closet and direct access to one of three baths. The bayed master bath boasts two pedestal sinks.
- Note the bright alcove extending from the bedroom immediately off the stairs.

Plan L-774-VSB	
Bedrooms: 4+	**Baths:** 3½
Living Area:	
Upper floor	1,418 sq. ft.
Main floor	1,354 sq. ft.
Total Living Area:	**2,772 sq. ft.**
Garage and storage	499 sq. ft.
Exterior Wall Framing:	2x4
Foundation Options:	
Slab	

(All plans can be built with your choice of foundation and framing. A generic conversion diagram is available. See order form.)

BLUEPRINT PRICE CODE: D

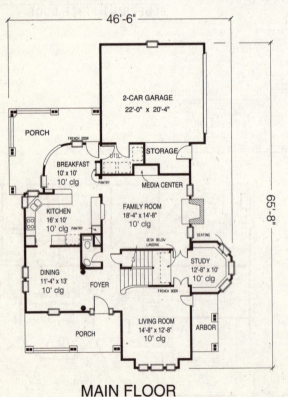

MAIN FLOOR

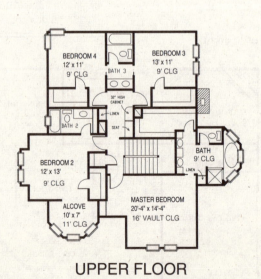

UPPER FLOOR

Plan L-774-VSB
Plan copyright held by home designer/architect

ORDER BLUEPRINTS ANYTIME!
CALL TOLL-FREE 1-800-820-1296

PRICES AND DETAILS ON PAGES 12-15

Vivacious Victorian

- The facade of this classic Victorian home is enhanced by a covered veranda bordering three sides.
- Inside, the modern interior begins with an airy two-story foyer that flows directly into a cozy bayed parlor.
- Past a bright window wall and a door to the side yard, the bay-windowed formal dining room boasts a wonderful built-in china hutch.
- Behind bifold doors, the island kitchen sports a nifty built-in desk and a cheery bayed morning room with speedy access to the veranda.
- Beautiful views are also offered from the family room, which flaunts a handsome fireplace, a wet bar and a wine rack.
- French doors access a bayed study that may be used as an extra bedroom.
- At the top of the angled staircase, three secondary bedrooms promise plenty of private space for everyone in your family. A compartmentalized bath and a laundry room are nearby.
- At the end of the hall, the master bedroom features a long, private deck. The gorgeous master bath offers a stunning, bay-windowed bathing area.

Plan L-3163	
Bedrooms: 4+	**Baths:** 2½
Living Area:	
Upper floor	1,598 sq. ft.
Main floor	1,565 sq. ft.
Total Living Area:	**3,163 sq. ft.**
Detached garage	576 sq. ft.
Exterior Wall Framing:	2x4

Foundation Options:
Slab
(All plans can be built with your choice of foundation and framing. A generic conversion diagram is available. See order form.)

BLUEPRINT PRICE CODE: E

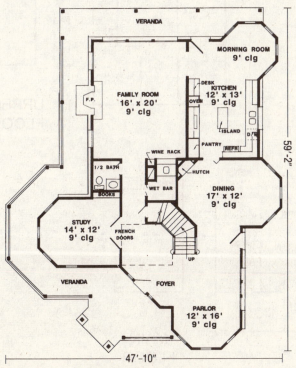

MAIN FLOOR

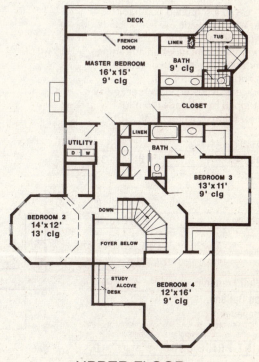

UPPER FLOOR

ORDER BLUEPRINTS ANYTIME!
CALL TOLL-FREE 1-800-820-1296

Plan L-3163
Plan copyright held by home designer/architect

PRICES AND DETAILS ON PAGES 12-15

Warm Family Memories

- This inviting four-bedroom design will provide your family with lots of room to breathe. The wraparound porch heightens the home's traditional feel.
- On cold winter nights, memories will be made around the fireplace in the family room. During warm weather you can move the events to the backyard deck.
- The foyer and family room feature impressive vaulted ceilings.
- You'll love the spacious kitchen with its central island and snack counter. The breakfast area features a handy pantry and access to a screened porch for summer meals outside.
- Enjoy your privacy in the master bedroom, which includes an adjoining bath with double sinks, two walk-in closets and a whirlpool tub.
- The garage is accessed via a breezeway and is topped by a bonus room for storage or future development.

REAR VIEW

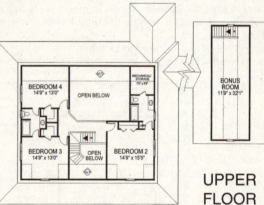

UPPER FLOOR

Plan APS-2913	
Bedrooms: 4	**Baths:** 3½
Living Area:	
Upper floor	986 sq. ft.
Main floor	1,986 sq. ft.
Total Living Area:	**2,972 sq. ft.**
Bonus room	396 sq. ft.
Daylight basement	1,986 sq. ft.
Garage	799 sq. ft.
Exterior Wall Framing:	2x4
Foundation Options:	
Daylight basement	
(All plans can be built with your choice of foundation and framing. A generic conversion diagram is available. See order form.)	
BLUEPRINT PRICE CODE:	**D**

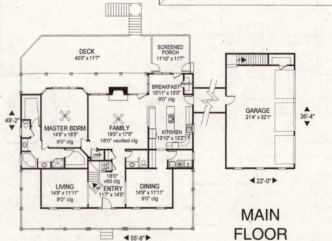

MAIN FLOOR

Plan APS-2913
Plan copyright held by home designer/architect

Very Victorian

- Distinctive characteristics reminiscent of the Queen Anne era are evident in this home's exterior: a rounded tower, a curved wraparound veranda and steeply pitched intersecting rooflines.
- Front doors of leaded glass open to a grand foyer with an elegant stairway and overlooking balcony. Beautiful and durable hardwood floors extend throughout the main floor.
- The spacious living room's circular sitting area has panoramic views of the veranda, which is arrived at through French doors. Pedestal columns set off the adjoining formal dining room.
- With a warm fireplace, a media center, a wet bar and twin serving counters, the family room, breakfast and kitchen areas lavishly fulfill your casual entertaining needs.
- Among the four upper-floor bedrooms is a romantic master suite with a private sitting area, balcony and skylighted bath; space for a sauna and an optional exercise loft atop a spiral stairway is also available.
- Each of the secondary bedrooms has a walk-in closet and its own bath.

Plan L-437-VSC

Bedrooms: 4	Baths: 4½
Living Area:	
Upper floor	1,818 sq. ft.
Main floor	1,617 sq. ft.
Total Living Area:	**3,435 sq. ft.**
Garage and storage	638 sq. ft.
Exterior Wall Framing:	2x4

Foundation Options:
Slab
(All plans can be built with your choice of foundation and framing. A generic conversion diagram is available. See order form.)

BLUEPRINT PRICE CODE: E

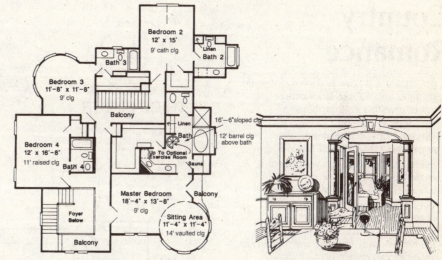

UPPER FLOOR

VIEW INTO DINING ROOM AND LIVING ROOM BEYOND

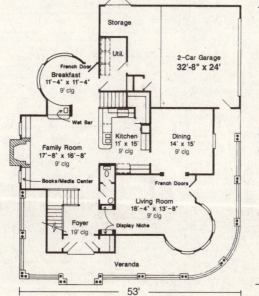

MAIN FLOOR

ORDER BLUEPRINTS ANYTIME!
CALL TOLL-FREE 1-800-820-1296

Plan L-437-VSC
Plan copyright held by home designer/architect

PRICES AND DETAILS ON PAGES 12–15

Country Romance

- A wraparound covered porch, fishscale shingles and a three-story octagonal tower give this country home a wonderfully romantic presence.
- The interior is dominated by the enormous Great Room. All your special events will naturally gravitate to this remarkably spacious spot.
- If your party gets too big for even the Great Room, take it outside to an equally huge backyard deck.
- Highlighted by a sizable pantry, the kitchen is ready for anything the family gourmet can dream up.
- The generous study makes a pleasant spare bedroom when needed.
- The elegant master suite boasts a walk-in closet, a private deck and lots of interesting nooks and crannies.
- Two additional bedrooms and a recreation loft are on the upper floor.
- The library inhabits the third floor. Indulge yourself and turn it into your very own writing loft.

Plan SUN-2580

Bedrooms: 3+	Baths: 3
Living Area:	
Third floor	268 sq. ft.
Second floor	828 sq. ft.
Main floor	2,022 sq. ft.
Total Living Area:	**3,118 sq. ft.**
Exterior Wall Framing:	2x6

Foundation Options:
Crawlspace
Slab
(All plans can be built with your choice of foundation and framing. A generic conversion diagram is available. See order form.)

BLUEPRINT PRICE CODE: E

THIRD FLOOR

REAR VIEW

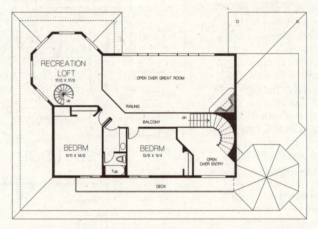
SECOND FLOOR

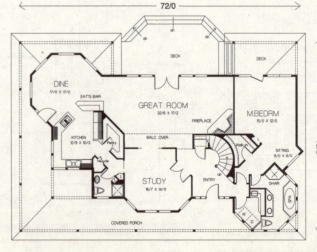
MAIN FLOOR

GRACEFUL VICTORIANS

ORDER BLUEPRINTS ANYTIME!
CALL TOLL-FREE 1-800-820-1296

Plan SUN-2580
Plan copyright held by home designer/architect

PRICES AND DETAILS ON PAGES 12-15

Absolute Luxury

- This home's folksy, Victorian facade conceals absolute luxury within.
- A metal-roofed front porch introduces the sidelighted foyer. The foyer spills into the living room, which expands past columned half-walls to the bayed formal dining room.
- A few steps away, the island kitchen flaunts an angled serving bar that interacts with the family room and a cute breakfast nook.
- The family room's fireplace spreads warmth throughout the home. French doors open to a study with built-in shelves and cabinets.
- In the breakfast nook, French doors open to the backyard. A sunken media room promises raucous fun, while a hobby room offers solitude.
- Upstairs, the posh master bedroom has a central fireplace, built-in cabinets, a coffered ceiling and French doors to a private deck.
- The master bath enjoys a Jacuzzi tub beneath a gazebo ceiling, and an exciting exercise room.
- Three more bedrooms boast private access to two full baths.

Plan L-841-VSC	
Bedrooms: 4+	**Baths:** 3½
Living Area:	
Upper floor	1,891 sq. ft.
Main floor	1,948 sq. ft.
Total Living Area:	**3,839 sq. ft.**
Garage and storage	600 sq. ft.
Exterior Wall Framing:	2x4

Foundation Options:
Slab
(All plans can be built with your choice of foundation and framing. A generic conversion diagram is available. See order form.)

BLUEPRINT PRICE CODE: F

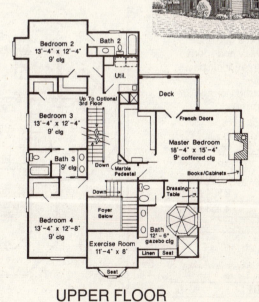

REAR VIEW

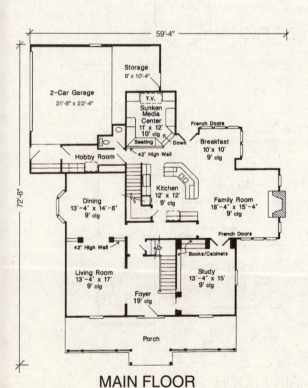

MAIN FLOOR

UPPER FLOOR

ORDER BLUEPRINTS ANYTIME!
CALL TOLL-FREE 1-800-820-1296

Plan L-841-VSC
Plan copyright held by home designer/architect

PRICES AND DETAILS ON PAGES 12-15

GRACEFUL VICTORIANS

Rambling Comfort

- Comfort rambles throughout this big, beautiful traditional home.
- Beyond a wraparound veranda and an ornate entrance, sprawling living spaces parade along the main floor.
- At the center, an expansive living room welcomes guests with its handsome fireplace, built-in entertainment center and sweeping views of the outdoors.
- With abundant counter space, a built-in desk and a walk-in pantry, the kitchen accommodates all of your storage needs—and then some.
- A hobby room and a study add function and versatility to the home.
- The master suite is enveloped in luxury with its romantic sitting area, fireplace, private garden bath and sauna!
- Three large upstairs bedrooms, each with a walk-in closet and a personal dressing area, offer privacy and room for growth. Exciting recreational spaces fulfill your leisure time.
- Plans for a two-car detached garage are included with the blueprints.

Plan L-4053-VC

Bedrooms: 4+	Baths: 3½
Living Area:	
Upper floor	1,529 sq. ft.
Main floor	2,524 sq. ft.
Total Living Area:	**4,053 sq. ft.**
Exterior Wall Framing:	2x4

Foundation Options:
Slab
(All plans can be built with your choice of foundation and framing. A generic conversion diagram is available. See order form.)

BLUEPRINT PRICE CODE: G

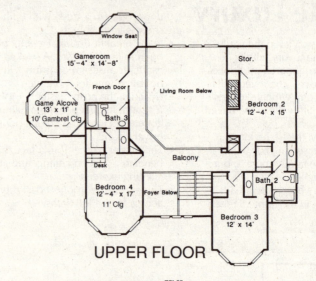

UPPER FLOOR

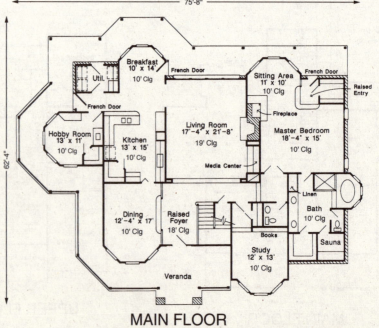

MAIN FLOOR

Plan L-4053-VC
Plan copyright held by home designer/architect

STATELY COLONIAL-STYLE HOMES

Open Spaces, Private Places

- This home's floor plan features open, light-filled common areas and private sleeping quarters.
- The foyer—topped by a stylish plant shelf and a high ceiling—is flanked by the formal living and dining rooms. The nearby kitchen is nicely arranged to serve both the dining room and the breakfast nook. The bayed nook has a built-in desk and a pantry.
- A serving bar opens out to the family room, which features a fireplace and a wall of windows that includes a French door opening to the backyard.
- Upstairs, the master suite boasts a tray ceiling and lots of bright windows in the sleeping area. The private, vaulted bath offers a dual-sink vanity, a glorious garden tub and a separate shower.
- Two more bedrooms feature walk-in closets. They share a full hall bath.

Plan FB-5045-MILL

Bedrooms: 3+	Baths: 2½
Living Area:	
Upper floor	897 sq. ft.
Main floor	989 sq. ft.
Total Living Area:	**1,886 sq. ft.**
Future area	272 sq. ft.
Daylight basement	989 sq. ft.
Garage and storage	508 sq. ft.
Exterior Wall Framing:	2x4
Foundation Options:	
Daylight basement	
Crawlspace	

(All plans can be built with your choice of foundation and framing. A generic conversion diagram is available. See order form.)

BLUEPRINT PRICE CODE: B

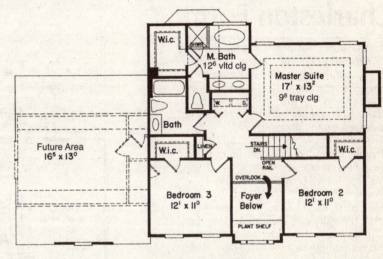

UPPER FLOOR

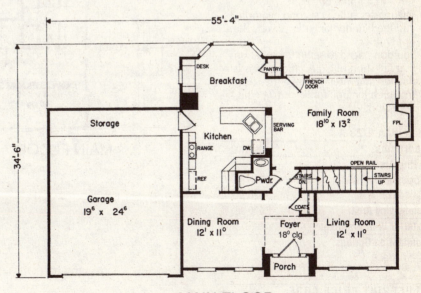

MAIN FLOOR

ORDER BLUEPRINTS ANYTIME!
CALL TOLL-FREE 1-800-820-1296

Plan FB-5045-MILL
Plan copyright held by home designer/architect

PRICES AND DETAILS ON PAGES 12-15

185

STATELY COLONIAL-STYLE HOMES

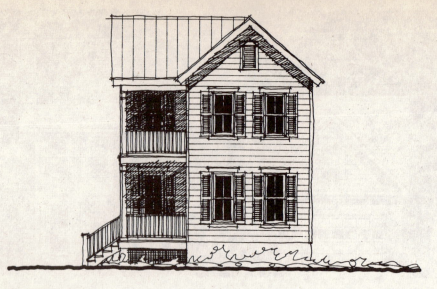

Charleston Form

- This charmer is a classic example of a "Charleston side yard" home. The side yard, in this case, would be located to the left of the home, overlooked by the stacked porches. If your lot so dictates, the plan could be "flipped" to place the overlook on the opposite side.
- The home's porches are deep and livable, with plenty of room for chairs or even a dinette set.
- Inside this well-proportioned home, you'll find a modern floor plan that suits your lifestyle. The living room unfolds from the entry porch and flows into the dining area and the kitchen. Access is easy from here to a backyard deck that's deep enough for a hungry family to dig into a barbecue.
- The foremost bedroom could easily serve as a home office.
- The master suite, a second bedroom and the laundry facilities occupy the upper floor.
- You don't need to settle for imitations that fall short of expectations. This is a flawless interpretation of a tried-and-true architectural form, and it could be yours today.

Plan WAA-9723-A	
Bedrooms: 2+	Baths: 3
Living Area:	
Upper floor	786 sq. ft.
Main floor	820 sq. ft.
Total Living Area:	**1,606 sq. ft.**
Exterior Wall Framing:	2x4
Foundation Options:	
Crawlspace	
(All plans can be built with your choice of foundation and framing. A generic conversion diagram is available. See order form.)	
BLUEPRINT PRICE CODE:	B

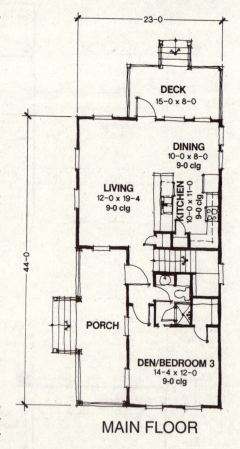

MAIN FLOOR

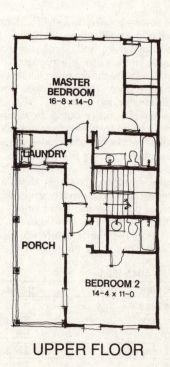

UPPER FLOOR

Plan WAA-9723-A
Plan copyright held by home designer/architect

STATELY COLONIAL-STYLE HOMES

Class with Comfort

- Twin gables, great window treatments and the rich look of brick lend a sophisticated air to this design.
- Inside, the floor plan is comfortable and unpretentious. The foyer is open to the formal spaces, which flow freely into the casual living areas.
- The kitchen, breakfast nook and family room combine to create a highly livable area with no wasted space.
- The kitchen's angled serving bar accommodates those in the family room and in the nook. The bay-windowed nook has a convenient, space-saving laundry closet. The family room's fireplace warms the entire area.
- The upper floor is highlighted by an irresistible master suite featuring a tray ceiling, his-and-hers walk-in closets and a vaulted bath with a garden tub.

Plan FB-1744-L	
Bedrooms: 4	Baths: 2½
Living Area:	
Upper floor	860 sq. ft.
Main floor	884 sq. ft.
Total Living Area:	**1,744 sq. ft.**
Daylight basement	884 sq. ft.
Garage	456 sq. ft.
Exterior Wall Framing:	2x4

Foundation Options:
Daylight basement
Crawlspace
Slab
(All plans can be built with your choice of foundation and framing. A generic conversion diagram is available. See order form.)

BLUEPRINT PRICE CODE: B

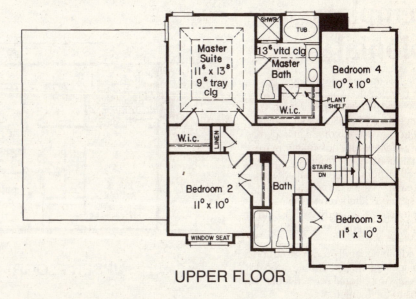

UPPER FLOOR

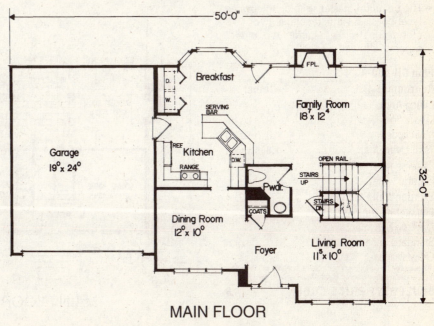

MAIN FLOOR

ORDER BLUEPRINTS ANYTIME!
CALL TOLL-FREE 1-800-820-1296

Plan FB-1744-L
Plan copyright held by home designer/architect

PRICES AND DETAILS ON PAGES 12-15

STATELY COLONIAL-STYLE HOMES

Exemplary Colonial

- Inside this traditionally designed home is an exciting floor plan for today's lifestyles. The classic center-hall arrangement of this Colonial allows easy access to each of the living areas.
- Plenty of views are possible from the formal rooms at the front of the home, as well as from the informal areas at the rear.
- The spacious kitchen offers lots of counter space, a handy work island, a laundry closet and a sunny bayed breakfast nook.
- The adjoining family room shows off a fireplace and elegant double doors to the rear. An optional set of double doors opens to the living room.
- The beautiful master suite on the upper level boasts a vaulted ceiling, two closets, dual sinks, a garden tub and a separate shower.

Plan CH-100-A

Bedrooms: 4	Baths: 2½
Living Area:	
Upper floor	923 sq. ft.
Main floor	965 sq. ft.
Total Living Area:	**1,888 sq. ft.**
Basement	952 sq. ft.
Garage	462 sq. ft.
Exterior Wall Framing:	2x4

Foundation Options:
Daylight basement
Standard basement
Crawlspace
(All plans can be built with your choice of foundation and framing. A generic conversion diagram is available. See order form.)

BLUEPRINT PRICE CODE: B

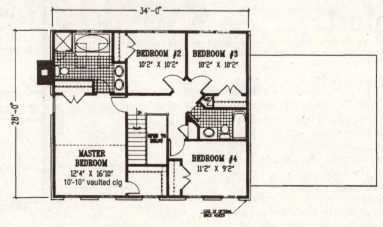

UPPER FLOOR

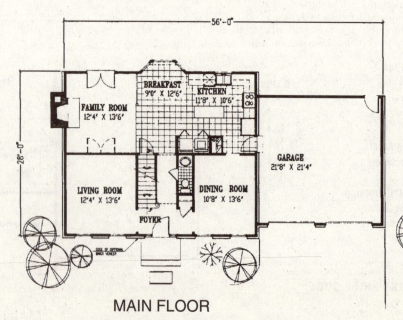

MAIN FLOOR

188   ORDER BLUEPRINTS ANYTIME!
CALL TOLL-FREE 1-800-820-1296

Plan CH-100-A
Plan copyright held by home designer/architect

PRICES AND DETAILS
ON PAGES 12-15

STATELY COLONIAL-STYLE HOMES

Spacious and Open

- A brilliant wall of windows invites guests into the two-story-high foyer of this striking traditional home.
- At the center of this open floor plan, the sunken family room boasts a vaulted ceiling and a striking fireplace with flanking windows.
- The cozy dinette merges with the family room and the island kitchen, creating a spacious, open atmosphere. A pantry closet, a laundry room, a half-bath and garage access are all nearby.
- The formal living and dining rooms are found at the front of the home. The living room boasts a cathedral ceiling and a lovely window arrangement.
- The main-floor master bedroom has a tray ceiling, a walk-in closet and a lush bath designed for two.
- Upstairs, two bedrooms share another full bath and a balcony landing that overlooks the family room and foyer.

Plan A-2207-DS	
Bedrooms: 3	**Baths:** 2½
Living Area:	
Upper floor	518 sq. ft.
Main floor	1,389 sq. ft.
Total Living Area:	**1,907 sq. ft.**
Standard basement	1,389 sq. ft.
Garage	484 sq. ft.
Exterior Wall Framing:	2x6
Foundation Options:	
Standard basement	

(All plans can be built with your choice of foundation and framing. A generic conversion diagram is available. See order form.)

BLUEPRINT PRICE CODE: B

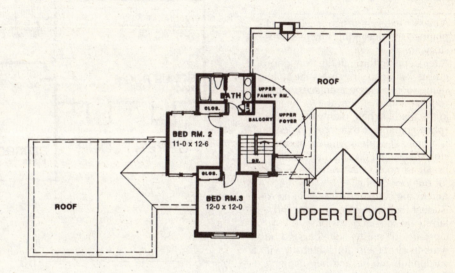

UPPER FLOOR

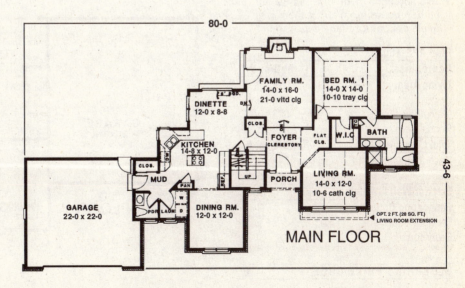

MAIN FLOOR

ORDER BLUEPRINTS ANYTIME!
CALL TOLL-FREE 1-800-820-1296

Plan A-2207-DS
Plan copyright held by home designer/architect

PRICES AND DETAILS ON PAGES 12-15

STATELY COLONIAL-STYLE HOMES

Timeless Two-Story

- A classic exterior design meets a well-planned interior in this timeless two-story home.
- After stepping through the front door, guests will head straight for the spacious living room. A large fireplace warms the rooms on chilly fall evenings.
- In the tiled kitchen, plenty of counter space guarantees that meal preparation is a breeze, while a window above the sink sheds light on clean-up. A sunny breakfast nook opens onto a rear deck for outdoor dining.
- Across the entry, the formal dining room is ideal for entertaining visitors and family on special occasions.
- Upstairs, the master suite boasts a huge walk-in closet and a private bath with a garden tub and his-and-hers vanities.
- Two additional bedrooms share a full bath. A bonus room above the garage offers options for future expansion.

Plan APS-1603	
Bedrooms: 3+	Baths: 2½
Living Area:	
Upper floor	837 sq. ft.
Main floor	816 sq. ft.
Bonus room	296 sq. ft.
Total Living Area:	**1,949 sq. ft.**
Daylight basement	744 sq. ft.
Garage	440 sq. ft.
Exterior Wall Framing:	2x4
Foundation Options:	
Daylight basement	
Crawlspace	
(All plans can be built with your choice of foundation and framing. A generic conversion diagram is available. See order form.)	
BLUEPRINT PRICE CODE:	B

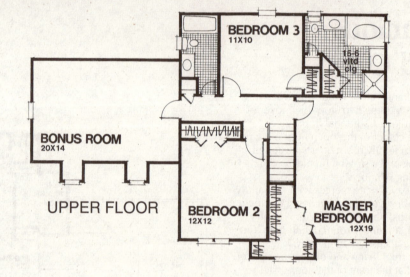

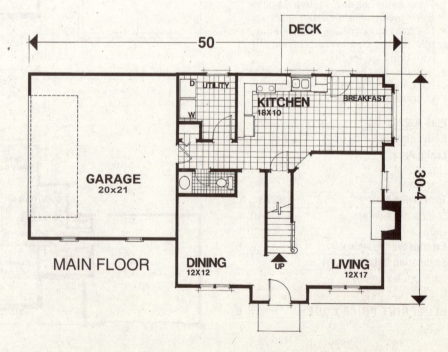

ORDER BLUEPRINTS ANYTIME!
CALL TOLL-FREE 1-800-820-1296

Plan APS-1603
Plan copyright held by home designer/architect

PRICES AND DETAILS ON PAGES 12-15

Colonial for Today

- Designed for a growing family, this handsome traditional home offers four bedrooms plus a den and three complete baths. The Colonial exterior is updated by a front entry porch with a fanlight window above.
- The dramatic tiled foyer is two stories high and provides direct access to all of the home's living areas. The spacious living room has an inviting brick fireplace and sliding pocket doors to the adjoining dining room.
- Overlooking the backyard, the huge combination kitchen/family room is the home's hidden charm. The kitchen features a peninsula breakfast bar with seating for six.
- The family room includes sliding glass doors that open to an enticing terrace. A built-in entertainment center and bookshelves line another wall.
- The adjacent mudroom houses a pantry closet and the washer/dryer. A full bath and a big den complete the main floor.
- The upper floor is highlighted by a beautiful balcony that overlooks the foyer below. The luxurious master suite boasts a skylighted dressing area and two closets, including an oversized walk-in closet. The private master bath offers a whirlpool tub and a dual-sink vanity.

Plan AHP-7050	
Bedrooms: 4+	**Baths:** 3
Living Area:	
Upper floor	998 sq. ft.
Main floor	1,153 sq. ft.
Total Living Area:	**2,151 sq. ft.**
Standard basement	1,067 sq. ft.
Garage and storage	439 sq. ft.
Exterior Wall Framing:	2x4 or 2x6

Foundation Options:
Standard basement
Crawlspace
Slab
(All plans can be built with your choice of foundation and framing. A generic conversion diagram is available. See order form.)

BLUEPRINT PRICE CODE: C

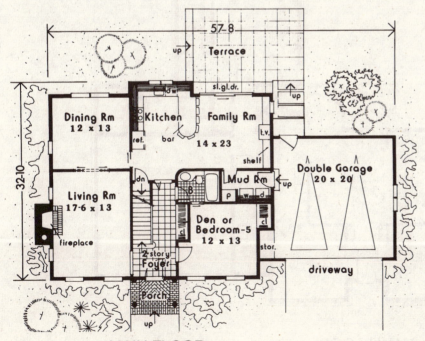

MAIN FLOOR

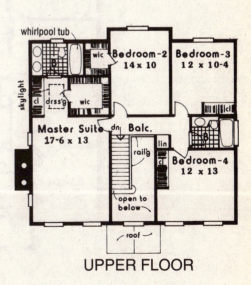

UPPER FLOOR

ORDER BLUEPRINTS ANYTIME!
CALL TOLL-FREE 1-800-820-1296

Plan AHP-7050
Plan copyright held by home designer/architect

PRICES AND DETAILS ON PAGES 12-15

STATELY COLONIAL-STYLE HOMES

Interior Angles Add Excitement

- Interior angles add a touch of excitement to this one-story home.
- A pleasantly charming exterior combines wood and stone to give the plan a solid, comfortable look for any neighborhood.
- Formal living and dining rooms flank the entry, which leads into the large family room, featuring a fireplace, a vaulted ceiling and built-in bookshelves. A covered porch and a sunny patio are just steps away.
- The adjoining eating area with a built-in china cabinet angles off the roomy kitchen. Note the pantry and the convenient utility room.
- The master bedroom suite is both spacious and private, and includes a dressing room, a large walk-in closet and a secluded bath.
- The three secondary bedrooms are also zoned for privacy, and share a compartmentalized bath.

Plan E-1904	
Bedrooms: 4	Baths: 2½
Living Area:	
Main floor	1,997 sq. ft.
Total Living Area:	**1,997 sq. ft.**
Garage	484 sq. ft.
Storage	104 sq. ft.
Exterior Wall Framing:	2x4

Foundation Options:
Crawlspace
Slab
(All plans can be built with your choice of foundation and framing. A generic conversion diagram is available. See order form.)

BLUEPRINT PRICE CODE: B

MAIN FLOOR

Plan E-1904
Plan copyright held by home designer/architect

ORDER BLUEPRINTS ANYTIME! CALL TOLL-FREE 1-800-820-1296

PRICES AND DETAILS ON PAGES 12-15

Updated Classic

- Light-filled and airy, this classic country-style home is filled with modern amenities.
- Brightened by high transom windows, the inviting two-story-high foyer flows into the spacious living room and the formal dining room.
- The efficient kitchen features a breakfast bar and a window over the sink. The adjoining dinette offers sliding glass doors to a backyard terrace. The nearby mudroom/laundry room has garage and backyard access.
- The friendly family room enjoys a view of the backyard through a row of three windows. The handsome fireplace is flanked by glass.
- Upstairs, the spectacular master bedroom boasts a cathedral ceiling and a roomy walk-in closet. The skylighted master bath showcases a whirlpool tub, a separate shower and a dual-sink vanity.
- Another skylighted bath services the three remaining bedrooms.

Plan AHP-9402

Bedrooms: 4	Baths: 2½
Living Area:	
Upper floor	1,041 sq. ft.
Main floor	1,129 sq. ft.
Total Living Area:	**2,170 sq. ft.**
Standard basement	1,129 sq. ft.
Garage and storage	630 sq. ft.
Exterior Wall Framing:	2x4 or 2x6

Foundation Options:
Standard basement
Crawlspace
Slab
(All plans can be built with your choice of foundation and framing. A generic conversion diagram is available. See order form.)

BLUEPRINT PRICE CODE: C

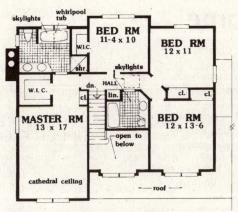

UPPER FLOOR

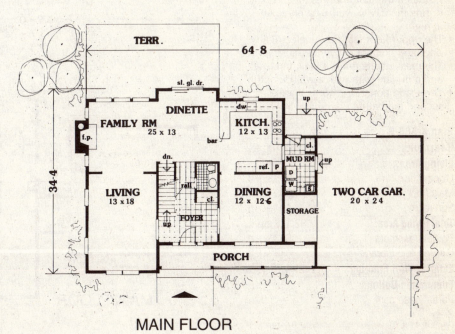

MAIN FLOOR

ORDER BLUEPRINTS ANYTIME!
CALL TOLL-FREE 1-800-820-1296

Plan AHP-9402
Plan copyright held by home designer/architect

PRICES AND DETAILS ON PAGES 12-15

Energy-Efficient Colonial Home

- This home combines classic Colonial styling with energy efficiency.
- An air-lock vestibule, which minimizes heat loss, leads into a spacious, elegant reception area.
- The bayed living room features optional folding doors to the family room, which offers a high-efficiency fireplace and two sets of sliding glass doors to a bright rear terrace.
- The expansive formal dining room leads into an efficient U-shaped kitchen, which boasts a pantry and a dinette with sliding glass doors to a glass-roofed sun room. The sun room's insulated thermal flooring collects heat during the day to warm the home later at night.
- The upper floor features an electrically operated skylight above the stairs.
- The master suite offers a walk-in closet and a private bath with a whirlpool tub.
- Three additional bedrooms share a second full bath.

Plan K-508-B

Bedrooms: 4	Baths: 2½

Living Area:

Upper floor	1,003 sq. ft.
Main floor	1,072 sq. ft.
Sun room	101 sq. ft.
Total Living Area:	**2,176 sq. ft.**
Partial basement	633 sq. ft.
Garage and storage	458 sq. ft.
Exterior Wall Framing:	2x4 or 2x6

Foundation Options:
Partial basement
Slab
(All plans can be built with your choice of foundation and framing. A generic conversion diagram is available. See order form.)

BLUEPRINT PRICE CODE: C

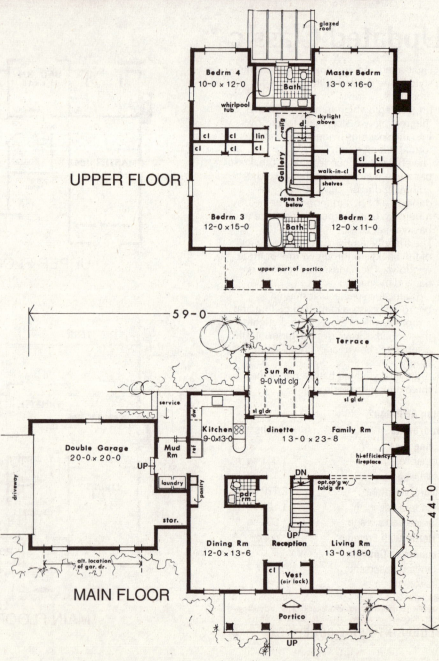

Plan K-508-B
Plan copyright held by home designer/architect

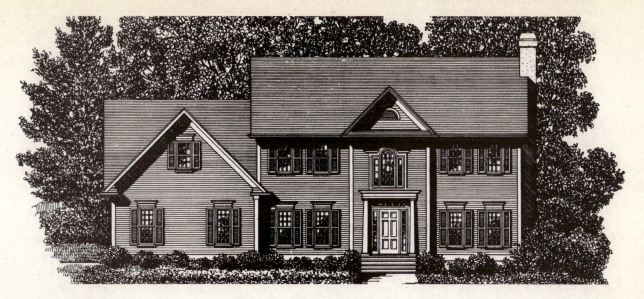

Distinctly Formal

- This attractive traditional home boasts room for up to four bedrooms plus formal living spaces that can be closed off from the informal areas.
- The two-story foyer features two handy coat closets and a decorative upper-level plant shelf.
- A large gourmet kitchen with a work island and an adjoining breakfast room each overlook an oversized rear deck. The breakfast room opens to the family room, which features a cozy fireplace.
- The laundry closet is conveniently located on the upper level, close to the bedrooms.
- The master bedroom has a tray ceiling and a private bath. The bath boasts his-and-hers walk-in closets, separate vanities and a toilet compartment.
- The bonus room can serve as a fourth bedroom, hobby room or playroom.

Plan APS-1905

Bedrooms: 3+	Baths: 2½
Living Area:	
Upper floor	915 sq. ft.
Main floor	1,084 sq. ft.
Bonus room	224 sq. ft.
Total Living Area:	**2,223 sq. ft.**
Standard basement	1,064 sq. ft.
Garage	440 sq. ft.
Exterior Wall Framing:	2x4

Foundation Options:
Standard basement
Crawlspace
(All plans can be built with your choice of foundation and framing. A generic conversion diagram is available. See order form.)

BLUEPRINT PRICE CODE: C

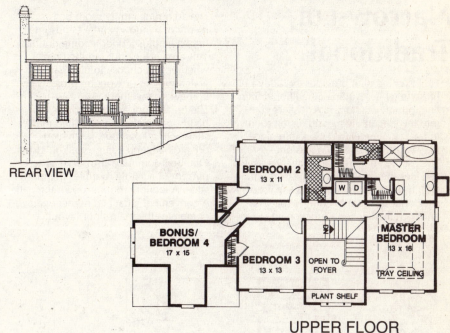

REAR VIEW

UPPER FLOOR

MAIN FLOOR

ORDER BLUEPRINTS ANYTIME!
CALL TOLL-FREE 1-800-820-1296

Plan APS-1905
Plan copyright held by home designer/architect

PRICES AND DETAILS ON PAGES 12-15

STATELY COLONIAL-STYLE HOMES

Narrow-Lot Traditional

- This exciting plan provides for today's lifestyle while exuding a traditional flair.
- The formal two-story foyer ushers guests into the elegant living and dining rooms to the left, where an optional fireplace may warm any special occasion.
- The roomy kitchen straight ahead easily services the skylighted breakfast room, which opens to the outdoors. A raised snack bar and ample counter space enhance the kitchen's functionality.
- The adjoining family room boasts plenty of windows and a handsome fireplace, plus a door leading out back. This area is ideal for family time, whether you choose to play games, watch movies or work on projects or homework together.
- The upper floor accommodates four bedrooms, including a vaulted master suite with a luxurious, skylighted private bath and a large walk-in closet. One bedroom may also serve as a nursery or a sitting room for the master suite. A laundry room is down the hall.
- A convenient, attached two-car garage completes the main-floor layout.

Plan CH-620-A	
Bedrooms: 3+	**Baths:** 2½
Living Area:	
Upper floor	1,104 sq. ft.
Main floor	1,134 sq. ft.
Total Living Area:	**2,238 sq. ft.**
Basement	1,134 sq. ft.
Garage	367 sq. ft.
Exterior Wall Framing:	2x4

Foundation Options:
Daylight basement
Standard basement
Crawlspace
(All plans can be built with your choice of foundation and framing. A generic conversion diagram is available. See order form.)

BLUEPRINT PRICE CODE: C

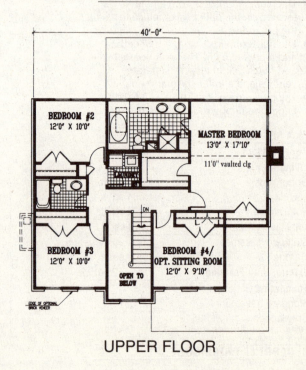

MAIN FLOOR

UPPER FLOOR

**ORDER BLUEPRINTS ANYTIME!
CALL TOLL-FREE 1-800-820-1296**

Plan CH-620-A
Plan copyright held by home designer/architect

**PRICES AND DETAILS
ON PAGES 12-15**

Welcome Home

- Recalling traditional hometown charm, this updated country-style home would be a welcome addition to any street.
- Stately columns highlight the inviting covered porch, while an arched transom accents the sidelighted entry.
- Inside, the open foyer is nestled between the formal living spaces. The foyer's hardwood floor extends into the living room, which is set off with striking columns.
- Past the foyer, the spacious family room flaunts a handsome fireplace. A French door provides access to the backyard.
- Bright and airy, the efficient U-shaped kitchen unfolds to a sunny breakfast area. A half-bath and a laundry room that opens to the garage are nearby.
- Upstairs, the master bedroom features a built-in desk and a tray ceiling. The master bath showcases a whirlpool tub, a separate shower, a dual-sink vanity and a roomy walk-in closet.
- Three additional bedrooms, a second full bath and a versatile bonus room complete the upper floor.

Plan APS-1908

Bedrooms: 4+	Baths: 2½
Living Area:	
Upper floor	985 sq. ft.
Main floor	1,013 sq. ft.
Bonus room	320 sq. ft.
Total Living Area:	**2,318 sq. ft.**
Garage and storage	480 sq. ft.
Exterior Wall Framing:	2x4

Foundation Options:
Crawlspace
(All plans can be built with your choice of foundation and framing. A generic conversion diagram is available. See order form.)

BLUEPRINT PRICE CODE: C

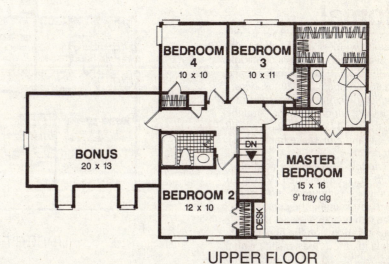

UPPER FLOOR

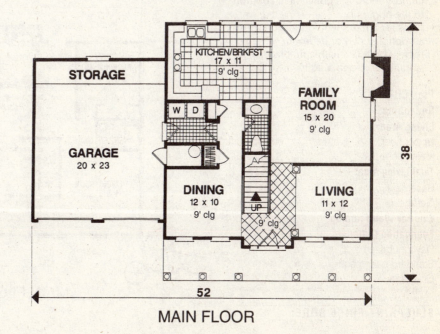

MAIN FLOOR

ORDER BLUEPRINTS ANYTIME!
CALL TOLL-FREE 1-800-820-1296

Plan APS-1908
Plan copyright held by home designer/architect

PRICES AND DETAILS ON PAGES 12-15

STATELY COLONIAL-STYLE HOMES

Contemporary Colonial

- A Palladian window and a half-round window give this Colonial a new look. Inside, the floor plan maximizes space, yet creates an open, airy atmosphere.
- The two-story foyer connects the formal areas at the front of the home. Straight ahead, the family room features a built-in wet bar and a fireplace framed by French doors.
- A bay window brightens the adjoining breakfast nook and kitchen. An angled counter looks to the nook and the family room, keeping the cook in touch with the family activities.
- The four bedrooms on the upper floor include a luxurious master suite with a vaulted ceiling and a skylighted bath. A laundry room is a convenient addition to the upper floor.
- Plans for a basement foundation show an optional den or bedroom, a recreation room with a fireplace, a storage room and a utility area.

Plan CH-320-A	
Bedrooms: 4+	Baths: 3
Living Area:	
Upper floor	1,164 sq. ft.
Main floor	1,293 sq. ft.
Total Living Area:	**2,457 sq. ft.**
Basement	1,293 sq. ft.
Garage	462 sq. ft.
Exterior Wall Framing:	2x4

Foundation Options:
Daylight basement
Standard basement
Crawlspace
(All plans can be built with your choice of foundation and framing. A generic conversion diagram is available. See order form.)

BLUEPRINT PRICE CODE: C

UPPER FLOOR

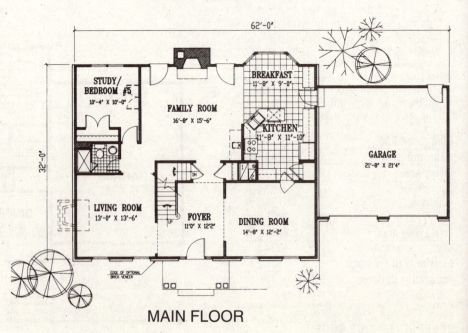

MAIN FLOOR

Plan CH-320-A
Plan copyright held by home designer/architect

STATELY COLONIAL-STYLE HOMES

Stately Colonial

- This stately Colonial features a covered front entry and a secondary entry near the garage and the utility room.
- The main foyer opens to a comfortable den with elegant double doors.
- The formal living areas adjoin to the left of the foyer and culminate in a lovely bay window overlooking the backyard.
- The open island kitchen has a great central location, easily accessed from each of the living areas. Informal dining can be extended to the outdoors through sliding doors in the dinette.
- A half-wall introduces the big family room, which boasts a high vaulted ceiling, an inviting fireplace and optional built-in cabinets.
- The upper floor is shared by four bedrooms, including a spacious master bedroom with a large walk-in closet, a dressing area for two and a private bath. An alternate bath layout is included in the blueprints.
- A bonus room may be added above the garage for additional space.

Plan A-2283-DS	
Bedrooms: 4+	Baths: 2½
Living Area:	
Upper floor	1,137 sq. ft.
Main floor	1,413 sq. ft.
Total Living Area:	**2,550 sq. ft.**
Optional bonus room	280 sq. ft.
Standard basement	1,413 sq. ft.
Garage	484 sq. ft.
Exterior Wall Framing:	2x6
Foundation Options:	
Standard basement	

(All plans can be built with your choice of foundation and framing. A generic conversion diagram is available. See order form.)

BLUEPRINT PRICE CODE: D

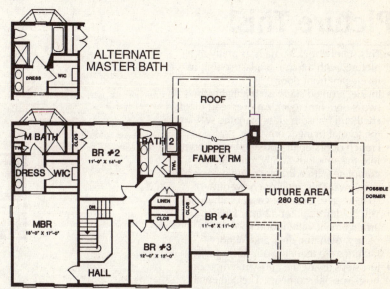

UPPER FLOOR

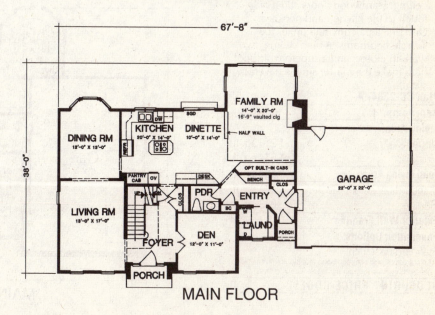

MAIN FLOOR

ORDER BLUEPRINTS ANYTIME!
CALL TOLL-FREE 1-800-820-1296

Plan A-2283-DS
Plan copyright held by home designer/architect

PRICES AND DETAILS
ON PAGES 12-15

199

STATELY COLONIAL-STYLE HOMES

Picture This!

- This stately brick home is as pretty as a picture, with a frame of glass setting off its elegant front door.
- Inside, a railed staircase highlights the two-story entry foyer. An overhead plant shelf and transom glass mark the way to the formal living room.
- French doors open from the living room into the spacious family room, which is complete with a fireplace and a bank of windows. This wide-open overflow space is also ideal for casual gatherings.
- You couldn't ask for a better kitchen arrangement—the island cooktop, pantry, planning desk and laundry facilities are there at your fingertips!
- Just steps away, the classy dining room hosts special moments. The octagonal breakfast nook provides sweeping views, and is expanded by a dome ceiling. Hardwood floors add a nice touch to the kitchen and nook.
- Upstairs, a balcony hall unites four sizable bedrooms. A high ceiling, two walk-in closets and a superb whirlpool bath make the master suite a haven.

Plan CC-2584-M

Bedrooms: 4	Baths: 2½
Living Area:	
Upper floor	1,210 sq. ft.
Main floor	1,374 sq. ft.
Total Living Area:	**2,584 sq. ft.**
Standard basement	1,374 sq. ft.
Garage	683 sq. ft.
Exterior Wall Framing:	2x4

Foundation Options:
Standard basement
(All plans can be built with your choice of foundation and framing. A generic conversion diagram is available. See order form.)

BLUEPRINT PRICE CODE: D

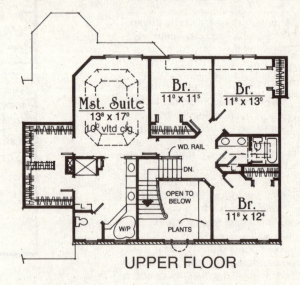

UPPER FLOOR

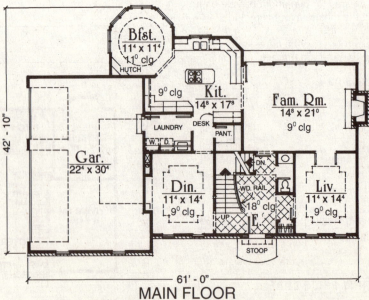

MAIN FLOOR

ORDER BLUEPRINTS ANYTIME! CALL TOLL-FREE 1-800-820-1296

Plan CC-2584-M
Plan copyright held by home designer/architect

PRICES AND DETAILS ON PAGES 12-15

Natural Attraction

- It's only natural that you should be attracted to this appealing home. With its timeless facade and Victorian-style touches, it may seem reminiscent of the pastoral countryside that inhabit your fondly remembered dreams.
- For your sophisticated nature, oversized formal rooms reside just off the raised foyer. What pleasure you'll feel as you usher your guests into these elegant yet inviting spaces!
- When it's time to unwind with your loved ones, head for the family room. If the evening calls for quiet, select a book from the built-in shelves and lose yourself in its pages. If your mood is just a tad more rambunctious than that, step into the media alcove, light a fire and catch the latest blockbuster movie.
- Warm summer days are the perfect excuse to step through the family room's fabulous French doors and enjoy an afternoon in the sun.
- The master suite's sitting area was made for reflection. Protect your personal time in this quiet, sunny retreat, or soak it up in the private bath's relaxing tub.

Plan L-649-HB

Bedrooms: 4		Baths: 2½	

Living Area:

Upper floor	1,284 sq. ft.
Main floor	1,363 sq. ft.
Total Living Area:	**2,647 sq. ft.**
Garage	504 sq. ft.
Exterior Wall Framing:	2x4

Foundation Options:
Slab
(All plans can be built with your choice of foundation and framing. A generic conversion diagram is available. See order form.)

BLUEPRINT PRICE CODE: D

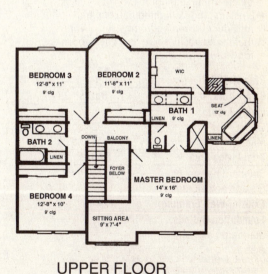

MAIN FLOOR

UPPER FLOOR

Plan L-649-HB
Plan copyright held by home designer/architect

STATELY COLONIAL-STYLE HOMES

Natural Beauty

VIEW INTO KITCHEN AND FAMILY ROOM

REAR VIEW

- Expansive windows and broad sliding glass doors fill this elegant home with dazzling natural light.
- In from the majestic, columned porch, the soaring gallery flows into the formal dining and living rooms. Beyond, a wide terrace beckons from behind sliding glass doors, promising fun times.
- The family room flaunts a casual fireplace and expands to the terrace.
- A circular snack bar makes the country kitchen a favorite with all family members. With plenty of space for the breakfast table, mornings will be a time for celebration!
- You'll soon realize the master suite is fit for royalty, with a private terrace, two closets and a dressing area with plenty of elbow room. The focal point of the master bath is its whirlpool tub, which is crowned by skylights and accented by gleaming glass block.
- Upstairs, the skylighted balcony hall introduces three bedrooms and a library that could easily serve as a guest room for those surprise visits!

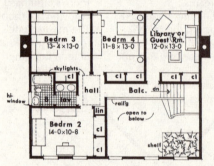

UPPER FLOOR

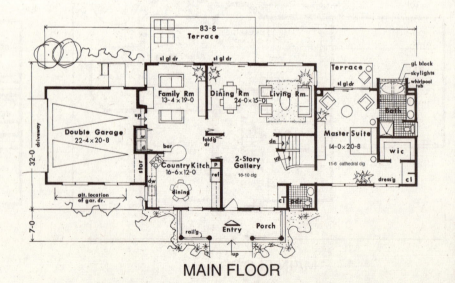

MAIN FLOOR

Plan K-693-T

Bedrooms: 4+	Baths: 2½
Living Area:	
Upper floor	934 sq. ft.
Main floor	1,723 sq. ft.
Total Living Area:	**2,657 sq. ft.**
Standard basement	1,710 sq. ft.
Garage and storage	470 sq. ft.
Exterior Wall Framing:	2x4 or 2x6
Foundation Options:	
Standard basement	
Slab	
(All plans can be built with your choice of foundation and framing. A generic conversion diagram is available. See order form.)	
BLUEPRINT PRICE CODE:	**D**

ORDER BLUEPRINTS ANYTIME! CALL TOLL-FREE 1-800-820-1296

Plan K-693-T
Plan copyright held by home designer/architect

PRICES AND DETAILS ON PAGES 12-15

Expansive and Exciting

- This home's expansive family room is sure to create excitement, with a charming focal-point fireplace flanked by windows overlooking the backyard.
- The comfy master suite boasts a nice-sized sleeping area and a luxurious master bath with two walk-in closets, a garden tub and a separate shower.
- At the front of the home, a versatile study could easily serve as a nursery, a guest room or a home office.
- A well-appointed kitchen with an island cooktop features a handy pantry and a convenient snack bar serving the adjoining bayed breakfast nook.
- A spacious game room highlights the upper floor of this home. With a high, coffered ceiling and plenty of room to play, this room is sure to be a hit with the whole family.
- The upper floor also features three good-sized bedrooms that share a full compartmentalized bath.

Plan KLF-9723

Bedrooms: 4+	Baths: 2½–3½
Living Area:	
Upper floor	960 sq. ft.
Main floor	1,748 sq. ft.
Total Living Area:	**2,708 sq. ft.**
Future areas	411 sq. ft.
Garage	551 sq. ft.
Exterior Wall Framing:	2x4

Foundation Options:
Slab
(All plans can be built with your choice of foundation and framing. A generic conversion diagram is available. See order form.)

BLUEPRINT PRICE CODE: D

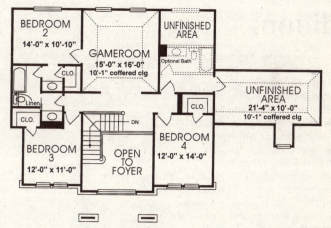

UPPER FLOOR

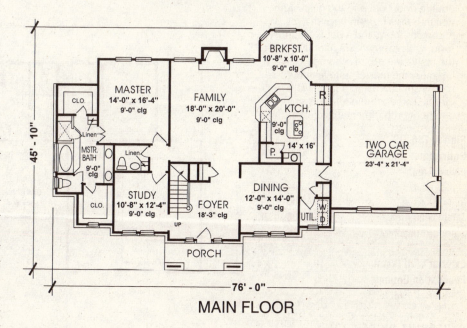

MAIN FLOOR

STATELY COLONIAL-STYLE HOMES

Plan KLF-9723

A Family Tradition

- This traditional design has clean, sharp styling, with family-sized areas for formal and casual gatherings.
- The sidelighted foyer is graced with a beautiful open staircase and a wide coat closet, a convenience when you are entertaining. Flanking the foyer are the spacious formal living areas.
- The everyday living areas include an island kitchen, a bayed dinette and a large family room with a fireplace. Openness between these rooms allows for a feeling of togetherness, even while everyone is doing their own thing.
- Just off the entrance from the garage, double doors open to the quiet study, which boasts built-in bookshelves.
- A powder room and a deluxe laundry room with cabinets are handily part of the active areas of the home.
- Upstairs, the master suite features a roomy split bath and a large walk-in closet. Three more bedrooms share another compartmentalized bath.

Plan A-118-DS

Bedrooms: 4+	Baths: 2½
Living Area:	
Upper floor	1,344 sq. ft.
Main floor	1,556 sq. ft.
Total Living Area:	**2,900 sq. ft.**
Standard basement	1,556 sq. ft.
Garage	576 sq. ft.
Exterior Wall Framing:	2x4

Foundation Options:
Standard basement
(All plans can be built with your choice of foundation and framing. A generic conversion diagram is available. See order form.)

BLUEPRINT PRICE CODE: D

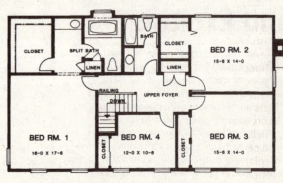

UPPER FLOOR

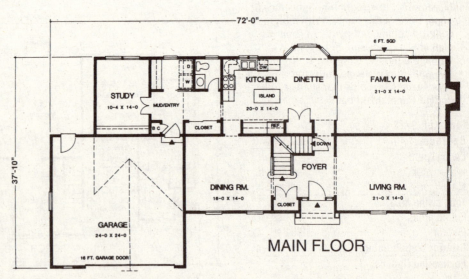

MAIN FLOOR

Plan A-118-DS
Plan copyright held by home designer/architect

Live in Luxury

- This luxurious home's arched windows and majestic entry accent the stucco finish. Plans for an alternate brick exterior are included in the blueprints.
- A graceful curved stairway anchors the two-story foyer, which is flanked by formal areas. The spacious living room hosts an inviting fireplace. Double doors close off the adjoining study, which has functional built-in shelves.
- The central family room boasts a second fireplace, a wet bar and two sets of French doors that open to the backyard.
- A pantry and an island cooktop with an eating bar offer extra storage and work space in the kitchen. The attached breakfast room is awash in natural light.
- The spacious master suite and three secondary bedrooms are located on the upper floor. The master suite offers two walk-in closets and a skylighted private bath with twin vanities and an oval spa tub. A second full bath services the secondary bedrooms.

Plan CH-360-A	
Bedrooms: 4	**Baths:** 2½
Living Area:	
Upper floor	1,354 sq. ft.
Main floor	1,616 sq. ft.
Total Living Area:	**2,970 sq. ft.**
Basement	1,616 sq. ft.
Garage	462 sq. ft.
Exterior Wall Framing	2x4
Foundation Options:	
Daylight basement	
Standard basement	
Crawlspace	
(All plans can be built with your choice of foundation and framing. A generic conversion diagram is available. See order form.)	
BLUEPRINT PRICE CODE:	**D**

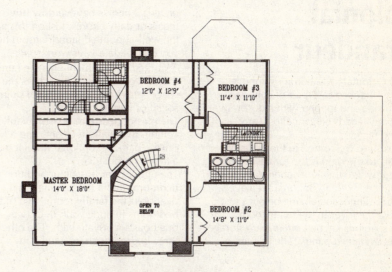

UPPER FLOOR

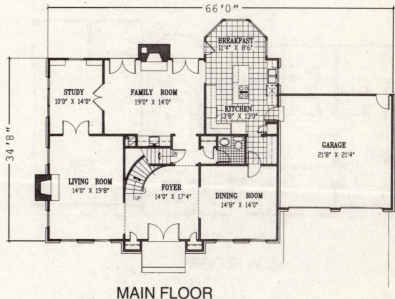

MAIN FLOOR

ORDER BLUEPRINTS ANYTIME!
CALL TOLL-FREE 1-800-820-1296

Plan CH-360-A
Plan copyright held by home designer/architect

PRICES AND DETAILS ON PAGES 12-15

STATELY COLONIAL-STYLE HOMES

Colonial Grandeur

- This Colonial-style home's stunning entry—flanked by a pair of columns on each side and topped with a decorative balcony—adds elegance to a truly grand facade.
- Guests are welcomed in the two-story foyer. To the right is the formal dining room, where the atmosphere may be enhanced with an optional fireplace. Before-dinner socializing belongs just across the foyer in the living room.
- The spacious kitchen offers extra storage in its oversized pantry. The adjoining breakfast nook's bay window brightens meals or daily chores. Just off this area, the well-appointed laundry room helps you consolidate your work space.
- A vaulted ceiling highlights the family room. A cozy fireplace anchors the space, providing a warm focal point for social or family gatherings.
- The master bedroom boasts a vaulted ceiling, two walk-in closets and a private bath. An optional fireplace adds a touch of romance.
- The upper floor hosts four additional bedrooms and a balcony hall that overlooks the family room. Two of the bedrooms include walk-in closets, and one boasts a private bath. The other three bedrooms share a full bath.

Plan CH-482-A	
Bedrooms: 5+	**Baths:** 3½
Living Area:	
Upper floor	1,031 sq. ft.
Main floor	2,006 sq. ft.
Total Living Area:	**3,037 sq. ft.**
Partial daylight basement	1,397 sq. ft.
Garage	722 sq. ft.
Exterior Wall Framing:	2x4

Foundation Options:
Partial daylight basement
Crawlspace
(All plans can be built with your choice of foundation and framing. A generic conversion diagram is available. See order form.)

BLUEPRINT PRICE CODE: E

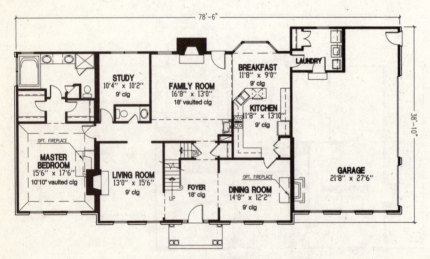

MAIN FLOOR

UPPER FLOOR

206 — ORDER BLUEPRINTS ANYTIME! CALL TOLL-FREE 1-800-820-1296

Plan CH-482-A
Plan copyright held by home designer/architect

PRICES AND DETAILS ON PAGES 12-15

STATELY COLONIAL-STYLE HOMES

Ornate Design

- This exciting home is distinguished by an ornate facade with symmetrical windows and a columned entry.
- A beautiful arched window highlights the two-story-high foyer, with its open-railed stairway and high plant shelf. The foyer separates the two formal rooms and flows back to the family room.
- The family room is brightened by corner windows and warmed by a central fireplace.
- Columns introduce the sunny breakfast area and the adjacent gourmet kitchen, which features an angled island and serving bar, and a butler's pantry that serves the nearby dining room.
- Upstairs, a dramatic balcony overlooks the family room and the foyer.
- The master suite boasts a tray ceiling, a sitting room and an opulent garden bath with an airy vaulted ceiling. Three more bedrooms, each with a walk-in closet and private bath access, complete the upper floor.

Plan FB-5347-HAST

Bedrooms: 4+	Baths: 4
Living Area:	
Upper floor	1,554 sq. ft.
Main floor	1,665 sq. ft.
Total Living Area:	**3,219 sq. ft.**
Daylight basement	1,665 sq. ft.
Garage	462 sq. ft.
Exterior Wall Framing:	2x4

Foundation Options:
Daylight basement
Crawlspace
(All plans can be built with your choice of foundation and framing. A generic conversion diagram is available. See order form.)

BLUEPRINT PRICE CODE: E

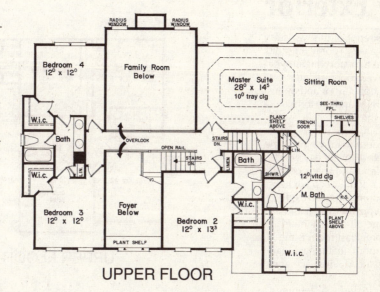

UPPER FLOOR

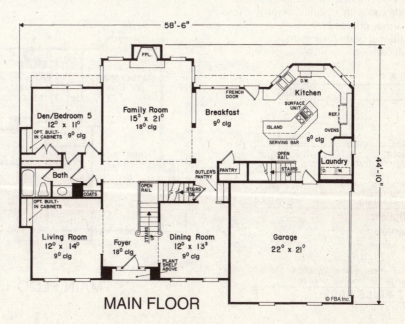

MAIN FLOOR

ORDER BLUEPRINTS ANYTIME!
CALL TOLL-FREE 1-800-820-1296

Plan FB-5347-HAST
Plan copyright held by home designer/architect

PRICES AND DETAILS ON PAGES 12-15

STATELY COLONIAL-STYLE HOMES

Stately Exterior

- The exquisite exterior of this two-story home opens to a very roomy interior.
- The magnificent two-story-high foyer shows off a curved, open-railed stairway to the upper floor and opens to a study on the right and the formal living areas on the left.
- The spacious living room flows into a formal dining room that overlooks the outdoors through a lovely bay window.
- A large work island and snack counter sits at the center of the open kitchen and breakfast room. An oversized pantry closet, a powder room and a laundry room are all close at hand.
- Adjoining the breakfast room is the large sunken family room, featuring a high vaulted ceiling, a cozy fireplace and outdoor access.
- The upper floor includes a stunning master bedroom with a vaulted ceiling and a luxurious private bath.
- Three additional bedrooms share a second full bath.

Plan CH-280-A	
Bedrooms: 4+	**Baths:** 2½
Living Area:	
Upper floor	1,262 sq. ft.
Main floor	1,797 sq. ft.
Total Living Area:	**3,059 sq. ft.**
Basement	1,797 sq. ft.
Garage	462 sq. ft.
Exterior Wall Framing:	2x4
Foundation Options:	
Daylight basement	
Standard basement	
Crawlspace	
(All plans can be built with your choice of foundation and framing. A generic conversion diagram is available. See order form.)	
BLUEPRINT PRICE CODE:	E

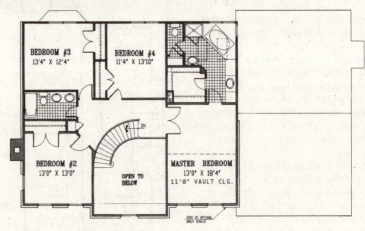

UPPER FLOOR

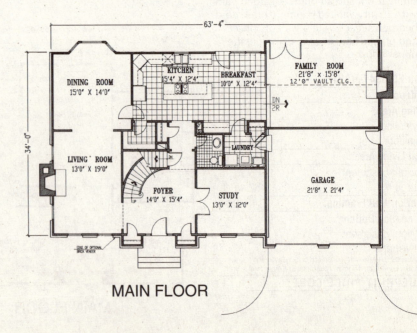

MAIN FLOOR

208 ORDER BLUEPRINTS ANYTIME! CALL TOLL-FREE 1-800-820-1296

Plan CH-280-A
Plan copyright held by home designer/architect

PRICES AND DETAILS ON PAGES 12-15

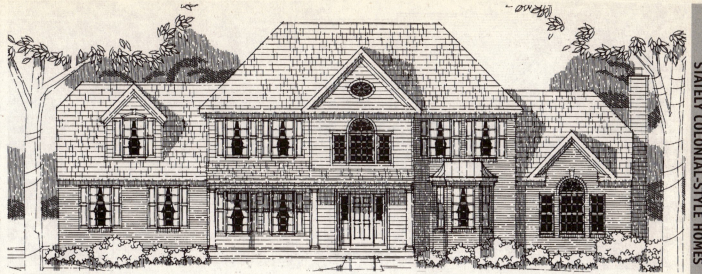

STATELY COLONIAL-STYLE HOMES

Fabulous!

- This fabulous home speaks of simple elegance and grace. Stately columns and a Palladian window lend an air of grandeur to the facade.
- Inside, a two-story foyer with a winding staircase will wow first-time visitors.
- On either side of the foyer, the living and dining rooms provide a stunning backdrop for your formal gatherings. A bay window and a tray ceiling in the dining room set a dignified tone for hors d'oeuvres and sit-down meals.
- The home's informal living spaces make a fun gathering area, and the combined kitchen and breakfast nook allows family members to concentrate on different tasks, yet spend time together.
- A cathedral ceiling crowns the family room, where you will spend hours with loved ones recapping the day's events. Double doors introduce a study that would be an ideal office.
- Upstairs, the opulent master suite serves as an oasis from the hectic world. A writer or artist will love the secluded sitting room off the master suite. Three more bedrooms share the upper floor.

Plan OH-255

Bedrooms: 4+	Baths: 2½
Living Area:	
Upper floor	1,433 sq. ft.
Main floor	1,874 sq. ft.
Total Living Area:	**3,307 sq. ft.**
Standard basement	1,874 sq. ft.
Garage	637 sq. ft.
Exterior Wall Framing:	2x4

Foundation Options:
Standard basement
(All plans can be built with your choice of foundation and framing. A generic conversion diagram is available. See order form.)

BLUEPRINT PRICE CODE: E

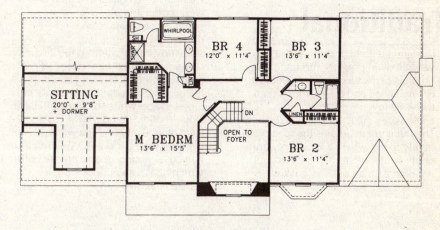

UPPER FLOOR

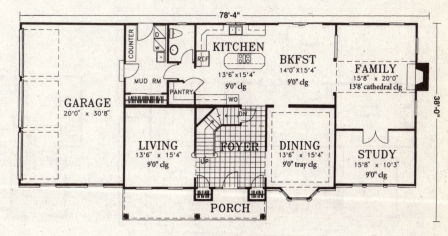

MAIN FLOOR

ORDER BLUEPRINTS ANYTIME!
CALL TOLL-FREE 1-800-820-1296

Plan OH-255
Plan copyright held by home designer/architect

PRICES AND DETAILS ON PAGES 12-15

STATELY COLONIAL-STYLE HOMES

Versatile and Traditional

- Designed with high ceilings and versatile living spaces, this traditional home is perfect for growing families.
- Formal living and dining rooms flank the wide foyer; a railed staircase emphasizes the foyer's soaring ceiling.
- The living room adjoins the spacious family room, where a fireplace warms chilly winter nights and a boxed-out window with an oak ledge takes advantage of summer sun.
- The adjacent dinette is open to the kitchen, which offers a huge island workstation and plenty of storage space. A four-season room off the dinette is a welcome haven, as is a study down the hall from the kitchen.
- Upstairs, four bedrooms form a private retreat. Three secondary bedrooms feature large windows and plenty of closet space, while sharing a full bath.
- Double doors introduce the master suite, where a boxed-out window overlooks the backyard. Walk-in closets flank the entrance to the private bath, which boasts a whirlpool tub, a separate shower and a vaulted ceiling.

Plan CL-3200-RE

Bedrooms: 4+	**Baths:** 3

Living Area:
Upper floor	1,318 sq. ft.
Main floor	1,955 sq. ft.
Four-season porch	176 sq. ft.
Total Living Area:	**3,449 sq. ft.**
Standard basement	1,955 sq. ft.
Garage	744 sq. ft.
Exterior Wall Framing:	2x6

Foundation Options:
Standard basement
Crawlspace
(All plans can be built with your choice of foundation and framing. A generic conversion diagram is available. See order form.)

BLUEPRINT PRICE CODE: E

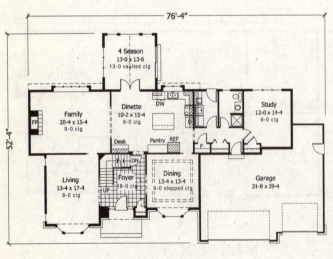

MAIN FLOOR

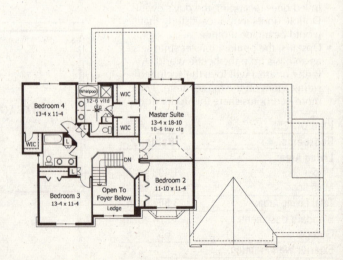

UPPER FLOOR

Plan CL-3200-RE
Plan copyright held by home designer/architect

Colonial Spirit

- This elegant two-story captures the spirit of the French Colonial home, with its brick exterior, columned entry, attic dormers and arched transom windows.
- The stately mood continues in the foyer, where a sweeping stairway and a plant shelf complement the soaring ceiling.
- Straight ahead, an abbreviated gallery leads to the high-traffic kitchen, which is intersected by each of the home's main living spaces; doors to the living room and dining room keep formal occasions quiet.
- Your guests will also appreciate the living room's inviting fireplace and refreshing wet bar.
- High half-round transoms beautifully frame the home's second fireplace in the relaxing family room.
- In the opposite wing resides a secluded study and a luxurious master suite with dual closets and vanities, plus a step-up tub under a dramatic arched window.
- An exciting game room serves the four secondary bedrooms upstairs.
- Also included in the blueprints is an optional two-car garage (not shown), which attaches at the utility room.

Plan L-505-GC

Bedrooms: 5+	Baths: 3½
Living Area:	
Upper floor	1,346 sq. ft.
Main floor	2,157 sq. ft.
Total Living Area:	**3,503 sq. ft.**
Garage	592 sq. ft.
Exterior Wall Framing:	2x4

Foundation Options:
Slab
(All plans can be built with your choice of foundation and framing. A generic conversion diagram is available. See order form.)

BLUEPRINT PRICE CODE: F

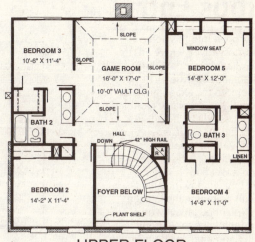

UPPER FLOOR

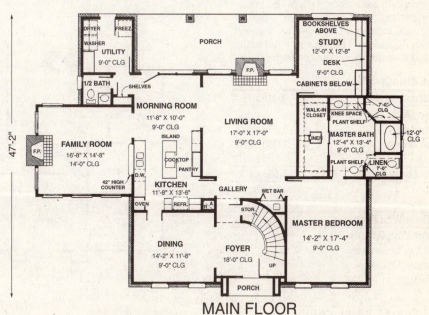

MAIN FLOOR

ORDER BLUEPRINTS ANYTIME!
CALL TOLL-FREE 1-800-820-1296

Plan L-505-GC
Plan copyright held by home designer/architect

PRICES AND DETAILS ON PAGES 12-15

STATELY COLONIAL-STYLE HOMES

Gracious Entry

- Double doors open into this home's gracious two-story foyer, where an upper-floor Palladian window throws light on a dramatic staircase.
- The living room, to the left of the foyer, includes an optional fireplace. Double doors close off a study with built-ins and a bright window arrangement.
- The huge family room boasts an impressive fireplace, access to the backyard and a wet bar.
- An extended bay window highlights a breakfast room adjoining the kitchen, where a well-planned layout works hard so you don't have to. A useful butler's pantry and a pocket door bridge the kitchen and the formal dining room.
- The isolated upper-floor master suite remains close enough to the other bedrooms for practical purposes, yet offers dual walk-in closets and a deluxe private bath, creating a secluded retreat.
- Three additional bedrooms, a full bath and a studio round out the upper floor.

Plan CH-361-A

Bedrooms: 4+	Baths: 2½
Living Area:	
Upper floor	1,382 sq. ft.
Main floor	1,695 sq. ft.
Studio	508 sq. ft.
Total Living Area:	**3,585 sq. ft.**
Basement	1,627 sq. ft.
Garage	511 sq. ft.
Exterior Wall Framing:	2x4

Foundation Options:
Daylight basement
Standard basement
Crawlspace
(All plans can be built with your choice of foundation and framing. A generic conversion diagram is available. See order form.)

BLUEPRINT PRICE CODE: F

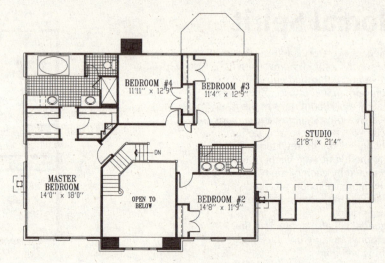

UPPER FLOOR

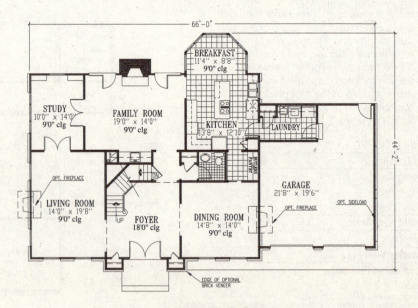

MAIN FLOOR

Plan CH-361-A
Plan copyright held by home designer/architect

STATELY COLONIAL-STYLE HOMES

Luxurious Inside and Out

- The beautiful exterior of this grand one-story home is a true indicator of the luxury within.
- Pillars accentuate the entrance of the home as well as the entrance to the exciting Grand Room. A gorgeous covered porch, featuring a summer kitchen, waits just beyond.
- The sunken Gathering Room boasts high, arched openings, a corner fireplace and a pretty window seat.
- Perfect for formal meals, the private dining room is sure to provide an extraordinary eating experience. Nearby, the island kitchen also serves the sunny morning room.
- The spectacular master suite has a sunken entertainment retreat, a two-way fireplace and access to the outside. The master bath offers a sinfully elegant tub and a sunken shower. A huge walk-in closet fits any wardrobe.
- Quiet and peaceful, the corner library easily converts to a bedroom, if needed.
- A guest suite also features a courtyard, a walk-in closet and its own bath.

Plan EOF-1	
Bedrooms: 4+	**Baths:** 4
Living Area:	
Main floor	3,903 sq. ft.
Total Living Area:	**3,903 sq. ft.**
Garage	748 sq. ft.
Exterior Wall Framing:	2x4

Foundation Options:
Slab
(All plans can be built with your choice of foundation and framing. A generic conversion diagram is available. See order form.)

BLUEPRINT PRICE CODE: F

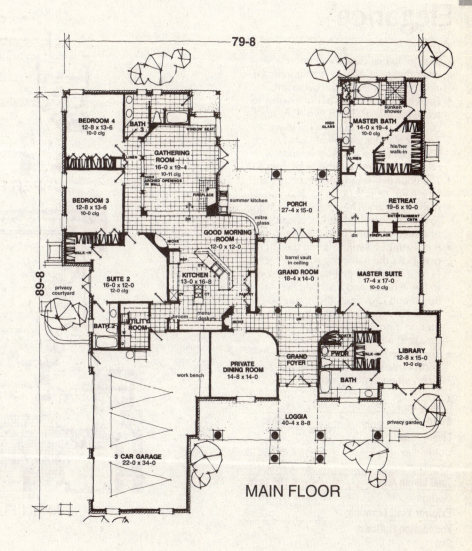

MAIN FLOOR

ORDER BLUEPRINTS ANYTIME!
CALL TOLL-FREE 1-800-820-1296

Plan EOF-1
Plan copyright held by home designer/architect

PRICES AND DETAILS
ON PAGES 12-15

STATELY COLONIAL-STYLE HOMES

Ultimate Elegance

- The ultimate in elegance and luxury, this home begins with an impressive foyer that reveals a sweeping staircase and a direct view of the backyard.
- The centrally located parlor, perfect for receiving guests, has a two-story-high ceiling, a spectacular wall of glass, a fireplace and a unique ale bar. French doors open to a covered veranda with a relaxing spa and a summer kitchen.
- The gourmet island kitchen boasts an airy 10-ft. ceiling, a menu desk and a walk-in pantry. The octagonal morning room has a vaulted ceiling and access to a second stairway to the upper level.
- A pass-through snack bar in the kitchen overlooks the gathering room, which hosts a cathedral ceiling, French doors to the veranda and a second fireplace.
- Bright and luxurious, the master suite has a 10-ft. ceiling and features a unique morning kitchen, a sunny sitting area and a lavish private bath.
- The curved staircase leads to three bedroom suites upstairs. The rear suites share an enchanting deck.

Plan EOF-3

Bedrooms: 4+	Baths: 5½

Living Area:
Upper floor	1,150 sq. ft.
Main floor	3,045 sq. ft.
Total Living Area:	**4,195 sq. ft.**
Garage	814 sq. ft.
Exterior Wall Framing:	2x6

Foundation Options:
Slab
(All plans can be built with your choice of foundation and framing. A generic conversion diagram is available. See order form.)

BLUEPRINT PRICE CODE: G

UPPER FLOOR

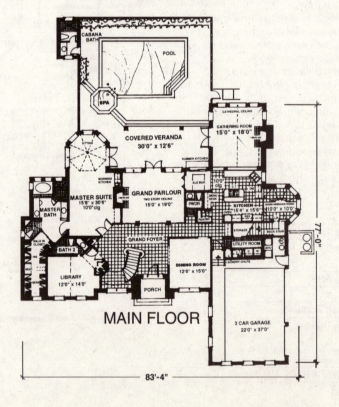
MAIN FLOOR

214 ORDER BLUEPRINTS ANYTIME! CALL TOLL-FREE 1-800-820-1296

Plan EOF-3
Plan copyright held by home designer/architect

PRICES AND DETAILS ON PAGES 12-15

Modern Craftsman

- Don't get turned around by the fact that this home has traditional Craftsman-style railings, classic shingles, decorative beams below the eaves—and a modern floor plan.
- What you will notice is that the floor plan itself appears to be upside down—all the primary living areas are located upstairs, atop a cute carport.
- The lower level hosts ample storage, including a mechanical room with laundry facilities, and a large secondary bedroom. A clever, angled closet and a corner sink make use of space in the bedroom, which has a private bath.
- Upstairs, the sunny, open living room blends seamlessly with the island kitchen and a cozy dining nook, as well as a sizable deck, lending a sense of spaciousness. A big pantry rounds out the space.
- The secluded master suite is a delightful retreat. It offers a large walk-in closet and private access to a full bath that features a generous tub.

Plan COA-1-0

Bedrooms: 2	Baths: 2
Living Area:	
Main floor	774 sq. ft.
Lower floor	438 sq. ft.
Total Living Area:	**1,212 sq. ft.**
Carport	230 sq. ft.
Exterior Wall Framing:	2x4

Foundation Options:
Slab
(All plans can be built with your choice of foundation and framing. A generic conversion diagram is available. See order form.)

BLUEPRINT PRICE CODE: A

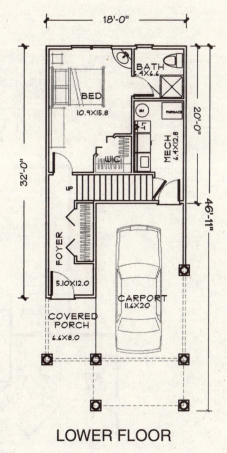

LOWER FLOOR

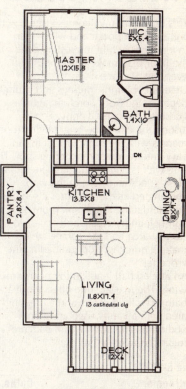

MAIN FLOOR

Plan COA-1-0
Plan copyright held by home designer/architect

Covered Porch Invites Visitors

- This nice home welcomes visitors with a grand front porch and wide-open living areas, while interesting angles in the floor plan make efficient use of every bit of space.
- Detailed columns, railings and shutters decorate the front porch that guides guests to the central entry.
- Just off the entry, the bright living room merges with the dining room for an easy entertaining or gathering spot. The side wall is lined with glass, including a glass door that opens to the yard.
- The angled kitchen features a serving counter facing the dining room. A handy laundry closet and access to a storage area and the garage are nearby, making quick work of unloading the groceries.
- An angled hall leads to the bedroom wing. The master suite offers a private bath, a walk-in closet and a dressing area with a vanity. Two additional bedrooms and another full bath are located down the hall.

Plan E-1217

Bedrooms: 3	Baths: 2
Living Area:	
Main floor	1,266 sq. ft.
Total Living Area:	**1,266 sq. ft.**
Garage and storage	550 sq. ft.
Exterior Wall Framing:	2x6
Foundation Options:	
Crawlspace	
Slab	

(All plans can be built with your choice of foundation and framing. A generic conversion diagram is available. See order form.)

BLUEPRINT PRICE CODE: A

SOUTHERN BELLES

VIEW INTO KITCHEN AND LIVING ROOM FROM DINING ROOM

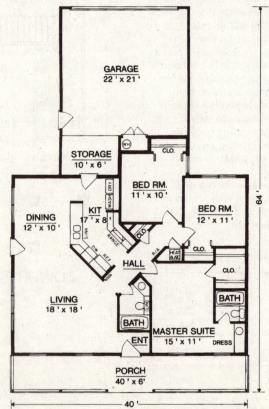

MAIN FLOOR

Plan E-1217
Plan copyright held by home designer/architect

216 — ORDER BLUEPRINTS ANYTIME! CALL TOLL-FREE 1-800-820-1296 — PRICES AND DETAILS ON PAGES 12-15

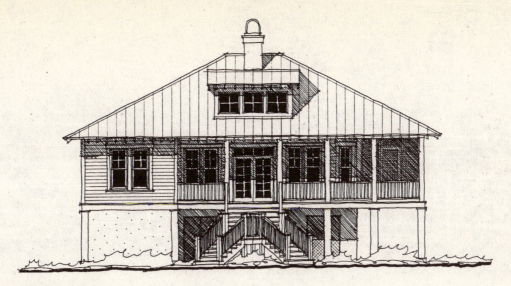

Ideal Getaway

- You'll have a ball in this cute, stylish and airy getaway home!
- A reverse Y-shaped staircase ascends to an expansive front porch that wraps around to a roomy screen porch.
- Dual doors lead to a gallery that connects the dining and living rooms. Joined also by a two-way fireplace, these rooms share an airy ceiling and are illuminated by numerous windows.
- The island kitchen may also be reached from the porch. Its layout manages all sorts of activity, from after-school antics to serious meal preparations.
- Down the hall, a secondary bedroom is a cozy place for the kids or for guests. A full bath and ample linen storage complement this room.
- Off the living room, the master suite is a peaceful haven. The private bath offers dual sinks, a garden tub, a separate shower and two walk-in closets.
- The lower floor has storage space on the left, plus an oversized two-car garage entered from the right. A wraparound porch mirrors the porches above.

Plan WAA-9738-C

Bedrooms: 2	Baths: 2
Living Area:	
Main floor	1,420 sq. ft.
Total Living Area:	**1,420 sq. ft.**
Screen porch	253 sq. ft.
Garage	848 sq. ft.
Storage	567 sq. ft.
Exterior Wall Framing:	2x4
Foundation Options:	

Pier
(All plans can be built with your choice of foundation and framing. A generic conversion diagram is available. See order form.)

BLUEPRINT PRICE CODE: A

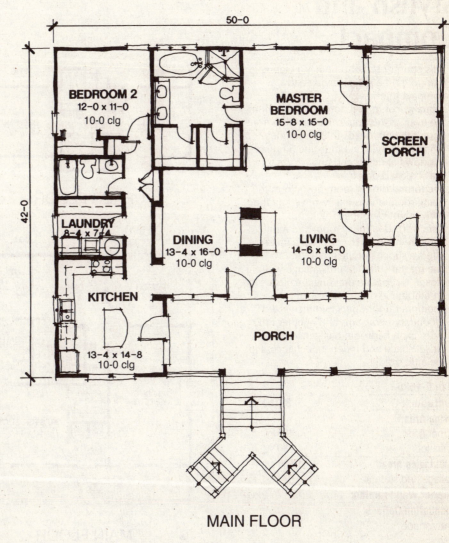

MAIN FLOOR

ORDER BLUEPRINTS ANYTIME!
CALL TOLL-FREE 1-800-820-1296

Plan WAA-9738-C
Plan copyright held by home designer/architect

PRICES AND DETAILS ON PAGES 12-15

Stylish and Compact

- This country-style home has a classic exterior and a space-saving and compact interior.
- A quaint columned porch extends along the front of the home. Through the front door, the entry leads to the spacious living room with a handsome fireplace, windows at either end and access to a big screened porch.
- The formal dining room flows from the living room and is easily served by the convenient U-shaped kitchen.
- A nice-sized laundry room and a full bath are nearby. The two-car garage offers a super storage area.
- The master suite features a huge walk-in closet. A separate dressing area leads to an adjoining, dual-access bath.
- The upper floor offers two nice-sized secondary bedrooms and another full bath. Each bedroom has generous closet space and independent access to the attic storage.

Plan E-1626

Bedrooms: 3	Baths: 2

Living Area:
Upper floor	464 sq. ft.
Main floor	1,136 sq. ft.
Total Living Area:	**1,600 sq. ft.**
Garage and storage	572 sq. ft.
Exterior Wall Framing:	**2x6**

Foundation Options:
Crawlspace
Slab
(All plans can be built with your choice of foundation and framing. A generic conversion diagram is available. See order form.)

BLUEPRINT PRICE CODE: B

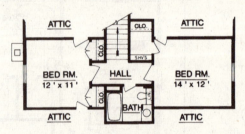

UPPER FLOOR

VIEW INTO LIVING ROOM

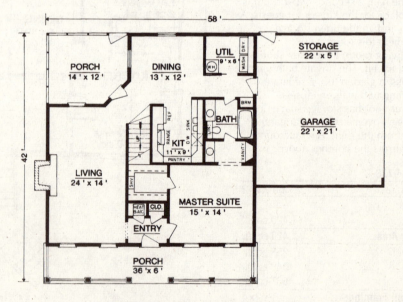

MAIN FLOOR

SOUTHERN BELLES

Plan E-1626
Plan copyright held by home designer/architect

Friendly Country Charm

- An inviting front porch welcomes you to this friendly one-story home.
- The porch opens to a spacious central living room with a warm fireplace and functional built-in storage shelves.
- The bay window of the adjoining dining room allows a view of the backyard.
- The dining area also enjoys an eating bar provided by the adjacent walk-through kitchen.
- The nice-sized kitchen also has a windowed sink and easy access to the laundry room and carport.
- Three bedrooms and two baths occupy the sleeping wing. The oversized master bedroom features a lovely boxed-out window, two walk-in closets and a private bath. The secondary bedrooms share the second full bath.

Plan J-8692

Bedrooms: 3	Baths: 2
Living Area:	
Main floor	1,633 sq. ft.
Total Living Area:	**1,633 sq. ft.**
Standard basement	1,633 sq. ft.
Carport	380 sq. ft.
Exterior Wall Framing:	2x4

Foundation Options:
Standard basement
Crawlspace
Slab
(All plans can be built with your choice of foundation and framing. A generic conversion diagram is available. See order form.)

BLUEPRINT PRICE CODE: B

VIEW INTO LIVING ROOM, DINING ROOM AND KITCHEN

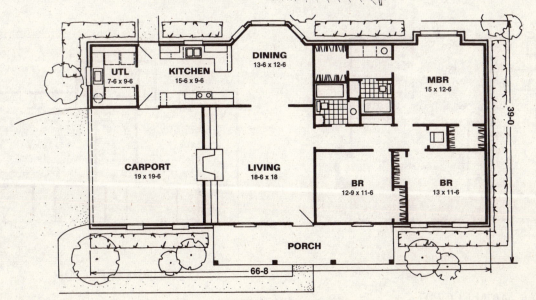

MAIN FLOOR

Plan J-8692
Plan copyright held by home designer/architect

ORDER BLUEPRINTS ANYTIME!
CALL TOLL-FREE 1-800-820-1296

PRICES AND DETAILS ON PAGES 12-15

Simple Beauty

- This unassuming country home projects a peaceful air to the world.
- The classic front porch is a perfect place to reminisce with old friends. Inside, the high vaulted entry unfolds to the family room, where a fireplace serves as a striking focal point.
- Possessing its own quiet elegance, the adjoining dining area is equally suited for both casual meals and important social gatherings. Double windows look out over the inviting backyard deck; a French door lets you step out for a breath of fresh air.
- Clever and efficient touches abound in the kitchen, and include a smart serving counter angled to face the family and dining rooms. A cheery skylight nicely punctuates the kitchen's vaulted ceiling, and a bright window gives the sink area visual appeal.
- A pocket door helps to segregate the laundry area and the master bedroom from the common living areas. In the master bath, a luxurious garden tub will help you to relax after a strenuous day.
- Your children will love their private upper-floor bedrooms, which offer dormers that are ideal for window seats. A split bath eases the bedtime routine and a balcony views the entry.
- A drive-under garage occupies half of the basement level.
- Upon request, a detached garage plan will be provided; a studio and bath above the garage measure 336 sq. ft.

Plan APS-1612

Bedrooms: 3	Baths: 2½
Living Area:	
Upper floor	579 sq. ft.
Main floor	1,064 sq. ft.
Total Living Area:	**1,643 sq. ft.**
Daylight basement	490 sq. ft.
Tuck-under garage	520 sq. ft.
Exterior Wall Framing:	2x4

Foundation Options:
Daylight basement
(All plans can be built with your choice of foundation and framing. A generic conversion diagram is available. See order form.)

BLUEPRINT PRICE CODE: B

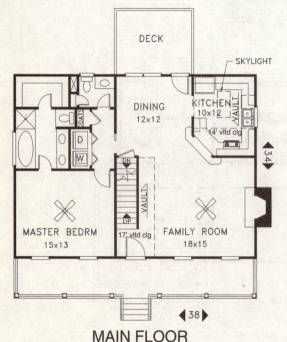

MAIN FLOOR

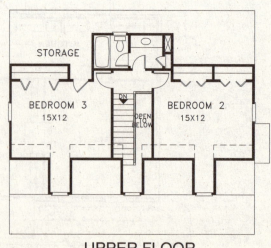

UPPER FLOOR

Plan APS-1612
Plan copyright held by home designer/architect

Take It Outside

- Take a breather on this country-style home's expansive front porch, or relax with loved ones out on the wide-open backyard patio.
- Opening directly from the front porch, the spacious Great Room showcases a soaring ceiling and built-in bookcases that flank an inviting fireplace.
- The kitchen's angled snack bar conveniently serves both the Great Room and the dining room, which offers access to the carport and the back patio. The nearby walk-in pantry and laundry facilities ease household duties.
- The secluded owner's suite boasts a spacious sleeping area and two walk-in closets. Its private bath has a dual-sink vanity, a wide garden tub and a separate shower.
- Two secondary bedrooms occupy the other side of the home. Both feature walk-in closets and share a full bath.
- Storage space adjoining the carport provides plenty of room for tools.

Plan J-9720	
Bedrooms: 3	Baths: 2
Living Area:	
Main floor	1,680 sq. ft.
Total Living Area:	**1,680 sq. ft.**
Standard basement	1,680 sq. ft.
Carport	484 sq. ft.
Storage	156 sq. ft.
Exterior Wall Framing:	2x4
Foundation Options:	

Standard basement
Crawlspace
Slab
(All plans can be built with your choice of foundation and framing. A generic conversion diagram is available. See order form.)

BLUEPRINT PRICE CODE: B

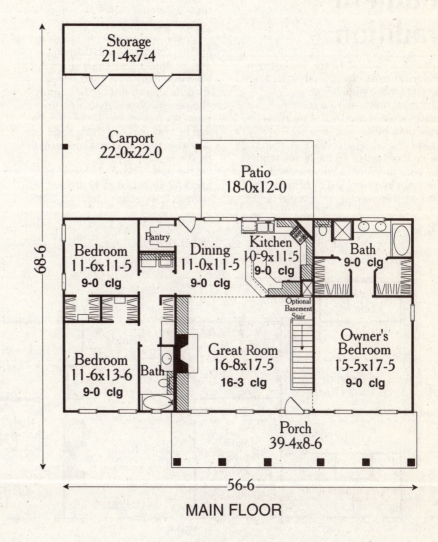

MAIN FLOOR

ORDER BLUEPRINTS ANYTIME!
CALL TOLL-FREE 1-800-820-1296

Plan J-9720
Plan copyright held by home designer/architect

PRICES AND DETAILS
ON PAGES 12-15

Southern Tradition

- Porches, a patio and a spacious carport make this traditional country-style home perfect for Southern living.
- Charming touches like a columned porch, shutters and oval glass in the front door evoke a bygone era.
- Inside, a soaring cathedral ceiling in the living room opens up the home, while the cozy fireplace provides warmth.
- Prepare a home-cooked meal in the open kitchen, then savor it in the bayed dining room. On warm summer nights, double doors invite you to dine on either the patio or the back porch.
- A convenient laundry room next to the kitchen offers access to the carport outside and keeps muddy shoes out of the main living area. Extra storage space is located just off the carport.
- The generous-sized master bedroom promises peaceful nights of slumber and relaxation. Dual sinks, a spa tub and a big walk-in closet complete the master bath.
- On the other side of the home, two good-sized secondary bedrooms with roomy closets share a full hall bath.

Plan J-9527

Bedrooms: 3	Baths: 2

Living Area:
Main floor — 1,689 sq. ft.

Total Living Area: — **1,689 sq. ft.**
Standard basement — 1,689 sq. ft.
Carport — 382 sq. ft.
Storage — 91 sq. ft.

Exterior Wall Framing: 2x4

Foundation Options:
Standard basement
Crawlspace
Slab
(All plans can be built with your choice of foundation and framing. A generic conversion diagram is available. See order form.)

BLUEPRINT PRICE CODE: B

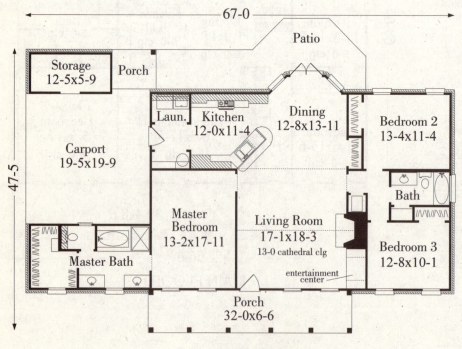

MAIN FLOOR

ORDER BLUEPRINTS ANYTIME!
CALL TOLL-FREE 1-800-820-1296

Plan J-9527
Plan copyright held by home designer/architect

PRICES AND DETAILS ON PAGES 12-15

Masterful Master Suite

- This gorgeous home features front and rear covered porches and a master suite so luxurious it deserves its own wing.
- The expansive entry welcomes visitors into the spacious, skylighted living room, which boasts a handsome fireplace. The adjacent formal dining room overlooks the front porch.
- The efficient kitchen features an angled snack bar and a bayed eating area. An all-purpose utility room is conveniently located off the kitchen.
- The kitchen, eating area, living room and dining room are all enhanced by high ceilings.
- The secluded master suite features a tub and a separate shower, a double-sink vanity, a walk-in closet with built-in shelves and a private toilet.
- The two secondary bedrooms share a hall bath at the other end of the home.
- The two-car garage features two built-in storage areas and access to unfinished attic space above.

Plan E-1811

Bedrooms: 3	Baths: 2

Living Area:
Main floor — 1,800 sq. ft.
Total Living Area: **1,800 sq. ft.**
Garage and storage — 574 sq. ft.
Enclosed storage — 60 sq. ft.
Exterior Wall Framing: 2x6
Foundation Options:
Crawlspace
Slab
(All plans can be built with your choice of foundation and framing. A generic conversion diagram is available. See order form.)

BLUEPRINT PRICE CODE: B

VIEW INTO LIVING ROOM

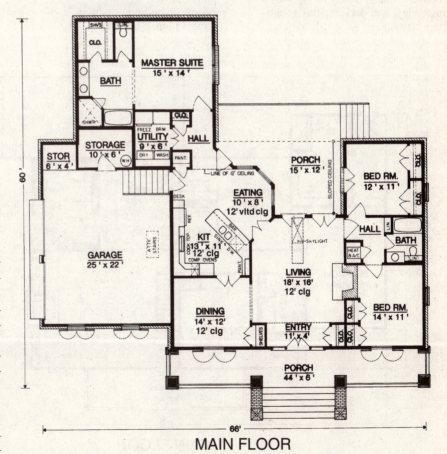

MAIN FLOOR

ORDER BLUEPRINTS ANYTIME!
CALL TOLL-FREE 1-800-820-1296

Plan E-1811
Plan copyright held by home designer/architect

PRICES AND DETAILS ON PAGES 12-15

SOUTHERN BELLES

Breezy Beauty

- A nostalgic covered front porch, a backyard deck and a sprawling screened porch combine to make this beautiful one-story home a breezy delight.
- The front entry opens into the Great Room, which is crowned by a soaring cathedral ceiling. A handsome fireplace is flanked by built-in bookshelves and cabinets.
- The large, bayed dining room offers a tray ceiling and deck access through French doors.
- The adjoining kitchen boasts plenty of counter space and a handy built-in recipe desk.
- From the kitchen, a side door leads to the screened porch. A wood floor and deck access highlight this cheery room.
- A quiet hall leads past a convenient utility room to the sleeping quarters.
- The secluded master bedroom is enhanced by a spacious walk-in closet. The private master bath includes a lovely garden tub, a separate shower and dual vanities.
- Two more bedrooms with walk-in closets share a hall bath.

Plan C-8905

Bedrooms: 3	Baths: 2

Living Area:
Main floor — 1,811 sq. ft.
Total Living Area: **1,811 sq. ft.**
Screened porch — 240 sq. ft.
Daylight basement — 1,811 sq. ft.
Garage — 484 sq. ft.

Exterior Wall Framing: 2x4

Foundation Options:
Daylight basement
Crawlspace
Slab
(All plans can be built with your choice of foundation and framing. A generic conversion diagram is available. See order form.)

BLUEPRINT PRICE CODE: B

MAIN FLOOR

Plan C-8905
Plan copyright held by home designer/architect

A Real Charmer

- A tranquil railed porch makes this country one-story a real charmer.
- The main entry opens directly into the Great Room, which serves as the home's focal point. A cathedral ceiling soars above, while a fireplace and a built-in cabinet for games make the space a fun gathering spot.
- Beautiful French doors expand the Great Room to a peaceful covered porch at the rear of the home. Open the doors and let in the fresh summer air!
- A bayed breakfast nook unfolds from the kitchen, where the family cook will love the long island snack bar and the pantry. The carport is located nearby to save steps when you unload groceries.
- Across the home, the master bedroom features a walk-in closet with built-in shelves. A cathedral ceiling tops the master bath, which boasts a private toilet, a second walk-in closet and a separate tub and shower.
- A skylighted hall bath services the two secondary bedrooms.

Plan J-9508	
Bedrooms: 3	**Baths:** 2½
Living Area:	
Main floor	1,875 sq. ft.
Total Living Area:	**1,875 sq. ft.**
Standard basement	1,875 sq. ft.
Carport	418 sq. ft.
Storage	114 sq. ft.
Exterior Wall Framing:	2x4
Foundation Options:	
Standard basement	
Crawlspace	
Slab	

(All plans can be built with your choice of foundation and framing. A generic conversion diagram is available. See order form.)

BLUEPRINT PRICE CODE: B

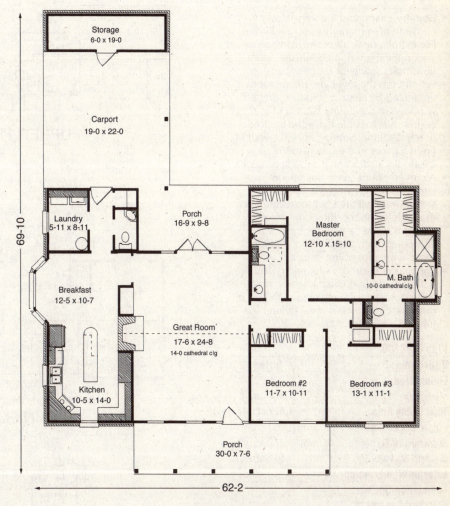

MAIN FLOOR

ORDER BLUEPRINTS ANYTIME!
CALL TOLL-FREE 1-800-820-1296

Plan J-9508
Plan copyright held by home designer/architect

PRICES AND DETAILS ON PAGES 12-15

Upscale Charm

- Country charm and the very latest in conveniences mark this upscale home. For extra appeal, all of the living areas are on the main floor, while the upper floor hosts space for future expansion.
- Set off from the foyer, the dining room is embraced by elegant columns. Arched windows in the dining room and in the bedroom across the hall echo the front porch detailing. Straight ahead, a wall of French doors in the family room overlooks a back porch and a large deck.
- A curved island snack bar smoothly connects the gourmet kitchen to the sunny breakfast area, which features a dramatic vaulted ceiling brightened by skylights. Other amenities include a computer room and a laundry/utility room with a recycling center.
- The master bedroom's luxurious private bath includes a dual-sink vanity and a large storage unit with a built-in chest of drawers. Other extras are a step-up spa tub and a separate shower.

Plan J-92100

Bedrooms: 3+	Baths: 2
Living Area:	
Main floor	1,877 sq. ft.
Total Living Area:	**1,877 sq. ft.**
Future upper floor	1,500 sq. ft.
Standard basement	1,877 sq. ft.
Garage and storage	551 sq. ft.
Exterior Wall Framing:	2x4

Foundation Options:
Standard basement
Crawlspace
Slab
(All plans can be built with your choice of foundation and framing. A generic conversion diagram is available. See order form.)

BLUEPRINT PRICE CODE: B

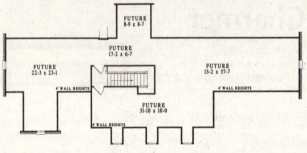

UPPER FLOOR

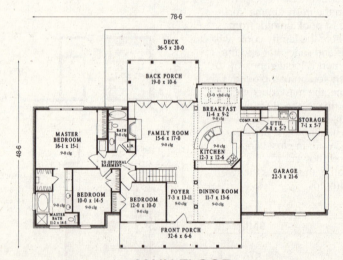

MAIN FLOOR

STAIRWAY AREA IN NON-BASEMENT VERSIONS

VIEW INTO FAMILY ROOM AND BREAKFAST NOOK

ORDER BLUEPRINTS ANYTIME! CALL TOLL-FREE 1-800-820-1296

Plan J-92100
Plan copyright held by home designer/architect

PRICES AND DETAILS ON PAGES 12-15

Southern Comfort

- This sprawling three-bedroom design exemplifies the comfort and charm of Southern-style architecture.
- The columned front porch beckons you to relax on a Sunday afternoon.
- Inside, the formal dining room opens to the left of the foyer, which leads to the home's focal point—the large living room. Complete with a built-in entertainment center, a cozy fireplace and a snack bar, this space will attract plenty of attention. Windows flanking the fireplace overlook the rear porch.
- Among the kitchen's many amenities are an island cooktop, a pantry closet and an adjoining breakfast area. The breakfast area accesses the rear porch through a French door.
- Secluded from the other bedrooms for privacy, the master suite is highlighted by two walk-in closets, a garden tub, a separate shower and a dual-sink vanity. The suite also enjoys private access to the rear porch.
- Across the home, two secondary bedrooms, one with a walk-in closet, share another full bath.

Plan L-1990-02A

Bedrooms: 3	Baths: 2½
Living Area:	
Main floor	1,990 sq. ft.
Total Living Area:	**1,990 sq. ft.**
Garage	522 sq. ft.
Exterior Wall Framing:	2x4

Foundation Options:
Slab
(All plans can be built with your choice of foundation and framing. A generic conversion diagram is available. See order form.)

BLUEPRINT PRICE CODE: B

MAIN FLOOR

ORDER BLUEPRINTS ANYTIME!
CALL TOLL-FREE 1-800-820-1296

Plan L-1990-02A
Plan copyright held by home designer/architect

PRICES AND DETAILS ON PAGES 12-15

Open Invitation

- The wide front porch of this friendly country-style home extends an open invitation to all who visit.
- Highlighted by a round-topped transom, the home's entrance opens directly into the spacious living room, which shows off a fireplace flanked by windows.
- The large adjoining dining area is enhanced by a lovely bay window and is easily serviced by the updated kitchen's angled snack bar.
- A bright sun room off the kitchen provides a great space for informal meals or relaxation. Access to a back porch is nearby.
- The good-sized master bedroom is secluded from the other sleeping areas. Its lavish private bath includes a separate shower, a dual-sink vanity, a garden tub and a nice-sized walk-in closet.
- Two more bedrooms share a second full bath. A convenient laundry/utility room is nearby.
- The upper floor offers opportunity for expanding into additional living space.
- The home's high ceilings add spaciousness.

Plan J-91078

Bedrooms: 3+	Baths: 2
Living Area:	
Main floor	1,879 sq. ft.
Total Living Area:	**1,879 sq. ft.**
Future upper floor	1,007 sq. ft.
Standard basement	1,846 sq. ft.
Garage	484 sq. ft.
Storage	132 sq. ft.
Exterior Wall Framing:	2x6

Foundation Options:
Standard basement
Crawlspace
Slab
(All plans can be built with your choice of foundation and framing. A generic conversion diagram is available. See order form.)

BLUEPRINT PRICE CODE: B

VIEW INTO DINING AND LIVING ROOMS

SOUTHERN BELLES

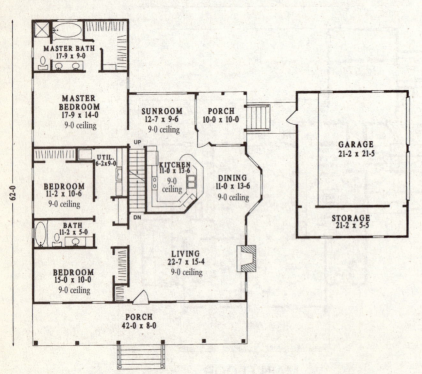

MAIN FLOOR

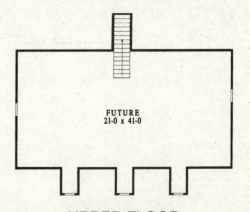

UPPER FLOOR

ORDER BLUEPRINTS ANYTIME!
CALL TOLL-FREE 1-800-820-1296

Plan J-91078
Plan copyright held by home designer/architect

PRICES AND DETAILS ON PAGES 12-15

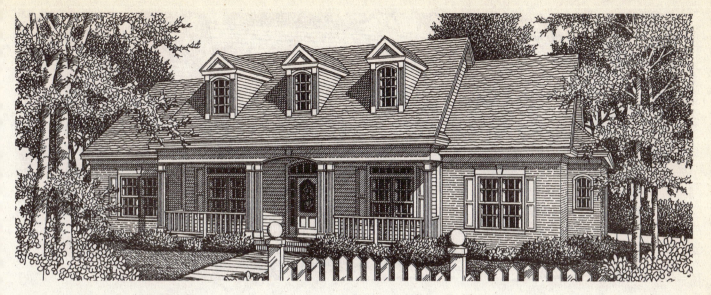

Outdoor Fête

- Who doesn't love an outdoor party? Front and rear porches and a spacious back deck make this design a natural for outside entertaining. The back porch features a spa and a summer kitchen.
- The interior is equally accommodating. Formal living and dining rooms flank the foyer, which leads into the stunning angled family room. A fireplace topped by a TV niche serves as the room's focal point. High above, a clerestory window illuminates the space.
- Columns define the entrance to the bright breakfast room and the kitchen, which boasts proximity to the two-car garage for easy unloading of groceries.
- When your guests are gone, relax in the master suite. A tray ceiling, a sitting area and a luxurious private bath make it a pampering retreat. A second bedroom is serviced by the hall bath.
- Plans are included for making the living room a third bedroom. Future area over the garage could be used as a studio.

Plan APS-1914

Bedrooms: 2+	Baths: 3
Living Area:	
Main floor	1,992 sq. ft.
Total Living Area:	**1,992 sq. ft.**
Future area	247 sq. ft.
Standard basement	1,992 sq.ft.
Garage	590 sq. ft.
Mechanical	19 sq. ft.
Exterior Wall Framing:	2x4

Foundation Options:
Standard basement
Slab
(All plans can be built with your choice of foundation and framing. A generic conversion diagram is available. See order form.)

BLUEPRINT PRICE CODE: B

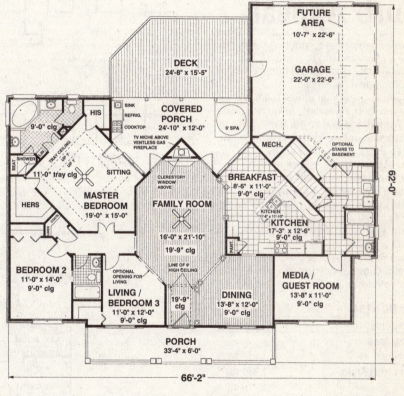

MAIN FLOOR

SOUTHERN BELLES

ORDER BLUEPRINTS ANYTIME!
CALL TOLL-FREE 1-800-820-1296

Plan APS-1914
Plan copyright held by home designer/architect

PRICES AND DETAILS ON PAGES 12-15

Traditional Curb Appeal

- With an expansive front porch topped by a charming trio of dormers, this traditional country-style home offers the curb appeal you seek.
- Open to the formal dining room and a bayed morning room, the kitchen boasts a work island and an attractive, bow-shaped counter serving the living room.
- Step through the spacious living room's French doors to the deck area. An optional barbecue and an outdoor spa make entertaining a breeze.
- The master suite enjoys a bayed sitting area, deck access, two walk-in closets and a private bath with separate vanities and a garden tub.
- Two more bedrooms share a full hall bath. Future space upstairs can be used as you desire.

Plan DD-1984

Bedrooms: 3+	Baths: 3

Living Area:
Main floor .... 1,994 sq. ft.
Total Living Area: .... **1,994 sq. ft.**
Future upper floor .... 1,316 sq. ft.
Standard basement ..... 1,994 sq. ft.
Garage and storage .... 466 sq. ft.
Exterior Wall Framing: 2x4

Foundation Options:
Standard basement
Crawlspace
Slab
(All plans can be built with your choice of foundation and framing. A generic conversion diagram is available. See order form.)
BLUEPRINT PRICE CODE: B

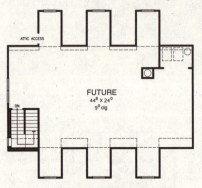

UPPER FLOOR

VIEW INTO LIVING ROOM

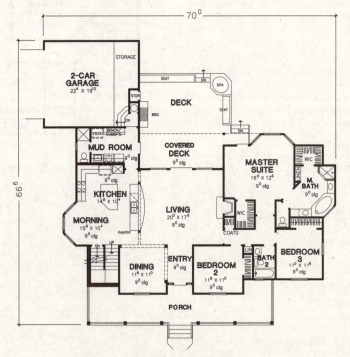

MAIN FLOOR

SOUTHERN BELLES

Plan DD-1984
Plan copyright held by home designer/architect

Clever Balance

- Beauty and balance are the hallmarks of this home's exterior, while a clever combination of openness and seclusion marks the floor plan.
- Columns and rails frame the front porch, which leads to the home's sidelighted entry. Inside, the Great Room's fireplace commands attention, situated at the center of the room between two sets of French doors. This area is perfect for large gatherings.
- The spacious dining room is equally accommodating for guests, while the breakfast nook is nice for casual dining.
- The kitchen is a dream for any gourmet. With a wide island workstation, a snack bar and a cavernous pantry, the family chef will have endless resources for preparing all sorts of meals and goodies.
- Hidden in a private corner of the home, the master suite is a pleasant retreat. It offers two walk-in closets and a sizable bath with a dual-sink vanity. Three additional bedrooms share a full bath.

Plan J-9816	
Bedrooms: 4	**Baths:** 2½
Living Area:	
Main floor	1,997 sq. ft.
Total Living Area:	**1,997 sq. ft.**
Standard basement	1,997 sq. ft.
Garage	465 sq. ft.
Storage	105 sq. ft.
Exterior Wall Framing:	2x4
Foundation Options:	
Standard basement	
Crawlspace	
Slab	
(All plans can be built with your choice of foundation and framing. A generic conversion diagram is available. See order form.)	
BLUEPRINT PRICE CODE:	**B**

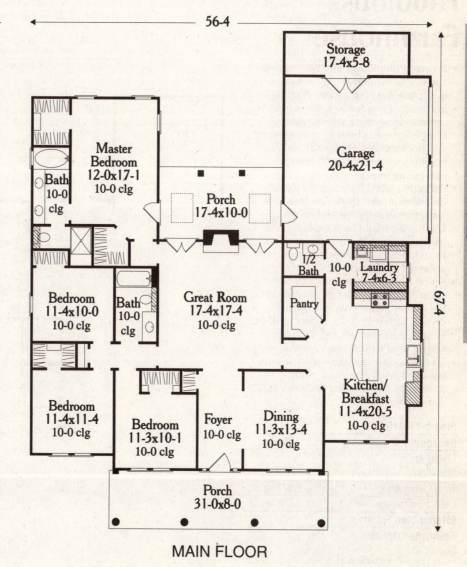

MAIN FLOOR

SOUTHERN BELLES

ORDER BLUEPRINTS ANYTIME!
CALL TOLL-FREE 1-800-820-1296

Plan J-9816
Plan copyright held by home designer/architect

PRICES AND DETAILS ON PAGES 12-15

231

Fabulous Farmhouse

- Tapered columns around the front porch and dormer windows set the tone for this sprawling country farmhouse.
- Inside, the foyer leads to the expansive central living room, which boasts a cozy fireplace, a built-in media center and bookshelves. Half-walls and columns set this space off from the other living areas.
- Perfectly placed between the formal dining room and the sunny breakfast area, the well-appointed kitchen features an island cooktop and a snack bar shared with the living room. A French door in the breakfast area accesses the rear porch.
- Set off from the living room by a solarium that doubles as a home office, the master bedroom offers a lavish private bath with his-and-hers walk-in closets, a garden tub and separate shower and a dual-sink vanity.
- The secondary bedroom sports a large walk-in closet. The study easily transforms into another bedroom for out-of-town guests.

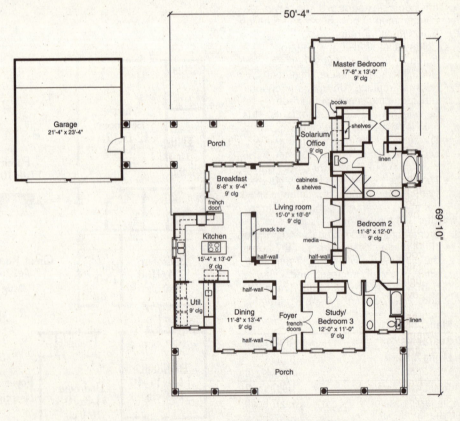

MAIN FLOOR

Plan L-77-01B

Bedrooms: 2+	Baths: 2
Living Area:	
Main floor	2,077 sq. ft.
Total Living Area:	**2,077 sq. ft.**
Detached garage	528 sq. ft.
Exterior Wall Framing:	2x4

Foundation Options:
Slab
(All plans can be built with your choice of foundation and framing. A generic conversion diagram is available. See order form.)

BLUEPRINT PRICE CODE: C

From the Past to Your Future

- With a trio of dormers up top and a classic porch out front, this stately traditional-style home steps straight from the past and into your future.
- Pass through the foyer into the living room, which features a tray ceiling and a window-flanked fireplace that warms not just that space, but the adjoining breakfast room, too.
- Mealtime is easy with a roomy kitchen offering lots of counter space, and with an angled counter serving both the living and breakfast rooms, you'll still be close by when guests come over.
- The owner's bedroom includes two walk-in closets and a private bath with a dual-sink vanity, while two secondary bedrooms share a full bath.
- Upstairs, future space abounds, with enough room for a wacky game room and even a home office.

Plan J-9513

Bedrooms: 3+	Baths: 2½

Living Area:

Main floor	2,127 sq. ft.
Total Living Area:	**2,127 sq. ft.**
Future upper floor	1,095 sq. ft.
Standard basement	2,127 sq. ft.
Garage and storage	546 sq. ft.

Exterior Wall Framing: 2x4

Foundation Options:
Standard basement
Crawlspace
Slab

(All plans can be built with your choice of foundation and framing. A generic conversion diagram is available. See order form.)

BLUEPRINT PRICE CODE: C

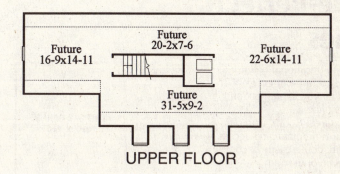

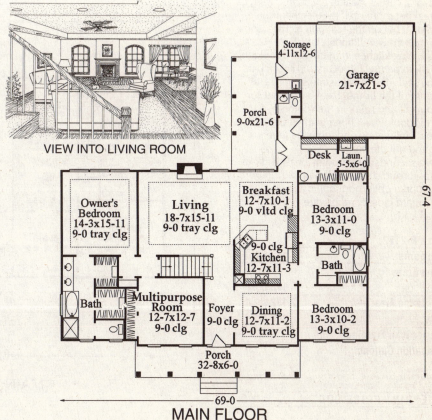

ORDER BLUEPRINTS ANYTIME!
CALL TOLL-FREE 1-800-820-1296

Plan J-9513
Plan copyright held by home designer/architect

PRICES AND DETAILS ON PAGES 12-15

Picture-Perfect Porches

- Come home to traditional country living, where picture-perfect front and rear porches let you stretch out and relax at day's end.
- The fantastic Great Room, with a tray ceiling, a warm fireplace and access to the rear porch, could easily become your family's favorite room.
- Savor a casual meal in the sunny breakfast room or, if the weather is nice, enjoy it out on the rear porch. The cook in the family will appreciate the adjoining kitchen with its island cooktop, walk-in pantry and oversized snack bar.
- The secluded master suite spans the depth of the home. Steal a moment for yourself and relax in the soothing whirlpool tub. A huge walk-in closet, a dual-sink vanity and a private toilet round out the bath.
- Two secondary bedrooms boast walk-in closets and share a full hall bath. A third secondary bedroom offers a large standard closet and private access to the hall bath.

Plan DP-2172

Bedrooms: 4	Baths: 2
Living Area:	
Main floor	2,172 sq. ft.
Total Living Area:	**2,172 sq. ft.**
Garage	480 sq. ft.
Exterior Wall Framing:	2x4
Foundation Options:	
Slab	

(All plans can be built with your choice of foundation and framing. A generic conversion diagram is available. See order form.)

BLUEPRINT PRICE CODE: C

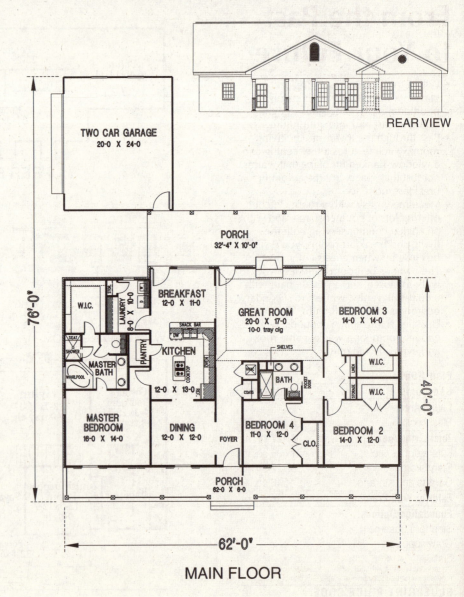

REAR VIEW

MAIN FLOOR

Plan DP-2172
Plan copyright held by home designer/architect

Fetching Facade

- A haven of comfort, this two-story design is filled with special features. The attractive facade sports a covered wraparound front porch, round-top windows and a trio of dormers.
- Airy and spacious, the Great Room houses a fireplace and a built-in TV cabinet, designed to enhance your at-home entertaining. French doors provide access to the living room in front and the large terrace in back.
- The roomy kitchen includes an island bar, a built-in menu desk and a pantry closet. The adjoining bayed dinette is perfect for casual meals.
- A mud room and a half-bath are located just off the kitchen. The mud room offers access to the garage.
- Retreat to the comfort of the master suite, ideally situated beyond the Great Room. It boasts a cathedral ceiling in the bedroom, a large walk-in closet and a well-equipped private bath with a dual-sink vanity, a whirlpool tub and a separate shower.
- Three good-sized secondary bedrooms and a full bath occupy the upper floor, completing the plan.

Plan AHP-9790

Bedrooms: 4	**Baths:** 2½
Living Area:	
Upper floor	672 sq. ft.
Main floor	1,505 sq. ft.
Total Living Area:	**2,177 sq. ft.**
Standard basement	1,505 sq. ft.
Garage and storage	468 sq. ft.
Exterior Wall Framing:	2x4 or 2x6

Foundation Options:
Standard basement
Crawlspace
Slab

(All plans can be built with your choice of foundation and framing. A generic conversion diagram is available. See order form.)

BLUEPRINT PRICE CODE: C

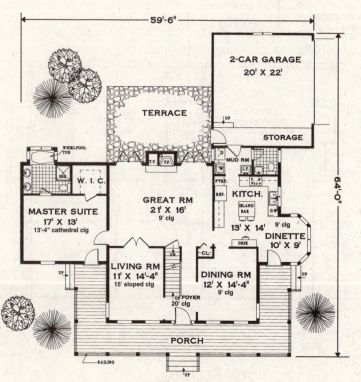

MAIN FLOOR

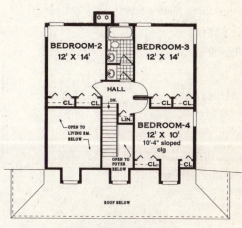

UPPER FLOOR

ORDER BLUEPRINTS ANYTIME! CALL TOLL-FREE 1-800-820-1296

Plan AHP-9790
Plan copyright held by home designer/architect

PRICES AND DETAILS ON PAGES 12-15

Spacious Country-Style

- This distinctive country-style home is highlighted by a wide front porch and multipaned windows with shutters.
- Inside, the dining room is defined by elegant columns and beams above, and it opens to the living room.
- The central living room boasts a cathedral ceiling, a fireplace and French doors to the rear patio.
- Designed for both work and play, the delightful kitchen and breakfast nook enjoy natural light from two kitchen windows and a large bay in the nook.
- A handy utility room and a half-bath flank a hallway leading to the carport.
- The master suite offers his-and-hers walk-in closets and an incredible bath that incorporates a plant shelf above a raised spa tub.
- The two remaining bedrooms share a hall bath that is compartmentalized to allow more than one user at a time.

Plan J-86140

Bedrooms: 3	Baths: 2½
Living Area:	
Main floor	2,177 sq. ft.
Total Living Area:	**2,177 sq. ft.**
Standard basement	2,177 sq. ft.
Carport	440 sq. ft.
Storage	120 sq. ft.
Exterior Wall Framing:	2x4

Foundation Options:
Standard basement
Crawlspace
Slab
(All plans can be built with your choice of foundation and framing. A generic conversion diagram is available. See order form.)

BLUEPRINT PRICE CODE: C

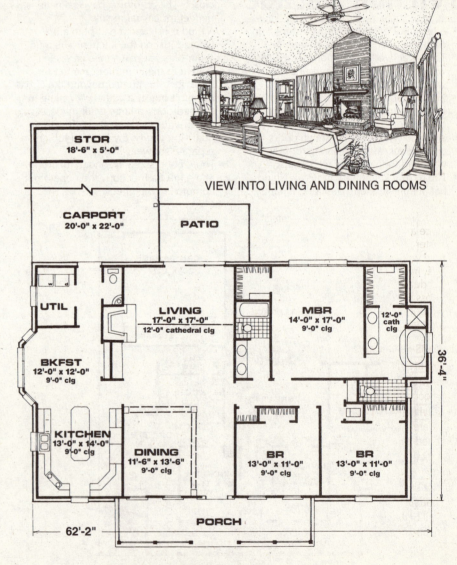

VIEW INTO LIVING AND DINING ROOMS

MAIN FLOOR

Plan J-86140

Inviting Design

- Lovely transoms and a deep, shady porch invite you into this welcoming home. The modest exterior hides a vast, open floor plan with soaring ceilings.
- Sprawling beneath a vaulted ceiling, the family room fills the heart of the home with lively activity. Double doors open into the more demure living room, which is perfect for formal gatherings.
- Across the foyer, the dining room features an elegant tray ceiling and tall windows. The grand country kitchen, only a step away, enjoys a huge walk-in pantry and spills into a sunny eating area overlooking a large patio or deck.
- Space and sunlight are the rule in the master suite, with its many windows, huge walk-in closets and pleasant sitting area. In the private bath, a garden tub and dual sinks add a luxurious touch.
- Across the home, two additional bedrooms—one with a private bath—boast generous walk-in closets.

Plan APS-2119	
Bedrooms: 3+	Baths: 3
Living Area:	
Main floor	2,184 sq. ft.
Total Living Area:	**2,184 sq. ft.**
Future area	379 sq. ft.
Screened porch	166 sq. ft.
Daylight basement	2,184 sq. ft.
Garage	548 sq. ft.
Exterior Wall Framing:	2x4
Foundation Options:	
Daylight basement	
Crawlspace	
Slab	

(All plans can be built with your choice of foundation and framing. A generic conversion diagram is available. See order form.)

BLUEPRINT PRICE CODE: C

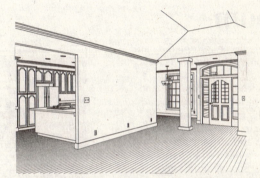

VIEW INTO KITCHEN, FAMILY ROOM AND FOYER

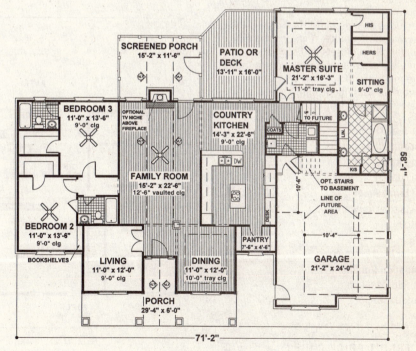

MAIN FLOOR

ORDER BLUEPRINTS ANYTIME!
CALL TOLL-FREE 1-800-820-1296

Plan APS-2119
Plan copyright held by home designer/architect

PRICES AND DETAILS ON PAGES 12-15

Versatile Sun Room

- This country-style home is fronted by an inviting front porch. The interior is just as welcoming.
- The living room features a fireplace and windows that overlook the porch.
- From here, the living room opens to a dining area, where French doors access a covered porch and a sunny patio.
- The island kitchen has a sink view, plenty of counter space, and a handy pass-through to the adjoining sun room. The bright sun room is large enough to serve as a formal dining room, a family room or a hobby room.
- Secluded to the rear of the home is the private master suite. A garden spa tub, dual walk-in closets and separate dressing areas are nice features found in the master bath.
- Two secondary bedrooms share a split bath, and each features a walk-in closet.

Plan J-90014

Bedrooms: 3	Baths: 2½
Living Area:	
Main floor	2,190 sq. ft.
Total Living Area:	**2,190 sq. ft.**
Standard basement	2,190 sq. ft.
Garage	465 sq. ft.
Storage	34 sq. ft.
Exterior Wall Framing:	2x6

Foundation Options:

Standard basement
Crawlspace
Slab

(All plans can be built with your choice of foundation and framing. A generic conversion diagram is available. See order form.)

BLUEPRINT PRICE CODE: C

SOUTHERN BELLES

VIEW INTO KITCHEN AND LIVING ROOM

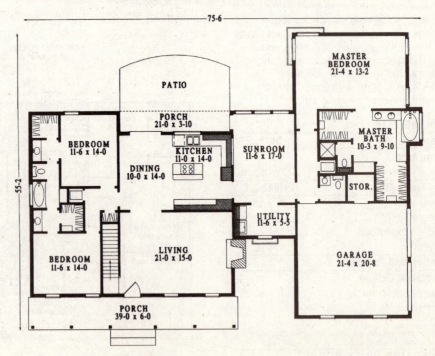

MAIN FLOOR

Plan J-90014

Plan copyright held by home designer/architect

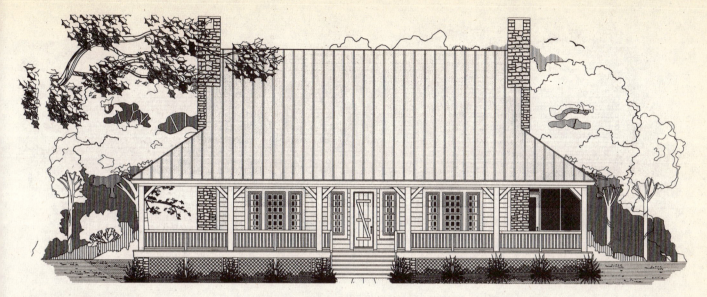

Outdoor Informality

- Surrounded by porches, this two-story home has the informal feel of a woodland lodge.
- Four doors on the main floor open to the porches. Family and friends can stroll outdoors to enjoy fresh mornings or warm evenings under the stars.
- In cool weather, everyone will want to gather around the fireplace in the generous family room, which is open to the dining area and the kitchen beyond.
- The kitchen pantry and a center island make cooking and serving easy.
- The big main-floor master suite, with a fireplace and a cathedral ceiling, echoes the family room's warmth.
- The luxurious master bath has a large walk-in closet and a handy linen closet.
- The upper-floor hall opens on an elegant loft with long bookshelves. Sit back with a novel and enjoy the view of the family room's fireplace.
- Each upper-floor bedroom has a wide closet and private access to the central bath. Attic storage areas allow you to stash seasonal clothing and gear out of sight until next year.

Plan SUL-1429	
Bedrooms: 3	**Baths:** 2½
Living Area:	
Upper floor	741 sq. ft.
Main floor	1,466 sq. ft.
Total Living Area:	**2,207 sq. ft.**
Screen porch	324 sq. ft.
Exterior Wall Framing:	2x4
Foundation Options:	
Crawlspace	

(All plans can be built with your choice of foundation and framing. A generic conversion diagram is available. See order form.)

BLUEPRINT PRICE CODE: C

SOUTHERN BELLES

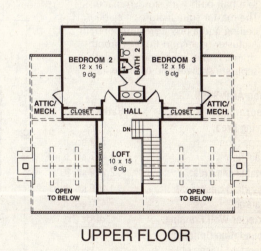

MAIN FLOOR

UPPER FLOOR

ORDER BLUEPRINTS ANYTIME!
CALL TOLL-FREE 1-800-820-1296

Plan SUL-1429
Plan copyright held by home designer/architect

PRICES AND DETAILS ON PAGES 12-15

239

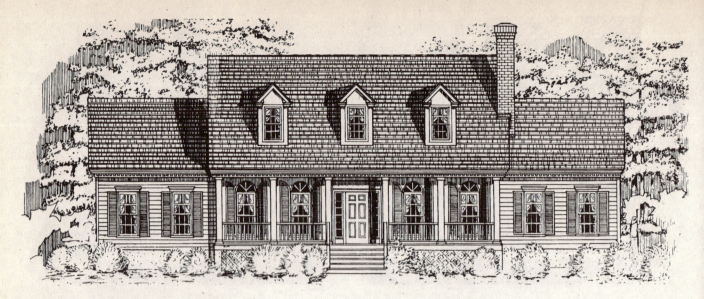

Graceful Facade

- Elegant half-round transoms spruce up the wood-shuttered facade of this charming traditional two-story.
- The wide front porch opens to a two-story foyer that flows between the formal dining room and a two-story-high library or guest room.
- Perfect for entertaining, the spacious Great Room shows off a handsome fireplace and a TV center. Beautiful French doors on either side extend the room to a large backyard deck.
- The adjoining dinette has its own view of the backyard through a stunning semi-circular glass wall, which sheds light on the nice-sized attached kitchen.
- A pantry and a laundry room are neatly housed near the two-car garage. The adjacent full bath could be downsized to a half-bath with storage space.
- The master suite features a cathedral ceiling and a private whirlpool bath.
- A cluster of second-floor bedrooms share another whirlpool bath with a separate shower and twin vanities.

Plan AHP-9490	
Bedrooms: 4+	**Baths:** 2½–3
Living Area:	
Upper floor	722 sq. ft.
Main floor	1,497 sq. ft.
Total Living Area:	**2,219 sq. ft.**
Standard basement	1,165 sq. ft.
Garage	420 sq. ft.
Exterior Wall Framing:	2x4 or 2x6
Foundation Options:	
Standard basement	
Crawlspace	
Slab	
(All plans can be built with your choice of foundation and framing. A generic conversion diagram is available. See order form.)	
BLUEPRINT PRICE CODE:	**C**

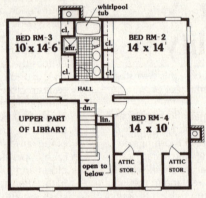

UPPER FLOOR

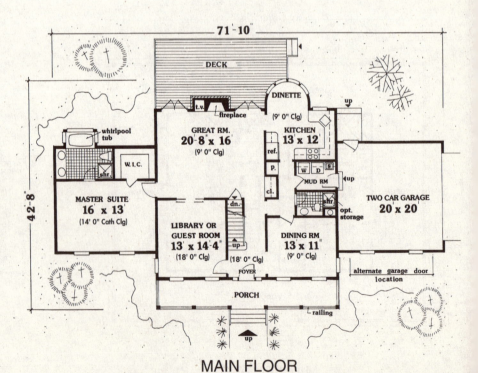

MAIN FLOOR

Plan AHP-9490

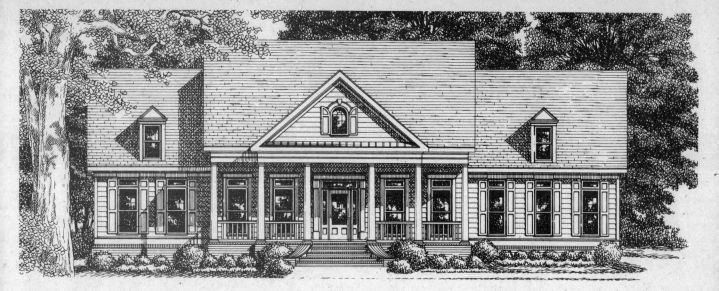

Ready for Fun?

- With an inviting front porch and a floor plan designed for entertaining, this home is ready for fun.
- A handsome fireplace—with interesting window treatments on either side—warms the spacious Great Room. A pass-through serving bar in the kitchen is the perfect way to serve appetizers and drinks, and built-ins on the other side of the room create a nice entertainment center.
- From breakfast to dinner and everything in between, this kitchen can handle it all. An extra-long island gives you more room to work, and you'll appreciate the double ovens and the roomy pantry when you expect company.
- Down the hall from the kitchen, enjoy a quiet afternoon in the study. With the nearby full bath, you might choose to make this room a secluded guest suite.
- When everyone goes home, take time for yourself in the beautiful master suite. A tiered ceiling adds height to the bedroom. French doors lead to the backyard. In the vaulted private bath, an oval bath and a separate shower promise relaxation.

Plan FB-5760-ALLE

Bedrooms: 3+	Baths: 3

Living Area:
Main floor	2,306 sq. ft.

Total Living Area: **2,306 sq. ft.**
Daylight basement	2,203 sq. ft.
Garage and storage	468 sq. ft.

Exterior Wall Framing: 2x4

Foundation Options:
Daylight basement
Crawlspace
(All plans can be built with your choice of foundation and framing. A generic conversion diagram is available. See order form.)

BLUEPRINT PRICE CODE: C

SOUTHERN BELLES

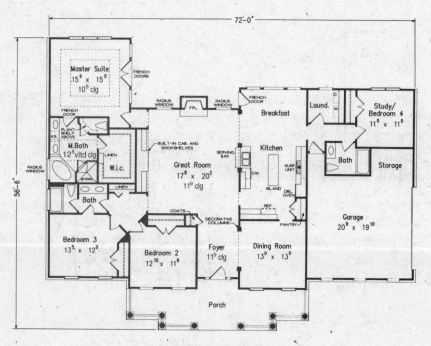

MAIN FLOOR

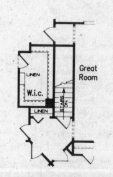

BASEMENT STAIRWAY LOCATION

ORDER BLUEPRINTS ANYTIME!
CALL TOLL-FREE 1-800-820-1296

Plan FB-5760-ALLE
Plan copyright held by home designer/architect

PRICES AND DETAILS ON PAGES 12-15

Versatility in Outdoor Living

- With a welcoming, wraparound front porch and a handsome terrace out back, this home offers versatile outdoor living spaces.
- Not to be outdone by its charming exterior, the interior of this home puts its best foot forward with a two-story foyer flanked by the formal living and dining rooms.
- The oversized Great Room features a fireplace, a media center and two sets of French doors that open to the inviting rear terrace.
- The well-planned kitchen includes a built-in desk and access to a useful mudroom with a convenient half-bath. An island eating bar makes casual meals easy to serve. Filled with natural light, the adjacent bayed dinette enjoys front-porch access.
- On the other side of the home, the master bedroom boasts a cathedral ceiling, a walk-in closet and a private bath with a garden tub, a separate shower and a dual-sink vanity.
- Upstairs, four additional bedrooms share a compartmentalized bath.

Plan AHP-9802	
Bedrooms: 5	**Baths:** 2½
Living Area:	
Upper floor	812 sq. ft.
Main floor	1,505 sq. ft.
Total Living Area:	**2,317 sq. ft.**
Standard basement	1,505 sq. ft.
Garage and storage	468 sq. ft.
Exterior Wall Framing:	2x4 or 2x6
Foundation Options:	
Standard basement	
Crawlspace	
Slab	

(All plans can be built with your choice of foundation and framing. A generic conversion diagram is available. See order form.)

BLUEPRINT PRICE CODE: C

SOUTHERN BELLES

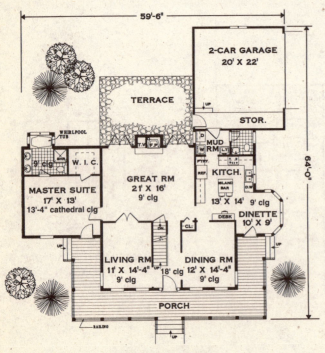

MAIN FLOOR

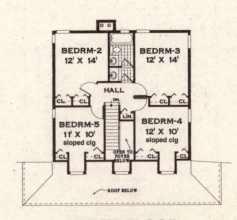

UPPER FLOOR

242   **ORDER BLUEPRINTS ANYTIME!** CALL TOLL-FREE 1-800-820-1296   **Plan AHP-9802** Plan copyright held by home designer/architect   **PRICES AND DETAILS ON PAGES 12-15**

Better by Design

- For the family that values an easygoing lifestyle, but also wants to impress friends with a beautiful home, this Southern-style design fits the bill.
- Hanging baskets dripping with vibrant flowers will dress up the front porch.
- Inside, handsome columns lend a look of distinction to the formal dining room, the ideal spot for classy meals. After dinner, guests can drift into the Great Room to continue their conversation. Plant shelves above display lush florals and greenery for all to admire.
- Casual meals have a place of their own in the breakfast nook and the kitchen, which features a distinctive bow window above the sink.
- The sitting room in the owner's bedroom provides an oasis of peace and quiet. The wet bar puts you steps closer to that first cup of coffee, while a skylight admits sunshine.
- Upstairs, an abundance of future space offers expansion possibilities.

Plan J-9320

Bedrooms: 3+	Baths: 2½

Living Area:

Main floor	2,348 sq. ft.
Total Living Area:	**2,348 sq. ft.**
Future upper floor	860 sq. ft.
Standard basement	2,348 sq. ft.
Garage	579 sq. ft.
Exterior Wall Framing:	2x4

Foundation Options:
Standard basement
Crawlspace
Slab
(All plans can be built with your choice of foundation and framing. A generic conversion diagram is available. See order form.)

BLUEPRINT PRICE CODE: C

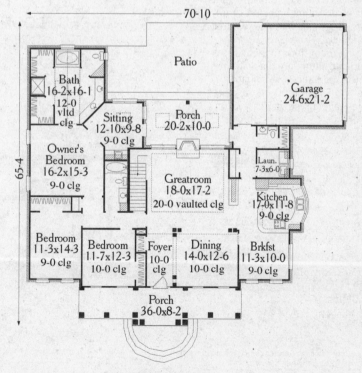

UPPER FLOOR

MAIN FLOOR

ORDER BLUEPRINTS ANYTIME!
CALL TOLL-FREE 1-800-820-1296

Plan J-9320
Plan copyright held by home designer/architect

PRICES AND DETAILS
ON PAGES 12-15

You Asked!

- Our most popular plan in recent years, E-3000, has now been downsized for affordability, without sacrificing character or excitement.
- Exterior appeal is created with a covered front porch with decorative columns, triple dormers and rail-topped corner windows.
- The floor plan has combined the separate living and family rooms available in E-3000 into one spacious family room with a corner fireplace and a vaulted ceiling. The area flows into the dining room via a columned gallery.
- The kitchen serves the breakfast room over an angled snack bar, and features a huge pantry.
- The stunning main-floor master suite offers a private sitting area, a walk-in closet and a dramatic, angled bath.
- There are two large bedrooms upstairs accessible via a curved staircase with a bridge balcony.

Plan E-2307

Bedrooms: 3	**Baths:** 2½

Living Area:
Upper floor	595 sq. ft.
Main floor	1,765 sq. ft.
Total Living Area:	**2,360 sq. ft.**
Standard basement	1,765 sq. ft.
Garage	484 sq. ft.
Storage	44 sq. ft.
Exterior Wall Framing:	2x6

Foundation Options:
Standard basement
Crawlspace
Slab
(All plans can be built with your choice of foundation and framing. A generic conversion diagram is available. See order form.)

BLUEPRINT PRICE CODE: C

SOUTHERN BELLES

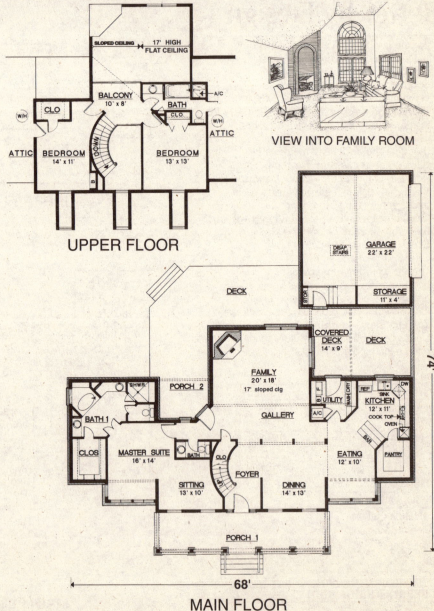

ORDER BLUEPRINTS ANYTIME!
CALL TOLL-FREE 1-800-820-1296

Plan E-2307
Plan copyright held by home designer/architect

PRICES AND DETAILS
ON PAGES 12-15

Journey's End

- As each night falls, you'll find yourself drawn to this home, knowing you've chosen the perfect abode for your immediate and extended family.
- Entertaining areas are not limited to the huge central living room. At the front of the home, a wide porch promises the prospect of calm; to the rear, another porch flows into two connected patios.
- Serving even the largest crowds is a simple trick. The galley-style kitchen offers an angled bar and access to the front porch.
- The kids have their own space in the right wing of the home. The master suite is situated far from the hubbub of daily living, and includes a sumptuous bath with a large walk-in closet and a dual-sink vanity.
- At the rear of the home, a complete suite resides, intended to house parents or in-laws. It includes a living room, a dining area, a full kitchen, and a sleeping chamber with a full bath and walk-in closet. A garage stall is also provided! The private porch adds a touch of charm.

Plan HOM-2400

Bedrooms: 4	Baths: 3

Living Area:

Main floor	2,400 sq. ft.
Total Living Area:	**2,400 sq. ft.**
Garage	672 sq. ft.
Exterior Wall Framing:	2x4

Foundation Options:
Crawlspace
Slab
(All plans can be built with your choice of foundation and framing. A generic conversion diagram is available. See order form.)

BLUEPRINT PRICE CODE: C

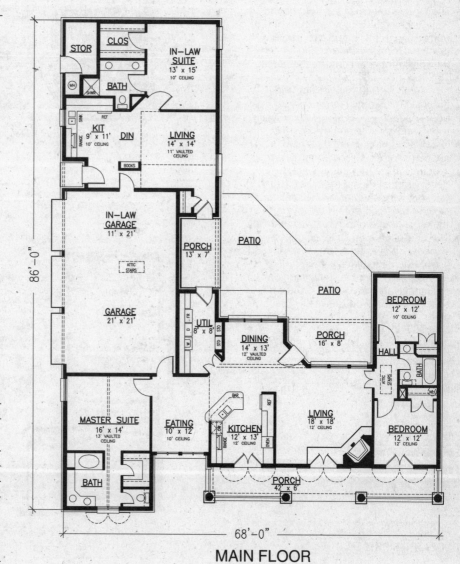

MAIN FLOOR

ORDER BLUEPRINTS ANYTIME!
CALL TOLL-FREE 1-800-820-1296

Plan HOM-2400
Plan copyright held by home designer/architect

PRICES AND DETAILS ON PAGES 12-15

SOUTHERN BELLES

245

Lovely Details

- The wonderfully detailed front porch, with its graceful arches, columns and railings, gives this home a character all its own. Dormer windows and arched transoms further accentuate the porch.
- The floor plan features a central living room with a 10-ft.-high ceiling and a fireplace framed by French doors. These doors open to a covered porch or a sun room, and a sheltered deck beyond.
- Just off the living room, the island kitchen and breakfast area provide a spacious place for family or guests. The nearby formal dining room has arched transom windows and a 10-ft. ceiling, as does the bedroom off the foyer. All of the remaining rooms have 9-ft. ceilings.
- The unusual master suite includes a window alcove, access to the porch and a fantastic bath with a garden tub.
- A huge utility room, a storage area off the garage and a 1,000-sq.-ft. attic space are other bonuses of this design.

VIEW INTO LIVING ROOM

Plan J-90019	
Bedrooms: 3	**Baths:** 2½
Living Area:	
Main floor	2,410 sq. ft.
Total Living Area:	**2,410 sq. ft.**
Standard basement	2,410 sq. ft.
Garage	512 sq. ft.
Storage	86 sq. ft.
Exterior Wall Framing:	2x4

Foundation Options:
Standard basement
Crawlspace
Slab
(All plans can be built with your choice of foundation and framing. A generic conversion diagram is available. See order form.)

BLUEPRINT PRICE CODE: C

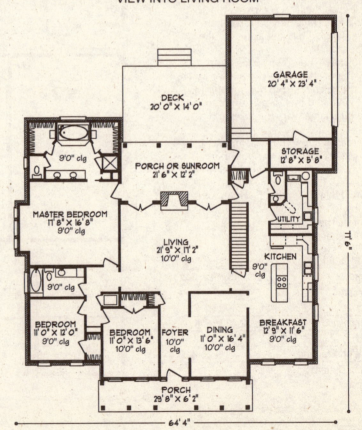

MAIN FLOOR

Plan J-90019
Plan copyright held by home designer/architect

The Look of Yesteryear

- A wraparound porch, quaint dormers and nostalgic window treatments give this home the look of yesteryear. Inside, you'll find a thoroughly modern floor plan that caters to today's families.
- The central living room enjoys a large hearth area and a door that leads to a covered backyard patio.
- Smells of delicious home-cooked meals will drift from the well-stocked kitchen into the sunny breakfast nook. The nook overlooks the patio and features a convenient serving bar.
- All bedrooms are located on the opposite side of the home, creating an effective separation between sleeping and living quarters.
- The master suite boasts a tray ceiling, a walk-in closet and a private bath with a tub that offers a lovely garden view.
- Two additional bedrooms with sloped ceilings and large closets share a hall bath with a dual-sink vanity.
- The fourth bedroom may be converted to a study or a home office. Double doors can be added so that the room is accessible from the foyer.

Plan DD-2495	
Bedrooms: 3+	Baths: 2½
Living Area:	
Main floor	2,420 sq. ft.
Total Living Area:	**2,420 sq. ft.**
Standard basement	2,420 sq. ft.
Exterior Wall Framing:	2x4

Foundation Options:
Standard basement
Crawlspace
Slab
(All plans can be built with your choice of foundation and framing. A generic conversion diagram is available. See order form.)

BLUEPRINT PRICE CODE: C

MAIN FLOOR

Plan DD-2495
Plan copyright held by home designer/architect

Clean Lines

- Clean lines, simple windows, shutters and a front porch accent the exterior of this timeless treasure.
- The soaring foyer lies between the front-facing living and dining rooms. The living room may also function as an office.
- The amenity-packed kitchen offers a snack bar that serves the bayed breakfast nook, which is a great place for family meals. A powder room and laundry facilities are down the hall.
- Invite friends into the family room for fireside chats, or spend warm evenings out back on the wood deck.
- Upstairs, the huge master bedroom adjoins a private bath, which boasts a spa tub with a garden view, as well as a separate shower and a dual-sink vanity.
- Two secondary bedrooms and a bonus room share a full hall bath.
- The side-entry garage preserves the home's traditional facade and offers a useful storage room.

Plan C-9905	
Bedrooms: 3+	Baths: 2½
Living Area:	
Upper floor	949 sq. ft.
Main floor	1,156 sq. ft.
Bonus room	329 sq. ft.
Total Living Area:	**2,434 sq. ft.**
Daylight basement	1,130 sq. ft.
Garage	496 sq. ft.
Storage	58 sq. ft.
Exterior Wall Framing:	2x4

Foundation Options:
Daylight basement
Crawlspace
(All plans can be built with your choice of foundation and framing. A generic conversion diagram is available. See order form.)

BLUEPRINT PRICE CODE: C

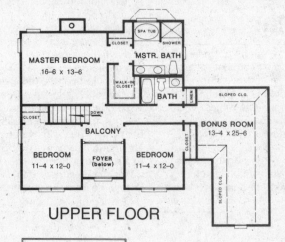

UPPER FLOOR

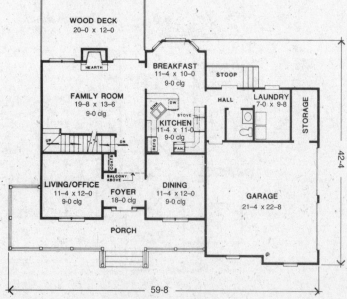

MAIN FLOOR

Plan C-9905
Plan copyright held by home designer/architect

Rapt in Country Memories

- This beautiful home's wraparound porch will carry you away to a time when all was right with the world.
- Triple dormers and nostalgic shuttered windows combine with gorgeous oval glass in the front door to make the facade charming indeed!
- Looks can be deceiving, however. The interior of the home is thoroughly up-to-date, with every conceivable feature.
- Beyond the foyer, a fireplace and tall windows under a cathedral ceiling make the living room a thing to behold.
- The roomy kitchen serves meals with minimal effort. A breakfast nook and a serving counter host quick snacks.
- Two corner porches are perfect for thoughtful moments. Or refresh yourself in the master suite's garden tub. A good book will keep you there for hours.
- Upstairs, the game room's balcony offers sweeping views; two big bedrooms share a nice bath.
- Plans for a detached garage will be sent with your blueprint order.

Plan L-2449-VC

Bedrooms: 3	Baths: 2½

Living Area:

Upper floor	780 sq. ft.
Main floor	1,669 sq. ft.
Total Living Area:	**2,449 sq. ft.**
Detached garage	545 sq. ft.
Exterior Wall Framing:	2x4

Foundation Options:

Slab
(All plans can be built with your choice of foundation and framing. A generic conversion diagram is available. See order form.)

BLUEPRINT PRICE CODE: C

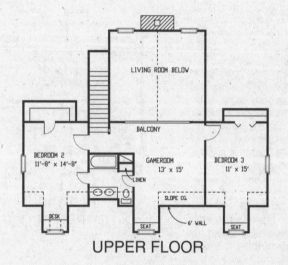

UPPER FLOOR

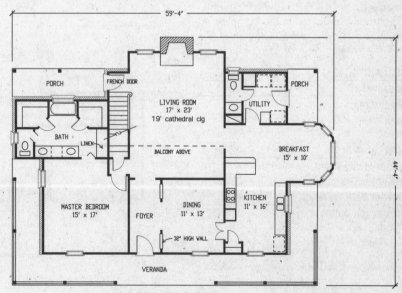

MAIN FLOOR

ORDER BLUEPRINTS ANYTIME!
CALL TOLL-FREE 1-800-820-1296

Plan L-2449-VC
Plan copyright held by home designer/architect

PRICES AND DETAILS
ON PAGES 12-15

Picture-Perfect

- Those tall, cold glasses of summertime lemonade will taste even better when enjoyed on the shady front porch of this picture-perfect home.
- Inside, the two-story, sidelighted foyer unfolds to the formal living areas and the Great Room beyond.
- Fireplaces grace the living room and the Great Room, which are separated by French pocket doors. A TV nook borders the fireplace in the Great Room. Four French doors reveal a rear deck.
- A glassy dinette with a bow window makes breakfasts cozy and comfortable.
- Restful nights will be the norm in the master suite, which boasts a cathedral ceiling. Next to the walk-in closet, the private bath has a whirlpool tub in a fabulous boxed-out window.
- At day's end, guests and children may retire to the upper floor, where four big bedrooms and a full bath—complete with a dual-sink vanity, a whirlpool tub and a separate shower—await them.

Plan AHP-9512

Bedrooms: 5	Baths: 2½
Living Area:	
Upper floor	928 sq. ft.
Main floor	1,571 sq. ft.
Total Living Area:	**2,499 sq. ft.**
Standard basement	1,571 sq. ft.
Garage and storage	420 sq. ft.
Exterior Wall Framing:	2x4 or 2x6

Foundation Options:
Standard basement
Crawlspace
Slab
(All plans can be built with your choice of foundation and framing. A generic conversion diagram is available. See order form.)

BLUEPRINT PRICE CODE: C

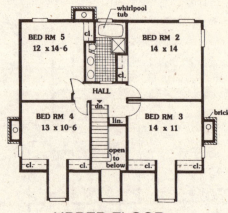

UPPER FLOOR

VIEW INTO GREAT ROOM

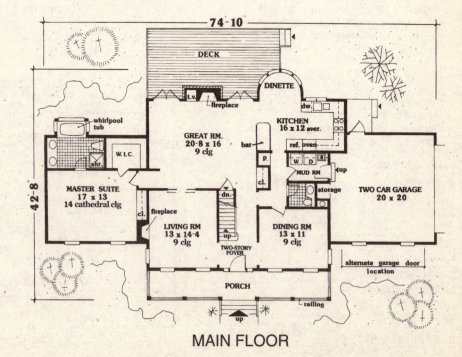

MAIN FLOOR

Plan AHP-9512

Elegant Interior

- An inviting columned porch welcomes guests into the elegant interior of this spectacular country-style home.
- Just past the entrance, the formal dining room boasts a stepped ceiling and a nearby server with a sink.
- The island kitchen has an eating bar that serves the breakfast room, which is enhanced by a cathedral ceiling and a bay window. Sliding glass doors lead to a covered side porch.
- Brightened by a row of windows, the spacious Great Room features a stepped ceiling, a built-in media center and a corner fireplace.
- The master bedroom has a tray ceiling and a cozy sitting area. The skylighted master bath boasts a whirlpool tub, a separate shower and a walk-in closet.
- A second main-floor bedroom, or optional study, offers private access to a split bath. Two more bedrooms share a third bath upstairs. Generous storage space is also included.

Plan AX-3305-B

Bedrooms: 3+	Baths: 3
Living Area:	
Upper floor	550 sq. ft.
Main floor	2,017 sq. ft.
Total Living Area:	**2,567 sq. ft.**
Upper-floor storage	377 sq. ft.
Standard basement	2,017 sq. ft.
Garage	415 sq. ft.
Exterior Wall Framing:	2x4

Foundation Options:
Standard basement
Crawlspace
Slab
(All plans can be built with your choice of foundation and framing. A generic conversion diagram is available. See order form.)

| **BLUEPRINT PRICE CODE:** | **D** |

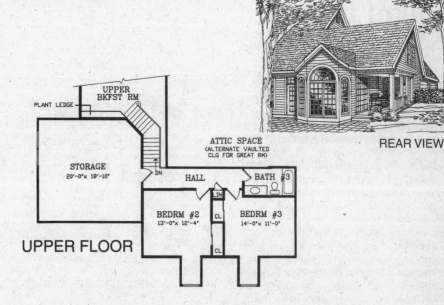

REAR VIEW

UPPER FLOOR

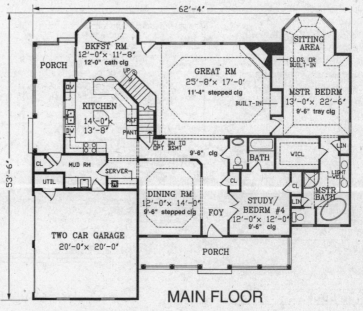

MAIN FLOOR

ORDER BLUEPRINTS ANYTIME!
CALL TOLL-FREE 1-800-820-1296

Plan AX-3305-B
Plan copyright held by home designer/architect

PRICES AND DETAILS ON PAGES 12-15

Full of Ideas

- Because of the numerous, clever design ideas found throughout this one-story home, it promises a comfortable, worry-free lifestyle for its occupants.
- Four handsome columns, three stately dormers and a pretty acorn pediment over the front door give this home's facade its distinguished air.
- Inside, the foyer flows into the living room, where friends will mingle before dinner. After some pleasant discourse, an arch framed by two columns ushers guests into the dining room for a sumptuous meal.
- Family members will frequent the kitchen, where a built-in desk, an island cooktop with a wine rack on the end and a snack bar accommodate them. In the nearby family room, books and entertainment equipment can be neatly stored alongside the fireplace.
- Across the home, the master suite presides over its own wing, enhanced by overhead plant shelves. The bedroom features private access to a rear porch. A super-posh, private bath flaunts his-and-hers walk-in closets, twin vanities, an oversized shower and a raised garden tub.

Plan HDS-99-294

Bedrooms: 3+	Baths: 3
Living Area:	
Main floor	2,636 sq. ft.
Total Living Area:	**2,636 sq. ft.**
Garage	789 sq. ft.
Exterior Wall Framing:	2x4

Foundation Options:
Slab
(All plans can be built with your choice of foundation and framing. A generic conversion diagram is available. See order form.)

BLUEPRINT PRICE CODE: D

VIEW INTO BREAKFAST NOOK, FAMILY ROOM AND KITCHEN

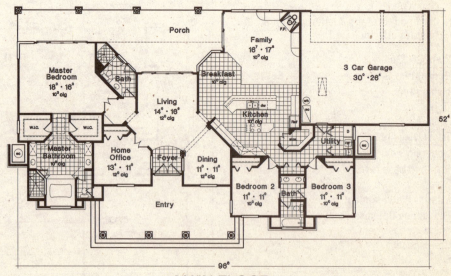

MAIN FLOOR

Plan HDS-99-294
Plan copyright held by home designer/architect

Columned Elegance

- Decorative columns frame the entrance to the two-story living room, adding a touch of elegance to this well-designed home.
- The living room also features a cozy fireplace flanked by windows looking into the backyard.
- An island cooktop highlights the modern kitchen, which also boasts a corner sink, a pantry closet and a handy snack bar that serves the sunny breakfast nook.
- The main-floor master suite has two walk-in closets, two sinks, a marble garden tub and a separate shower.
- A spacious bonus room above the garage would make a great guest room, home office or playroom for the kids.
- Upstairs, one of the two large bedrooms enjoys a built-in desk. Both rooms offer a walk-in closet; they share a full bath featuring a dual-sink vanity.

Plan RD-2656

Bedrooms: 4+	Baths: 3

Living Area:

Upper floor	687 sq. ft.
Main floor	1,969 sq. ft.
Bonus room	370 sq. ft.
Total Living Area:	**3,026 sq. ft.**
Garage and storage	629 sq. ft.
Exterior Wall Framing:	2x4

Foundation Options:
Standard basement
Crawlspace
Slab
(All plans can be built with your choice of foundation and framing. A generic conversion diagram is available. See order form.)

BLUEPRINT PRICE CODE: E

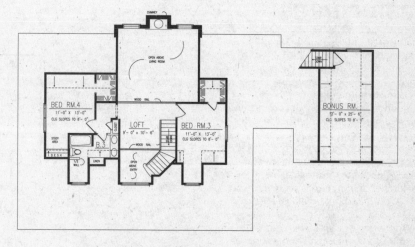

UPPER FLOOR

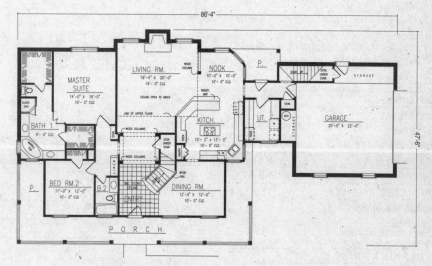

MAIN FLOOR

ORDER BLUEPRINTS ANYTIME!
CALL TOLL-FREE 1-800-820-1296

Plan RD-2656
Plan copyright held by home designer/architect

PRICES AND DETAILS ON PAGES 12-15

Country Masterpiece!

- A handsome railed veranda punctuated by symmetrical columns bids a warm welcome to this country-style home.
- Historic hardwood floors in the foyer and dining room coupled with an abundance of windows, glass doors and high ceilings give the interior the style and character of a masterpiece!
- Pocket doors isolate the study or guest room from the noise of incoming traffic.
- At the core of the informal spaces is an airy kitchen that interacts with the family room and the breakfast area over a snack counter.
- The sprawling master suite basks in the comfort of a garden bath and a sunny sitting area that opens to the backyard.
- A window seat is centered between built-in bookshelves in the second main-floor bedroom.
- The upper-floor bedrooms share the use of a full bath and a huge game room.
- A detached three-car garage is included with the blueprints.

Plan L-308-FC

Bedrooms: 4+	Baths: 3
Living Area:	
Upper floor	787 sq. ft.
Main floor	2,519 sq. ft.
Total Living Area:	**3,306 sq. ft.**
Detached three-car garage	942 sq. ft.
Exterior Wall Framing:	2x4

Foundation Options:
Slab
(All plans can be built with your choice of foundation and framing. A generic conversion diagram is available. See order form.)

BLUEPRINT PRICE CODE: E

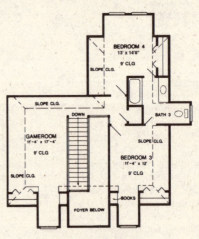

UPPER FLOOR

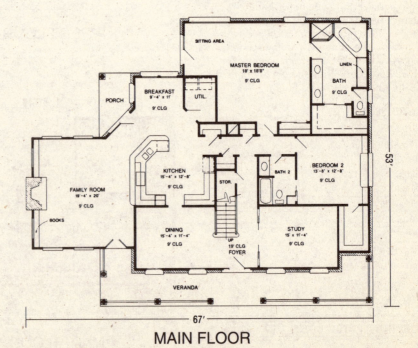

MAIN FLOOR

Plan L-308-FC

All Good Things

- This stone-sturdy home pleases the eye with a rustic, country facade and a multitude of interior luxuries.
- Designed with your loved ones in mind, the family room, island kitchen and bayed breakfast nook flow into each other for a feeling of togetherness. From the nook, a huge backyard deck is quickly accessible.
- For formal gatherings, the living and dining rooms serve effortlessly. The living room hosts a cozy fireplace, and columns distinguish the dining room.
- The master suite epitomizes comfort, with its private deck and adjoining office space. Opulence is apparent in the master bath, which features a spa tub, a separate shower, a dual-sink vanity and two walk-in closets.
- Two additional bedrooms share a full hall bath. The foremost bedroom boasts a cheery bay window, and could serve as a comfortable study.
- A stunning guest suite delivers a private deck and a kitchen area. With its full bath, it's the perfect spot for long-term guests or relatives who are enjoying their golden years.

Plan DD-3152

Bedrooms: 3+	Baths: 3½

Living Area:
Main floor — 3,152 sq. ft.
Total Living Area: — **3,152 sq. ft.**
Standard basement — 3,152 sq. ft.
Garage — 691 sq. ft.

Exterior Wall Framing: 2x4

Foundation Options:
Standard basement
Crawlspace
Slab
(All plans can be built with your choice of foundation and framing. A generic conversion diagram is available. See order form.)

BLUEPRINT PRICE CODE: E

SOUTHERN BELLES

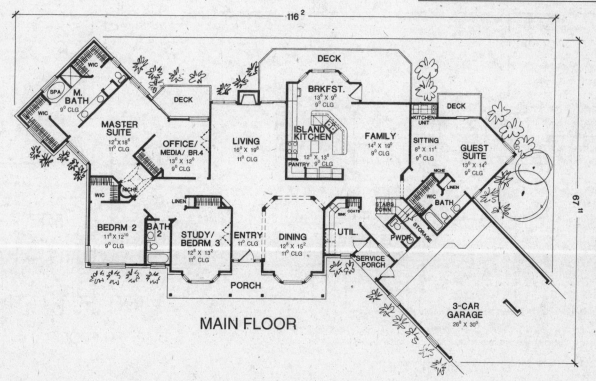

MAIN FLOOR

ORDER BLUEPRINTS ANYTIME!
CALL TOLL-FREE 1-800-820-1296

Plan DD-3152
Plan copyright held by home designer/architect

PRICES AND DETAILS ON PAGES 12-15

255

Rambling Romance

- The wonderful wraparound veranda of this rambling farmhouse provides hours of outdoor leisure and romance.
- Inside, there's plenty of space for the whole family to enjoy privacy, as well as conversation and togetherness.
- The airy foyer spills directly into the living room, which presents the first of the home's three handsome fireplaces. In the adjoining dining room, built-in glass cabinets attractively store china.
- The central kitchen includes a pantry and a snack bar; its location is ideal for hosting formal or casual occasions. Sunny views of the backyard are possible through the window wall of the attached breakfast room.
- A dramatic brick fireplace wall in the family room backs up to a much more private flame in the lavish master suite.
- Recreation and exercise are combined on the upper floor, which also offers three more bedrooms and two baths.

Plan L-337-VC	
Bedrooms: 4+	**Baths:** 3½
Living Area:	
Upper floor	1,169 sq. ft.
Main floor	2,166 sq. ft.
Total Living Area:	**3,335 sq. ft.**
Garage	588 sq. ft.
Exterior Wall Framing:	2x4
Foundation Options:	

Slab
(All plans can be built with your choice of foundation and framing. A generic conversion diagram is available. See order form.)

BLUEPRINT PRICE CODE: E

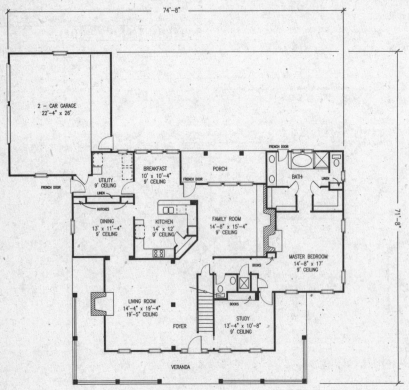

MAIN FLOOR

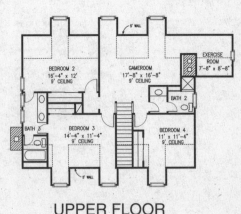

UPPER FLOOR

ORDER BLUEPRINTS ANYTIME! CALL TOLL-FREE 1-800-820-1296

Plan L-337-VC
Plan copyright held by home designer/architect

PRICES AND DETAILS ON PAGES 12-15

Adorable and Affordable

- This charming one-story home has much to offer, despite its modest size and economical bent.
- The lovely full-width porch has old-fashioned detailing, such as the round columns, decorative railings and ornamental molding.
- An open floor plan maximizes the home's square footage. The front door opens to the living room, where a railing creates a hallway effect while using very little space.
- Straight ahead, the dining room adjoins the island kitchen, while offering a compact laundry closet and sliding glass doors to a large rear patio.
- Focusing on quality, the home also offers features such as a tray ceiling in the living room and a stepped ceiling in the dining room.
- The three bedrooms are well proportioned. The master bedroom includes a private bathroom, while the two smaller bedrooms share a full bath.

Plan AX-91316	
Bedrooms: 3	**Baths:** 2
Living Area:	
Main floor	1,097 sq. ft.
Total Living Area:	**1,097 sq. ft.**
Basement	1,097 sq. ft.
Garage	461 sq. ft.
Exterior Wall Framing:	2x4

Foundation Options:
Daylight basement
Standard basement
Crawlspace
Slab
(All plans can be built with your choice of foundation and framing. A generic conversion diagram is available. See order form.)

BLUEPRINT PRICE CODE: A

VIEW INTO LIVING AND DINING ROOMS

NOTE: The above photographed home may have been modified by the homeowner. Please refer to floor plan and/or drawn elevation shown for actual blueprint details.

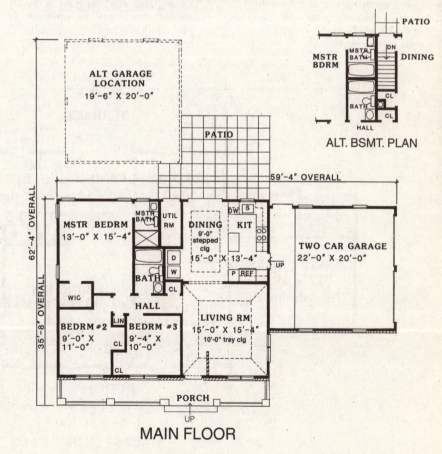

MAIN FLOOR

ALT. BSMT. PLAN

SOUTHERN BELLES

ORDER BLUEPRINTS ANYTIME!
CALL TOLL-FREE 1-800-820-1296

Plan AX-91316
Plan copyright held by home designer/architect

PRICES AND DETAILS ON PAGES 12-15

It's All in the Details

- It's the mouthwatering details that give this home its distinctively country character. Its facade is a marvel; the graceful columns, railings, dormer windows and high transoms accentuate the inviting porch.
- Brightened by radiant windows, the large living room hosts a warming fireplace. Two high dormers admit additional natural light.
- Straight back, a bay window punctuated by French doors livens the dining area. A snack bar links it to the kitchen, which you'll find adaptable to both casual and formal meals.
- A sizable terrace overlooking the backyard is the perfect arena for lazy summer picnics and frolicsome Sunday afternoons.
- The sprawling master bedroom is blessed with a pair of windows in the sleeping chamber that wake you with morning light. A private bath offers a zesty whirlpool tub and a separate shower for busy weekday mornings.

Plan AHP-9615

Bedrooms: 3	Baths: 2

Living Area:
Main floor — 1,331 sq. ft.

Total Living Area: **1,331 sq. ft.**

Standard basement — 1,377 sq. ft.
Garage — 459 sq. ft.

Exterior Wall Framing: 2x4 or 2x6

Foundation Options:
Standard basement
Crawlspace
Slab
(All plans can be built with your choice of foundation and framing. A generic conversion diagram is available. See order form.)

BLUEPRINT PRICE CODE: A

SOUTHERN BELLES

MAIN FLOOR

Plan AHP-9615
Plan copyright held by home designer/architect

ORDER BLUEPRINTS ANYTIME!
CALL TOLL-FREE 1-800-820-1296

PRICES AND DETAILS ON PAGES 12–15

258

Stylish Exterior, Open Floor Plan

- With its simple yet stylish exterior, this modest-sized design is suitable for country or urban settings.
- A covered front porch and a gabled roof extension accent the facade while providing plenty of sheltered space for outdoor relaxation.
- Inside, the open floor plan puts available space to efficient use.
- The living room, which offers a warm fireplace, is expanded by a cathedral ceiling. The addition of the kitchen and the bayed dining room creates an expansive gathering space.
- The master suite features a private bath and a large walk-in closet.
- Two more good-sized bedrooms share a second full bath.
- A utility area leads to the carport, which incorporates extra storage space.

Plan J-86155

Bedrooms: 3	Baths: 2
Living Area:	
Main floor	1,385 sq. ft.
Total Living Area:	**1,385 sq. ft.**
Standard basement	1,385 sq. ft.
Carport	380 sq. ft.
Storage	40 sq. ft.
Exterior Wall Framing:	2x4

Foundation Options:
Standard basement
Crawlspace
Slab
(All plans can be built with your choice of foundation and framing. A generic conversion diagram is available. See order form.)

BLUEPRINT PRICE CODE: A

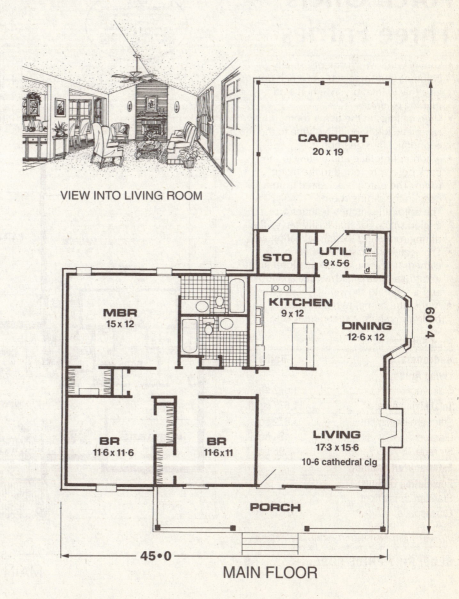

VIEW INTO LIVING ROOM

MAIN FLOOR

SOUTHERN BELLES

ORDER BLUEPRINTS ANYTIME!
CALL TOLL-FREE 1-800-820-1296

Plan J-86155
Plan copyright held by home designer/architect

PRICES AND DETAILS ON PAGES 12-15

Porch Offers Three Entries

- Showy window treatments, stately columns and three sets of French doors give this Plantation-style home an inviting exterior.
- High ceilings in the living room, dining room and kitchen add volume to the economically-sized home.
- A corner fireplace and a view to the back porch are found in the living room. The porch is accessed from a door in the dining room.
- The adjoining kitchen features an angled snack bar that easily serves the dining room and the casual eating area.
- The secluded master suite offers a cathedral ceiling, a walk-in closet and a luxurious private bath with a spa tub and a separate shower.
- Across the home, two additional bedrooms share a second full bath.

SOUTHERN BELLES

Plan E-1602	
Bedrooms: 3	Baths: 2
Living Area:	
Main floor	1,672 sq. ft.
Total Living Area:	**1,672 sq. ft.**
Standard basement	1,672 sq. ft.
Garage	484 sq. ft.
Storage	96 sq. ft.
Exterior Wall Framing:	2x6
Foundation Options:	
Standard basement	
Crawlspace	
Slab	
(All plans can be built with your choice of foundation and framing. A generic conversion diagram is available. See order form.)	
BLUEPRINT PRICE CODE:	B

NOTE: The above photographed home may have been modified by the homeowner. Please refer to floor plan and/or drawn elevation shown for actual blueprint details.

VIEW INTO LIVING ROOM

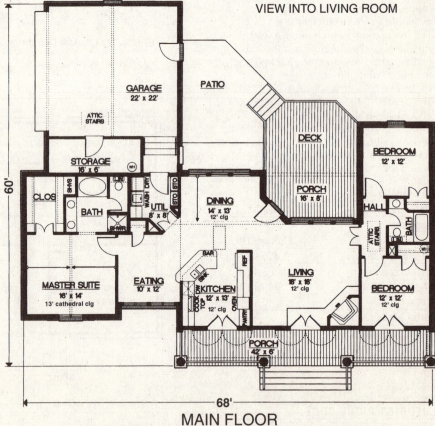

MAIN FLOOR

ORDER BLUEPRINTS ANYTIME!
CALL TOLL-FREE 1-800-820-1296

Plan E-1602
Plan copyright held by home designer/architect

PRICES AND DETAILS ON PAGES 12-15

Rustic, Relaxed Living

- The screened porch of this rustic home offers a cool place to dine on warm summer days. The covered front porch provides an inviting welcome and a place for pure relaxation.
- With its warm fireplace and surrounding windows, the home's spacious living room is ideal for unwinding indoors. The living room unfolds to a nice-sized dining area that overlooks a backyard patio and opens to the screened porch.
- The U-shaped kitchen is centrally located and features a nice windowed sink. A handy pantry and a laundry room adjoin to the right.
- Three large bedrooms make up the home's sleeping wing. The master bedroom boasts a roomy private bath with a step-up spa tub, a separate shower and two walk-in closets.
- The secondary bedrooms have ample closet space and share a compartmentalized hall bath.

Plan C-8650

Bedrooms: 3	Baths: 2

Living Area:
Main floor — 1,773 sq. ft.
Total Living Area: **1,773 sq. ft.**
Screened porch — 246 sq. ft.
Daylight basement — 1,773 sq. ft.
Garage — 441 sq. ft.

Exterior Wall Framing: 2x4

Foundation Options:
Daylight basement
Crawlspace
Slab
(All plans can be built with your choice of foundation and framing. A generic conversion diagram is available. See order form.)

BLUEPRINT PRICE CODE: B

SOUTHERN BELLES

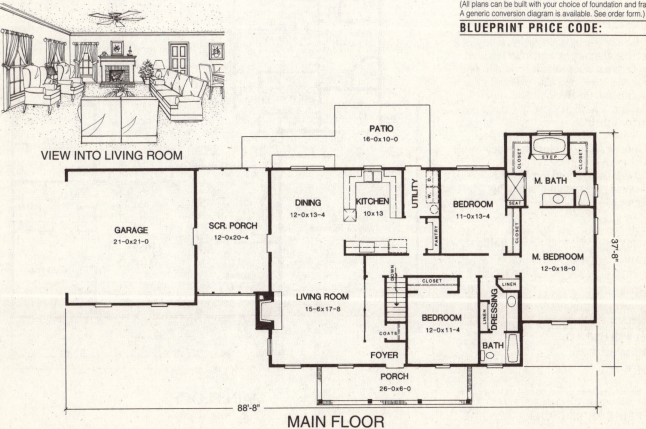

VIEW INTO LIVING ROOM

MAIN FLOOR

ORDER BLUEPRINTS ANYTIME!
CALL TOLL-FREE 1-800-820-1296

Plan C-8650
Plan copyright held by home designer/architect

PRICES AND DETAILS ON PAGES 12-15

Cozy Covered Porches

- Twin dormers give this raised one-story design the appearance of a two-story. Two porches and a deck supplement the main living areas with plenty of outdoor entertaining space.
- The large central living room features a dramatic fireplace, a high ceiling with a skylight and access to both porch areas.
- Double doors open to a bayed eating area, which overlooks the adjoining deck and includes a vaulted ceiling that tops the kitchen as well. An angled snack bar and a pantry are also featured.
- The elegant master suite is tucked to one side of the home and also overlooks the backyard and the deck. A dual-sink vanity and a walk-in closet are featured in the private bath.
- Handy laundry facilities, freezer space, and broom and coat closets are nearby.
- Across the home, two additional bedrooms share another full bath.
- Two storage areas complement the spacious two-car garage.

Plan E-1826

Bedrooms: 3	Baths: 2

Living Area:

Main floor	1,800 sq. ft.
Total Living Area:	**1,800 sq. ft.**
Garage and storage	574 sq. ft.
Enclosed storage	60 sq. ft.
Exterior Wall Framing:	2x6

Foundation Options:

Crawlspace
Slab
(All plans can be built with your choice of foundation and framing. A generic conversion diagram is available. See order form.)

BLUEPRINT PRICE CODE: B

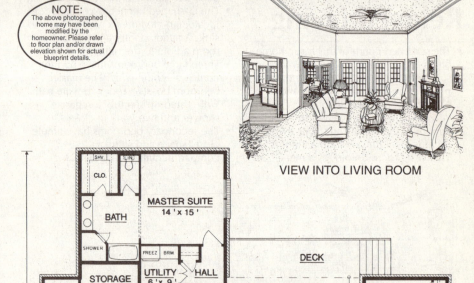

VIEW INTO LIVING ROOM

MAIN FLOOR

Plan E-1826
Plan copyright held by home designer/architect

Surrounded by Shade

- Comfort reigns in this delightful domicile, which boasts a shaded veranda that nearly surrounds the home. There's enough room for a porch hammock! When it rains during the family reunion, the festivities can be moved to this glorious covered area.
- Inside, a fireplace-blessed living room joins seamlessly with the welcoming foyer. Opposite, the big dining room will hold the largest dinner parties.
- Your whole family can participate in meal preparation, since the kitchen and connecting breakfast room flow into each other. A French door gives veranda access.
- In the master bedroom, an atrium door offers private passage to the veranda. The private bath includes a bubbly tub, a separate shower and a planter for your lush greenery.
- Upstairs, two more bedrooms flank a peaceful sitting area. A large split bath features a dual-sink vanity.
- All rooms in the home are topped by high ceilings, for optimal light and spaciousness.

Plan L-88-VB

Bedrooms: 3	**Baths:** 2½
Living Area:	
Upper floor	751 sq. ft.
Main floor	1,308 sq. ft.
Total Living Area:	**2,059 sq. ft.**
Detached two-car garage	505 sq. ft.
Exterior Wall Framing:	2x4

Foundation Options:
Slab
(All plans can be built with your choice of foundation and framing. A generic conversion diagram is available. See order form.)

BLUEPRINT PRICE CODE: C

REAR VIEW

SOUTHERN BELLES

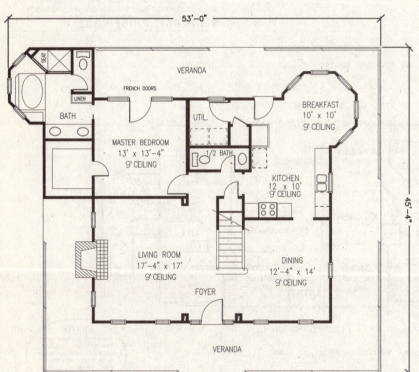

MAIN FLOOR

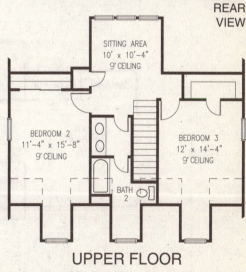

UPPER FLOOR

Plan L-88-VB
Plan copyright held by home designer/architect

Handsome Facade

- This distinguished home's facade boasts a trio of dormers above a handsome front porch, complete with columns and room enough to enjoy a glass of lemonade with the neighbors.
- Inside, the entry leads to the versatile study and the expansive Great Room, which features a stunning corner fireplace and three large windows overlooking a large covered patio.
- The modern kitchen enjoys an island workstation and a walk-in pantry. These, along with a snack bar, help to serve the formal dining room, the Great Room and the sunny morning room.
- The exquisite master suite offers a pair of walk-in closets and a private bath with a garden spa tub, a separate shower and dual sinks.
- One of the secondary bedrooms features a full, private bath. The others share a full hall bath and each enjoys a built-in desk, making them perfect for the kids. A workshop off the garage is great for the family carpenter.

Plan DD-2096	
Bedrooms: 4+	**Baths:** 3
Living Area:	
Main floor	2,088 sq. ft.
Total Living Area:	**2,088 sq. ft.**
Standard basement	2,088 sq. ft.
Garage and workshop	552 sq. ft.
Storage	64 sq. ft.
Exterior Wall Framing:	2x4
Foundation Options:	
Standard basement	
Crawlspace	
Slab	

(All plans can be built with your choice of foundation and framing. A generic conversion diagram is available. See order form.)

BLUEPRINT PRICE CODE: C

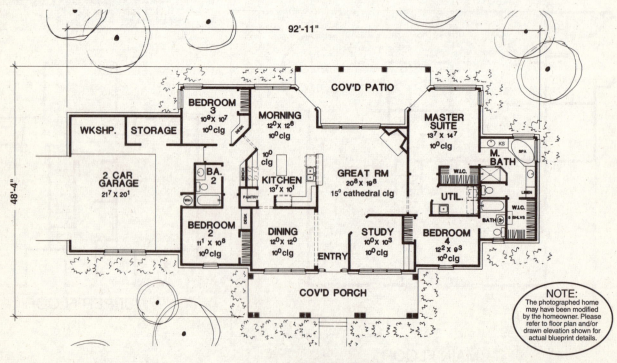

MAIN FLOOR

NOTE: The photographed home may have been modified by the homeowner. Please refer to floor plan and/or drawn elevation shown for actual blueprint details.

Plan DD-2096

Plan copyright held by home designer/architect

Picture Perfect!

- With graceful arches, columns and railings, this home's wonderful front porch makes it the picture of country charm. Decorative chimneys, shutters and dormers complete the portrait.
- Illuminated by sidelights and a fantail transom, the foyer enjoys a dramatic view of the living room and the back porch. Extra-high ceilings adorn the living room, the foyer and the adjoining dining room and bedroom.
- French doors nicely frame the living room's grand fireplace while they offer access to the skylighted porch.
- The L-shaped kitchen has a big island cooktop and a sunny breakfast nook.
- A Palladian window arrangement brightens the sitting alcove in the master suite, which also has its own entrance to the porch. The fantastic garden bath includes dual walk-in closets and a handy double-sink vanity.
- Future expansion space is available on the upper floor.

Plan J-9401

Bedrooms: 3+	Baths: 2½
Living Area:	
Main floor	2,089 sq. ft.
Total Living Area:	**2,089 sq. ft.**
Future upper floor	878 sq. ft.
Standard basement	2,089 sq. ft.
Garage	492 sq. ft.
Storage	38 sq. ft.
Exterior Wall Framing:	2x4
Foundation Options:	
Standard basement	
Crawlspace	
Slab	

(All plans can be built with your choice of foundation and framing. A generic conversion diagram is available. See order form.)

BLUEPRINT PRICE CODE: C

VIEW INTO KITCHEN AND BREAKFAST NOOK

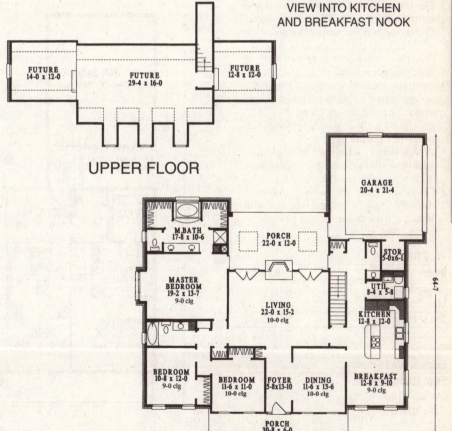

UPPER FLOOR

MAIN FLOOR

SOUTHERN BELLES

ORDER BLUEPRINTS ANYTIME!
CALL TOLL-FREE 1-800-820-1296

Plan J-9401
Plan copyright held by home designer/architect

PRICES AND DETAILS ON PAGES 12-15

Porch Paradise

- You'll be tempted to spend all your time on the huge front porch of this perfect one-story home!
- Great for outdoor parties or relaxing on a rocking chair, the front porch has an endless variety of uses. The pretty railing makes a handy footrest.
- The interior offers room for casual and formal entertaining. The healthy-sized Great Room is the natural location for all your large gatherings. It features a chic tray ceiling and access to a spacious back patio.
- Centrally located, the island kitchen serves both the casual breakfast nook and the formal dining room. An enormous walk-in pantry provides lots of space for storage.
- With a bubbly whirlpool bath and a sizable walk-in closet, the master suite adds a pleasant dose of luxury.
- On the opposite end of the home are the secondary bedrooms, each of which boasts a walk-in closet and private access to a full bath.

SOUTHERN BELLES

Plan DP-2108	
Bedrooms: 3+	Baths: 3
Living Area:	
Main floor	2,156 sq. ft.
Total Living Area:	**2,156 sq. ft.**
Standard basement	2,108 sq. ft.
Garage	480 sq. ft.
Exterior Wall Framing:	2x4
Foundation Options:	
Standard basement	
Crawlspace	
Slab	
(All plans can be built with your choice of foundation and framing. A generic conversion diagram is available. See order form.)	
BLUEPRINT PRICE CODE:	**C**

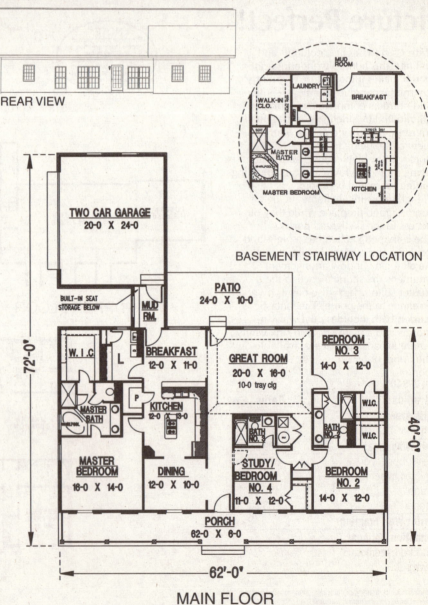

266   **ORDER BLUEPRINTS ANYTIME! CALL TOLL-FREE 1-800-820-1296**

Plan DP-2108
Plan copyright held by home designer/architect

PRICES AND DETAILS ON PAGES 12-15

Classic Exterior

- This classic exterior is built around an interior that offers all the amenities desired by today's families.
- In from the covered front porch, the entry features a curved stairway and a glass-block wall to the dining room.
- A step down from the entry, the Great Room boasts a dramatic cathedral ceiling and provides ample space for large family gatherings.
- The formal dining room is available for special occasions, while the vaulted breakfast nook serves everyday needs.
- The adjoining island kitchen offers plenty of counter space and opens to a handy utility room and a powder room.
- The deluxe main-floor master suite features a cathedral ceiling and an opulent private bath with a garden spa tub and a separate shower.
- Upstairs, two secondary bedrooms share a full bath and a balcony overlooking the Great Room below.
- Plans for a two-car garage are available upon request.

Plan DW-2112

Bedrooms: 3	Baths: 2½
Living Area:	
Upper floor	514 sq. ft.
Main floor	1,598 sq. ft.
Total Living Area:	**2,112 sq. ft.**
Standard basement	1,598 sq. ft.
Detached garage	508 sq. ft.
Exterior Wall Framing:	2x4

Foundation Options:
Standard basement
Crawlspace
Slab
(All plans can be built with your choice of foundation and framing. A generic conversion diagram is available. See order form.)

BLUEPRINT PRICE CODE: C

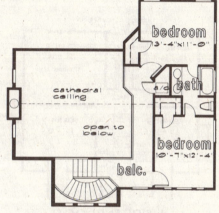

UPPER FLOOR

VIEW INTO GREAT ROOM

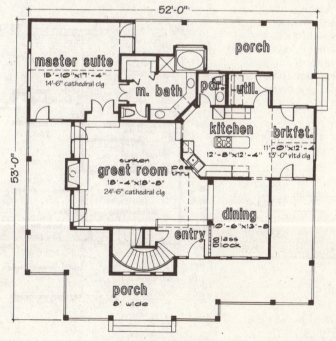

MAIN FLOOR

ORDER BLUEPRINTS ANYTIME!
CALL TOLL-FREE 1-800-820-1296

Plan DW-2112
Plan copyright held by home designer/architect

PRICES AND DETAILS ON PAGES 12-15

SOUTHERN BELLES

REAR VIEW

Stunning Spaces, Fantastic Facade

- Matching dormers and a generous covered front porch give this home its fantastic facade. Inside, the open living spaces are just as stunning.
- A two-story foyer bisects the formal living areas. The living room offers three bright windows, an inviting fireplace and sliding French doors to the Great Room. The formal dining room overlooks the front porch and has easy access to the kitchen.
- The Great Room is truly grand, featuring a fireplace and a TV center flanked by French doors that lead to a large deck.
- A circular dinette connects the Great Room to the kitchen, which is handy to a mudroom and a powder room.
- The main-floor master suite boasts a cathedral ceiling, a walk-in closet and a private bath with a whirlpool tub.
- Upstairs, four large bedrooms share another whirlpool bath. One bedroom offers a sloped ceiling.

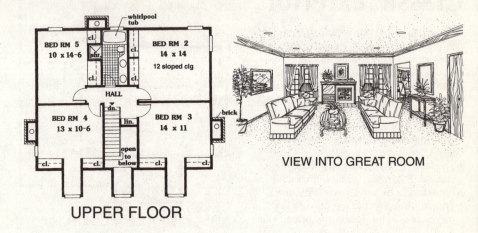

UPPER FLOOR

VIEW INTO GREAT ROOM

Plan AHP-9397	
Bedrooms: 5	**Baths:** 2½
Living Area:	
Upper floor	928 sq. ft.
Main floor	1,545 sq. ft.
Total Living Area:	**2,473 sq. ft.**
Standard basement	1,545 sq. ft.
Garage and storage	432 sq. ft.
Exterior Wall Framing:	2x4 or 2x6
Foundation Options:	
Standard basement	
Crawlspace	
Slab	
(All plans can be built with your choice of foundation and framing. A generic conversion diagram is available. See order form.)	
BLUEPRINT PRICE CODE:	**C**

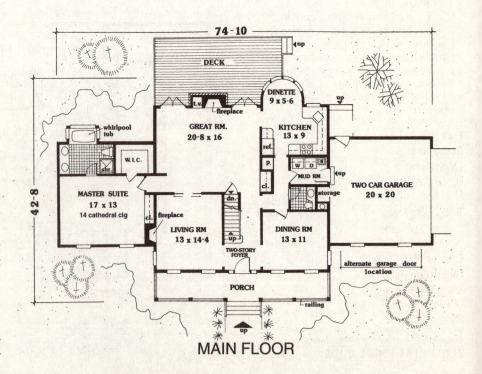

MAIN FLOOR

SOUTHERN BELLES

268   **ORDER BLUEPRINTS ANYTIME! CALL TOLL-FREE 1-800-820-1296**

Plan AHP-9397
Plan copyright held by home designer/architect

PRICES AND DETAILS ON PAGES 12-15

Classic Creole

- Grand symmetry and a livable floor plan mark this classic Creole home—one of our most popular designs.
- A deep porch fronts the home, helping to cool the interior and dramatically extending the living space.
- Inside, formal spaces flank the entry and flow through double doors into the casual family room, which features a prominent fireplace. French doors flank the fireplace for quick outdoor access.
- The secluded master suite boasts a quiet sitting area and a luxurious bath topped by a skylighted sloped ceiling.
- A peninsula cooktop and a sunny eating nook highlight the kitchen.
- At the back, the home's floor plan encloses a porch and deck, creating a large, private area for fresh-air fun.
- To avoid disturbing the design's countenance, the side-loaded garage is placed at the rear of the home.
- The upper floor houses three more bedrooms and two full baths.

Plan E-3000

Bedrooms: 4	Baths: 3½

Living Area:
Upper floor	1,027 sq. ft.
Main floor	2,008 sq. ft.
Total Living Area:	**3,035 sq. ft.**
Standard basement	2,008 sq. ft.
Garage	484 sq. ft.
Storage	96 sq. ft.

Exterior Wall Framing:	2x6

Foundation Options:
Standard basement
Crawlspace
Slab
(All plans can be built with your choice of foundation and framing. A generic conversion diagram is available. See order form.)

BLUEPRINT PRICE CODE: E

NOTE: The above photographed home may have been modified by the homeowner. Please refer to floor plan and/or drawn elevation shown for actual blueprint details.

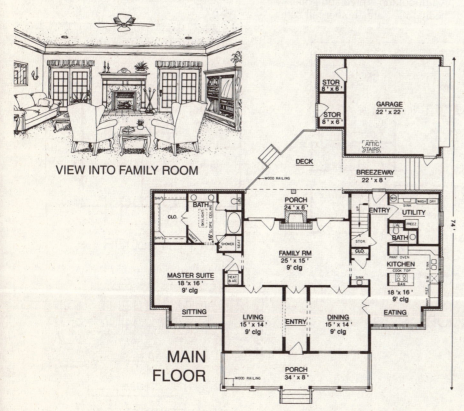

VIEW INTO FAMILY ROOM

MAIN FLOOR

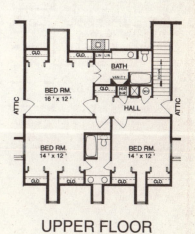

UPPER FLOOR

SOUTHERN BELLES

ORDER BLUEPRINTS ANYTIME!
CALL TOLL-FREE 1-800-820-1296

Plan E-3000
Plan copyright held by home designer/architect

PRICES AND DETAILS
ON PAGES 12–15

Innovative Floor Plan

- The wide front porch, arched windows and symmetrical lines of this traditional home conceal the modern, innovative floor plan found within.
- A two-story-high foyer guides guests to the front-oriented formal areas, which offer views to the front porch.
- The hot spot of the home is the Great Room, with one of the home's three fireplaces and a media wall. Flanking doors open to a large backyard deck.
- The island kitchen and glassed-in eating nook overlook the deck and access a handy mudroom. High ceilings add to the aura of warmth and hospitality found on the main floor of this home.
- Another of the fireplaces is offered in the master suite. This private oasis also boasts a soaring cathedral ceiling and a delicious private bath with a luxurious garden tub.
- Upstairs, one bedroom has a sloped ceiling and a private bath with a whirlpool tub. Three additional bedrooms share another full bath.

Plan AHP-9360

Bedrooms: 5	**Baths:** 3½
Living Area:	
Upper floor	970 sq. ft.
Main floor	1,735 sq. ft.
Total Living Area:	**2,705 sq. ft.**
Standard basement	1,550 sq. ft.
Garage and utility area	443 sq. ft.
Exterior Wall Framing:	2x4 or 2x6

Foundation Options:
Standard basement
Crawlspace
Slab

(All plans can be built with your choice of foundation and framing. A generic conversion diagram is available. See order form.)

BLUEPRINT PRICE CODE: D

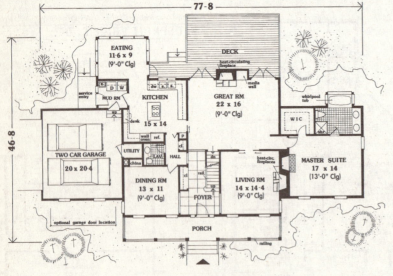

MAIN FLOOR

UPPER FLOOR

VIEW INTO GREAT ROOM

ORDER BLUEPRINTS ANYTIME!
CALL TOLL-FREE 1-800-820-1296

Plan AHP-9360
Plan copyright held by home designer/architect

PRICES AND DETAILS ON PAGES 12-15

Formal, Casual Entertainment

- This charming home has plenty of space for both formal and casual entertaining.
- On the main floor, the huge central living room will pamper your guests with an impressive fireplace, a wet bar and two sets of French doors that expand the room to a backyard porch.
- The large formal dining room hosts those special, sit-down dinners.
- There's still more space in the roomy island kitchen and breakfast nook to gather for snacks and conversation.
- For quiet evenings alone, the plush master suite offers pure relaxation! A romantic two-way fireplace between the bedroom and the bath serves as the focal point, yet the whirlpool garden tub is just as inviting.
- All rooms are enhanced by high ceilings for added spaciousness.
- The kids' recreation time can be spent in the enormous game room on the upper floor. Private baths service each of the vaulted upper-floor bedrooms.

Plan L-105-VC	
Bedrooms: 4+	**Baths:** 4
Living Area:	
Upper floor	1,077 sq. ft.
Main floor	1,995 sq. ft.
Total Living Area:	**3,072 sq. ft.**
Garage	529 sq. ft.
Storage	184 sq. ft.
Exterior Wall Framing:	2x4

Foundation Options:
Slab
(All plans can be built with your choice of foundation and framing. A generic conversion diagram is available. See order form.)

BLUEPRINT PRICE CODE: E

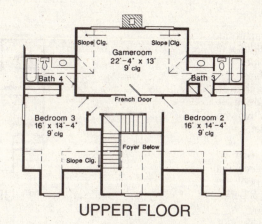

UPPER FLOOR

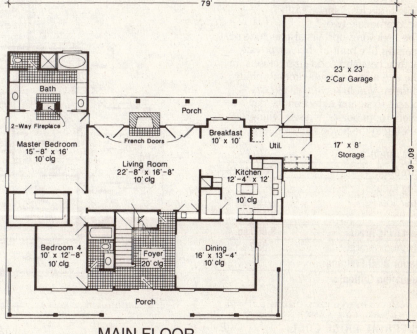

MAIN FLOOR

ORDER BLUEPRINTS ANYTIME!
CALL TOLL-FREE 1-800-820-1296

Plan L-105-VC
Plan copyright held by home designer/architect

PRICES AND DETAILS ON PAGES 12-15

SOUTHERN BELLES

Blend of Old and New

- In this design, a traditional wraparound porch surrounds a floor plan filled with the best features in today's homes.
- Inside, columns and bookshelves introduce the living room, which hosts gatherings in style. A sunny garden room shares the living room's two-way fireplace, and would be a quiet, pleasant spot for reading.
- For most activities, the family room is quite suitable, as it interacts nicely with the kitchen and the breakfast nook.
- In the master suite, a number of perks offer you special treatment. The secluded patio provides a private spot for coffee, while twin vanities and bountiful closet space easily accommodate two.
- The bedrooms upstairs also include neat features like built-in shelves, private bath access and good-sized closets. In the two front-facing bedrooms, pretty dormers would serve well as cozy places to sit and reflect on the day.
- Every room boasts a raised ceiling, adding to the home's airiness.

Plan L-3050-C

Bedrooms: 4	Baths: 3½
Living Area:	
Upper floor	787 sq. ft.
Main floor	2,263 sq. ft.
Total Living Area:	**3,050 sq. ft.**
Detached garage	552 sq. ft.
Exterior Wall Framing:	2x4

Foundation Options:
Slab
(All plans can be built with your choice of foundation and framing. A generic conversion diagram is available. See order form.)

BLUEPRINT PRICE CODE: E

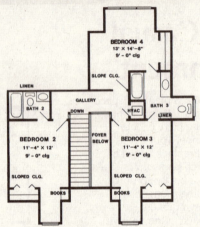

UPPER FLOOR

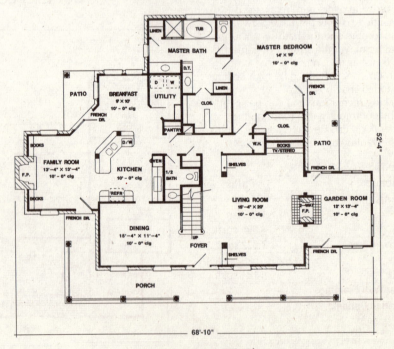

MAIN FLOOR

Plan L-3050-C
Plan copyright held by home designer/architect

The symbols pictured here denote optional products designed to enhance your home-building experience. To determine which products are available for a particular plan, refer to the symbol(s) appearing beneath the heading **Product Options** in the specifications box accompanying that plan. Turn to pages 12–15 for detailed information about each product, including pricing.

 Planning Set

 Reproducible Set

 Itemized List of Materials

 Full-Reverse Plan

FHA/VA Description of Materials

Next-Day Delivery

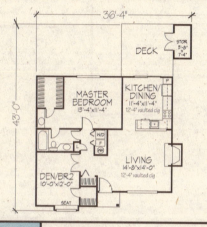

The Osseo

Plan B-8315 **Price Code AA**

890 sq. ft.	Main floor:	890 sq. ft.
1+ Bedrooms	Exterior Framing:	2x4
1 Bath		

Product Options:

Foundations: Slab

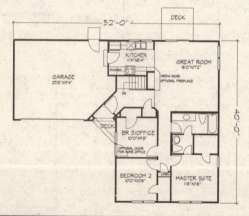

Plan LS-95888-DD **Price Code A**

The Northome

1,068 sq. ft.	Main floor:	1,068 sq. ft.
2+ Bedrooms	Basement:	1,040 sq. ft.
1½ Baths	Garage:	482 sq. ft.
	Exterior Framing:	2x4

Product Options:

Foundations: Daylight basement or Standard basement

ORDER BLUEPRINTS ANYTIME!
CALL TOLL-FREE 1-800-820-1296

Plan copyright held by home designer/architect

PRICES AND DETAILS ON PAGES 12-15

The Hansford

Plan L-22-VA   **Price Code A**

An expansive central living room warmed by a handsome fireplace serves as the hub of activity in this cozy home.

1,078 sq. ft.
3 Bedrooms
2 Baths

Main floor: 1,078 sq. ft.
Garage: 431 sq. ft.
Exterior Framing: 2x4

Product Options:

Foundations: Slab

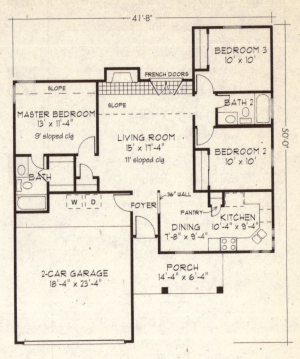

The Sartell

Plan B-88054   **Price Code A**

This traditional home's stone-and-siding exterior gives way to an open, family-friendly floor plan.

1,154 sq. ft.
2+ Bedrooms
2 Baths

Main floor: 1,154 sq. ft.
Garage: 426 sq. ft.
Exterior Framing: 2x4

Product Options:

Foundations: Slab

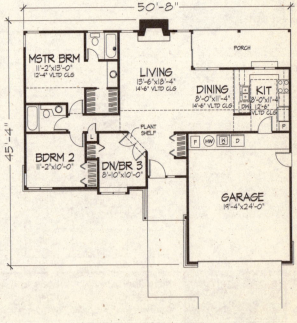

STYLISH NEWCOMERS

ORDER BLUEPRINTS ANYTIME!
CALL TOLL-FREE 1-800-820-1296

Plan copyright held by home designer/architect

PRICES AND DETAILS ON PAGES 12-15

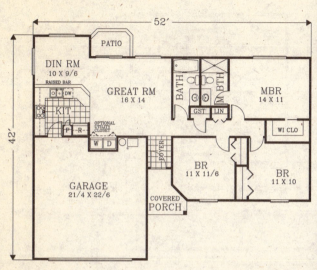

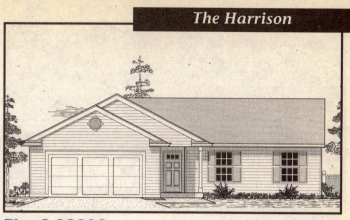

The Harrison

Plan S-82898 — **Price Code A**

This home's smart kitchen serves the adjoining dining room via a snack bar; nearby, sliding glass doors open to a patio.

1,155 sq. ft.	Main floor:	1,155 sq. ft.
3 Bedrooms	Garage:	479 sq. ft.
2 Baths	Exterior Framing:	2x6

Product Options:

Foundations: Crawlspace

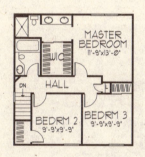

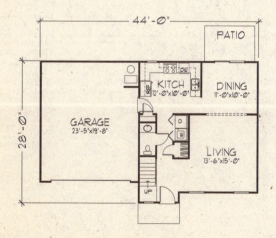

The Lindstrom

Plan LS-98849-GW — **Price Code A**

An economical combination of Early American influences and simple construction, this two-story is sure to please.

1,249 sq. ft.	Upper floor:	608 sq. ft.
3 Bedrooms	Main floor:	641 sq. ft.
2½ Baths	Garage:	480 sq. ft.
	Exterior Framing:	2x4

Product Options:

Foundations: Slab

ORDER BLUEPRINTS ANYTIME!
CALL TOLL-FREE 1-800-820-1296

Plan copyright held by home designer/architect

PRICES AND DETAILS ON PAGES 12-15

STYLISH NEWCOMERS

The Monroeville

Plan BSA-1298-A **Price Code A**

Graced by a welcoming front porch, this nostalgic design reveals a spacious Great Room with a cheery fireplace.

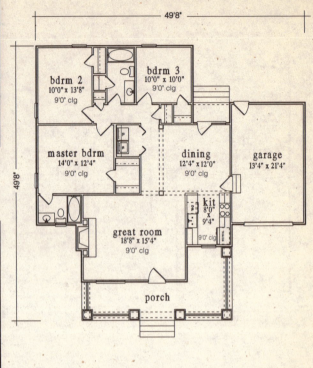

1,298 sq. ft.	Main floor:	1,298 sq. ft.
3 Bedrooms	Garage:	301 sq. ft.
2 Baths	Exterior Framing:	2x4

Product Options:

Foundations: Slab

The Maurice

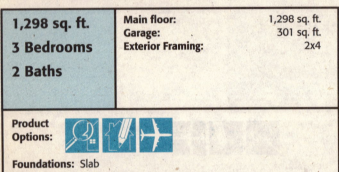

Plan B-89022 **Price Code B**

Simple living is made easy with a vaulted Great Room that opens to the dining room and offers a view of the rear deck.

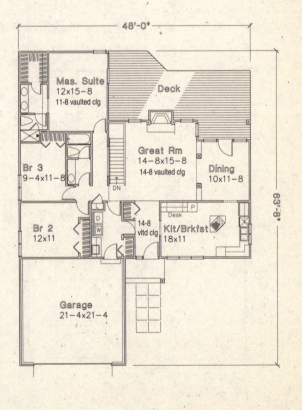

1,571 sq. ft.	Main floor:	1,571 sq. ft.
3 Bedrooms	Basement:	1,571 sq. ft.
2 Baths	Garage:	455 sq. ft.
	Exterior Framing:	2x4

Product Options:

Foundations: Standard basement

ORDER BLUEPRINTS ANYTIME!
CALL TOLL-FREE 1-800-820-1296

PRICES AND DETAILS ON PAGES 12-15

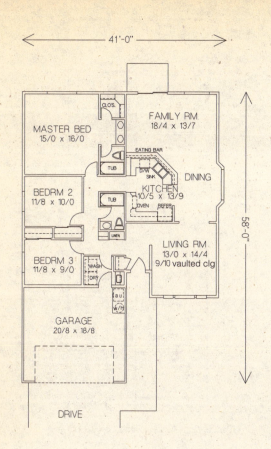

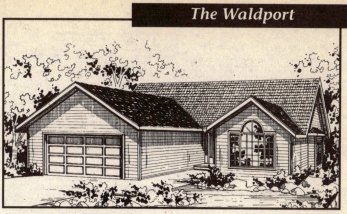

The Waldport

Plan SUN-1360-B   **Price Code B**

For your peace and quiet, this home nicely separates the free-flowing living areas from the secluded sleeping wing.

1,582 sq. ft.	Main floor:	1,582 sq. ft.
3 Bedrooms	Garage:	404 sq. ft.
2 Baths	Exterior Framing:	2x6

Product Options:

Foundations: Crawlspace or Slab

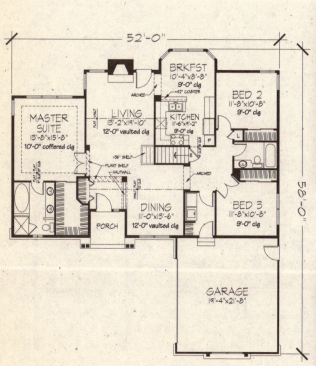

The Koochiching

Plan LS-1112-BSB   **Price Code B**

Make the most of this home's high ceilings by displaying knickknacks on the plant ledges above doorways.

1,612 sq. ft.	Main floor:	1,612 sq. ft.
2+ Bedrooms	Basement:	1,612 sq. ft.
2 Baths	Garage:	440 sq. ft.
	Exterior Framing:	2x6

Product Options:

Foundations: Standard basement

ORDER BLUEPRINTS ANYTIME!
CALL TOLL-FREE 1-800-820-1296

Plan copyright held by home designer/architect

PRICES AND DETAILS ON PAGES 12-15

STYLISH NEWCOMERS

The Mora

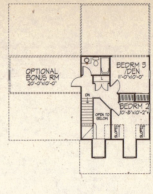

Plan LS-98818-GW **Price Code B**

The blueprints for this flexible home show details for a screen porch, a bonus room and an alternate master bath.

1,579 sq. ft.	Upper floor:	392 sq. ft.
2+ Bedrooms	Main floor:	1,187 sq. ft.
	Optional bonus room:	214 sq. ft.
2½ Baths	Optional screen porch:	104 sq. ft.
	Garage:	400 sq. ft.
	Exterior Framing:	2x4

Product Options:

Foundations: Slab

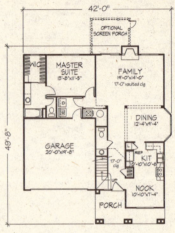

The Kelton

Plan KD-1612 **Price Code B**

Enhanced by a coffered ceiling, this home's central Great Room features a handsome fireplace and access to a rear patio.

1,612 sq. ft.	Main floor:	1,612 sq. ft.
3 Bedrooms	Garage and storage:	438 sq. ft.
2 Baths	Exterior Framing:	2x4

Product Options:

Foundations: Slab

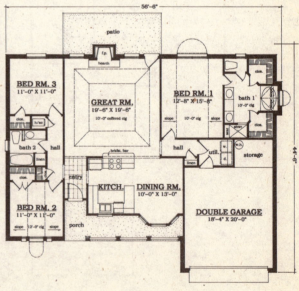

ORDER BLUEPRINTS ANYTIME!
CALL TOLL-FREE 1-800-820-1296

Plan copyright held by home designer/architect

PRICES AND DETAILS ON PAGES 12-15

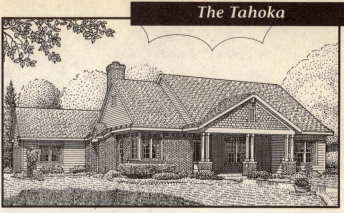

The Tahoka

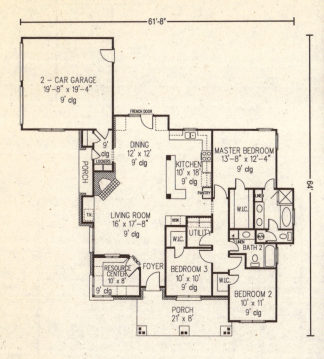

Plan L-9903-UDA **Price Code B**

A resource center adjoining this home's spacious living room makes a perfect home office or study.

1,616 sq. ft.	Main floor:	1,616 sq. ft.
3 Bedrooms	Garage:	437 sq. ft.
2 Baths	Exterior Framing:	2x4

Product Options:

Foundations: Slab

The Cedar Hill

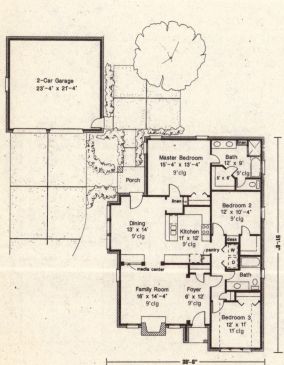

Plan L-1673-BA **Price Code B**

Old-world charm wraps a floor plan that includes a family room with a fireplace and a built-in media center.

1,673 sq. ft.	Main floor:	1,673 sq. ft.
3 Bedrooms	Garage:	498 sq. ft.
2 Baths	Exterior Framing:	2x4

Product Options:

Foundations: Slab

ORDER BLUEPRINTS ANYTIME!
CALL TOLL-FREE 1-800-820-1296

Plan copyright held by home designer/architect

PRICES AND DETAILS ON PAGES 12-15

The Celina

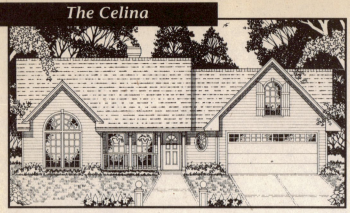
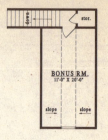

Plan KD-1348 **Price Code B**

This home's master suite is one tempting retreat. It showcases a coffered ceiling and a soothing garden tub.

1,632 sq. ft.	Main floor:	1,348 sq. ft.
3+ Bedrooms	Bonus room:	284 sq. ft.
2 Baths	Garage:	419 sq. ft.
	Exterior Framing:	2x4

Product Options:

Foundations: Crawlspace or Slab

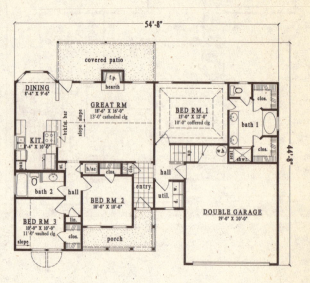

The Amagansett

Plan K-820-D **Price Code B**

From the vaulted entryway, head into the reception hall and marvel at the living and dining room's backyard view.

1,638 sq. ft.	Main floor:	1,638 sq. ft.
3 Bedrooms	Basement:	1,595 sq. ft.
2½ Baths	Garage:	394 sq. ft.
	Exterior Framing:	2x4 or 2x6

Product Options:

Foundations: Standard basement, Crawlspace or Slab

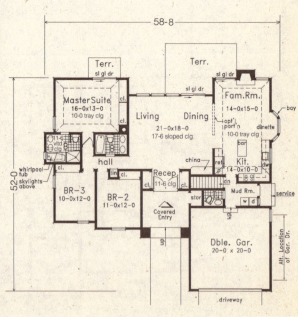

ORDER BLUEPRINTS ANYTIME!
CALL TOLL-FREE 1-800-820-1296

Plan copyright held by home designer/architect

PRICES AND DETAILS ON PAGES 12-15

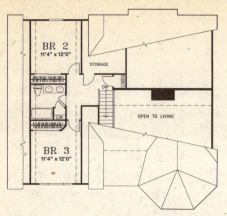
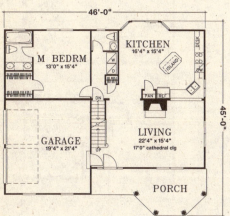

The Kenilworth

Plan OH-241 | **Price Code B**

A multipurpose living room and a bayed country kitchen make this home perfect for plenty of family time.

1,689 sq. ft.	Upper floor:	508 sq. ft.
3 Bedrooms	Main floor:	1,181 sq. ft.
	Basement:	1,181 sq. ft.
2½ Baths	Garage:	428 sq. ft.
	Exterior Framing:	2x4

Product Options:

Foundations: Standard basement

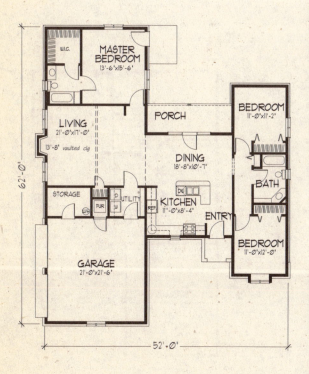

The Montevideo

Plan LS-94136-E | **Price Code B**

Tudor-style touches on the outside hint at this home's fantastic interior, highlighted by a huge, vaulted living room.

1,696 sq. ft.	Main floor:	1,696 sq. ft.
3 Bedrooms	Garage:	548 sq. ft.
	Storage (approx.):	60 sq. ft.
2 Baths	Exterior Framing:	2x6

Product Options:

Foundations: Crawlspace

ORDER BLUEPRINTS ANYTIME!
CALL TOLL-FREE 1-800-820-1296

Plan copyright held by home designer/architect

PRICES AND DETAILS ON PAGES 12-15

STYLISH NEWCOMERS

The Aleman

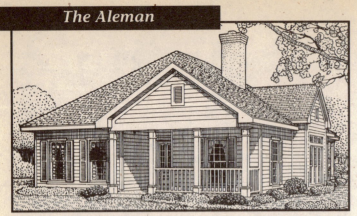

Plan L-97143-UDA   **Price Code B**

Your family will surely enjoy this home's living room, which features a handsome fireplace and a built-in media center.

1,649 sq. ft.	Main floor:	1,649 sq. ft.
2+ Bedrooms	Garage:	567 sq. ft.
2 Baths	Exterior Framing:	2x4

Product Options: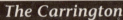

Foundations: Slab

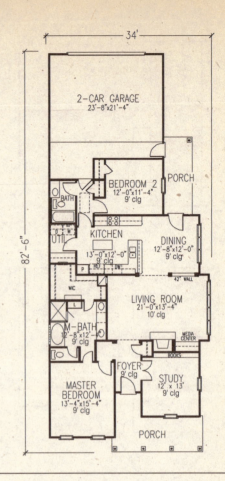

The Carrington

Plan S-3295-M   **Price Code B**

This home's fantastic Great Room shows off a vaulted ceiling, a corner fireplace and access to the backyard patio.

1,691 sq. ft.	Main floor:	1,691 sq. ft.
3 Bedrooms	Garage and storage:	480 sq. ft.
2 Baths	Exterior Framing:	2x6

Product Options:

Foundations: Crawlspace

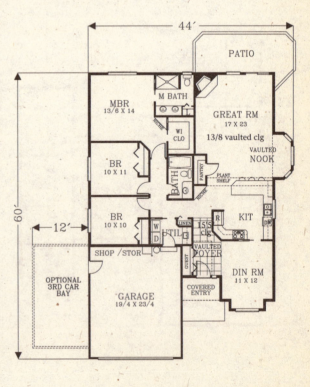

STYLISH NEWCOMERS

ORDER BLUEPRINTS ANYTIME!
CALL TOLL-FREE 1-800-820-1296

Plan copyright held by home designer/architect

PRICES AND DETAILS ON PAGES 12-15

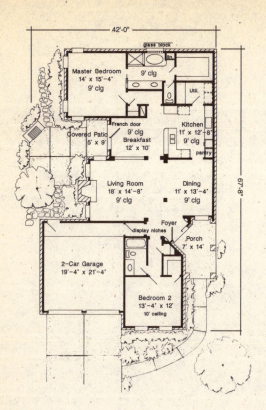

The Higginbotham

Plan L-303-HCC   **Price Code B**

This home's private front porch is ideal for outdoor relaxation, while the covered side patio is great for entertaining.

1,706 sq. ft. 2 Bedrooms 2 Baths	Main floor: 1,706 sq. ft. Garage: 456 sq. ft. Exterior Framing: 2x4

Product Options:

Foundations: Slab

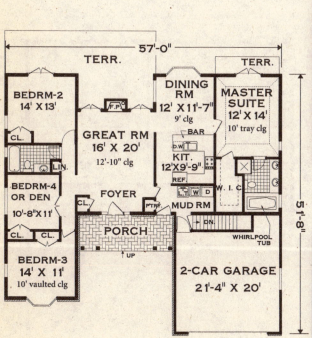

The Galeville

Plan AHP-2011   **Price Code B**

Both indoor and outdoor entertaining are a breeze with this home's impressive Great Room and large backyard terrace.

1,748 sq. ft. 3+ Bedrooms 2 Baths	Main floor: 1,748 sq. ft. Basement: 1,800 sq. ft. Garage: 520 sq. ft. Exterior Framing: 2x4 or 2x6

Product Options:

Foundations: Standard basement, Crawlspace or Slab

ORDER BLUEPRINTS ANYTIME!
CALL TOLL-FREE 1-800-820-1296

Plan copyright held by home designer/architect

PRICES AND DETAILS ON PAGES 12-15

The Richland Springs

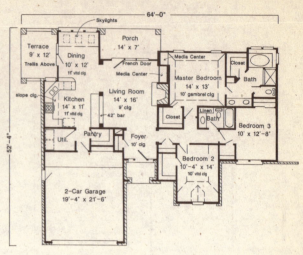

Plan L-698-FA **Price Code B**

Every meal is a picnic in this home's skylighted dining room, which enjoys an impressive view of a trellised terrace.

1,696 sq. ft.	Main floor:	1,696 sq. ft.
3 Bedrooms	Garage:	460 sq. ft.
2 Baths	Exterior Framing:	2x4

Product Options:

Foundations: Slab

The Loma Alta

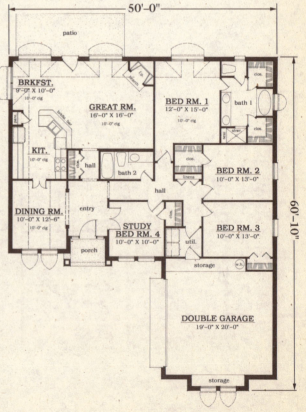

Plan KD-1795 **Price Code B**

Exciting windows and glorious ceilings set this smart home apart by making the most of natural light.

1,795 sq. ft.	Main floor:	1,795 sq. ft.
3+ Bedrooms	Garage and storage:	484 sq. ft.
2 Baths	Exterior Framing:	2x4

Product Options:

Foundations: Slab

ORDER BLUEPRINTS ANYTIME!
CALL TOLL-FREE 1-800-820-1296

PRICES AND DETAILS ON PAGES 12-15

Plan copyright held by home designer/architect

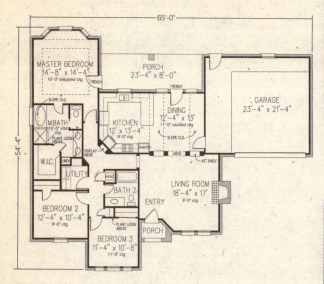

The Raymondville

Plan L-9908-UDA   **Price Code B**

A dramatic archway leads into the bright dining room, which is complete with a French door to the back porch.

1,711 sq. ft.	Main floor:	1,711 sq. ft.
3 Bedrooms	Garage:	567 sq. ft.
2 Baths	Exterior Framing:	2x4

Product Options:

Foundations: Slab

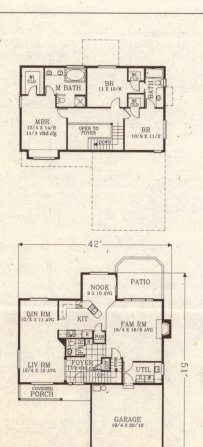

The Yamhill

Plan S-63095-D   **Price Code B**

With a striking balcony overlook and a sumptuous master suite, this home's modest exterior reveals a slew of surprises.

1,789 sq. ft.	Upper floor:	800 sq. ft.
3 Bedrooms	Main floor:	989 sq. ft.
2½ Baths	Garage:	400 sq. ft.
	Exterior Framing:	2x6

Product Options:

Foundations: Crawlspace

ORDER BLUEPRINTS ANYTIME!
CALL TOLL-FREE 1-800-820-1296

Plan copyright held by home designer/architect

PRICES AND DETAILS ON PAGES 12-15

STYLISH NEWCOMERS

The Ellsworth

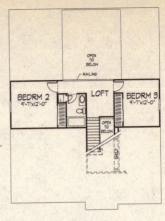

Plan LS-98847-GW **Price Code B**

This home's well-appointed kitchen adjoins both the formal dining room and the casual breakfast nook.

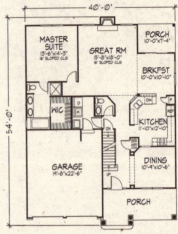

1,710 sq. ft.	Upper floor:	386 sq. ft.
3 Bedrooms	Main floor:	1,324 sq. ft.
	Basement:	1,317 sq. ft.
2½ Baths	Garage:	460 sq. ft.
	Exterior Framing:	2x4

Product Options:

Foundations: Standard basement

The Faribault

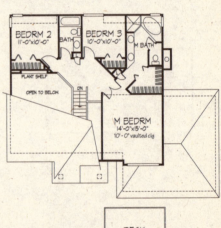

Plan B-89017 **Price Code B**

Double doors lead into the vaulted master suite; the lavish private bath boasts a corner tub with sparkling windows.

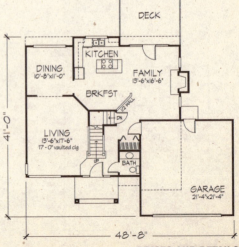

1,866 sq. ft.	Upper floor:	872 sq. ft.
3 Bedrooms	Main floor:	994 sq. ft.
	Basement:	994 sq. ft.
2½ Baths	Garage:	455 sq. ft.
	Exterior Framing:	2x4

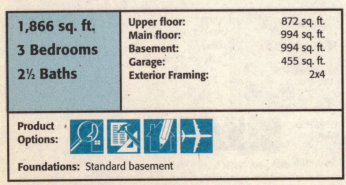

Product Options:

Foundations: Standard basement

ORDER BLUEPRINTS ANYTIME!
CALL TOLL-FREE 1-800-820-1296

Plan copyright held by home designer/architect

PRICES AND DETAILS ON PAGES 12-15

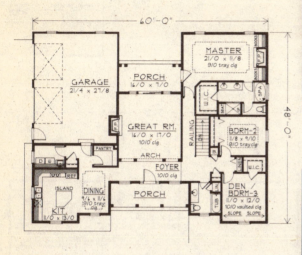

Plan Y-1809   Price Code B

This home's fetching island kitchen and adjoining dining area is the right spot for family and friends to gather.

1,809 sq. ft. 2+ Bedrooms 2 Baths	Main floor: 1,809 sq. ft. Basement: 1,809 sq. ft. Garage: 600 sq. ft. Exterior Framing: 2x6

Product Options:

Foundations: Standard basement

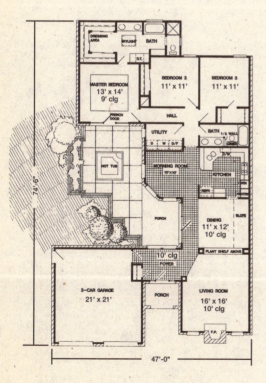
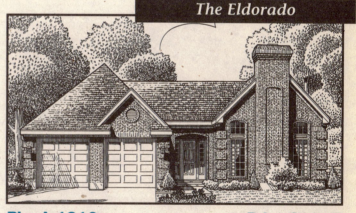

The Eldorado

Plan L-1910   Price Code B

This wide-open home includes a spacious living room and a stunning master bedroom that opens onto a beautiful patio.

1,910 sq. ft. 3 Bedrooms 2 Baths	Main floor: 1,910 sq. ft. Garage: 458 sq. ft. Exterior Framing: 2x4

Product Options:

Foundations: Slab

ORDER BLUEPRINTS ANYTIME!
CALL TOLL-FREE 1-800-820-1296

Plan copyright held by home designer/architect

PRICES AND DETAILS ON PAGES 12-15

The Forbes

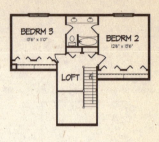

Plan LS-95855-HB   **Price Code B**

With its formal living and dining rooms, plus a sizable sun porch, this home has plenty of space for entertaining.

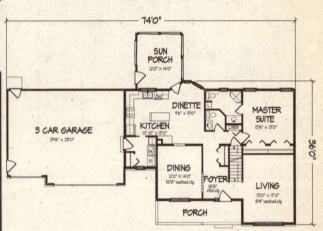

1,824 sq. ft.	Upper floor:	572 sq. ft.
3 Bedrooms	Main floor:	1,252 sq. ft.
	Sun porch:	165 sq. ft.
2½ Baths	Basement:	1,251 sq. ft.
	Garage:	700 sq. ft.
	Exterior Framing:	2x6

Product Options:

Foundations: Standard basement

The Dadeville

Plan BSA-1856   **Price Code B**

The sunny study off this home's Great Room can easily be converted into an efficient home office or a cozy den.

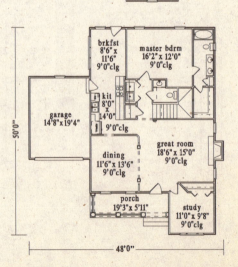

1,856 sq. ft.	Upper floor:	498 sq. ft.
3+ Bedrooms	Main floor:	1,358 sq. ft.
	Garage:	300 sq. ft.
2½ Baths	Exterior Framing:	2x4

Product Options:

Foundations: Slab

ORDER BLUEPRINTS ANYTIME!
CALL TOLL-FREE 1-800-820-1296

Plan copyright held by home designer/architect

PRICES AND DETAILS ON PAGES 12-15

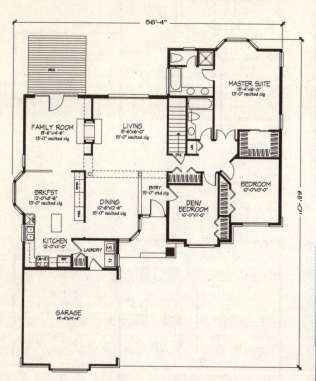

The Soudan

Plan B-90030 **Price Code B**

A crackling see-through fireplace connects the living room and the family room, forming the heart of this cozy home.

1,923 sq. ft.	Main floor:	1,923 sq. ft.
2+ Bedrooms	Basement:	1,904 sq. ft.
2 Baths	Garage:	374 sq. ft.
	Exterior Framing:	2x6

Product Options:

Foundations: Standard basement

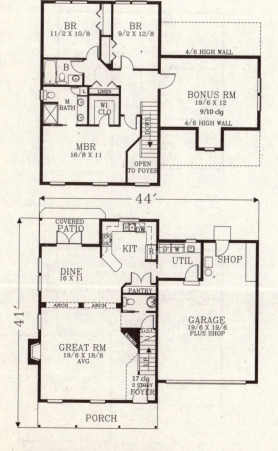

The Hawthorne

Plan S-111197 **Price Code B**

This ideal family home offers a spacious Great Room as well as three bedrooms and a bonus room.

1,955 sq. ft.	Upper floor:	775 sq. ft.
3+ Bedrooms	Main floor:	865 sq. ft.
2½ Baths	Bonus room:	315 sq. ft.
	Garage and shop:	458 sq. ft.
	Exterior Framing:	2x6

Product Options:

Foundations: Crawlspace

ORDER BLUEPRINTS ANYTIME!
CALL TOLL-FREE 1-800-820-1296

Plan copyright held by home designer/architect

PRICES AND DETAILS ON PAGES 12-15

The Vantage

Plan Y-1881 — **Price Code C**

The formal parlor of this charming Victorian-style home shares a see-through fireplace with the spacious family room.

2,221 sq. ft.	Upper floor:	883 sq. ft.
3+ Bedrooms	Main floor:	998 sq. ft.
2½ Baths	Bonus room:	340 sq. ft.
	Basement:	963 sq. ft.
	Garage:	518 sq. ft.
	Exterior Framing:	2x6

Product Options:

Foundations: Standard basement or Crawlspace

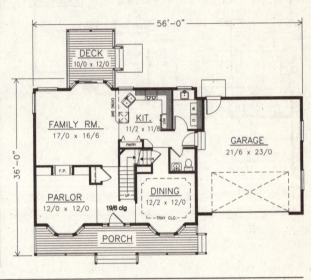

The Bois Fort

Plan LS-98827-GW — **Price Code B**

This home boasts a majestic fireplace in the spacious family room, which is sure to be a haven on chilly nights.

1,913 sq. ft.	Upper floor:	905 sq. ft.
4 Bedrooms	Main floor:	1,008 sq. ft.
2½ Baths	Garage:	440 sq. ft.
	Exterior Framing:	2x6

Product Options:

Foundations: Slab

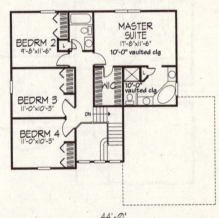

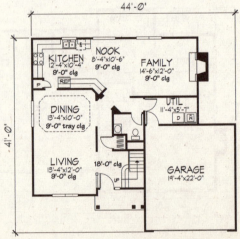

ORDER BLUEPRINTS ANYTIME!
CALL TOLL-FREE 1-800-820-1296

Plan copyright held by home designer/architect

PRICES AND DETAILS ON PAGES 12-15

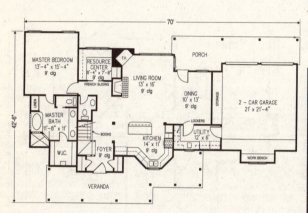

The Garnett

Plan L-9902-UDA **Price Code B**

A front veranda and a back porch easily merge with this pretty home's open, shared living spaces.

1,986 sq. ft.	Upper floor:	646 sq. ft.
3 Bedrooms	Main floor:	1,340 sq. ft.
2½ Baths	Garage, storage, workbench:	479 sq. ft.
	Exterior Framing:	2x4

Product Options:

Foundations: Slab

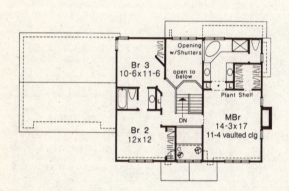
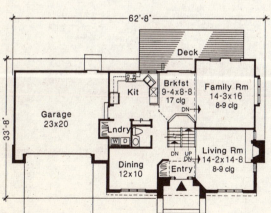

The Parnell

Plan B-87114 **Price Code B**

A fetching front porch accents this home's clean lines and practical, straightforward plan.

1,995 sq. ft.	Upper floor:	910 sq. ft.
3 Bedrooms	Main floor:	1,085 sq. ft.
2½ Baths	Basement:	1,085 sq. ft.
	Garage:	460 sq. ft.
	Exterior Framing:	2x4

Product Options:

Foundations: Standard basement

ORDER BLUEPRINTS ANYTIME!
CALL TOLL-FREE 1-800-820-1296

Plan copyright held by home designer/architect

PRICES AND DETAILS ON PAGES 12-15

The James

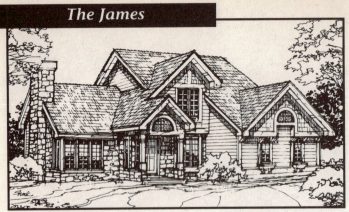
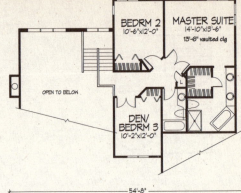
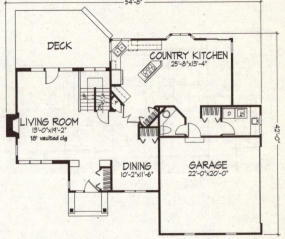

Plan B-87161 **Price Code B**

This home's floor plan works well for a growing family, with a large country kitchen and a vaulted living room.

1,957 sq. ft.	Upper floor:	797 sq. ft.
2+ Bedrooms	Main floor:	1,160 sq. ft.
	Basement:	1,160 sq. ft.
2½ Baths	Garage:	440 sq. ft.
	Exterior Framing:	2x4

Product Options:

Foundations: Standard basement

The Conley

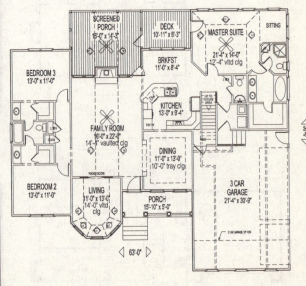

Plan APS-1913 **Price Code B**

Whether you're inside cozying up to the fire or outside enjoying the breeze, this classic home is sure to please.

1,982 sq. ft.	Main floor:	1,982 sq. ft.
3+ Bedrooms	Bonus room:	386 sq. ft.
	Screened porch:	225 sq. ft.
2½ Baths	Garage:	681 sq. ft.
	Exterior Framing:	2x4

Product Options:

Foundations: Crawlspace

ORDER BLUEPRINTS ANYTIME!
CALL TOLL-FREE 1-800-820-1296

Plan copyright held by home designer/architect

PRICES AND DETAILS ON PAGES 12-15

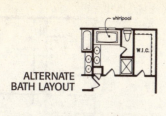
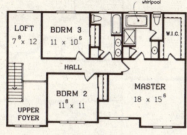
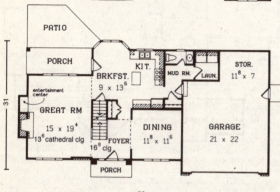
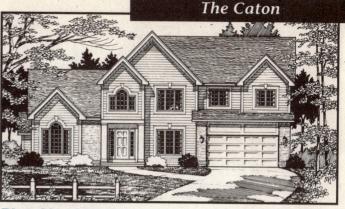

The Caton

Plan GL-1997-3 **Price Code B**

A backyard porch and patio, plus an upper-floor loft, expand this design's thoughtful, practical living spaces.

1,997 sq. ft.	Upper floor:	1,031 sq. ft.
3 Bedrooms	Main floor:	966 sq. ft.
2½ Baths	Basement:	932 sq. ft.
	Garage and storage:	544 sq. ft.
	Exterior Framing:	2x4

Product Options:

Foundations: Standard basement

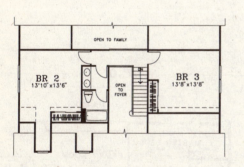
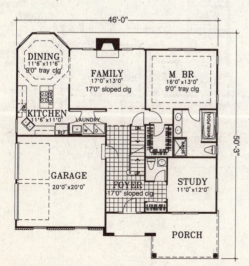

The Jordanville

Plan OH-301 **Price Code C**

This livable home's pleasing roofline and tidy, arched entry lend it an air of grace and simplicity.

2,011 sq. ft.	Upper floor:	639 sq. ft.
3+ Bedrooms	Main floor:	1,372 sq. ft.
2½ Baths	Basement:	1,372 sq. ft.
	Garage:	415 sq. ft.
	Exterior Framing:	2x4

Product Options:

Foundations: Standard basement

ORDER BLUEPRINTS ANYTIME!
CALL TOLL-FREE 1-800-820-1296

Plan copyright held by home designer/architect

PRICES AND DETAILS ON PAGES 12-15

The Tatum

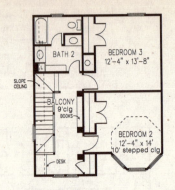
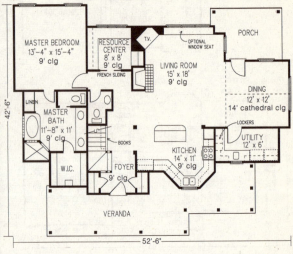

Plan L-9907-UDA **Price Code C**

This adorable home flaunts a roomy island kitchen that opens to the sunny living room with a fireplace and a media center.

2,056 sq. ft.	Upper floor:	646 sq. ft.
3 Bedrooms	Main floor:	1,410 sq. ft.
2½ Baths	Exterior Framing:	2x4

Product Options:

Foundations: Slab

The Marcola

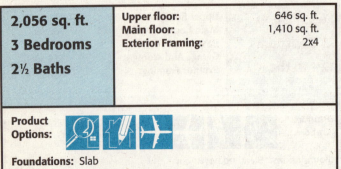

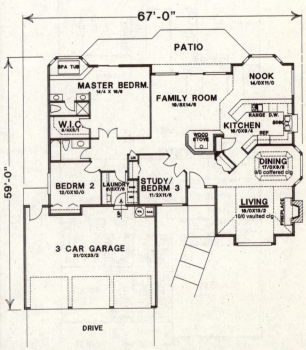

Plan SUN-1020 **Price Code C**

This home's crowning glory is its palatial master suite, which flaunts private patio access and a spa tub.

2,073 sq. ft.	Main floor:	2,073 sq. ft.
2+ Bedrooms	Garage:	450 sq. ft.
2 Baths	Exterior Framing:	2x6

Product Options:

Foundations: Crawlspace or Slab

ORDER BLUEPRINTS ANYTIME! CALL TOLL-FREE 1-800-820-1296

Plan copyright held by home designer/architect

PRICES AND DETAILS ON PAGES 12-15

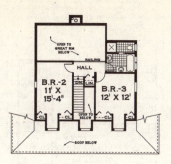
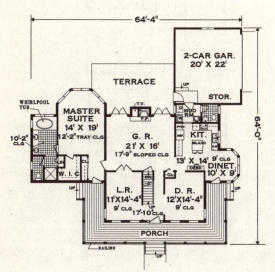

The Holbrook

Plan AHP-2007   **Price Code C**

Enjoy a quiet afternoon on the sprawling wraparound porch or the back terrace of this distinguished family home.

2,252 sq. ft.	Upper floor:	524 sq. ft.
3 Bedrooms	Main floor:	1,728 sq. ft.
	Basement:	1,728 sq. ft.
2½ Baths	Garage and storage:	468 sq. ft.
	Exterior Framing:	2x4 or 2x6

Product Options:

Foundations: Standard basement, Crawlspace or Slab

The Catalina

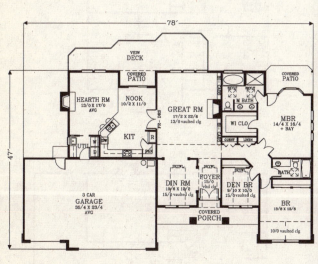

Plan S-112795-D   **Price Code C**

This home's fantastic master bedroom features a private patio, a large walk-in closet and a spacious skylighted bath.

2,090 sq. ft.	Main floor:	2,090 sq. ft.
2+ Bedrooms	Garage:	864 sq. ft.
2 Baths	Exterior Framing:	2x6

Product Options:

Foundations: Crawlspace

ORDER BLUEPRINTS ANYTIME!
CALL TOLL-FREE 1-800-820-1296

Plan copyright held by home designer/architect

PRICES AND DETAILS ON PAGES 12-15

The Belmont

Plan S-62094   **Price Code C**

This home's wonderful dining options include a backyard deck, a bayed dining area and a sunny, vaulted nook.

2,178 sq. ft.	Main floor:	1,623 sq. ft.
3+ Bedrooms	Basement (finished):	555 sq. ft.
	Basement (unfinished):	367 sq. ft.
3 Baths	Garage:	400 sq. ft.
	Exterior Framing:	2x6

Product Options:

Foundations: Partial basement

The Cobble Creek

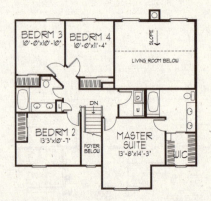

Plan LS-98821-GW   **Price Code C**

A large, bright office at the front of this home is the perfect quiet spot for studying or conducting business.

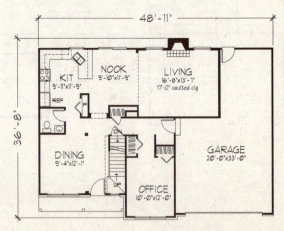

2,201 sq. ft.	Upper floor:	1,159 sq. ft.
4+ Bedrooms	Main floor:	1,042 sq. ft.
	Basement:	812 sq. ft.
2½ Baths	Garage:	545 sq. ft.
	Exterior Framing:	2x4

Product Options:

Foundations: Standard basement

ORDER BLUEPRINTS ANYTIME!
CALL TOLL-FREE 1-800-820-1296

Plan copyright held by home designer/architect

PRICES AND DETAILS ON PAGES 12-15

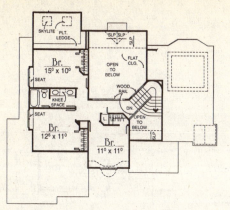

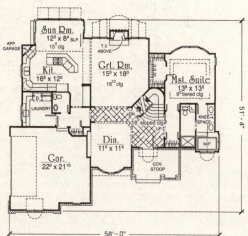

The Glenvil

Plan CC-2234   **Price Code C**

Double doors, a bay window and a tiered ceiling make the master bedroom in this attractive home airy and bright.

2,234 sq. ft.	Upper floor:	660 sq. ft.
4 Bedrooms	Main floor:	1,574 sq. ft.
	Basement:	1,434 sq. ft.
2½ Baths	Garage:	477 sq. ft.
	Exterior Framing:	2x4

Product Options:

Foundations: Standard basement

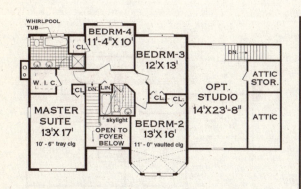

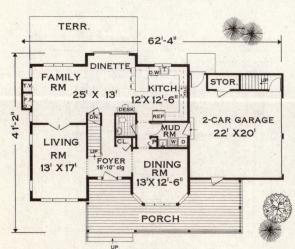

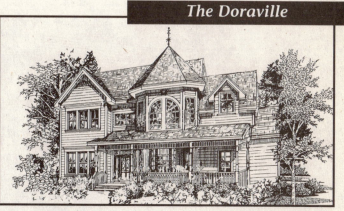

The Doraville

Plan AHP-9913   **Price Code C**

This charming Victorian has it all, featuring a dramatic two-story foyer and a huge family room with a fireplace.

2,270 sq. ft.	Upper floor:	1,093 sq. ft.
4+ Bedrooms	Main floor:	1,177 sq. ft.
	Opt. studio:	379 sq. ft.
2½ Baths	Basement:	1,177 sq. ft.
	Garage:	487 sq. ft.
	Storage:	25 sq. ft.
	Exterior Framing:	2x4 or 2x6

Product Options:

Foundations: Standard basement, Crawlspace or Slab

ORDER BLUEPRINTS ANYTIME!
CALL TOLL-FREE 1-800-820-1296

Plan copyright held by home designer/architect

PRICES AND DETAILS ON PAGES 12-15

The Spring Valley

Plan HDC-2111 **Price Code C**

Shared living spaces flow through this home's center, while private areas are tucked along the perimeter.

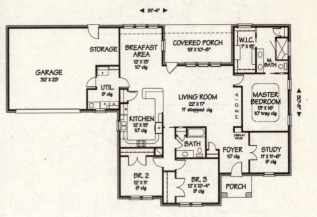

2,209 sq. ft.	Main floor:	2,209 sq. ft.
3+ Bedrooms	Garage and storage:	684 sq. ft.
2 Baths	Exterior Framing:	2x4

Product Options:

Foundations: Slab

The Gladwyne

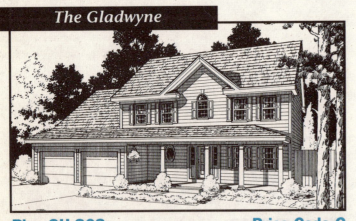

Plan OH-303 **Price Code C**

The upper floor's huge master bedroom, with two walk-in closets and a lush whirlpool bath, dominates this home.

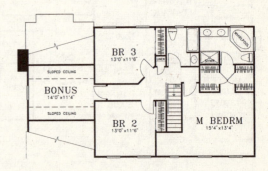

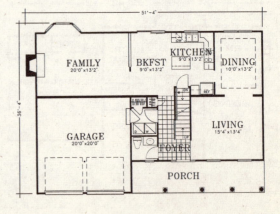

2,239 sq. ft.	Upper floor:	968 sq. ft.
3+ Bedrooms	Main floor:	1,099 sq. ft.
2½ Baths	Bonus room:	172 sq. ft.
	Basement:	1,099 sq. ft.
	Garage:	416 sq. ft.
	Exterior Framing:	2x4

Product Options:

Foundations: Standard basement

ORDER BLUEPRINTS ANYTIME!
CALL TOLL-FREE 1-800-820-1296

Plan copyright held by home designer/architect

PRICES AND DETAILS ON PAGES 12-15

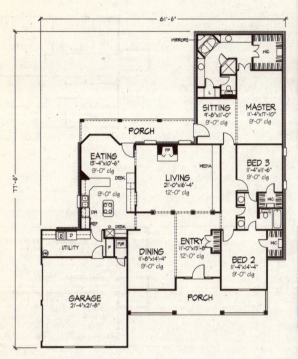

The Kelliher

Plan LS-96201-E   **Price Code C**

This home's extravagant master suite includes a separate sitting area and mirrors above a garden tub.

2,271 sq. ft. 3 Bedrooms 2 Baths	Main floor: 2,271 sq. ft. Garage: 484 sq. ft. Exterior Framing: 2x4

Product Options:

Foundations: Slab

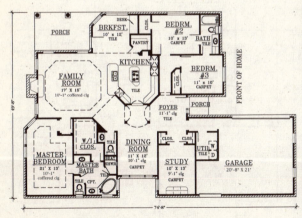

The Amherst

Plan KLF-981   **Price Code C**

Designed for comfort, this home's large, bright family room is augmented by a coffered ceiling and a fireplace.

2,272 sq. ft. 3+ Bedrooms 2½ Baths	Main floor: 2,272 sq. ft. Garage: 525 sq. ft. Exterior Framing: 2x4

Product Options:

Foundations: Slab

The Farwell

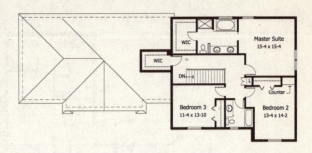

Plan CL-2303-RE **Price Code C**

The kitchen/dinette blends with a breezy family room while keeping formal areas separate in this classy home.

2,329 sq. ft.	Upper floor:	1,111 sq. ft.
3+ Bedrooms	Main floor:	1,218 sq. ft.
	Basement:	1,218 sq. ft.
2½ Baths	Garage:	745 sq. ft.
	Exterior Framing:	2x6

Product Options:

Foundations: Standard basement or Crawlspace

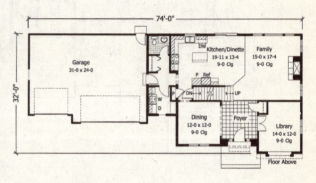

The Catalina

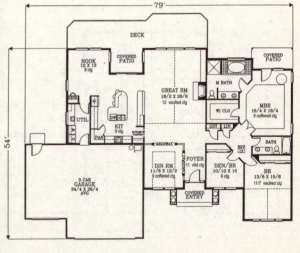

Plan S-112795-E **Price Code C**

A butler's pantry and an eating bar in this home's top-notch kitchen ease everything from snacks to formal dinners.

2,335 sq. ft.	Main floor:	2,335 sq. ft.
2+ Bedrooms	Garage:	848 sq. ft.
	Exterior Framing:	2x6
2 Baths		

Product Options:

Foundations: Crawlspace

ORDER BLUEPRINTS ANYTIME! CALL TOLL-FREE 1-800-820-1296

PRICES AND DETAILS ON PAGES 12-15

Plan copyright held by home designer/architect

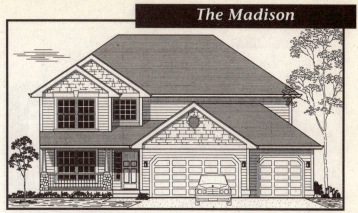

The Madison

Plan S-62998   **Price Code C**

Separation of formal and casual areas is upheld in this space-wise home, providing ample entertaining options.

2,346 sq. ft.	Upper floor:	1,047 sq. ft.
3+ Bedrooms	Main floor:	1,299 sq. ft.
	Garage:	682 sq. ft.
2½ Baths	Exterior Framing:	2x6

Product Options:

Foundations: Crawlspace

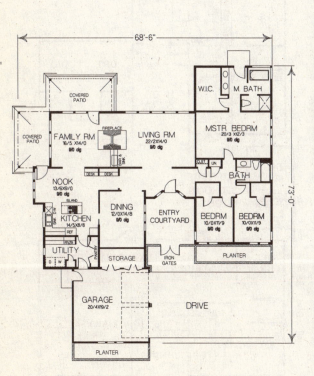

The Beatty

Plan SUN-1075   **Price Code C**

Special touches, such as an entry courtyard and transom-topped windows, enhance this elegant home.

2,370 sq. ft.	Main floor:	2,370 sq. ft.
3 Bedrooms	Garage:	409 sq. ft.
	Storage:	58 sq. ft.
2 Baths	Exterior Framing:	2x6

Product Options:

Foundations: Crawlspace or Slab

ORDER BLUEPRINTS ANYTIME!
CALL TOLL-FREE 1-800-820-1296

Plan copyright held by home designer/architect

PRICES AND DETAILS ON PAGES 12-15

The Sherando

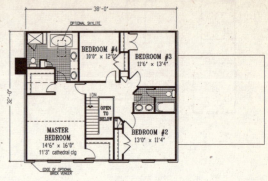

Plan CH-124-A **Price Code C**

This home's master suite features a luxurious private bath and a sleeping area with a cathedral ceiling.

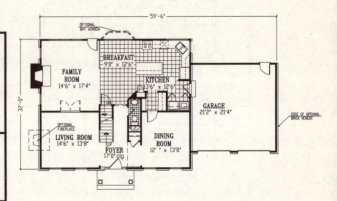

2,364 sq. ft.	Upper floor:	1,148 sq. ft.
4 Bedrooms	Main floor:	1,216 sq. ft.
2½ Baths	Basement:	1,240 sq. ft.
	Garage:	452 sq. ft.
	Exterior Framing:	2x4

Product Options:

Foundations: Daylight basement, Standard basement or Crawlspace

---

The Weatherly

Plan OH-277 **Price Code C**

An optional studio beyond this handsome home's master suite could host an easel, a writing desk or a yoga mat!

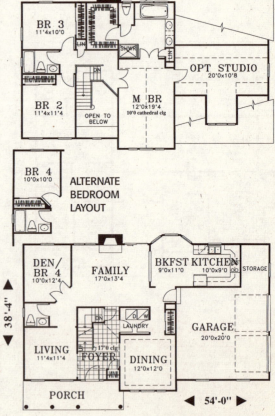

2,374 sq. ft.	Upper floor:	913 sq. ft.
3+ Bedrooms	Main floor:	1,187 sq. ft.
2½–3 Baths	Optional studio:	274 sq. ft.
	Basement:	1,187 sq. ft.
	Garage and storage:	476 sq. ft.
	Exterior Framing:	2x4

Product Options: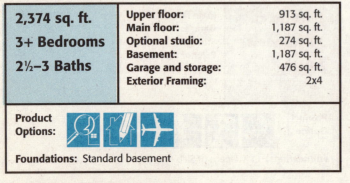

Foundations: Standard basement

ORDER BLUEPRINTS ANYTIME! CALL TOLL-FREE 1-800-820-1296

Plan copyright held by home designer/architect

PRICES AND DETAILS ON PAGES 12–15

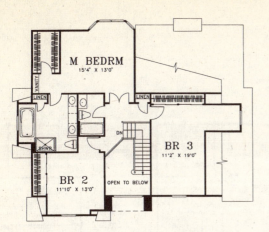

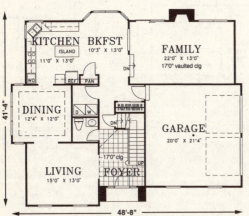

The Royersford

Plan OH-275   **Price Code C**

This home's sunken family room, topped by a vaulted ceiling, boasts a window-flanked fireplace.

2,380 sq. ft. 3 Bedrooms 2½ Baths	Upper floor: 1,109 sq. ft. Main floor: 1,271 sq. ft. Basement: 973 sq. ft. Garage: 440 sq. ft. Exterior Framing: 2x4

Product Options:

Foundations: Standard basement

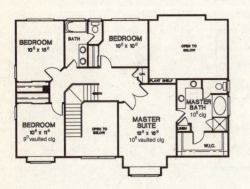

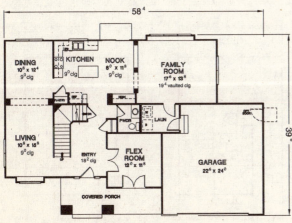

The Lombard

Plan KP-2103-B   **Price Code C**

Promising snug sanctuaries, bright and cozy window seats are scattered throughout this roomy home.

2,396 sq. ft. 4+ Bedrooms 2½ Baths	Upper floor: 1,072 sq. ft. Main floor: 1,324 sq. ft. Basement: 1,192 sq. ft. Garage: 506 sq. ft. Exterior Framing: 2x4 and 2x6

Product Options:

Foundations: Standard basement

ORDER BLUEPRINTS ANYTIME!
CALL TOLL-FREE 1-800-820-1296

Plan copyright held by home designer/architect

PRICES AND DETAILS ON PAGES 12-15

The Braselton

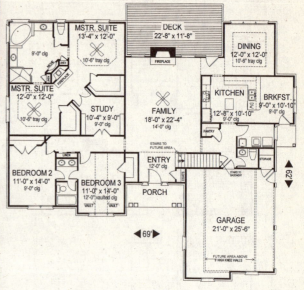

Plan APS-2316 **Price Code C**

This home's posh master suite is fit for royalty, with a deluxe bath, a study and dual sleeping quarters.

2,398 sq. ft.	Main floor:	2,398 sq. ft.
3+ Bedrooms	Future area:	302 sq. ft.
	Basement:	2,398 sq. ft.
2½ Baths	Garage:	538 sq. ft.
	Storage:	16 sq. ft.
	Exterior Framing:	2x4

Product Options:

Foundations: Daylight basement

The Tiderunner

Plan SDC-001-B **Price Code C**

Front and rear porches, a rear balcony and plenty of windows make this home perfect for a lot with a view.

2,423 sq. ft.	Upper floor:	889 sq. ft.
3+ Bedrooms	Main floor:	1,834 sq. ft.
	Future lower floor:	665 sq. ft.
2 Baths	Garage:	869 sq. ft.
	Exterior Framing:	2x4

Product Options:

Foundations: Pole

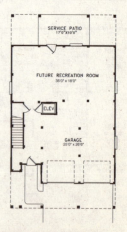

ORDER BLUEPRINTS ANYTIME!
CALL TOLL-FREE 1-800-820-1296

Plan copyright held by home designer/architect

PRICES AND DETAILS ON PAGES 12-15

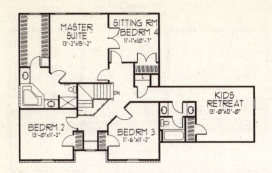

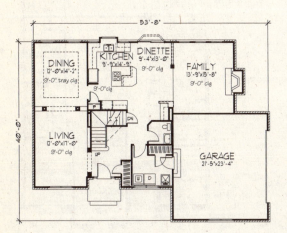

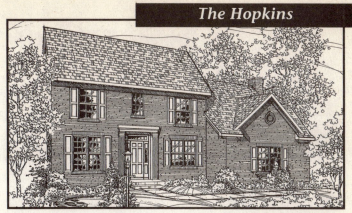

The Hopkins

Plan LS-98839-GW **Price Code D**

A cozy kids' retreat on the upper floor and a big family room on the main floor make this an ideal family home.

2,565 sq. ft.	Upper floor:	1,005 sq. ft.
3+ Bedrooms	Main floor:	1,287 sq. ft.
	Kids' retreat:	273 sq. ft.
2½ Baths	Basement:	588 sq. ft.
	Garage:	525 sq. ft.
	Exterior Framing:	2x6

Product Options:

Foundations: Partial basement

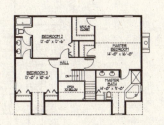

The Elmhurst

Plan MIN-9822 **Price Code D**

A cathedral ceiling, a shared fireplace and three walls of windows highlight this home's pretty sun room.

2,526 sq. ft.	Upper floor:	946 sq. ft.
3 Bedrooms	Main floor:	1,580 sq. ft.
	Basement:	1,517 sq. ft.
3½ Baths	Garage and storage:	880 sq. ft.
	Exterior Framing:	2x6

Product Options:

Foundations: Standard basement

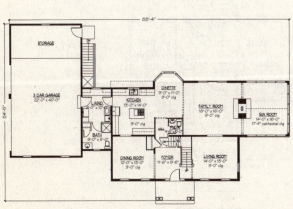

ORDER BLUEPRINTS ANYTIME!
CALL TOLL-FREE 1-800-820-1296

Plan copyright held by home designer/architect

PRICES AND DETAILS ON PAGES 12-15

The Simonton

Plan HDC-2538-A   **Price Code D**

The large, central living room serves as the home's hub while providing easy passage to a secluded back porch.

2,538 sq. ft.	Main floor:	2,538 sq. ft.
3+ Bedrooms	Garage:	540 sq. ft.
3 Baths	Exterior Framing:	2x4

Product Options:

Foundations: Slab

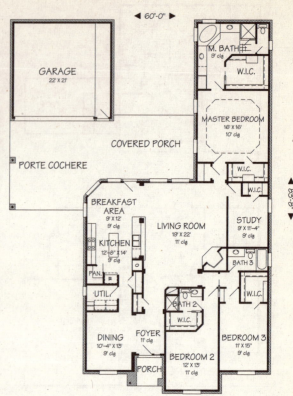

The Isle of Palms

Plan SDC-010-B   **Price Code D**

Featuring an impressive front porch and a glorious two-story Great Room, this home is great for hosting guests.

2,592 sq. ft.	Upper floor:	980 sq. ft.
3 Bedrooms	Main floor:	1,612 sq. ft.
3½ Baths	Tuck-under garage/storage:	1,612 sq. ft.
	Exterior Framing:	2x4

Product Options:

Foundations: Pole

STYLISH NEWCOMERS

ORDER BLUEPRINTS ANYTIME!
CALL TOLL-FREE 1-800-820-1296

Plan copyright held by home designer/architect

PRICES AND DETAILS ON PAGES 12-15

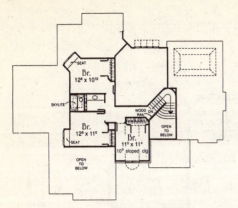

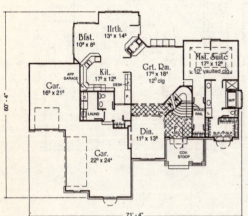

The Huntley

Plan CC-2453   **Price Code D**

With its hearth room and spacious Great Room, this home is the very picture of comfort and ease.

2,539 sq. ft.	Upper floor:	666 sq. ft.
4 Bedrooms	Main floor:	1,873 sq. ft.
	Basement:	1,734 sq. ft.
2½ Baths	Garage:	880 sq. ft.
	Exterior Framing:	2x4

Product Options:

Foundations: Standard Basement

The Madisonville

Plan L-0002-UDA   **Price Code D**

With a snack counter serving the living room, this home's well-planned island kitchen is a treat for cooks.

2,628 sq. ft.	Main floor:	2,368 sq. ft.
3+ Bedrooms	Bonus suite:	260 sq. ft.
	Garage:	532 sq. ft.
3 Baths	Exterior Framing:	2x4

Product Options:

Foundations: Slab

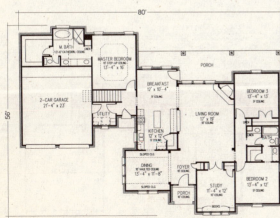

ORDER BLUEPRINTS ANYTIME!
CALL TOLL-FREE 1-800-820-1296

Plan copyright held by home designer/architect

PRICES AND DETAILS ON PAGES 12-15

STYLISH NEWCOMERS

The Moravia

Plan HDC-2634   **Price Code D**

The quiet, isolated sleeping wing of this home allows entertaining and resting to occur simultaneously.

2,634 sq. ft.	Main floor:	2,634 sq. ft.
4 Bedrooms	Detached garage:	770 sq. ft.
2½ Baths	Carport:	414 sq. ft.
	Exterior Framing:	2x4

Product Options:

Foundations: Slab

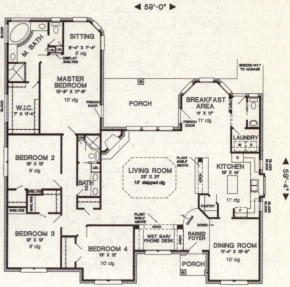

The Millville

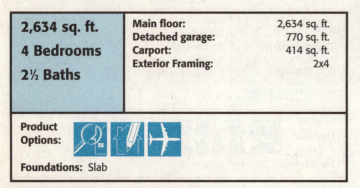

Plan CL-2603-RE   **Price Code D**

This Colonial-style holds some surprises beyond its formal facade, including a garden room and an upper-floor study.

2,655 sq. ft.	Upper floor:	1,134 sq. ft.
3+ Bedrooms	Main floor:	1,380 sq. ft.
3 Baths	Garden room:	141 sq. ft.
	Basement:	1,521 sq. ft.
	Garage:	517 sq. ft.
	Exterior Framing:	2x6

Product Options:

Foundations: Standard basement or Crawlspace

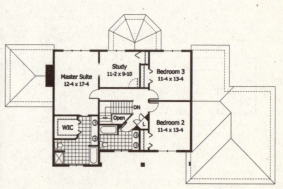

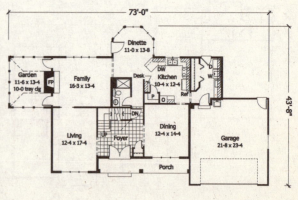

ORDER BLUEPRINTS ANYTIME!
CALL TOLL-FREE 1-800-820-1296

Plan copyright held by home designer/architect

PRICES AND DETAILS ON PAGES 12-15

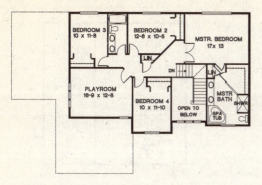
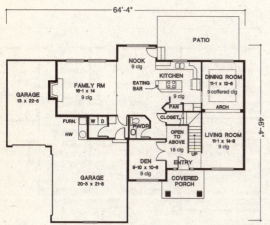
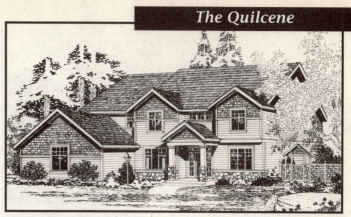

The Quilcene

Plan GS-2056   **Price Code D**

Kids rule in this spacious two-story! A large family room and an upstairs playroom offer options for rainy days.

2,674 sq. ft.	Upper floor:	1,311 sq. ft.
4+ Bedrooms	Main floor:	1,363 sq. ft.
2½ Baths	Garage:	803 sq. ft.
	Exterior Framing:	2x6

Product Options:

Foundations: Crawlspace

The Winona

Plan LS-95907-MC   **Price Code D**

A bay window in the bedroom and a split bath with a corner tub highlight this home's fabulous master suite.

2,697 sq. ft.	Upper floor:	1,229 sq. ft.
4+ Bedrooms	Main floor:	1,468 sq. ft.
2½ Baths	Upper-floor storage:	95 sq. ft.
	Basement:	1,468 sq. ft.
	Garage:	704 sq. ft.
	Exterior Framing:	2x6

Product Options:

Foundations: Daylight basement

ORDER BLUEPRINTS ANYTIME!
CALL TOLL-FREE 1-800-820-1296

Plan copyright held by home designer/architect

PRICES AND DETAILS ON PAGES 12-15

STYLISH NEWCOMERS

The Westmere

Plan AHP-2005 **Price Code D**

This traditional home's well-appointed kitchen serves a sunny dinette via a handy island snack bar.

2,717 sq. ft.	Upper floor:	855 sq. ft.
4 Bedrooms	Main floor:	1,862 sq. ft.
2½ Baths	Basement:	1,862 sq. ft.
	Garage:	467 sq. ft.
	Exterior Framing:	2x4 or 2x6

Product Options:

Foundations: Standard basement, Crawlspace or Slab

The Windsor

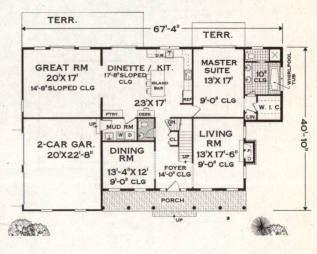
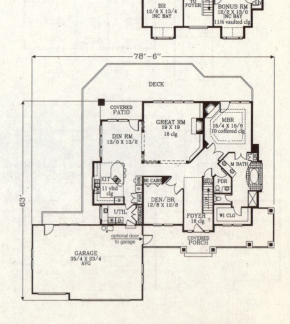

Plan S-3294-H **Price Code D**

Whether you're hosting a barbecue or relaxing on a lazy afternoon, this home's rear deck offers ideal outdoor space.

2,754 sq. ft.	Upper floor:	725 sq. ft.
3+ Bedrooms	Main floor:	1,873 sq. ft.
2½ Baths	Bonus room:	156 sq. ft.
	Garage:	840 sq. ft.
	Exterior Framing:	2x6

Product Options:

Foundations: Crawlspace

ORDER BLUEPRINTS ANYTIME!
CALL TOLL-FREE 1-800-820-1296

Plan copyright held by home designer/architect

PRICES AND DETAILS ON PAGES 12-15

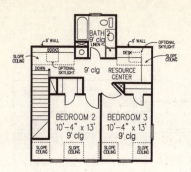
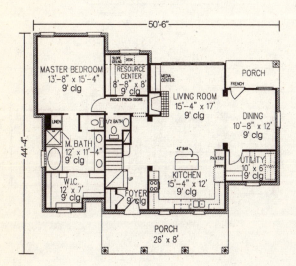
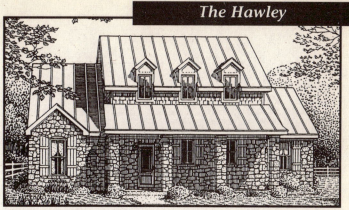

The Hawley

Plan L-9911-UDA **Price Code C**

There's plenty of space for work, play or study in this charming stone home, with its two resource centers.

2,071 sq. ft.	Upper floor:	588 sq. ft.
3 Bedrooms	Main floor:	1,483 sq. ft.
2½ Baths	Exterior Framing:	2x4

Product Options:

Foundations: Slab

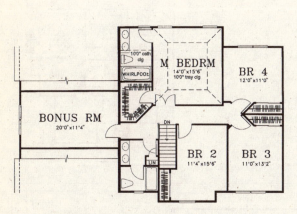
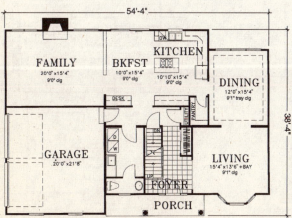
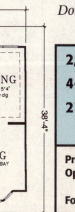

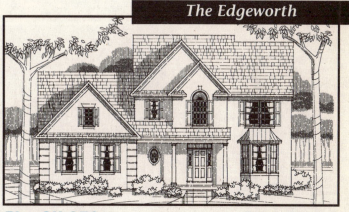

The Edgeworth

Plan OH-272 **Price Code D**

Double doors introduce the master suite, which is topped by a grand tray ceiling and features a whirlpool bath.

2,790 sq. ft.	Upper floor:	1,102 sq. ft.
4+ Bedrooms	Main floor:	1,444 sq. ft.
2½ Baths	Bonus room:	244 sq. ft.
	Basement:	1,444 sq. ft.
	Garage:	450 sq. ft.
	Exterior Framing:	2x4

Product Options:

Foundations: Standard basement

ORDER BLUEPRINTS ANYTIME!
CALL TOLL-FREE 1-800-820-1296

Plan copyright held by home designer/architect

PRICES AND DETAILS ON PAGES 12-15

STYLISH NEWCOMERS

311

The Evington

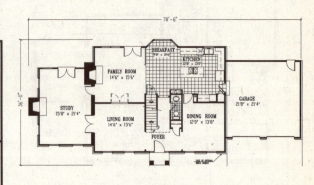

Plan CH-121-A   **Price Code D**

The master suite features a cathedral ceiling, a private bath and a sitting room that's accented by charming dormers.

2,877 sq. ft.	Upper floor:	1,381 sq. ft.
4+ Bedrooms	Main floor:	1,496 sq. ft.
2½ Baths	Basement:	1,140 sq. ft.
	Garage:	462 sq. ft.
	Exterior Framing:	2x4

Product Options:

Foundations: Daylight basement, Standard basement or Crawlspace

---

The Waterman

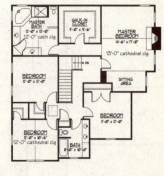

Plan MIN-9749   **Price Code D**

Enjoy home-cooked meals in this home's formal dining room, sunny breakfast nook or breezy screen porch.

2,957 sq. ft.	Upper floor:	1,395 sq. ft.
4+ Bedrooms	Main floor:	1,562 sq. ft.
2½ Baths	Basement:	1,422 sq. ft.
	Garage:	588 sq. ft.
	Screen porch:	182 sq. ft.
	Exterior Framing:	2x4

Product Options:

Foundations: Standard basement

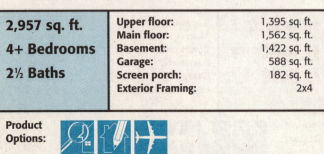

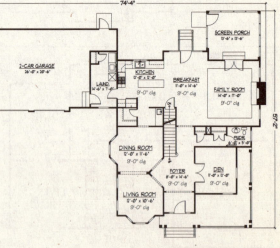

ORDER BLUEPRINTS ANYTIME!
CALL TOLL-FREE 1-800-820-1296

Plan copyright held by home designer/architect

PRICES AND DETAILS ON PAGES 12-15

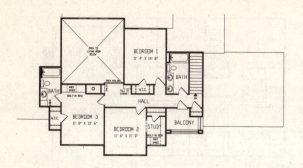

The Indianola

Plan L-9806-UDA **Price Code D**

With three porches, a hobby room and a fireplace, this home offers something for every member of the family.

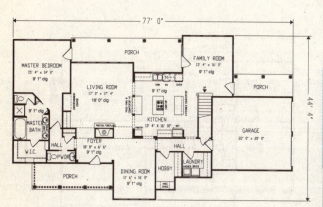

2,920 sq. ft.	Upper floor:	982 sq. ft.
4 Bedrooms	Main floor:	1,938 sq. ft.
3½ Baths	Basement:	1,938 sq. ft.
	Garage:	442 sq. ft.
	Exterior Framing:	2x4

Product Options:

Foundations: Standard basement, Crawlspace or Slab

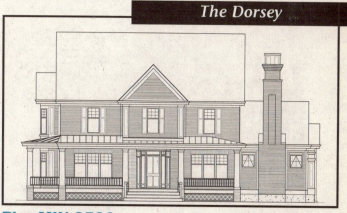

The Dorsey

Plan MIN-9530 **Price Code D**

This ideal family home features ample storage, flexible spaces, wide-open living areas and quiet bedrooms.

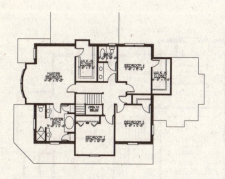
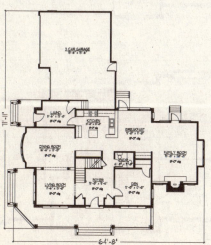

2,974 sq. ft.	Upper floor:	1,349 sq. ft.
4+ Bedrooms	Main floor:	1,625 sq. ft.
2½ Baths	Basement:	1,563 sq. ft.
	Garage:	717 sq. ft.
	Exterior Framing:	2x4

Product Options:

Foundations: Standard basement

ORDER BLUEPRINTS ANYTIME!
CALL TOLL-FREE 1-800-820-1296

Plan copyright held by home designer/architect

PRICES AND DETAILS ON PAGES 12-15

The Manassas

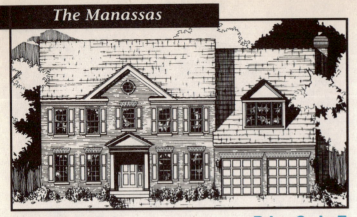
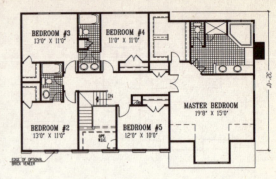

Plan CH-245-A   **Price Code E**

Perfect for a large family, this attractive home offers a huge master suite, plus four additional bedrooms.

3,056 sq. ft.	Upper floor:	1,723 sq. ft.
5+ Bedrooms	Main floor:	1,333 sq. ft.
	Basement:	1,434 sq. ft.
3½ Baths	Garage:	384 sq. ft.
	Exterior Framing:	2x4

Product Options:

Foundations: Standard basement or Crawlspace

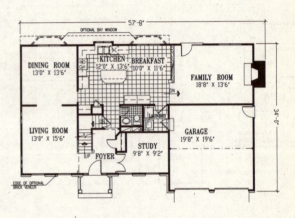

The Danbury

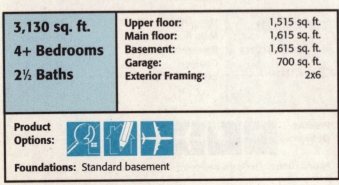
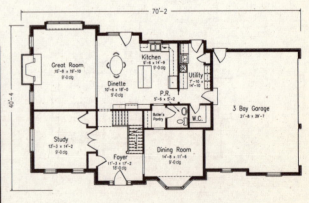

Plan LLM-251   **Price Code E**

On chilly nights, you'll love curling up next to a crackling fire in this home's spacious Great Room.

3,130 sq. ft.	Upper floor:	1,515 sq. ft.
4+ Bedrooms	Main floor:	1,615 sq. ft.
	Basement:	1,615 sq. ft.
2½ Baths	Garage:	700 sq. ft.
	Exterior Framing:	2x6

Product Options:

Foundations: Standard basement

STYLISH NEWCOMERS

ORDER BLUEPRINTS ANYTIME!
CALL TOLL-FREE 1-800-820-1296

PRICES AND DETAILS ON PAGES 12-15

Plan copyright held by home designer/architect

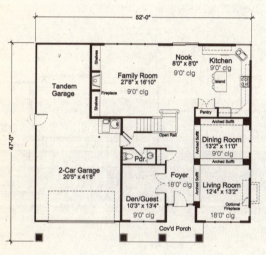

The Wilsonville

Plan TS-2151-A **Price Code E**

A huge bonus room, an optional loft and a flexible den help this versatile home fit your family's needs.

3,173 sq. ft.	Upper floor:	1,337 sq. ft.
3+ Bedrooms	Main floor:	1,431 sq. ft.
	Bonus room:	287 sq. ft.
2½ Baths	Optional loft:	118 sq. ft.
	Garage:	742 sq. ft.
	Exterior Framing:	2x6

Product Options:

Foundations: Crawlspace

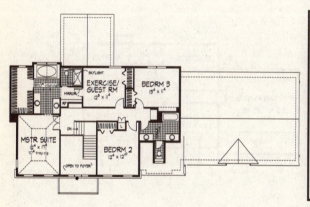
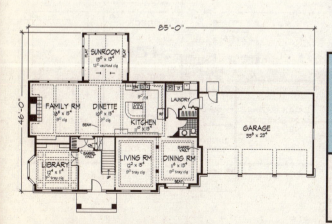

The Brevik

Plan LS-97838-RE **Price Code E**

This home features plenty of bedrooms, including a well-appointed master suite with an opulent garden tub.

3,296 sq. ft.	Upper floor:	1,514 sq. ft.
3+ Bedrooms	Main floor:	1,586 sq. ft.
	Sun room:	196 sq. ft.
2½ Baths	Basement:	1,782 sq. ft.
	Garage:	816 sq. ft.
	Exterior Framing:	2x6

Product Options:

Foundations: Standard basement or Crawlspace

ORDER BLUEPRINTS ANYTIME!
CALL TOLL-FREE 1-800-820-1296

Plan copyright held by home designer/architect

PRICES AND DETAILS ON PAGES 12-15

The Pennington

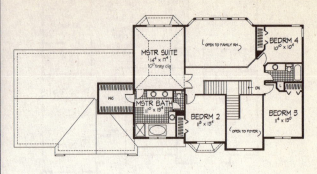
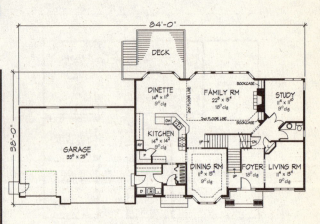

Plan LS-97832-RE   **Price Code E**

This appealing home showcases a spacious family room with built-in bookcases and an inviting gas fireplace.

3,194 sq. ft.	Upper floor:	1,485 sq. ft.
4+ Bedrooms	Main floor:	1,709 sq. ft.
	Basement:	1,709 sq. ft.
2½ Baths	Garage:	928 sq. ft.
	Exterior Framing:	2x6

Product Options:

Foundations: Standard basement or Crawlspace

The Altona

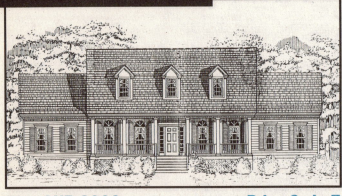
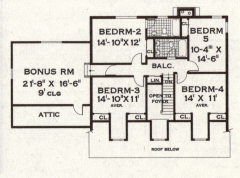
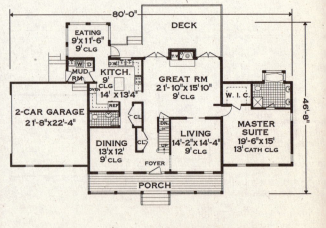

Plan AHP-2006   **Price Code E**

This home's upper floor boasts four good-sized bedrooms, two full baths and a versatile bonus room.

3,246 sq. ft.	Upper floor:	1,030 sq. ft.
5+ Bedrooms	Main floor:	1,842 sq. ft.
	Bonus room:	374 sq. ft.
3½ Baths	Basement:	1,842 sq. ft.
	Garage:	484 sq. ft.
	Exterior Framing:	2x4 or 2x6

Product Options:

Foundations: Daylight bsmt., Standard bsmt., Crawlspace or Slab

ORDER BLUEPRINTS ANYTIME!
CALL TOLL-FREE 1-800-820-1296

PRICES AND DETAILS ON PAGES 12-15

Plan copyright held by home designer/architect

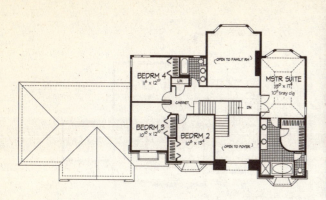
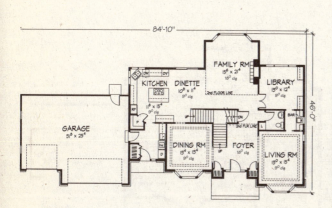
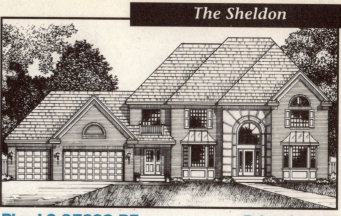

The Sheldon

Plan LS-97833-RE **Price Code E**

Bay windows in the common areas and the master bedroom lend this home a bit of space and a lot of class.

3,301 sq. ft.	Upper floor:	1,511 sq. ft.
4+ Bedrooms	Main floor:	1,790 sq. ft.
2½ Baths	Basement:	1,790 sq. ft.
	Garage:	784 sq. ft.
	Exterior Framing:	2x6

Product Options:

Foundations: Standard basement or Crawlspace

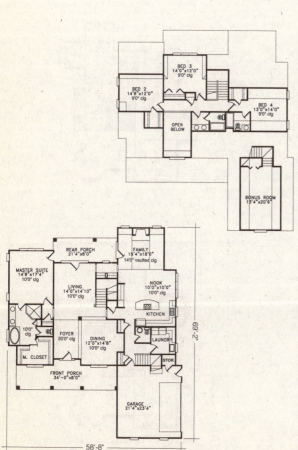

The Cherry Lane

Plan SDC-005-B **Price Code F**

Featuring an open layout and expansive counter space, this home's island kitchen is every cook's dream.

3,642 sq. ft.	Upper floor:	1,231 sq. ft.
4+ Bedrooms	Main floor:	2,095 sq. ft.
3½ Baths	Bonus room:	316 sq. ft.
	Garage:	520 sq. ft.
	Storage:	18 sq. ft.
	Exterior Framing:	2x4

Product Options:

Foundations: Crawlspace

ORDER BLUEPRINTS ANYTIME!
CALL TOLL-FREE 1-800-820-1296

Plan copyright held by home designer/architect

PRICES AND DETAILS ON PAGES 12-15

The Crosshill

Plan LLM-262 **Price Code F**

Bookworms will happily while away a rainy afternoon in this charming home's spacious main-floor library.

3,650 sq. ft.	Upper floor:	1,370 sq. ft.
3+ Bedrooms	Main floor:	2,280 sq. ft.
	Basement:	2,280 sq. ft.
2½ Baths	Garage:	760 sq. ft.
	Exterior Framing:	2x6

Product Options:

Foundations: Standard basement

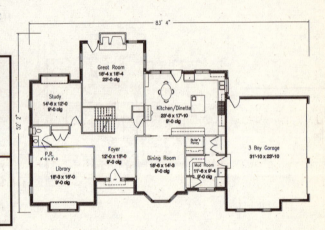

The Dassel

Plan LS-98152-L **Price Code G**

A loft area above this stunning Victorian-style home's master suite is perfect as an exercise room or a quiet study.

4,124 sq. ft.	Upper floor:	1,842 sq. ft.
5+ Bedrooms	Main floor:	2,128 sq. ft.
	Loft:	154 sq. ft.
4½ Baths	Basement:	2,128 sq. ft.
	Garage:	441 sq. ft.
	Exterior Framing:	2x6

Product Options:

Foundations: Standard basement

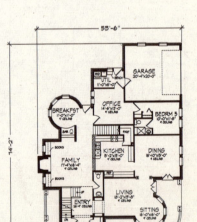

ORDER BLUEPRINTS ANYTIME!
CALL TOLL-FREE 1-800-820-1296

Plan copyright held by home designer/architect

PRICES AND DETAILS ON PAGES 12-15

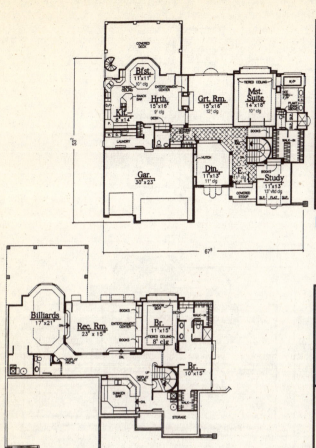

The Chambers

Plan CC-2175-P **Price Code F**

Grab a cocktail from the sunken bar area before shooting a game of pool in this home's billiard room.

3,955 sq. ft.	Main floor:	2,175 sq. ft.
3+ Bedrooms	Basement:	1,780 sq. ft.
	Garage:	720 sq. ft.
2 Full,	Storage:	138 sq. ft.
2 Half Baths	Exterior Framing:	2x4

Product Options:

Foundations: Daylight basement

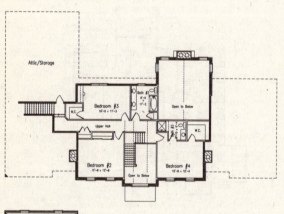

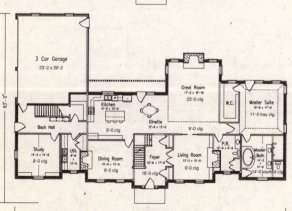

The Georgian Grand Manor

Plan LLM-265 **Price Code G**

With a gourmet kitchen, a soaring Great Room and a three-car garage, this manor-style home is fit for a king.

4,100 sq. ft.	Upper floor:	1,145 sq. ft.
4+ Bedrooms	Main floor:	2,955 sq. ft.
	Basement:	2,955 sq. ft.
3½ Baths	Garage:	720 sq. ft.
	Exterior Framing:	2x6

Product Options:

Foundations: Standard basement

ORDER BLUEPRINTS ANYTIME!
CALL TOLL-FREE 1-800-820-1296

Plan copyright held by home designer/architect

PRICES AND DETAILS ON PAGES 12-15

The Swansonville

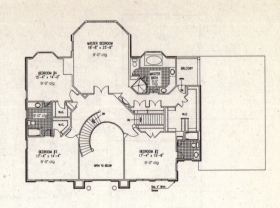

Plan CH-910-A — **Price Code H**

No need for a weekend getaway! Simply pamper yourself in the master suite, complete with a private balcony.

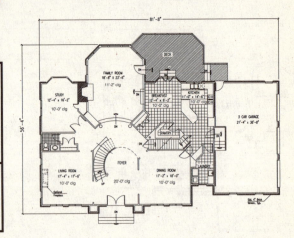

4,921 sq. ft.	Upper floor:	2,307 sq. ft.
4+ Bedrooms	Main floor:	2,614 sq. ft.
3½ Baths	Basement:	2,641 sq. ft.
	Garage:	782 sq. ft.
	Exterior Framing:	2x4

Product Options:

Foundations: Daylight basement, Crawlspace or Slab

The Rockport

Plan L-215-OLE — **Price Code I**

A home theater, a snack bar, game and exercise rooms and two covered decks make returning to this home a real treat.

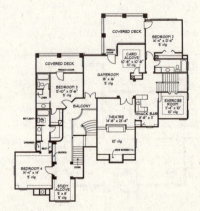

5,229 sq. ft.	Upper floor:	2,353 sq. ft.
4+ Bedrooms	Main floor:	2,876 sq. ft.
4½ Baths	Garage (one-car):	225 sq. ft.
	Garage (two-car):	528 sq. ft.
	Exterior Framing:	2x4

Product Options:

Foundations: Slab

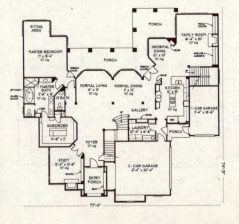

ORDER BLUEPRINTS ANYTIME!
CALL TOLL-FREE 1-800-820-1296

Plan copyright held by home designer/architect

PRICES AND DETAILS ON PAGES 12-15